Praise for Keith Gilyard

Voices of the Self: A Study of Language Competence, winner of the American Book Award

"An effective mixed-genre discussion of issues in sociolinguistics, language policy, and literacy education that should be of interest to English and language arts teachers at all levels."

—National Council of Teachers of English

"This book is a classic that should appeal to parents, students of sociolinguistics and education, and those interested in the language challenges that face youth. Strongly recommended."

—*Humanities*

Let's Flip This Script: An African American Discourse on Language, Literature, and Learning

"Gilyard is a knowledgeable, diplomatic lecturer on issues of language and education pertaining to African Americans. Gilyard's writing style is provocative, and he brings an astute, different viewpoint to American social commentary."

—*Community Review*

"This latest book by Keith Gilyard is a brilliant, inspiring collection of personal essays about freedom and literacy, and the life forces that can empower us in our quest to 'flip the script.' There are profound truths in this visionary work from a major voice in the field. Written in an engaging style by a homeboy scholar, the book is a must-read for those of us engaged in the educational enterprise."

—Geneva Smitherman, University Distinguished Professor Emerita, Michigan State University

"The collection of eleven essays displays a remarkable breadth of knowledge, an inventive and playful use of language, provocative thoughts, wisdom and insight."

—*Composition Forum*

Liberation Memories: The Rhetoric and Poetics of John Oliver Killens

"Gilyard demonstrates that Killens's persistent themes are the imperative need for Black solidarity, empowerment, resistance, self-defense, and heroism, and the centrality of the community and family in the cause of Black liberation."

—*Choice*

"Keith Gilyard has done an impressive job! This excellent and long overdue introduction to the work of an important writer and literary activist allows us to carefully reevaluate John Oliver Killens's place in the history of postwar American and African American literature. Keith Gilyard's thoughtful and informed study is required reading for anyone who wants to understand the vibrant, controversial, and often deliberately misinterpreted Black Arts Movement."

—Lorenzo Thomas, Poetry Foundation Award winner

"Though Killens no longer has a significant readership, he played a large part in the postwar development of African American literature, a point that is made convincingly in *Liberation Memories*."

—*The Washington Post*

"Gilyard's holistic approach to Killens—as novelist, essayist, teacher, sociopolitical activist, and organizer of literary conferences—posits him as heir to the likes of Frederick Douglass and W. E. B. Du Bois, for the latter's insistence on the compatibility of aesthetics and propaganda in particular. Gilyard underscores the literary distinction and integrity Killens achieves through a deft, at times unique adaptation of African American vernacular art forms and modes of expression to the aesthetic uses of his fiction."

—Alvin Aubert, professor emeritus, Wayne State University Press

"A masterwork by a master scholar. An important reappraisal of John O. Killens, a literary visionary whose influence on African American letters is both unprecedented and unsung. In *Liberation Memories*, Keith Gilyard has produced a visionary work worthy of its subject matter. A masterful fusion of heart and scholarship that illuminates Killens's works and his unrelenting efforts as an ideological orchestrator in an evocative text that questions and clarifies the historical/cultural/destinic dynamics of literature and the visionary artists. In doing so, Gilyard suggests a seminal griotic paradigm for approaching and assessing African American literature, letters, writers, and thinkers."

—Arthur Flowers, professor emeritus, Syracuse University

Discourse in Black

African American Life Series

A complete listing of the books in this series can be found online at wsupress.wayne.edu.

SERIES EDITOR

Melba Joyce Boyd
Department of Africana Studies, Wayne State University

Discourse in Black

VOICES OF THE SELF, *LET'S FLIP THE SCRIPT*, AND *LIBERATION MEMORIES*

THREE ESSENTIAL WORKS BY

Keith Gilyard

WAYNE STATE UNIVERSITY PRESS
DETROIT

ISBN 9780814351925 (paperback)

Library of Congress Control Number: 2024941777

Cover design by Nathaniel Roy.

Published with support from the Arthur L. Johnson Fund for African American Studies and with the assistance of a fund established by Thelma Gray James of Wayne State University for the publication of folklore and English studies.

Wayne State University Press rests on Waawiyaataanong, also referred to as Detroit, the ancestral and contemporary homeland of the Three Fires Confederacy. These sovereign lands were granted by the Ojibwe, Odawa, Potawatomi, and Wyandot Nations, in 1807, through the Treaty of Detroit. Wayne State University Press affirms Indigenous sovereignty and honors all tribes with a connection to Detroit. With our Native neighbors, the press works to advance educational equity and promote a better future for the earth and all people.

Wayne State University Press
Leonard N. Simons Building
4809 Woodward Avenue
Detroit, Michigan 48201-1309

Visit us online at wsupress.wayne.edu.

Contents

Preface

When *Voices of the Self* appeared thirty-four years ago, the esteemed language scholar Bob Shuman labeled the volume a "classic." The comment reflected his typical generosity, although I deemed it inaccurate because there had not been enough time or reception to substantiate the claim. Even after receiving an American Book Award from the Before Columbus Foundation, I still shied away from the praise. However, I do consider *Voices* to be part of a classic *wave* of books published in the 1980s and 1990s that became popular among writing teachers and researchers. Texts include Gloria Anzaldúa's *Borderlands / La Frontera*, Mike Rose's *Lives on the Boundary*, and Victor Villanueva's *Bootstraps*. Numerous compositionists, Mary Soliday prominent among them, argued that the study of published literacy autobiographies and the production of student literacy narratives were important to a project of centering students in the academy and constructing more inclusive and dialogic curriculums.

I argue the same today. However, composition teachers were never my primary intended audience. As the product of an English Education department, I thought of my work more in terms of it having value in teacher preparation programs. Spurred by the late Gordon Pradl, my dissertation advisor at NYU, and later by the nonpareil Geneva Smitherman, my immediate writing goal was to intervene productively in the conversation about language and public-school education relative to urban African American students. I aimed to speak to the value of African American Vernacular English (AAVE) in schools and against the vernacular-eradicating trends in education policy and pedagogy. As I have continued to maintain, nothing in the vernacular itself accounts for failure in school or justifies deficit approaches. The most-cited section of *Voices* has been the section on eradicationism, pluralism, and bidialectalism, in which I asserted that linguistic pluralism is the superior approach. I also continue to view so-called student failure more in terms of resistance. These dispositions fueled my memoir-analytic method. Looking back at some point, I realized that I never should have bothered to think about an Education-English divide. Indeed, given that I have taught in both education departments and English departments, I have been concerned with language pedagogy at all levels of schooling.

After the publication of *Voices*, I received several invitations to speak and write about issues of language and education. My responses led to *Let's Flip the Script*, a collection of essays each written upon request. Among a variety of related topics such as politics, so-called dialect interference, the role of literature, racism, and resistance, I remarked about the participant structure of writing courses, drawing several distinctions between authoritarian and democratic classrooms. I criticized the view of knowledge strictly as lore, adherence only to teacher purposes, language-deficit models, and nonnegotiable writing standards. Countering practices include beliefs that student motive is vital, students can co-construct knowledge, an equality model of language is requisite, and standards can be adjusted. Reviewer Xin Liu Gale commented that I presented "an unsettling polemic which challenges the meaning of democracy in America, tests the depth of our humanity, and persuades us to open our eyes to others' sufferings in our comfortable institutional confinements."

Script was published in 1996, a few months before the Oakland School Board issued its Ebonics resolution, calling for Ebonics to be recognized as legitimate and incorporated into teaching materials and practices. The new book had a definite side to be on—the Oakland School Board's. As was the case following the release of *Voices*, a number of people, including media types, contacted me for my opinion or to invite me to professional gatherings. One newspaper editor asked me to pen the "pro" answer to the question of whether incorporating Ebonics programs into curriculums was a good idea. He told me that it would be a difficult essay to write because all "my" leaders thought Ebonics was bad. Of course, the article was simple enough to write. A reporter contacted me to get quotes criticizing the school officials in Oakland. Our conversation was a very short and disappointing one for her. A highlight for me occurred before a symposium in New York when I roomed with psychologist Robert Williams, who was credited with coining the term Ebonics, a portmanteau derived from "ebony" and "phonics." Williams did not make that claim to me. Instead, he played for me a cassette tape of the discussion during which the term was created in 1973. It was a group effort. This occurred at a conference, "The Cognitive and Language Development of Black Children," held in St. Louis.

Back in graduate school, as I was exposed to work by sociolinguistics and educational linguists and as I explored concepts that would be articulated in *Voices* and *Script*, I began to examine literature, particularly African American literature, through a "language lens"—that is, an intense focus on how language-as-subject served as a topic, theme, motif, or plot element. I read numerous texts in that manner and began to teach accordingly in both literature and writing courses. For example, as recounted in *Script*, I used some of Charles Chesnutt's Uncle Julius stories as writing prompts for college students who had been classified as remedial. The stories, which are about language empowerment, at least the way I saw them, always sparked lively discussion and writing.

Earlier, in 1974, the Conference on College Composition and Communication (CCCC) adopted a resolution affirming "the students' right to their own patterns and varieties of language" and that "teachers must have the experience and training that will enable them to respect diversity and uphold the right of students to their own language." In the source material accompanying the published version of the resolution, it was suggested that *The Cotillion*, a 1971 novel by John Oliver Killens, with its shifts among language varieties, including AAVE, could serve as model writing for composition students. Of course, I considered *The Cotillion*, with its signifying writer-narrator Ben Ali Lumumba and characters such as Billy "Bad Mouth" Williams, to be an intriguing language story. It so happens that I knew Killens during my years in graduate school and read his other major novels, *Youngblood*, *And Then We Heard the Thunder*, and *'Sippi*, finding them also to be notable language stories as well as politically informative. For me, then, to write *Liberation Memories*, a book focused on the rhetoric and poetics in Killens's texts, represented, in 2003, the completing of an education–linguistics–politics–writing studies–literature–rhetoric chain.

Killens, a major figure during the Black Arts Movement during the 1960s and 1970s, needed to be promoted more widely, and I was pleased that a few weeks after the release of *Liberation Memories*, the critic Jonathan Yardley published a largely positive article about Killens in the *Washington Post*. Although Yardley's main concern was to review Killens's *Thunder*, as part of his setup he quoted from my book, including my observation that the author took "every opportunity he could to push the idea that African American writers should place their creative energies in the service of Black liberation efforts." I suspect that my volume prompted him to produce the piece and garner new attention for Killens.

Nowadays, in an educational landscape teeming with diversity, the need still exists, as a casual observer could discern, to combat language and cultural discrimination, anti-dialogic practices, and monocultural initiatives. We all should test the limit to which education and culture can contribute to a more substantive, multicultural democracy and greater social justice. Of course, in doing so, we should contribute the best we can to the cultivation of informed, expressive, critical, and culturally sensitive student voices. I am gratified that Wayne State University Press considers *Voices of the Self*, *Let's Flip the Script*, and *Liberation Memories* to have continuing relevance with respect to these essential tasks and has committed to seeking an expanded audience for the work.

References

Anzaldúa, G. (1987). *Borderlands / la frontera: The new mestiza*. Aunt Lute Books.

Corbett, E. P. J. (Ed.) (1974). Students' right to their own language. [Special issue] *CCC* 25(3).

Gale, X. L. Review. Review. *Composition Forum* 8(2), 42–44.

Killens, J. O. (1954). *Youngblood*. Dial.

———. (1963). *And then we heard the thunder*. Knopf.

———. (1967). *'Sippi*. Trident.

———. (1971). *The cotillion: or, one good bull is half the herd*. Trident.

Soliday, M. (1994). Translating self and difference through literacy narratives. *College English*, (56)5, 511–26.

Rose, M. (1989). *Lives on the boundary: The struggles and achievements of America's underprepared*. Free Press.

Shuman, R. B. (1992). Review. *Choice*, January 1992, 73.

Villanueva, V., Jr. (1993). *Bootstraps: From an American academic of color*. NCTE.

Yardley, J. (2003, July 24). The thunder of protest without the lightning of art. *Washington Post*, pp. C1, C8.

Voices of the Self

A STUDY OF
LANGUAGE COMPETENCE

*To Andre, Taneha, Kahlil, Kaamilah, Matthew,
Tyrell, Jerome, Amina, Asha, and Tiffany*

The essay portions of this book were written under the auspices of the Program in English Education at New York University.

Special thanks to Gordon Pradl.

Contents

1

Introduction

Over the past quarter century few problems in education have received as much media, professional, and parental attention as the fact that, by and large, young urban African-Americans have not achieved Standard English competence in public schools. The reasons for this are complex and, as expected, explanations abound and many solutions have been readily proposed. But there have been few, if any, unqualified success stories, and the proponents of theory themselves have been vehemently at odds with one another.

Such writers as Geneva Smitherman (1977), Jim Haskins and Hugh Butts (1973), and J. L. Dillard (1973) have condemned the public school system's traditional nonrecognition and nonacceptance of the separate and legitimate language variety, popularly labeled Black English, spoken by the majority of inner-city Black youth.* In their view, this implicit and explicit rejection of language communicates a rejection of both Black children and the culture that has produced them. The school characteristically fails, the argument continues, to capitalize on the linguistic competencies the children have already developed. When, predictably, these students seem less than enthusiastic about formal education, they are portrayed as slow learners. Little is expected of them academically, and academically these students produce very little—yet another example of the self-fulfilling prophecy.

The use of Black English in schools, therefore, has seemed plausible to many educators. One response, for example, was the 1974 resolution passed by members of the Conference on College Composition and Communication advocating the "students' right to their own language." Of course such resolutions, not being binding, are frequently ignored. Legions of teachers and other citizens (many of them Black) have

*Although "African-American" and "Black" are used interchangeably, the author acknowledges that the former term is more accurate.

considered all this talk about Black English to be mere "Black nonsense" and have insisted all along that there is no place for Black English, if such a thing exists, in the curriculum. Marva Collins, for one, founded a private school in Chicago in which any positive mention of Black English is eschewed. Her approach has been heralded by many, and her story was the subject of a docudrama that appeared on national television. In a similar vein, conservatives inside the National Council of Teachers of English have conspired to abrogate the students' right resolution (see Sledd 1983).

However, keeping in spirit with Smitherman, Haskins, Butts, Dillard, and company, Judge Charles W. Joiner ruled, in a precedent-setting case in 1979, that Black English is indeed a distinct linguistic form and must have an officially established place within the educational environment of the Martin Luther King Jr. Elementary School in Ann Arbor, Michigan. Joiner's decision was hailed as a great victory by those who considered themselves progressive.

Throughout all these developments, amid this cacophony of voices, African-American students in large numbers continue not to master Standard English. Oddly enough, conspicuously absent are the voices of the students themselves. I am not speaking about the street stories or the recorded snatches of conversation that typically have provided some researcher with his or her data, but the articulate opinion of those African-American students who face the task of public school language education. It is not being idealistic to expect at least some students to be able to furnish such information if encouraged to do so. One would not expect the elaborate speculation that a writer such as Smitherman can provide but, nonetheless, much valuable knowledge could be gathered. I know that I, had I been asked in, say, 1964, could have told someone something about this clash between cultures, this problem of being Black and attempting to cope with the instruction offered in a school controlled by those of another background. But of course I was never asked by anyone in authority to speak about the conflict. I was just asked to survive it.

Years later, in 1979, I finally got around to discussing that earlier period. Between jobs and (though I didn't know it at the time) careers, with my first child on the way, I decided to fashion a gift of experience, of my education. I became obsessed with beginning to organize the things I would need to say as a father. In tune with many prospective parents I planned to be "hard" on my child, but I also wanted things to be easier for him or her than they were for me.

I began to write a story of my life. Although I changed certain names and locations (freeing up my composing process), the writing is still undeniably autobiographical, as most long-term acquaintances of mine can attest. Despite working at breakneck pace, I had only completed the eighth grade again when Kahlil, a seven-pound, fifteen-ounce manchild, burst upon the scene. The text remained that way until I was later persuaded to add more.

As I reviewed my writing during the weeks following Kahlil's birth, I viewed the manuscript, entitled *Primary School*, as a story of educational survival cast mainly in racial terms. Only later, after I had become an English instructor and graduate student of sociolinguistics, did the realization set in that I had spun much of my record, developed that very theme of survival, around the acquisition and mastery of various communicative competencies. That survival, race consciousness, and communicative skill form a conceptual triangle in that writing is now very interesting to me, but not surprising. Wasn't it communication skill that brought the manuscript itself into existence? Wasn't the acute exercise of it my chief response to the stress I felt of welcoming a child into a world filled with race-related perils?

In 1980 I became an English teacher. On the college level I have worked with Black students who, for the most part, have been ill-prepared by the public schools to write the Standard English demanded of them. So while it has been an immediate responsibility to instruct the students in my basic writing courses the best I can, I feel that prevention in education is worth, at the very least, one ton of cure and, as such, I am concerned with language pedagogy along the full length of the curriculum. I have plunged into the sea of theoretical controversy described above, choosing to swim alongside those who see the legitimacy of Black verbal expression in formal educational contexts. My interest is not merely in the ways Black students can learn; I am also concerned about the psychic costs they pay. A pedagogy is successful only if it makes knowledge or skill achievable while at the same time allowing students to maintain their own sense of identity.

I have chosen to write about the various voices I have come to possess, to speak of my own psychic payments. Using my autobiographical narrative (the even-numbered chapters of this book) as a focal point, I have explored how I, as a native Black English speaker in an urban public school environment, acquired Standard English language skills. In addition I have addressed the broader subject of what was involved in acquiring certain strategies beyond strictly linguistic skills, namely mainstream *sociolinguistic competence*, which I employed in order to be a successful participant in certain settings. Such ability involves, as Philips (1972) suggests, "knowledge of when and in what style one must present one's utterances" (p. 372).

I developed my analytic approach out of the beliefs that, first, autobiographical artifacts serve as fairly accurate historical documents and, second, that human behavior is sensibly studied within the framework of a *transactional* model. I will elaborate on these two conceptions below.

An autobiographical account, despite its subjectivity, provides an important record of events the author has responded to—in short, what has shaped him or her as a social being. In a quest for such significance, the chronological facts of an individual's existence are not nearly as important as the psychological facts of forging a life, something autobiographies reveal quite well. Analysis of details presented in my autobiographical narrative, therefore, is crucial to an adequate understanding of my sociolinguistic development.

Although the personal narrative has been the primary database, I have scrutinized my accumulated school record obtained from the Board of Education of the City of New York. Several documents appear in the Appendix of this volume. This step was not taken for the purposes of corroboration in any strict sense. The intent was to elaborate on the personal narrative—not to confirm it.

Eisner (1981) also addresses this issue:

> In artistic approaches to research, the cannons of test reliability and sampling do not apply. While one might consider or question a writer's or film producer's reliability, there is no formalized set of procedures to measure writer reliability; one doesn't really want the mean view of four writer's observations about the mental hospital in Oregon which served as the subject-matter for Ken Kesey's play [*One Flew Over The Cuckoo's Nest*]. One simply wants Ken Kesey's view. Its validity, if that is the appropriate term, is to be determined by our view of its credibility,

> and not by reducing his work to some average by using only that portion that it shares with the views of others. Validity in the arts is the product of the persuasiveness of a personal vision; its utility is determined by the extent to which it informs. There is no test of statistical significance, no measure of construct validity in artistically rendered research. What one seeks is illumination and penetration. The proof of the pudding is the way in which it shapes our conception of the world or some aspect of it. (p. 6)

Once I became convinced that my personal narrative was legitimate subject matter for a study of language development, I sought to specify social-psychological and linguistic principles that would guide my probing. In this light a transactional model, in which humans are viewed as continually negotiating with an evolving environment, appeared attractive. From this perspective, behavior is neither the exclusive acting out of inner drives, nor is it shaped solely by external forces. One has personal traits and a belief system that set one's expectations and guide one's actions. The results of these actions in turn modify that belief system. The modified belief system governs further action and so on. Such a model of human action is described in the work of George A. Kelly (1963). He terms it the *psychology of personal constructs*. In examining the data, I have not restricted myself to a consideration of my past sociolinguistic performances in and of themselves; rather, I have tried to determine the conceptions I held that caused me to perform as I did.

Noam Chomsky's viewpoint is similar (1957, 1972). He stresses that an active, scientific intellect lies at the center of the language acquisition process. Rather than merely absorbing and reproducing the speech surrounding them, children manipulate patterns and experiment with language choices as they come to grips with language on their own terms. I have evaluated the data from a compatible outlook, having related as far as possible my sociolinguistic development to my accompanying perception of self-interest.

This analysis of my autobiographical materials should prove useful to all those concerned with helping African-American students develop their ability to communicate in mainstream settings, for I have also dealt with issues of language pedagogy in more universal terms. This discussion is reported in chapters 3, 5, 7, and 9.

In chapter 3 I focus on language development up until the first grade. I inspect some of the differences between Black English and Standard English, and I indicate how code-switching develops as a communicative strategy. Reading theories and the growth of nonverbal skill also are considered.

Chapter 5 deals with linguistic and educational progress through the third grade. I look at how such progress, or lack thereof, may be affected by the social (with emphasis on race) climate of the school. My own progress is seen as the outcome of successful negotiation with classmates, school officials, family members, and community residents. I detail my response to educational proposals for dialect eradication, linguistic pluralism, and bidialectalism.

In chapter 7 I am concerned primarily with the relatively advanced self-concept students have formed by the close of elementary school. I demonstrate ways in which linguistic ability, societal awareness, political events, and various demands by peers may relate to that sense of self. Additionally, I explore how both the willingness and reluctance to code-switch on the part of students may cause problems for teachers and researchers.

Chapter 9, the conclusion, is not a mere summary of results. It mostly pertains to my journey through high school, my reflections on that passage, and the way in which that experience helped to shape my views on language education.

None of the issues raised in this book are original areas for investigation, nor is this work intended to be unique in that sense. I sought to present an account that will further illuminate matters for those involved with the education of African-American students. The noted anthropologist, Clifford Geertz (1973), conveys the spirit intended here:

> The essential vocation of interpretive anthropology is not to answer our deepest questions, but to make available to us answers that others, guarding other sheep in other valleys, have given, and thus to include them in the consultable record of what man has said. (p. 30)

2

First Lessons

Some events come before the memory. Completely beyond the veil of vagueness. Just no way to recall. The only knowledge I have of the times came through eavesdropping. I could not deal with direct questioning because it was clear that made me a bug. Try to open up the past and I would get shrugged off with stares like roach spray. So I just kept listening and observing and drawing my own conclusions, trying to get a sense of what the pre-memory was all about. That's important to me because it's a part of life too and it's a lot like the wind, you know, you can't see it but it can kick your rump pretty good if it blows hard enough.

I hit the scene uptown in 1952 on a Sunday afternoon. I think I started out as a good reason for all to be happy, but there was a curious error on the take-home copy of my birth certificate. In the space where the name of the father belongs my own name was written in. His was left off the document altogether. That error, however committed, was my first omen.

I hadn't yet cut a tooth when I received omen number two. A fire broke out in our apartment. Started in back of the refrigerator. My mother detected it first, yanked my one-year-old sister out of her bed, snatched me up from the crib, and hustled on outdoors. She didn't bother to arouse her husband/my dad. It's a blessing he managed to get out on his own. I've always thought that was a horrible thing for her to do although by the time I heard the story, with the influence I was under, I felt he probably deserved it. And I have chuckled about the event on numerous occasions since. But at other times I have pictured my father lying dead in a robe of bright yellow flames and felt my own palms moisten with fear. There was no doubt something cruel going on in our little world.

The signs persisted like ragweed. Sad events that would be revealed to me in tale. The tale of the perfectly thrown frying pan, you know, it's more feistiness than I would like to see in a woman of mine. Sherry and I were, in one sense, beneath it all. Down on the floor knocking over and spilling everything. But we also assumed a role in the power play as it was we who became its center. Mama took that battle also; as far back as we can remember we had the distinct impression that we belonged to her exclusively. We were her objects of adornment and possession, always dressed for compliments. Pops could get no primary billing in that setup. When I think back now to my earliest remembrances I sense him only as a haze in the background. And even as I reel forward again and he begins to crystallize for me, it's quite some time before he appears essential. Moms, on the other hand, was ranked up there next to sunlight from the beginning.

That's a long way to come from Ashford, Alabama. Way down by the Chipola River. Little Margie, with stubbornness her most celebrated trait. Might as well whip a tree, they would say, if you were figuring on whipping her for a confession. At least you spare your own self some pain. And she was real close to her few chosen friends. If she liked you she could bring you loyalty in a million wheelbarrows. Labeled "good potential," she worked far below it. Skated her way through school. Folks have camped just outside her earshot for years whispering, "She's smart so she could do better if. . . ."

Ammaziah, though bright, didn't have a chance to skate through school. He had to work on a farm northeast of Ashford, going up toward the Chattahoochee. "He's just a plain nice man" is the worst thing I have ever heard anybody outside of our own household say about him. And I guess it would be hard not to like a big and gentle Baptist with a basic decency who could hold his liquor and had a name you could make fun of.

He liked to watch all the horses run and all the New York women too. Couldn't lick either gamble. He hadn't developed enough finesse for the big town. I know he tried hard at times but whenever he put together two really good steps irresponsibility would rear up and knock him back three. He couldn't be any Gibraltar for you.

All this going on around our heads. The big folks. Both destined to be enshrined in the best-friend-you-could-possibly-have hall of fame, provided they could keep each other off the selection committee. But they still hung out together. Hadn't fully understood the peace that can crop up here and there amid the greatest confusion. And right in the middle of 1954 came daughter number two. Judy ate well and slept a lot, then less, and grew to be a good partner to knock around with as we caromed off the walls of the Harlem flat and tumbled forward.

In the early reaches of memory events swirl about like batches of stirred leaves. No order or sequence. I remember we had two pet turtles. One had a yellow shell. The other's was red. We kept them in a bowl with a little plastic palm tree and tiny cream-colored pebbles. Sherry fed them and I poured in the fresh water. Well the turtles were a bit frisky. They often climbed out of the bowl and we had to overturn tables and cushions and chairs to find them. I don't recall how many times we went on this chase but it was all over one morning when they were found under the sofa with their bellies ripped open by rats. For a long time afterward I would associate rats with turtlemeat first, rather than cheese, which I guess isn't exactly a good start toward a high IQ.

So the turtles died early on. But I can't tell you whether that was before the back of my head was split open on the front stoop. There was a bunch of us out there preparing to run a dash down 146th Street. Victory wasn't the main thing in these races. Just please don't come in last or you would be the first one to get your mother talked about and everything. I had poor position inside along the rail next to this chubby girl, but as we came thundering past the front of the building I began to pull away from her. I was getting away from the last spot for sure when she reached out and pushed me down. My head banged hard into the edge of a concrete step and the blood started dripping down the back of my neck and I started screaming like crazy. Then I had to get shaven bald in one spot and look like a jerk so I could get patched up right. But that was better still than being last. I mean I had heard Pee Wee Thomas, who was in school already, tell Tyrone that the reason he was so slow was because whoever Tyrone's father was had to be slow too not to have been able to get away from Tyrone's ugly damn mama.

There was a babysitter we went to sometimes down on Seventh Avenue. Her name was Janine and she had boy-girl twins, Diane and Darnell, who were a few months older than Sherry. She was real nice and let us drag our toys all over the house, but whenever her husband, Butch, would come home early in the afternoon she would round us up quickly and herd us into the kids' room. We were under strict orders not to come out and of course we didn't. But she never said anything about peeping. The first time was at Darnell's suggestion. We crept up to the door and cracked it with the stealth of cat burglars. I couldn't see over Sherry and the twins so I crouched to the floor and never did get a look at the action. Darnell almost burst out laughing and we retreated to the farthest corner of the room. We sent Judy off to play with some blocks.

"What is they doin Sherry?" I whispered as I took a seat atop Darnell's wagon.

"Oh you so stupid Keith."

"Well I ain't see so good."

"Oh you just so stupid. Tell him Darnell." She and Diane were giggling.

"No you Sherry."

"No Darnell you."

"It's your brother. You 'pose to."

"I can't. I don't know for real."

"You know for real."

"No I don't."

"Then why you laughin?"

"I was laughin at you." And they all started laughing at each other. Then Darnell came and whispered in my ear: "They doin nasty."

"NASTY OOOOH NAS—." Darnell clamped his hand over my mouth. "You gotta be quiet Keith or we can't go no more."

I was quiet. And got to go many times before I decided, or was it Diane who decided, that we could do some nasty of our own. But we announced our intentions first and Sherry squealed and Janine gave both of us a spanking. Barely five, I was mad I had to wait.

I remember one Saturday we were coming home from the beauty parlor with my mother. I had on my cowboy get up, six-shooters at my sides. We were walking well up in front of her as usual, trained to stop at the corner. That morning, however, I took it into my head to go dashing across Eighth Avenue on my own. I think I saw my father but I'm not sure. I know I didn't look for any traffic lights. I tripped about halfway across and couldn't get to my feet again. I was struggling hard but my coordination had deserted me. Like scrambling on ice. There was a screeching of brakes and then the most gigantic bus imaginable was hovering over me. I still couldn't get the feet to work together. I was somehow yanked from under the bus, dragged the rest of the way across the street and, with my own pistols, beaten all the way up the block. It was a fierce thrashing and there were folks out there imploring my mother to stop. But verbal support was all I received. Wasn't anybody out there going to risk tangling with Moms. I have never fallen in any roadway, nor been pistol-whipped, since.

One evening we were digging into some fruit cocktail after dinner and heard a great ruckus out in the hallway. The cops were chasing these two drug addicts and they were headed for the roof. "They's junkies I know," said a man across the hall. Sherry had mentioned something about junkies to me before, but when the police paraded them down the stairs stark naked with their hands cuffed behind their backs it was the first time I had a good opportunity to see what they actually looked like. It was somewhat disappointing, however, for they looked just about like everybody else.

I was bringing a loaf of bread home from the store when I saw this gray dog getting his neck chewed off in a dogfight on the corner. I dropped my bag to go save him and was trying to push my way through the circle of gamblers and spectators when this huge man hoisted me up onto his shoulder. He thought I merely wanted a better view. Before I could figure a way to get down another man rescued the dog, though he was cursing the poor animal, and green bills changed hands around the circle.

Sherry had gone off to kindergarten and I decided to give Judy a sex change operation while our mother was asleep. I slipped her into a change of my clothing as I kept reassuring her. "You know it gon be more fun. You know it right?" She was properly willing. We had to roll the pants up at the bottom and her feet couldn't make it down into the toes of my sneakers but we could live with that. But we were dissatisfied with her hair. Such soft long braids. Boys get away with that now but not in '57.

"You gotta cut it."

"Then I be a boy Keith? I finish that I be a boy?"

"Yeah you'll be one. It gon be more fun too."

Scissors please. She wouldn't cut it in one fell swoop like I wanted her to do. She started nibbling at the edges. Tiny dark patches falling gently to the floor. As she became more relaxed, however, she began to clip at a faster pace and made a clearing on one side all the way to the scalp. I was urging her to clip even faster, "go head Judy go head," when Sherry came charging into the apartment, saw what was taking place, let out a long and soulful "Ooooooooooh I'm gonna tell Ma," and ran into the other room to awaken her. I began to sweat.

"You made me," Judy accused.

"No I didn't and you gon git in trouble and git a beatin too."

"You made me."

"I did not."

"Yes you did."

"I DID NOT." I had to get loud to prove my innocence. Moms was already approaching fast like an enraged lioness and I wanted no part of her fury. She slashed me across the legs with her strap and cast me aside. I was getting off light. Unbelievably so. But Judy got it all.

Maybe I could have stood up for Judy, but by then I was taking the vast majority of the whippings in the household. So I guess I figured what the heck, Judy could stand to share some of the weight. She may have become a trifle less eager to pursue my ideas of fun but I was sort of growing bored with running around the house with her all morning anyway. I mean Sherry was bringing home books and finger paintings all the time and making kindergarten seem like the hip thing.

It was all right I suppose. Artwork and musical chairs and fairy tales. The biggest kindergarten thrill for me, however, was the chance to come home along Eighth Avenue unescorted. Sherry didn't get out until three o'clock and my mother didn't embarrass me by picking me up like I was a baby, so every day I had a three-and-a-half-block distance to negotiate as I pleased. Or at least I took it that way.

Some of us would go scampering along the Avenue. Anything could happen out there. The side streets were tall and narrow with hallways no more interesting than our own. But Eighth Avenue, well, that was the real world. We stuck our noses into the barber shop, the shoe repair shop, the fish market, the bars. The conversation was mostly baseball and whores. Willie Mays was clearly the Prince of Uptown, and the next best thing you could be was a pimp. We threw stones at sleeping winos and followed the vegetable wagon all the way down to 140th Street waiting for the horse to move his bowels in the middle of the street. Then we'd stay and watch the cars run over the large piles of dung. Every time a tire scored a bull's-eye we'd shout "Squish" and spin about with glee. Don't let it be a truck that scored. Ecstasy. Sometimes we would run straight across 148th Street to Colonial Park to play tag and rock fight and climb the hill until the guilt snuck up on us one by one and then, each according to his conscience, we would begin to head for home.

From the very beginning my mother couldn't understand why it should take me over an hour to walk less than four blocks, especially when it meant showing up with my new jacket all muddy or my pants ripped at the knee, you know, the kinds of things you never notice until your mother points them out. And she made all her points clear with that belt. I tried telling her that the clock on the kitchen wall must be broken or something because I always ran straight home, but she wouldn't buy it. I eventually had to come around. And that's when I really got jammed.

There was a substitute teacher for our class one day and she didn't know the proper time to dismiss us. It must have been going on 12:30 and she was still reading us a story about Curious George. Our class was at the end of the hall, so when the other classes let out we couldn't hear them. There was no impatient parent to rescue us. The substitute just kept on and on about this wonderful monkey.

Finally she sensed something was wrong and asked us what time we were supposed to let out.

"Twelve o'clock" we chorused.

"Oh no" she exclaimed. "Are you sure?"

"We get out twelve o'clock" some of us repeated, as general chatter erupted about the room. Louis went up to her and said, "We get out when the two hands is straight up. That's twelve o'clock right?" She ran out of the room. When she returned a few moments later she was shouting "Hats and coats everybody. Hats and coats now. We're late."

Late was the last word I needed to hear. She couldn't let us out of there fast enough to suit me. I sprinted home as swiftly as possible, scaled the six flights of stairs in record time, and as I burst into the apartment out of breath my mother, as I knew she would be, was waiting for me belt in hand. She backed me up against the door with her stern voice.

"Haven't I told you about not coming straight home from school?" I caught my breath. I was sure glad I was armed with the truth.

"Ma we had a substitute. We had a substitute Ma and she didn't know what time to let us out. I ran all the way home."

"Boy don't tell that barefaced lie. I'll take the skin off your backside for lyin to me."

"But I ain't lyin Ma. I ain't."

"Shut up boy! Ain't no teacher can keep no class late like that."

"But she was readin us a story."

"Shut up I said. Don't be standin there and givin me no cold-ass argument." She drew back the strap and I cringed in terror. I sidestepped her, as the first blow crashed against my thigh, and took off for the living room. She was right behind me. I dove to my knees and stuck my head under the couch. It was one of the several defensive maneuvers I had developed by then. I was always mortgaging my rear to save my head. Wasn't going to let anybody beat me in the head. Which was all right with Moms.

"You ain't accomplishin nothing by stickin that behind up there like that boy. That's the part I want any old how. I'll teach you yet about not payin me no mind." She had that talking-beating rhythm in high gear. You know how you had to receive a lecture to go along with your whipping. And can't anyone on earth hand out a more artistic ass whipping than a Black woman can. Syncopated whippings: Boy didn't I lash lash tell you about lash lash lying to me? Lash lash lash lash hunh? Lash hunh boy? Lash lash lash hunh boy? Hunh? I was always supposed to answer these questions although my answering them never stopped anything and sometimes made matters worse, especially if I was giving the wrong answers as I was that day. Although I was hollering my head off I still managed to insist upon my innocence. To no avail. Lash lash lash I will break your behind lash if necessary lash boy. Do you hear me? Do you lash lash hear me?

I heard and I felt and it hurt both ways. After the beating I continued to proclaim my innocence. Only stopped when she became angry all over again and threatened me with more punishment. Afterward I complained to my sisters on occasion, but it was weeks before I mentioned the incident to my mother again. She just gave me a warm smile and said, "I'll tell you something Keith. It all evens out."

Sibling rivalry stalked me from behind. I was getting intensive reading lessons from Sherry and had made progress to the point where I was ready to show off for Moms. We had her cornered on the sofa and I was holding the book out in front of me. Sherry was on my right, ready to help if I faltered, so I started reading something like:

> "See here," said Don. "Here are blue flowers. We want blue flowers. Let us get blue flowers."

It was something along those lines, you know, and I was performing well. My mother was beaming and I had her undivided attention until Judy came out of somewhere, slid the edge of a razor blade into the side of my face clear to the bone, narrowly missing my eye, and ripped a deep diagonal clean past my ear.

Blood popped out everywhere. I spent what seemed like hours with my head ducked under a running faucet. Towels. Compresses. Mercurochrome. Bandages. Then my mother seized a high-heeled shoe and beat Judy worse than she had beaten me for almost getting myself killed out on the Avenue.

My little sister never apologized. In fact she used to taunt me about this incident as she was later becoming a favorite target for my aggression. No matter what I did to her. Kick her, trip her, whatever. She would just keep repeating, "So I cut you in the face."

"Do it again" I would retort most angrily.

"I did it already."

"I dare you to do it again. I'll push you out the window."

"No you won't."

"Yes I will."

"No you won't."

"I will so."

"Then I'll cut you in your face again."

"Then come on. Come on if you still think you so big and bad."

"I ain't scared."

"Come on then sucker."

"I'll cut you right in the face again."

"What you waitin for then fraidy cat?"

"I did it already."

She was about as mean a three year old as you will ever find.

Actually I had my hardest battles with Sherry. She was good for teaching me things but when her mood shifted I had to watch out. She gave me my next permanent scar by pressing a hot steam iron to the back of my hand. Burned off a circle of flesh. I later shattered a lightbulb against the bridge of her nose but she escaped unharmed. I think you can say we were taking this rivalry thing a bit too seriously.

At times my sisters would double-team me. We were heavily into words now and when my sisters discovered that to stifle mine was the best weapon they could use against me, it led to some of the unhappiest moments I can recall. They had found my fledgling sensitivity, clutched it about the windpipe, and squeezed. They teased me and baited me but whenever I began to reply they would shout as loudly as they could to obscure what I was saying. Their favorite lines were "Am sam sam sam sam. Am sam sam sam sam." As soon as I parted my lips they would start chanting and send me straight to tears. I would wipe aside the water, swallow hard to compose myself, and fall apart all over again. I could rumble and accept insults but I couldn't ever deal with not being allowed to speak. Their am sam curse was too devastating. I had neither the sense to ignore nor the strength to attack.

I don't recall much about a whole pregnancy, but when my mother left for the hospital one night in June of '58 there was only a single wish ringing in my consciousness: BOY. And I knew I would get a brother because it was the only thing that could even the score. He would be my guarantee to be heard because wasn't anybody going to brainwash little brother but me. I alone would teach him how to bound down the stairs two at a time and sneak to the park. And he'd be the real thing. No imitation like Judy. No turncoat like Sherry. I knew I would have to handle his fights for him but that was fine as long as he listened to me and helped me beat the am sam curse. We'd start our own "Ooma booma booma booma" or something like that. Fix them good.

When the phone rang my grandmother, who was up from Alabama, reached it first. I watched her smile as she spoke. As she turned toward me she was saying, "Yeah he standin right here. You know he can't wait to hear the news." She handed me the receiver.

"Hi Ma."

"Hi," she answered dreamily. "You finally have another sister."

I was condemned. I dropped the receiver and walked out of the room in a daze. Debra Lynn showed up a few days later with a head full of wild hair. She was a beauty, and from that day to this she has never been out of my heart. But she couldn't be a brother.

I had just one more summer to pass on 146th Street. Farmer Gray cartoons in the morning. The Jocko Show in the afternoon. Sit down and rock Debra Lynn for a spell or jump up and go wild to the rhythm of my first favorite record, "Tequila," by the Champs. And I was beginning to tread more lightly about the apartment, trying to avoid all scars and bruised feelings, overjoyed at any opportunity to go outside. Just give me the playground or send me to the corner grocery so I can squeeze in as much Eighth Avenue as possible before I have to hurry back. I couldn't shoot a basketball high enough to make a goal but I began learning how to dribble and saw my first pair of dead wide open eyes on a fat man lying amid a crowd in front of the fish market with a thin jagged line of blood across the width of his throat.

On Sundays, for religion, we went up on the hill. Skipping along the hexagon-shaped tile in Colonial Park. Darting up the steps to Edgecomb Avenue. Stopping in the candy store on St. Nicholas to load up. Leaning forward for leverage to finish the climb up to the church. I was always impressed by this particular house of the Lord. Tremendous gray and white cinder blocks. Polished maple pews in the main service room. Red carpet, stained windows, and gigantic organ pipes. And the Lord, he owned the best singers available. There was nothing like a gorgeous soprano wailing and sweating under influence of the spirit and a hot wig. There were always old women with blue dye in their hair shrieking and swooning during the sermon as folks around them grabbed hold of them while exclaiming, "Yes Lord. I see you done come to us." With women like that falling out in droves you had to believe. And Pops was up in the front row with the rest of the deacons. A broad-shouldered frame in a gray or blue suit. Sometimes wore white gloves to serve communion. He always winked at us when he passed by.

The first grade brought a teacher, Miss Novick, who we thought was the top genius on the planet. She was going to turn us all into little scientists she would say. And there was invariably one experiment or another for us to observe.

She placed a glass jar, two small candles in holders, and a box of matches on her desk. She raised the jar and candles over her head and waved them slowly for all to see.

"I have here a glass jar and two simple candles. Can everyone see them?"

"Yes Miss Novick," we replied, speaking as everyone.

"See them James?"

"Yeah."

"See them Karen?"

"Uh hunh."

"See them John?"

"I sees it."

"OK." She returned the objects to her desk, lit the candles and held them overhead. Our eyes were transfixed with magic show expectations.

"Now the candles are lit. You see? Rosanne? Ryan? Keith?" I gave a nod of affirmation. Then she lowered the candles to the desk and lifted the jar, upside down, as we inched forward in our seats.

"Now who can tell me what will happen if I set this jar down over one of these flames? Can anyone tell me? James?" He could not. He was smart but stumped. Sat looking dumb with his face greased and his eyes bulged and his index finger glued to his chin.

"How about you Barbara?"

"You gonna catch the des' on fire Miss Novick."

"YEAAHHHHHHHH. . . ."

"No, little scientists. No. No. No. We will not harm the desk. Anyone else? . . . No? . . . Well let us observe."

She placed the jar over one of the candles and we stared eagerly at both flames until the one inside the jar died out. Miss Novick surveyed our puzzled faces and smiled.

"Now why did that happen class?"

"You mean why it went out?"

"Yes Harold. Can you tell me why?"

"Because you put that jar on there. You made it go out Miss Novick. You did it."

"Sure Harold. But how could I do it with only the jar?"

"I don't know. Was there some water in there?"

"There wasn't Harold. We all looked at the jar together, remember?"

"Oh yeah."

"Anyone else?" Miss Novick was extremely patient and thoroughly flustered us all before giving us our first formal explanation concerning oxygen.

I liked the prospect of becoming a resident scientist up at P.S. 90 (strange what faith I had in the public school system up there), and when the announcement came later that fall that we were moving into a house out in Queens I was, at first, a bit disheartened. I knew there were scientific experiments elsewhere but I wasn't so sure I could get another Miss Novick or even more important, in a related field, another Eighth Avenue.

I wasn't anti-Queens; all I knew about the place was that it was over a bridge somewhere. But I surely had no beef with Harlem. I didn't recoil at the sight of its streets as I would at other times later in life. I had no sense of society being so terrible. I was there and I fit.

On another level, however, I guess I did welcome a chance to leave the apartment I was associating more and more with misunderstanding and pain. *House* sounded like more space to stay out of the way of others.

So at the age of six it was time for a crossing. My young mind poised for any game that came along. Could play the middle or skirt the fringe as I saw fit. Just come out stepping light and easy, you know, and if it gets hectic remember to cover in the clinch. The point was to hold the defense together while all about me from complex fabrics of frustration and rejection and sensitivity and conflict and hope and loneliness and resignation and reticence and wonderment and bewilderment and romantic notions and romantic disappointments, from all this and more, the imposing offense was being woven.

And the bridge bowed gracefully and beckoned. Bore me upon its majestic back and arched me high above the cold and swirling dark waters of that November toward another shore, and another truth, which all should know: Most times a bridge is just another two-way street.

3

Rapping, Reading, and Role-Playing

Early Language

The speech of a large group of African-Americans has been given many labels, including Ebonics, Black English Vernacular, and just plain Black English. The last term is by far the most popular. I will use it throughout this text to refer to my native tongue—that is, the language variety I first acquired and the one I have always been able to use with greatest facility.

The idea of Black English is still controversial despite research dating back three decades, which documents that it is a legitimate linguistic system and not merely a collection of verbal aberrations arrived at by the reckless violation of the rules of a so-called superior variety of English. But let us presently make an end run around that debate. The intent here is not to argue the existence or overall merits of Black English. The case has been made quite well by scholars such as Smitherman (1977), Dillard (1973), and Haskins and Butts (1973). The most pressing purpose at this point is to demonstrate how the dialogue of the Keith character (me) is reflective of that language variety.* The analysis is meant to be indicative rather than exhaustive. As such, a thorough review of the rules of Black English will not be required. Structural explanations will be offered only to further illuminate the specific portions of the text being considered. Perhaps it is instructive, however, to include a general definition. Smitherman's should suffice: "Black Dialect is an Africanized form of English reflecting Black America's linguistic-cultural heritage and the conditions of servitude, oppression and life in America" (p. 2).

In the previous chapter, as the four youngsters are engaged in the Peeping Tom scene, we find the following snatches of dialogue.

*Again, the premise is that these sequences, while not actual, are certainly plausible.

(1) "What is they doin Sherry?" (Keith speaking)
(2) "Oh you so stupid Keith." (Sherry speaking)
(3) "Then why you laughin?" (Darnell speaking)
(4) "They doin nasty." (Darnell speaking)

The *is they* combination in sentence 1 would be identified as an error in noun-verb agreement under the rules of Standard English; however, this construction exemplifies the Black English convention of simplifying the conjugation of the verb *to be*. Smitherman again explains: "When the forms of *be* are used, they are simplified so that *is* and *was* usually serve for all subjects of sentences, whether the subjects are singular or plural, or refer to *I*, *you*, *we* or whatever" (p. 21).

Skeptics may suggest that this speech is not an example of some Black English rule but simply the utterance of a child who has yet to master this element of agreement. After all, the speaker in this case is only five, an age at which noun-verb agreement errors are likely still to be numerous for any speaker of English. However, I must counter that the type of noun-verb error committed by a five year old in the process of acquiring Standard English is of a different nature than constructions like *is they*. Consider the description by Beck (1979) of the language of the five- to six-year-old child relative to noun-verb combinations:

> The child should be advancing in use of the full verb system, although errors, particularly in noun and verb number agreement, are still prevalent. . . . The kindergarten child is as likely to say "There is flowers" as to say "There are flowers," the head word sounding singular to the child, who incorrectly anticipates the major noun's number. (p. 96)

The puzzlement that exists for the child in Beck's presentation is not to be found in the case of *is they* or, by transformation to the declarative form, *they is*. Here there is no question that the noun, *they*, is plural. The choice of the accompanying verb, *is*, is definitely not based on a perception of singularity as opposed to plurality and thus cannot be said to epitomize number confusion. Furthermore, and a more obvious rebuttal, I made *they is* "mistakes" long past the age that the speaker of strictly Standard English eventually masters even the most difficult aspects of noun-verb agreement. In fact, I am still making them. But my *they is* type of talk is not merely a transitory stage in the acquisition of Standard English. It clearly points to a deeply held rule, one I already was adhering to at the age of five. The simplification of the verb *to be*, like several other features of Black English, can only erroneously be viewed as representing a stage, or worse, an arrest in the acquisition of an alternate linguistic system.

Operative in sentences 2, 3, and 4 is the much discussed zero copula rule—that is, the omission of *be* when it would only refer to events fixed in time and nonrepeating (Smitherman, p. 21). Thus we get in sentence 2 *you so* and not *you are so*; in 3, *why you* and not *why are you*; in 4, *they doin* and not *they are doin*. Although these lines are not exact quotations, it is obvious that, as a member of that peer group, I produced these types of utterances. This is not, by the way, to suggest that language learning is solely an imitative activity. We understand from Kelly (1963) that the essential nature of human learning lies not in imitating but in active construing. Fortunately, I speak so many zero copula phrases, both real and literary, that the claim above does not have to be based solely on the evidence so far chosen. I have opted to make the case at this juncture for purposes of organization.

Let us look at sentence 1 from another angle. Although the speaker of *is they* conforms to a rule of Black English, he ignores the zero copula rule, which he also uses on occasion. The zero copula rule is a nonobligatory rule, whereas the simplification of *to be* is required. Put another way, one may use a form of *to be* and still be speaking Black English, but that form must be *is* or *was*. It is interesting enough to ponder why he chose to bypass the zero copula rule while his sister and friends were using it. But matters become even more intriguing when one is aware that yet another rule of Black English was bypassed, that of question formation. Questions in Black English can be asked by means of rising intonation (Burling 1973). Thus one could hear "What they is doin?" as well as "What is they doin?" So the issue now is to determine what significance can be attached to sentence 1 in light of the fact that it reflects two choices to ignore certain rules of Black English. More on this a little later.

In the haircut scene, there is a two-sentence response to an inquiry by Judy.

(5) "Yeah you'll be one."
(6) "It gon be more fun too."

Note the use of the auxiliary in sentence 5, *you'll*, while in 6 it is ignored (an instance of zero copula). Sentence 5 is not Black English at all, although we can discern from the grammar of the following sentence that the speaker surely had the ability to say, "Yeah you gon be one." The contrast is even greater than that spotted in the earlier dialogue. Also note that *gon* represents a strong Black English phonology pattern. The sound system of Black English is relatively difficult to capture in print, but the contraction *gon* in place of *going to* is, nevertheless, a stark indicator. Smitherman describes its formation: "Here the *to* is omitted altogether, and the nasal sound at the end is shortened, producing a sound that is somewhat like an abbreviated form of *gone*" (p. 18). To reiterate though, this option was not chosen in sentence 5.

In the whipping scene, we see that the mother initiates the dialogue with a question that is clearly Standard English. The reply is equally standard. But when the story is flatly rejected and the physical threat becomes immediate, whatever coolness has been maintained gives way and the dialect changes.

(7) "Boy don't tell that barefaced lie."
(8) "I'll take the skin off your backside for lyin to me."
(9) "But I ain't lyin Ma."
(10) "I ain't."

In part the child, in sentences 9 and 10, is following the lead of his mother who not only has added to his stress but has actually shifted, in 7 and 8, into an alternate vernacular. Great variance in grammatical structure is not apparent in this speech, nor is the huge phonological shift evident. However, the semantics are telling. This is clearly the talk of Black folks. And it is not at all surprising that very quickly we come across a multiple (triple or more) negation.

(11) "Ain't no teacher can keep no class late like that."

This pattern of negation, distinct from the double negatives that appear commonly in all nonstandard forms of English, occurs quite frequently in Black English and is perhaps the most noncontroversial marker of that language variety.

My mother is a bidialectal speaker, capable of producing Black English and Standard English as well. And it should be obvious, with the examples so far adduced, that even in the preschool years my own move toward bidialectalism was well underway, made possible no doubt by my awareness of my mother's verbal maneuvering. I had seen how she could speak to a grocer, a salesman, a doctor, or a stranger in one manner (Standard) and then turn around, watch me carelessly knock a bowl of cereal on the floor, and exclaim, "Now look what you done did!" She was displaying and I was learning a technique linguists refer to as code-switching. Elgin (1979) defines this phenomenon as the "ability to move back and forth among languages, dialects, and registers with ease, as demanded by the social situation" (p. 109). Although this is a pretty fair description of the skill involved, the word *ease* is objectionable, as it seems to imply that the whole process is somehow psychically neat. I have often chosen to switch, rather than fight, but the routine hasn't always implied any emotional ease. For a definition that is essentially similar yet allows the appropriate room for pain, one may consult Penalosa (1981). He defines code-switching as "a strategy by which the skillful speaker uses his knowledge of how language choices are interpreted in his community to structure the interaction so as to maximize outcomes favorable to himself" (p. 77).

That my mother was the chief agent helping me learn to code-switch should not raise any eyebrows. She was, after all, the dominant person in my life. There appears, however, to have been some specific sociolinguistic principle operative as well. Labov (1981) contends that women generally employ more prestige forms than men and tend to exhibit much greater fluctuation in the modes they employ. The fact that my mother achieved the status of number-one role model for bidialectal speech patterns in both the text and my present recollection was only, as Labov indicates, the most likely outcome.

Despite this discussion of bidialectalism, bear in mind that such discourse does no damage to the claim that Black English is my native tongue. It merely demonstrates that I was not growing up as a speaker of the basilect or most uncontaminated form of the language (see Stewart 1969). Relatively few Blacks are. A child, indeed a whole community, would have to exist in extreme isolation for any language variety to remain pure. I would expect, therefore, most Blacks to be bidialectal to some extent.

But if we accept another contention of Labov, that no one is ever perfectly bidialectal—that is, even-handed in a linguistic sense—I think we can safely assert, based on the evidence then and now, that for me Black English was developing as the dominant tongue while Standard English, though quite significant, was not wielded as handily.

With this information to augment the text, we can return to the dialogue cited earlier and more firmly avow that it is authentic in that it captures the reality that forms of Standard English were also being acquired. What initially may seem to be blundering manipulations of voice are better understood as accurate portrayals of an emerging bidialectalism. To render the speech only in Black English would not have been genuine. Therefore we should expect sentences like number 1. There is no doubt that this is Black English, but the use of the auxiliary *is* and its placement immediately preceding the subject, *they*, displays competence (subject-auxiliary inversion) in forming interrogatives along the lines of Standard English. Similarly, the use of *you'll* in sentence 5 manifests mastery of the contraction system. Beck indicates that both of these capabilities generally come to be distinct, indeed, in the speech of the five to six year old.

With this in mind, it should startle no one that sentence 6, a decidedly Black English sentence, follows sentence 5, for it highlights the juxtaposing of dialects that was occurring. Of great importance, in addition, is that each case of shifting or mixing happens as the child is experiencing conflicting social demands. In the Peeping Tom scene, he must appear knowledgeable even while being forced to ask a question of slightly older peers; the haircut scene requires that he talk down to a three year old yet coax her into action; and in the whipping scene, it is necessary that he try to inject some special combination of caution and urgency into his voice in an attempt to avoid physical punishment. This implies an awareness of the social relevance of dialects, a skill often assigned by scholars to a later stage of development. Smitherman, for example, indites that "among school-age blacks, one would find a greater degree of bi-dialectalism among older adolescents than among younger black children, for adolescents have begun to get hip to the social sensitivities associated with different kinds of languages and dialects" (pp. 31–32). I think folks get hip long before that age. The crucial dynamic is choice. Younger children, mostly out of self-defense, are not on the whole as willing to "play the game." But they can perceive much of the game and could play a lot of it if they so desired.

Troike (1972) asserts that even the youngest schoolchildren pay a great deal of attention to the social significance of dialect differences. Speaking of the child's ability to alternate between linguistic systems, he reasons that "despite cultural beliefs to the contrary, even very young children are often quite aware of the social relevance of stylistic and dialect differences" (p. 305). He proceeds to give the example of a first grader who was given a picture in a magazine and asked to tell a story about it to a researcher.

> The girl drew herself up, began "Once upon a time, . . ." and launched into a very formal narrative which was notable for containing no contractions. At the end of the story, she visibly relaxed, and from there on freely used contractions for the remainder of the interview. The whole subject of the range of styles and dialects in the productive and receptive repertory of children is only just beginning to receive attention, and a great deal yet remains to be learned. Nevertheless, it is clear that even pre-first-graders are far from linguistically naive and have already learned a great deal about the adaptive significance of linguistic behavior within their own very real social world. (p. 309)

The whole question of the child's social awareness of dialect differences will be of major concern, of course, throughout this work. At present, the essential notion to understand is that this social awareness on my part was considerably sharpened even during the preschool years.

I carried with me a tremendously empowering repertoire of speaking and listening skills when I shuffled off to public school and continued to expand it once I arrived. Included in my bag of communicative tricks were that prize stratagem, Black English, a productive (speaking) biloquialism, and a broader receptive (listening) bidialectalism. There was also an adroitness at responding to the perceived need to match each dialect to different sets of social circumstances. All this achievement may appear quite marvelous and, I guess, actually is. But it represents nothing miraculous beyond the basic miracle of existing, nothing special among Black children, nothing that should not be the case if a developing mind is pretty much left alone. Put more succinctly, it really ain't no new news.

Reading Acquisition

As the story indicates, I literally shed blood in the process of learning how to read. Such action should not become the basis for educational policy (though perhaps on a symbolic level it has), but it does indicate, in a way that only blood can, just how important I felt reading was. Being able to comprehend print allowed me to participate in my environment on yet another level; it was a skill I just had to have. Naturally, therefore, I kept close tabs on whatever progress my older sister was making toward literacy, and I was, in fact, doing a considerable amount of reading before I received any formal school instruction. (Such instruction could not have come before first grade, at which point I was already six and a half.)

I will attempt here to sketch how this reading acquisition transpired. First I will speak about the reading process in broad, general terms; then I will pay particular attention to the controversy that inevitably surrounds a discussion of initial reading instruction. I will consider then the role that literature (such as the fairy tales mentioned three times in the text) played in my personal attempts to read. And finally I will elaborate on the notion, alluded to above, of literacy in the context of social relations.

THE READING PROCESS

Frank Smith (1971, 1979) asserts that since there are no unique physical structures in the brain that specifically account for the ability to read, there is nothing special to say about reading once a correct assessment of human learning in general has been made (1979, p. 2). In his view, when we look at print we derive meaning from it in much the same way as we derive meaning from other objects in the world. We recognize it, which is an alternate way of saying that we reduce all our relevant uncertainty about what it is, and we make informed predictions as to its meaning, which rule out unlikely occurrences. Smith realizes that "prediction is not a new and artificial skill that has to be learned but the *natural* way to make sense of the world" (1979, p. 77). We will make mistakes of course, but the point is that the mistakes are insignificant if they don't interfere with actual meaning. Or as Smith himself asks, "If a mistake makes no difference, then what difference can it make?" (1979, p. 34). A fluent reader, he gathers, will probably bother with only one-fifth of the graphic information on the page.

Smith further argues that if one, in fact, tries to make too precise an identification of individual words or letters while reading, this increases his or her chance of error. By analogy he explains:

> The situation is rather similar for a sentry on duty on a dark night who hears approaching footsteps but who cannot reveal his own position by asking questions. His alternatives are to shoot or hold his fire. If he shoots and the intruder is indeed hostile, then the sentry will get a medal. If he holds his fire and the stranger is friendly his decision is also commendable. But a miss (letting through an enemy) or a false alarm (shooting a friend) are less desirable consequences. Yet the nature of the world is such that sentries always have to settle for some level of probability for the undesirable consequences; the man anxious to stop every enemy is going to shoot a friend from time to time, while the sentry anxious not to shoot a friend is occasionally going to let an enemy slip through. . . . The skilled reader cannot afford to set his criterion too high for deciding on word or meaning identification; we see that if he demands too much visual information, he will often be unable to get it fast enough to overcome memory limitations and read for sense. (1971, pp. 24–25)

Making sense, of course, is the single most important thing about reading, for it is the urge that motivates us to read in the first place. And within the limits of his general conception, which clearly argues the centrality of an anticipatory psychology to an understanding of the reading process, Smith offers several specific insights into the act of reading that merit attention here. First is that efficient readers do not decode to sound. If this were not so, if they did decode to sound, then they could read no faster than the rate of speech or the rate at which they could hear the words inside their heads. It is known that skilled readers (perhaps like yourself) can read several times faster than the average rate of speech. So Smith's stance appears to be correct. A related insight is that one cannot read one word at a time and read for sense. This is due, as alluded to above, to the physical limitations of short-term memory. If a person is reading at such a slow pace, he or she cannot hold enough strands of information in his or her brain simultaneously in order to make necessary connections, to make sense. A third belief that logically follows is that the most fluent readers are the ones who require the least visual information. And fourth is the notion that "meaningful language is transparent; we look through words for the meaning beyond" (Smith 1979, p. 123).

Some affirmation of Smith's approach can be found in the work of Isakson (1979). His research, in which the performances of college students on a reaction-time test were measured, indicates that sense is indeed extracted directly from print in meaning units as opposed to word units:

> The reader seems to be searching actively for the information which, combined with his general world knowledge, will allow him to identify the structural relationships between the words he has encountered. When the information is sufficient for at least a tentative identification of structure, processing activity increases so as to integrate the words received up to that point. (p. 164)

Kenneth Goodman (1967) has offered a view of the reading process, which he terms a "psycholinguistic guessing game," that also supports Smith's position. He specifically criticizes Spache (1964) and McCracken and Walcutt (1963) for having forwarded the notion of reading as a linear, cumulative process rather than as a selective leap toward meaning.

THE NOT-SO-GREAT DEBATE

Much has been made of the argument between those who favor a global (reading for meaning) approach to reading instruction and those who favor a code approach (usually phonics). Scholars of the Smith-Goodman ilk favor the global method of course. Their view is a logical extension of the theoretical stance described above. Let us consider specifically how this conception informs their pedagogical position.

Smith (1980) asserts that the only basic insights necessary for learning how to read are (a) print is meaningful and (b) print is different from speech. Once these two insights have been achieved and children are exposed to a variety of interesting and complex material, then reading acquisition should, Smith believes, proceed as naturally as oral language acquisition. As he states:

> I have argued that children need two basic insights to begin to learn to read. Also, I have implied that with these insights children can solve all

> the other problems associated with print by themselves provided that no extraneous confusion or hindrance is put in their way. They must be able to predict and make sense of language in the first place, and they can do this only by bringing meaning to it. This is certainly the way that all children learn spoken language and is probably the reason that many of them succeed in learning to read despite the instructional method used. (p. 423)

Smith's notions seem plausible, but they are totally rejected by prophets of the "phonics first" approach. Chief among these individuals is Rudolf Flesch, author of *Why Johnny Can't Read* (1955) and *Why Johnny Still Can't Read* (1981). He advances an argument long on acerbic rhetoric but decidedly short on substance.

My first objection to Flesch's conception is that he misrepresents the position of the psycholinguists, namely Smith and Goodman. He says that psycholinguistics is only look-and-say in shiny new garments (1981, pp. 23–24). But look-and-say, in the sense of focusing on one word at a time, giving word lists to memorize, and restricting vocabulary development, is definitely *not* what psycholinguistics is about at all. So any attack on those methods, and they certainly are restrictive, cannot simultaneously be a criticism of, say, Smith, who seems to be Flesch's favorite target.

Aside from this, Flesch's perception of reading failure is much too simplistic. He analyzes the phenomenon without any regard to the surrounding social or social-psychological circumstances. His argument, simply put, is that reading failure is rampant because of look-and-say instruction and would be eliminated if everyone were taught by the "phonics first" method. The fallacy here, of course, is to think that any instructional method alone can guarantee students success, for any such method is but an abstraction in and of itself. Its worth can be ascertained only in a social arena of real teachers and real students. (Note that Smith's primary concern is with the nature of reading, not the teaching of reading.)

Flesch persists in his distortion by presenting the following picture of reading acquisition. Before one learns to read, the argument goes, one must know the "mechanics" of reading. In the case of phonics, one must first learn all the rules for spelling-to-sound correspondences (roughly

180 of them). Once one knows the rules one can sound out, and therefore read, any print. Typically, then, after one or two years of instruction a child can read 24,000 words, whereas a child taught another way can only read 1,000 or so words.

Again, Flesch is a proponent of sophism. If one defines reading as making sense of print, then the mere sounding out of words does not assure that such activity is taking place. But perhaps even more basic is the question of whether one can actually sound out words accurately on the basis of phonics alone. Smith submits that one cannot because the spelling-to-sound correspondences in English are not one to one but many to many. In fact, Smith asserts, the chances of successfully sounding out a word phonetically is only one in four (1979, p. 55). He illustrates the problem:

> Here are eleven common words in each of which the initial *ho* has a different pronunciation—*hot, hope, hook, hoot, house, hoist, horse, horizon, honey, hour, honest*. Can anyone really believe that a child could learn to identify any of these words by sounding out the letters? (1979, p. 56)

He goes on to add that "phonics works if you know what a word is likely to be in the first place. . . . It is not surprising that children who are best at phonics are the best readers—they have to be" (1979, pp. 56–57).

Smith overstates his case somewhat by arguing that a program based on phonics would be too complex for even a computer to read. Flesch has countered by citing that a Kurzweil Reading Machine can, in fact, "read" by using a phonics-based program fed into a computer. But I fail to see the relevance of this information. For, alas, children are not Kurzweils, and the machine is doing what machines are made for: to do work that humans cannot do efficiently. Reading by phonics is some of that work.

The last problematic claim by Flesch is that other children will be severely limited in the number of words they can read as opposed to phonics-first readers. He has reached this conclusion by inspecting the word lists of nonphonics reading books. But I know of no evidence to show that children read only the words in their readers. Counting word lists, therefore, is by no means an accurate measure of how many words children know. If children have it set in mind to read and are actually reading in some instances, they will not allow themselves to be restricted to any reading book. Nor, I hope, will they be constrained by any teacher. Any method that tries to force them to focus on only one aspect of the reading process is harmful.

All this is not to say that phonics is irrelevant. It is one strategy for figuring out text, and as a child assembles a repertoire of strategies, there is some place for it. The essential point, however, is that a child is searching for sense, and at no point should that search be hindered by dogmatic instruction. Just as one learns spoken language by total immersion in it, so it must be with reading. And so it was, I am sure, for me. Bissex (1980) has made a similar discovery. Reporting on her assiduous observation of her son, she writes:

> Development—and Paul's development in particular—is not evenly paced. There is more rapid movement through the earlier strategies and concepts because these are more limited and incomplete in relation to the demands of the tasks. Especially at the beginning, quite drastic change seems essential for progress. It may not matter so much where a child begins in reading (phonics, sight words, language experience) as that he begins *somewhere* that works for him and soon moves somewhere *else*. Later strategies, being more inclusive and complex, allow room for more extended development. (p. 168)

Bissex, as is proper, sees a child's active intellect in control of the reading acquisition process. It is a blessing that children have such intellects, as well as the strength to persevere in the face of all the not-so-great debates around them.

OF LITERATURE

> Sentimental things are said about the magical world of literature and the imagination, but few think of applying this driving force to the basic learning of literacy tasks. Nor do they think of remedying the situation for those children who have not learned to operate imaginatively. For such children, half their motivation for becoming literate is paralyzed, and so learning to read must be like learning to walk with one leg. (Holdaway 1979, pp. 55–56)

Don Holdaway understands that the story and the poem address and in turn spur our curiosity in ways more powerful than our own immediate experience. The world of fantasy opens to us whole new vistas. This is particularly true of small children, always our most eager seekers. The lure of the story is what kept me and my kindergarten class transfixed when we should have been on our way home. In listening to *Curious George*, we all wanted to know what this monkey could encounter in the way of adventure, of ups and downs. Most important, we wanted to find out what we could make of his ups and downs, for by then we, of course, were having a few ups and downs ourselves. It is in such a way that literature can enlighten young lives and, in fact, all lives. As Rouse (1978) tells us, "life will never be a substitute for literature, it's not long enough" (p. 92).

When listening to a story and thus expanding the limits of their conception, children receive valuable assistance in their own quests to apprehend print. Britton (1972) develops this idea:

> The children who listen are gaining experience of written forms of the English language, and this aspect of the process is of particular importance to those who cannot yet read for themselves. There is an art of listening to reading that is very different from the process of listening to somebody talking to you—and this art contributes to the art of reading. (p. 150)

The young listener even before attending school can put together, in Holdaway's terms, a literacy set (p. 62). On an emotional level, this involves having a high expectation of print, of viewing it as a source of pleasure and fulfillment. Linguistically the child is picking up on the types of intonation patterns, idioms, and vocabulary that are found more in print than in speech. On an operational level, the child has become aware of such predictive operations as using the context to fill in particular language slots and can also follow plot and other logical arrangements. Concerning the conventions of print itself, the child may know that it is composed from left to right, from top to bottom, left page before right page. The child may also know some letters, understand some phonetic principles, and may have some concept of "words" and "spaces."

Looking back at "First Lessons," we see every indication that the development of a literacy set as described above was well underway. I mentioned earlier that I was reading before formal school instruction. By doing so I probably saved myself, in a sense, from such instruction. With respect to reading I had a little edge on the school, a leg up if you will. You might even say that up there on 146th Street, I had a "head start."

OF FAMILY

Denny Taylor (1983), in describing her approach to ethnographic literacy research, reports: "My task was to develop systematic ways of looking at reading and writing as activities that have consequences and are affected by family life" (p. xiii). The implication is that much literacy acquisition (like mine) goes on in the home, for which the home is not given proper credit. That oversight will not be a problem here.

If I ever had a true reading teacher, it was my older sister. If anyone were explicitly manipulating my attempts to comprehend print, it was mainly she. Or perhaps I was manipulating her (probably both). For as determined as she was to show off what she knew, I was just as determined to make her display it. She was not going to leave me behind, participate on a broader level than I, share anything, especially with our mother, that I could not share. So apart from any incentive a school might provide, reading took on great significance within the confines of our very own family. It was not only a way of widening and deepening perspectives through a self-regulated encounter with story; it was a way of enhancing social status. This use of reading as a tool of social growth is seen by Taylor to be essential:

> The question emerges of whether we can seriously expect children who have never experienced or have limited experience of reading and writing as complex cultural activities to successfully learn to read and write from the narrowly defined pedagogical practices of our schools. Can we teach children on an individual level of intrapersonal processes what they have never experienced on a social level as interpersonal processes of functional utility in their everyday lives? I would submit that we cannot. (pp. 90–91)

It is clear that my early reading skills, like my oral ones, developed largely within a family context. Familial relations dictated that these skills were to be regarded as cherished possessions. My younger sister at three, poised with blade in hand, obviously understood a great deal about the social value of reading.

Impression Management

On one level this entire chapter has been about linguistic role-playing, the use of certain conventions of language to sustain various relationships. I have discussed my doing what we all do: using language as a way of adapting to situations and, to some extent, as a means of defining and controlling situations. We all practice, in Goffman's (1959) terms, the art of impression management. It is important to realize, however, that such a display of verbal ability as described above grows directly out of and then evolves alongside a general social competence. Or as Byers and Byers (1972) indicate:

> And when we examine a human relationship such as a simple conversation between two people, we almost immediately discover that there are multiple modalities or channels operating in addition to language. We discover that the modalities, verbal and nonverbal, are learned as patterns of the culture (as language is learned) and that they are systematic (as language has grammar, for example). Furthermore we discover that they all fit together: they are systematically interrelated. (p. 6)

What we see, therefore, is that there is a nonverbal grammar (or grammars) to be acquired. More will be made of this later on. But even with respect to the character we have been considering thus far, the conception is certainly convenient, and it should not be surprising that I have made quite specific remarks in the narrative about this particular set of skills.

At the close of "First Lessons," I assert that I "could play the middle or skirt the fringe as I saw fit." It was easier written than done, of course, but it is evident that I had some idea of how much an actor I had to be and had confidence that I could handle the part. I had a clear (we might even say conscious) notion of how important even nonverbal adaptation or impression management was in protecting my own developing identity. If I had landed in Rome, I certainly would have been about the business of doing as the Romans were doing—if I had thought it would help matters. I later took this heightened awareness into a dominant White environment, and because I was afforded a certain measure of participation, I picked up certain elements of the grammar of White, middle-class, particularly Jewish, nonverbal communication (such as when to make eye contact and when not to), which I in turn used to guide the impressions the residents of that environment formed (while they were of course trying to figure out and outmaneuver me). It may be an open question as to who acted better, but I undoubtedly did all right.

"All the world," Goffman writes, "is not, of course, a stage, but the crucial ways in which it isn't are not easy to specify" (p. 72). He does, nevertheless, proceed to detail the most significant difference. "An action staged in a theater is a relatively contrived illusion and an admitted one: unlike ordinary life, nothing real or actual can happen to the performed characters" (p. 254). Art may imitate life, then, but it is not nearly as difficult. The curtain was always up for me, as for most, and I was a young lad as busy as the next child learning lines, mastering gestures, working on all levels to manage impression.

While I am being so direct about impression management let me offer, in closing out this chapter, a few more phrases in trying to shape yours. The home in Harlem from which I was catapulted into the larger world was one that was, in a sociolinguistic sense, enabling—not disabling. Tensions existed that obviously helped to shape my personality in ways I have yet to fully understand, but such tensions alone did not, in fact could not, impede the acquisition of the sociolinguistic ability that has been examined in this chapter. There was a *consistency* in that habitat and, I submit, it is the apprehension of consistency that is the cognitive key to communicative development. The prime affective requirement, of course, is that the use of such skills helps to establish some social relation that is gratifying. My home, no matter what else it was, took care of me on both counts.

4

Semivoices

We came to Corona when the garbage trucks still ran three or four times a week. But it wouldn't continue that way for long. The White evacuation, of mostly Irish and Italians, was nearly complete, and all community services would eventually tail off leaving Blacks and blight hand in hand, wondering if they caused each other. Folks who stayed in Harlem, Brooklyn, or the Bronx would say we had moved out to Long Island. With a twenty-minute cab ride they thought we had reached outer suburbia. It wasn't nearly so great of course, but I could see how it seemed like a decent deal to families fleeing from tenements. Back then you could purchase a respectable two-family house for ten to fifteen thousand dollars, probably under the GI bill, rent out the top floor, and maybe see a comparatively rosy future. In our case we even got new furniture on credit. And we were on one of the nicest blocks in the neighborhood, treelined 34th Avenue, a block and a half east of Junction Boulevard. That was a street most aptly named, for it served as a border between two neighborhoods, Corona and Jackson Heights, and between two worlds—a Black one and a White one. Junction Boulevard was often referred to as the Mason-Dixon Line in Queens.

I was fairly pleased. The basement and backyard held good possibilities for hideaway and play, and there was a park right in the next block with seesaws, swings, the works. No Eighth Avenue. But not all that bad.

We were located virtually equidistant between P.S. 92 on 99th Street in Corona and P.S. 149 on 94th Street in Jackson Heights. They were both located on 34th Avenue, and Sherry and I could spot them from in front of the house. We had no idea which way to go until our mother came outside with the baby carriage and headed east toward the dark-complexioned 92. I kept right on her heels, excited. We were turned away from that school, something about overcrowding and new zoning, and directed to 149. I kept on her heels, still excited, across the Mason-Dixon.

After Sherry and I were registered, the principal, Mr. Price, escorted us to class. His pants were too baggy and long. The back of the cuffs flapped up under his heels as he walked. We thought it was funny that he should want to ruin his pants that way, and all the way down the hall we fought the urge to burst out laughing. I didn't feel very humored, though, when he ushered me into Class 1-1 and exposed me to a room full of White kids. I trembled. I wanted to grab hold of one of Mr. Price's baggy trouser legs like it was a mother's apron, but I couldn't allow myself to show that much fear. I wished Sherry would come in but when I realized she wouldn't I wished the same shock on her wherever she went. Or worse. It's like they were trying to stare me back out of the room. Goldstein. Rubin. Landau. Weiss. Cohen. I knew next to nothing about kids like that. Only saw them on the subway a couple of times and in the doctor's office downtown. My eyes frantically searched theirs, trying to find some sign I could translate into friendliness. There was one Black student, a girl in pigtails, and she stared as hard as anyone else. Mr. Price spoke at last.

"Hello class, this is Raymond Keith Gilyard." The name suddenly sounded important to me. "He's a fine enough young man, isn't he?" They answered in synchronized yesses. The principal continued. "What shall we call you, young Master Gilyard? Shall we call you Raymond or Keith?"

Nobody had ever called me Raymond before. Uptown it was always Keith or Keithy or Little Gil. Raymond was like a fifth wheel. A spare. And that's what I decided to make these people call me. *They cannot meet Keith now. I will put someone else together for them and he will be their classmate until further notice. That will be the first step in this particular survival plan.* Of course it wasn't thought out in those specific terms, but the instinct and action were there. And from that day on, through all my years in public school, all White folks had to call me Raymond.

The point was to have a plot. To keep a part of myself I could trust. A way to pull myself through. Be a Raymond, a brother, a son, a Keith, a son, a Raymond, a son, a brother. Keep juggling and save myself. So along with handwriting drills, simple addition, simple subtraction, and readings from the primer, I began getting familiar with these strange people around me. Peeping into their lives while trying to keep their strange pale noses out of mine.

One day Sherry and I were nearing Junction Boulevard while walking home when I noticed that the moon was up already. The sun, of course, was shining brightly. I was startled because I had always thought that their relationship was strictly causal. The moon came up because the sun went down or the sun went down because the moon had to come up, you know, I had that kind of notion. This was weird.

"Hey Sherry, you see that?"

"See what?"

"See the moon, Sherry. See it's up already."

"Oh yeah, I see it."

"But the sun is still up. I don't see how they can be up at the same time." She looked back over her shoulder to check. Remained silent as I continued. "You ever seen it like this before, Sherry? You ever seen this?"

"No," she finally replied. "I don't look at the sky all that much in the daytime. That's dumb. I like the stars at night. It's just like this today anyway, that's all. Just today."

"Wonder if Ma knows about this."

"You know she does. She knows about stuff like this."

"You'll ask her?"

"You can ask her, Keith."

"No, you. It'll be better. She won't get mad."

"Oh Keith, she won't get mad if you ask her something like this."

"I don't know. She might . . . you know it too!" She reflected a moment, knowing I was right.

Moms patiently explained to Sherry that her observation wasn't anything all that unusual, just the natural movement of heavenly bodies. She told her that if she would watch the sky more often, she would see it occur more often, and if she lived long enough she would see far more stranger things than that.

Indeed, I have. But imagine again how I felt. The sun and the moon out together.

Sky-watching became more serious in the second grade. The Space Bug had bitten America, artificial satellites and such, and the schools had caught a fever. We were given a frenzied assortment of data about Venus, Mars, red and yellow stars, Big and Little Dippers, and Halley's comet. Seemed like I could spend all evening gazing at the stars and yakking about the universe. And I heard people say I was as bright as a star myself. I guess they meant I was motivated. I had to be to keep up with the smarter pupils in my class. And I definitely meant to keep up. To fit in.

I was the only Black in the one-level class because Saundra Meritt, whom I had grown to like during our time together in first grade, was placed in 2-3. Nowadays in public schools they may designate classes by room numbers like 2-301 or 2-315. There may be differences in performance levels among the classes but the students, at least the younger ones, may not be acutely aware of them. Probably better that way. But back in '59 I knew I was in with the so-called cream of my grade level. Even without the class numbers, the few dark faces I saw in each of the other classes made it easy to figure out what was going on. I had been "identified." I was, however, gaining more and more confidence in my role as student.

Along with Eddie Goldstein I became a class clown. We came up with the funniest quips and made the funniest faces. But we both wanted to be laughed with, not laughed at, so we scored highly on all our tests and raised our hands as vigorously as anyone else. I liked being able to play it either way. I also began expressing a certain physical dominance in the schoolyard, as I could outwrestle any of my classmates. This was as much due to aggression as to my skill. I could handle these people. And Mrs. Lehrman didn't hassle me much. She occasionally had to put my clowning in check, but her main beef seemed to be the way I would dot an *i*. I still hear her sometimes: They're just dots, Raymond. Not giant colored-in circles. Dots. Dots. Dots. Not anything so terribly important. If that was her major complaint against me, I knew I had to be progressing satisfactorily. I even had an opportunity to show off for my father.

He showed up on one of those parents' observation days in a brown suit with a gray Ban-Lon shirt and a tan raincoat. When he came through the door all heads turned toward me. Then Linda Katz, as if she alone knew the scoop, tapped me on the shoulder from behind and whispered the obvious: "There goes your father, Raymond." Pops didn't bother to look my way, simply nodded to the teacher and strode swiftly to the back of the room where several other parents were already gathered.

We were working with the calendar. It was the fourteenth, and Mrs. Lehrman wanted to know who could show her which date was exactly one week away. Hands shot up all around the room. Nearly everyone wanted to pounce on such an easy question, and I was among the most desperate. Waving my hand wildly and straining forward half out of my seat, squirming like I had to go to the bathroom or something, moaning, "Ooh ooh ooh Mrs. Lehrman, ooh!" She studied the contorted pleas on our faces, in our eyes. She hesitated as if she were trying to select a proper head of lettuce and then settled on Helen Rubin, who hadn't even raised her hand. Her mother was in the back, yet the girl still wasn't eager. It didn't seem fair she should be called on before I was.

I tried to attract my father's attention to let him know I knew the answer, but he was staring straight ahead. It was ironic because I had learned what I knew about the calendar from watching him run his finger down the left margin of the one in our kitchen in order to count the Sundays. There just couldn't have been any easier question for me.

But Helen had it. She accepted the rubber-tipped pointer from the teacher and stuck it straight in the box marked 20. I couldn't believe she blew it like that. Hands shot up all over again, even more urgently, and Helen was told to sit down. I didn't bother raising my hand this time because I had become more interested in Helen's mother. She was wringing her hands. She lowered her head, then lifted it slowly and blew a thin stream of air from her mouth. I imagined her in a cartoon with steam spouting from her ears, forming a scowling mist over her graying head. I was still having fun with this vision as Bernie Cohen went up and pointed to 15. Eddie called him stupid, and Bernie's father was in the back smiling. Fake. I could feel it. I turned my eyes back to Mrs. Rubin's anger.

"RAYMOND." I whirled to face the teacher. I was nervous because I thought she was going to reprimand me for not paying attention and it was certainly no time for that, but when she asked "Can you show us?" it took all the control I could muster to refrain from howling with laughter.

"I think I can show you, Mrs. Lehrman."

"Well let's hop to it then." She looked back at the group of observers and asked rhetorically, "We are having our little adventures today, aren't we?"

I fidgeted with my notebook, opened and shut my inkwell a few times, you know, appearing uncertain so I could build the suspense. I slowly rose to my feet, very deliberately tucked in my shirt, and hitched my trousers. Show time. I took the pointer from Mrs. Lehrman, switched it from hand to hand, tapped the floor with the rubber tip a couple of times, and picked out that glorious 21.

"Thank you, Raymond," said Mrs. Lehrman in relief. She smiled and I poked out my chest and headed for my seat. Cast a glance at Pops. He wasn't one for the big grin, but his faint nod of approval let me know he was pleased.

It would have been better still if Pops could have caught my act a few weeks later when Mrs. Lehrman asked if anyone knew the difference between a house and a home. No one else in the class even attempted an answer. The perfect stage for me. I mean getting called on and supplying the correct response was exciting enough, but you knew there were other young knights who could have handled the question. To dominate the floor completely, however, was to be top royalty. And there I was, the king.

"A house can be anywhere you live with walls and ceilings and floors. But it's not a home until there is love." This answer seemed to really excite the teacher.

"That is well put, Raymond. Very, very interesting." I sat down as my classmates stared in amazement, probably wondering where I picked up this information. I wouldn't tell them I had learned it in Sunday School. And I was really somewhat amazed myself that not a single one of them could answer that question. I began to wonder more seriously about what these Jews were learning in those synagogues and those one-afternoon-a-week Hebrew School classes. What were the few Catholics, who got out early on Wednesdays for religious instruction, learning over at Blessed Sacrament?

I felt I was coming along nicely. Sang "America the Beautiful" and "My Country, 'Tis of Thee" as loudly as anyone. Recited the Pledge of Allegiance at a time when it was mandatory to do so. Related strongly to "Jack and the Beanstalk" and felt great admiration for both Androcles and the lion. Thought Miles Standish was a hero for fighting Indians and beheading Wituwamat. Respected wig-wearing, silver dollar-slinging George Washington, Honest Abe, and President Eisenhower. Showed the proper concern for the Cold War, was glad Red China was denied entry to the U.N., and was properly upset when a spying Francis Gary Powers was shot down from the Russian skies. Smooth sailing on into 3-1. Where I punched Susan Goldberg straight in her eye.

The boys, mainly John Greenberg and Michael Stein, conned me into it. They had some kind of running feud with the girls and wanted to end it, so they drew up this peace treaty that they wanted the girls to approve. The whole thing was silly to me because I never categorically hated girls. I also knew that over at P.S. 92 that type of thing couldn't be happening because for those boys, like myself, there wasn't a hate-girls phase to emerge from. Hell, some guys over there were hard pursuing the girls right from jumpstreet. Trying to corner them on the back stairs or in the wardrobe closet. A boy-girl feud, in and of itself, didn't appeal to me at all. Nor did resolving one. White girls' acceptance wasn't what I needed anyway. I would long for a certain measure of it later on at classroom parties when, although I knew I could dance rings around everyone else, I had to pretend to dislike dancing. I knew no girl could really be comfortable with me as a partner. So I left them alone. But I had to be tight with the boys, so when John told me during lunch hour that I could be their general if I could get Susan, the leader of the girls, to sign the treaty, I agreed to give it a try. Couldn't turn down a generalship, not even a peacetime one, and I kept sending Susan notes all that afternoon to persuade her to sign. She ripped up all the notes and stuffed the pieces into her desk. I sent her the treaty itself and she ripped that also. I had to send Michael a message to write another one. When I approached Susan after school, she was in the middle of a group of girls heading farther into Jackson Heights. I blocked her path and offered the replacement treaty.

"Look Susan, you don't really have to sign it but at least you could read it. You might change your mind." Without uttering a word, she stepped around me, leaving me to present my case to thin air if I so desired. The boys around me began giggling. Even John flashed his braces. I ran in front of her again and shoved the paper at her. "READ IT I SAID." She merely started around me again. I grabbed her by the shoulder while warning her, "You're not gonna just ignore me." She shook loose from my grasp, seemingly unafraid, chumping me off some more.

"I'm not reading that. It's so stupid."

"Oh yeah? Well you're still gonna read it. And you're gonna sign it too."

"I'm not signing anything."

"Yeah? Then I think I'll sign you." I uncorked a beauty of a right hand straight to her left eye. She went one way and her book bag went the other.

"You bastard," she screamed as she covered her eye momentarily with her hands. "You're a real bastard." I wanted to slug her again but my fear was swelling even faster than her eye was.

"You all right Susan?" I asked stupidly.

"Leave me alone you bastard! Leave me alone!" She picked up her bag and started running for home. I took off in the opposite direction, knowing I was in deep trouble, and figuring I had until morning to figure a way to escape it. Good thing neither Sherry nor Judy knew what had happened, so I could at least avoid the beating that night. After the next morning though, I would definitely be fair game if I failed to come up with a plan.

That next morning Susan was not in class. Nobody who was there offered me any conversation. The girls were mad I suppose, or scared. The boys were waiting to take their cue from me. Mrs. Rosen didn't seem to know what was going on. I remained silently worried, could see no way to get around what I imagined would be the most ferocious beating of my life. To get in trouble at home was bad enough, but to act up in public was the worst thing I could do to Moms. Wherever we traveled folks always commented on how well behaved my sisters and I were. Moms would usually reply, "They had better be." And that was the truth.

It was about an hour before I was summoned to the principal's office. Susan had a terrible shiner and turned her head to avoid my stare. Mr. Price sternly directed me to a seat facing her. Susan's parents had come and gone. Guess they had confidence in Mr. Price. I was glad I didn't have to face them.

"I won't beat around the bush, Raymond," said Mr. Price as he sank into his chair. "Is this what you are taught at home?"

"No Mr. Price," I replied humbly, glancing at the floor. "I just lost my temper and I feel sorry about it. I want Susan to know I'm sorry too." She still wouldn't look me in the eye. Mr. Price continued.

"An apology is nice, Raymond. But it won't help her eye feel any better. I'll have to inform your parents. You understand that, don't you?"

"Yes Mr. Price." I felt I was officially finished.

"What shall I tell them?"

"I don't know." I spoke in a forlorn semiwhisper, you know, doomed but looking for a miracle of sympathy. Then I looked Mr. Price fairly straight in the eye. "Probably have to tell them I was being real bad and punched a girl in the eye for nothing."

"For no reason at all?"

"No Mr. Price. I had a reason but it wasn't a good one."

"What reason is that, Raymond?"

"I was mad because she wouldn't listen to me."

"Oh I see. You mean she wouldn't acknowledge that whole peace treaty affair?"

"She wouldn't even read it."

"It's a free country," Susan cut in. "I don't have to do anything I don't want to do."

"But you could have listened," I retorted. I could feel my anger rising. BUT HAD TO CHECK IT. Susan countered sharply.

"I didn't want to. It was so stupid . . . and they made you do it."

"They did not," I blurted. "I did it myself."

"You're stupid then."

"I am not." I was ready to shine her other eye but I quickly put the emotion in harness. Had to appear remorseful. Mr. Price cut in.

"Now, now. No one is stupid here. What we have here is an example of what bad judgment and a lack of discipline can lead to. Do you know what discipline means, Raymond?"

"Yes Mr. Price. It's like self-control."

"Precisely. You know I can tell you a great deal about discipline because of my experiences in the Navy. Was your father ever in the service?"

"He was in the Navy too," I said proudly. Actually he had been in the Army but you know how I had to play it.

"Then I'm sure he can back me up. You see, I had to learn how to follow rules in the Navy. I had my own emotions; there were many things I did not like; I felt misunderstood a lot of the time, but I still had to follow the rules. Nothing was more important than the rules. If we didn't have rules, we couldn't have gotten anything accomplished. There would have been no cooperation, and without cooperation there would not have been any Navy. And that just wouldn't have been right. Can you understand that?"

"Yes." Sure I could. I knew there were few things in life worse than not having a navy.

"Now we can't have a school without cooperation either, without rules. And our rules state that we do not hit each other. Is that clear?"

"Yes Mr. Price." I struggled to gaze at him directly so he could read how sincere I was. "I know we're not supposed to fight."

"Of course not Raymond. And we certainly can't beat up the girls. Gentlemen don't do that. You do want to be a gentleman, don't you?"

"Yes Mr. Price. I want to be a gentleman."

"That's good." He paused briefly, seemed pleased that I was so agreeable. "So tell me, is there any chance this might happen again?"

"Not with me. I'll never do anything like this again."

"Are you sure?"

"Yes Mr. Price. I'd never do this again because I know it's bad." I had locked in on his eyes real good for a moment.

"I hope you're right. You know kids get thrown out of school for things like this. Would your parents wish that to happen to you?"

"No sir. My parents wouldn't like that at all."

"I think not." A fleeting smile passed over his face as he looked over at Susan, who was already focused in on him. "What do you think, Susan? Can you trust him? Has he ever done anything like this before?"

"No. This is the first time he ever bothered anybody."

"So maybe you can trust him now?"

"I don't know. He might try something else."

"Well I can't let him do that. I'd have to kick him out of here before I let him do that. As a matter of fact, if you don't think you can feel comfortable around him, I can still move him. Do you think I should do that?"

Susan pointed her shiner directly at me and I lowered my head. Might be kissing 149 good-bye. She spoke very deliberately.

"Let him stay. . . . He likes this school."

"And you'll feel safe? I want you to be sure."

"I'll be all right, Mr. Price."

"OK," he said smilingly. "We'll see how it goes."

The principal rose to escort Susan from the office. I rubbed my face with my hands. I had been played out of position by the boys and I knew it. As angry as I was, I thought they might need a peace treaty to ever talk to me again. I was sure wishing I could get Moms to sign one. After a few moments Mr. Price returned, patted me on the head, then resumed his seat.

"So you really feel sorry, don't you?" I locked in on his eyes again.

"Yes I do."

"I know you do. I believe that. Tell me, do you like it here?"

"I like it here a whole lot." Anybody in my world could have answered that one for him.

"Do you have friends in class?"

"Oh yeah. I have a lot of friends in the class. I like everybody."

He leaned back in his chair and looked upward, staring so intently at the ceiling that I looked up also. But wasn't anything up there I could see that was going to help me. Finally Mr. Price continued.

"I'm going to offer you a deal, Master Gilyard. If you promise to behave yourself, to practice more discipline from now on, I won't tell your parents about what happened yesterday. Do you think we can make an arrangement of that sort?"

Now you just know we could. I mean I was getting the biggest break since Noah was allowed to beat the flood. I floated all the way back to class, eager to maintain my end of the bargain. Which I did pretty well. I was still admonished here and there about chattering and clowning, but I never dared do anything serious enough to get Mr. Price involved again. Susan and I were forced together. Every time there was a group project, like reporting on the Northeastern states or something, Mrs. Rosen made sure to put us in the same group. I even had to go to her home for a couple of meetings, and she became my favorite girl in the class.

I was a hero with the boys and John said I could still be their general since I had the most courage. I flatly refused that commission. Didn't want to be a colonel either. Or a major. We finally decided that captain would be a good rank for me, you know, in the middle.

The boys and girls started working things out for themselves. As for myself, I was on course even steadier than ever. Spelling tests. Book reports. Multiplication. Division. History. Astronomy. Current events. Mr. Price came on the loudspeaker to request we give a moment of silence for U.N. Secretary-General Hammarskjold, who died in a plane crash while on the way to take care of some business in the Congo. Kennedy was in, took our class decisively, and we were in the era of manned space flights. We jammed the auditorium to listen to the radio broadcast of Alan B. Shepard's joy ride aboard the Freedom 7. I clapped in tune with everyone else. Yes sir, Raymond was doing fine.

Keith was developing well also. Found my first best friend, Lonnie Blair, while I was walking down 97th Street on the way to the store. He was in front of his house throwing pebbles up onto his own roof. He held the bunch in his left hand and plucked and tossed them with his right. He was a skinny, close-cropped young boy, very much like myself. When he noticed me approaching, he dropped the pebbles right where he stood and came up straight to my face.

"Hey boy, what's your name?"

"My name Keith."

"Oh yeah?"

"Yeah. What's your name?"

"Ain't none a your damn business. That's what the hell it is."

"Well mine ain't none a yours then."

"Is too 'cause you just told me your name stupid."

"I did not."

"Did so."

"What I say?"

"Said your name was Keith, dummy. Can't remember what you just said?"

"I was just foolin you."

"You wasn't foolin me, Keith. You can't."

He did have me on that one and I didn't like it one bit. I stepped around him and continued on my way. He kept following, paused to pick up a rock and hurl it up on a neighbor's roof, then pulled alongside.

"You know I seen you before in school."

"So I seen you too."

"Yeah Keith, but I seen you first 'cause I always see people first before they see me. Where you use to live at?"

"I come from Harlem."

"Harlem? I heard about that place. That means you 'pose to be tough or somethin? You ain't as tough as people from Brooklyn."

"That's where you from?"

"Yeah Keith, that's where I'm from!"

"So that don't make you so tough."

"Tougher than you."

"No you not."

"Yes I am Keith. What if I did somethin to you? What would you do?"

"Do somethin back to you."

"Like what?"

"You'll see. I'm use ta fightin. I been in gang fights."

"Aw man, get outa here. You ain been in no gang fights."

"I have so. Where you think I got this scar from?" I put a hand up to the left side of my face to really draw his attention to it. I closed in on him, but kept enough distance so that out of the corner of my eye I could watch his reaction. He really appreciated that scar. I had an edge on him, had him leaning toward belief.

"How that happen?"

"I told you I was in a gang fight. I got cut with a butcher knife. You don't know about stuff like that. You too little."

"I'm just as big as you," he said defiantly.

"Yeah but you couldn't get out like I could. When everybody in my house was sleepin I use to sneak out at midnight. That's when the big people had the gang fights. I was the only kid they let in. This big man cut me and I was bleeding a lot but my side got him."

"Did they kill him?" he asked eagerly.

"Yeah they killed him. What you think?"

"Well they 'pose to anyway. I was in gang fights too you know."

"Where's your scar then?"

"You don't have to have one."

"Yes you do. If you was in one you have to have a scar. If you was in a *real* one."

I knew I scored heavily with that tale, so did he, and we had set up a pretty good basis for a friendship. Neither one of us was going to be bullied.

On days when I would break off early from my classmates so I could catch up to the Black group heading toward Corona, I would always fall in stride next to Lonnie as we waited to see where the next fun would come from. We both had a lot of static, but for different reasons. Lonnie plain liked to rumble. Enjoyed it about as much as anything. I preferred to spar with words. Debate, you know, try to rank somebody out. I usually had to fight only when someone lost his temper because I was needling too good, getting too good an audience response. Of course I'd also fight if my target tried to ignore me. And sometimes I had to use my best rap to cop pleas to older kids who got a little too aggressive from time to time. I usually was able to be just humble enough to suit them and just assertive enough to save face within my own inner circle.

Lonnie and I often roamed Junction Park together. One day, when we were both nine, we were on the seesaw. Suddenly, while I was on the up end of the board, he jumped off, leaving me to crash painfully to the ground. I was jarred from head to toe. As soon as I shook off most of the pain I charged straight at Lonnie and we locked in one of our special tussles. We had our own ground rules; we only wrestled, never kicked or punched each other as we would an outsider. After a couple of rolls along the ground I managed to get him in a headlock. He yelled "I give" even before I could secure my hold and apply any serious pressure. Neither of us had ever given up that easily. I let him go but was prepared for some kind of trick. However, he just walked over to the nearest bench, sat down, and started laughing. I was still waiting for the trick when he spoke.

"You know somethin Keith? We should become blood brothers."

"Blood brothers? What's that?"

"What's that?" he mimicked. "You mean you don't even know what it is?"

"Yeah I know. I mean I used to know but I forgot. What we have to do?"

"It's easy. All we do is stick needles in our fingers and rub our blood together. That makes us like real brothers and we always help each other out with things."

"But we do that now."

"Yeah but this is a real special thing. You want a brother, don't you?" You know he couldn't get any argument from me.

"When can we do it?"

"Right now" he replied as he began pulling a wad of tissues from his pocket. There was a small sewing needle inside. "You ain scared, is you?"

"Naw I ain scared. It's just like a doctor's needle, that's all. I ain scared a no doctor's needle so I ain scared a this."

"Yeah all right. Gimme your left hand then. It's the one closer to your heart."

"How you know that?"

"I just know, man. Gimme the hand." I offered it promptly this time and Lonnie deftly pricked a hole in the tip of my index finger, setting forth a rush of adventure. He pricked his own finger and we pressed our blood together. "Now we brothers Keith."

That was perfect. Especially since it didn't look as though the real thing was coming along. Now if he could only be in my class. I always thought Lonnie Blair was as smart as any kid I knew. He just wouldn't take much of an interest in school. Back then I would still try to turn him around. I worked straight into my pitch.

"I'm glad we're like real brothers now. We ain gon let nobody mess with us. If you was in my class that would really be good."

"3-1 class? Not me. Here, take this tissue man. Your finger still bleedin." As I accepted the tissue Lonnie kept emphasizing his rejection of my idea. "Fuck the 3-1 class. Yall startin ta git too much homework. Shoot, that's what's takin you so long to git back outside now. Makin sure all them arithmetic problems git done right. We don't worry about all that in 3-4. I hardly ever do my homework and I still don't git in that much trouble. Shoot, you don't do yours one day and you might git a note home with your sister. Nah, I wouldn't want no one class. Don't want *no* class." Lonnie seemed to dive off into deep thought for a moment. Then he switched topics altogether. "Hey man, let's git back on the seesaw."

Sure. And it has been that way a lot of the time for me and Lonnie, my brother, my first best friend. On different planes of reality despite our closeness. Years and years on the seesaw. But whenever our feet hit the ground at the same time. Beautiful.

Home provided still more difficulties to resolve, and there were no easy resolutions. I had lumps to take there also. Especially during the 1960 World Series. Along with the rest of the boys in my class who cared about baseball, I had become an incurable New York Yankees fan even though I knew my mother would never approve. She was from the Ebbets Field Asylum, you know, if it wasn't Don Newcombe and Gil Hodges then it wasn't really baseball. The Dodgers had already left town, but she was still loyal. She would pull for them and every other team in the National League to smash the hated Yankees. That is, every team except the San Francisco Giants. Pops, you see, was a Giants fan. And although he was far less zealous about his loyalty than my mother was, there was no way I could drum up any support in our household for the local heroes. Moms said the Yankees were a prejudiced team, reluctant to sign Negroes. Well by then they had Elston Howard and Hector Lopez and that seemed to me to be Negro enough for a baseball team. I didn't know yet what the Jackie Robinson experiment had been all about. I simply wanted the Yankees to crush the upstart, overconfident Pittsburgh Pirates. And I was sure they would do it because they had such an awesome lineup and had been playing so well. Mantle, Maris, and company had cracked 193 homers for a new American League record, had finished the season with fifteen consecutive victories. I knew Dick Groat had hit .325 for the Pirates and was the man to keep a rally going, but I wasn't worried. We had too many home runs in our bats for their little rallies to overcome. No, no one should take the Pirates too seriously.

I panicked when the Pirates won the opener 6–4. But when Mickey Mantle knocked two over the wall the next day to key a 16–3 rout, my mental peace was restored. Now all we had to do was bring them up to the Stadium and polish them off. And when Mickey cracked another homer and Bobby Richardson weighed in with a grand slam behind the shutout pitching of Whitey Ford, I was ready for the celebration. It was inconceivable that the Yankees would drop the next two games. I was severely depressed, couldn't understand how we could score only four runs in two whole games when we often scored more than four runs in a single inning. Now we were only one loss away from losing the whole World Series. And Moms was ribbing me real good. She was on vacation and was a most interested spectator.

"Boy, I don't know what possessed you to like those Yankees." I don't know if it occurred to her that I was simply rooting for the home team. "You see they're nothing but clowns. Getting ready to lose the Series. Pirates gonna go bop bop bop tomorrow." She spoke while taking three swings with an imaginary bat to illustrate her point. Unwisely, I threw her a fast ball straight down the middle.

"The Yankees are gonna win the next game, Ma. You watch how they beat those Pirates."

"Beat them? Boy you need to stop babbling all that foolishness before folks come and lock you up. Beat the Pirates? Hmph. They couldn't beat them with a stick."

"Just watch Mickey Mantle, Ma. Just watch."

"Yeah. Watch him strike out some more."

"He doesn't always strike out. You see he has three home runs already. You know he's good."

"Yeah he's good. A good joke. Boy, you got too much faith in that Mickey Mantle, but I'll tell you something: Mickey Mantle couldn't hit the side of a barn with an ironing board. The Yankees will lose the next game, JUST LIKE THEY LOST THE LAST ONE, and then you'll see that the National League is the best."

"You just don't know, Ma."

"No you're the one who just doesn't know. I've already forgotten things you haven't even learned yet."

"Yeah I know, Ma. But what's gonna happen in the next game is the future."

"Sure it's the future. But it will be the sad, sad past for the Yankees soon enough." She laughed and went bop bop bop some more. I wasn't qualified to beat her with words. Nor could I break the hold she had on Sherry and Judy. Neither of them could tell you the difference between a curveball and a jock strap, but they hated the Yankees. And they were working on Debra Lynn.

Whitey Ford came through with another shutout to tie the Series at 3–3, and I was ecstatic. I didn't get a chance to gloat and brag too much because my mother, predictably, wouldn't permit it. When she heard me deriding Sherry and Judy she told me to be quiet so that I wouldn't wake up Debra Lynn. But I knew neither the noise nor my little sister's sleep was the real issue. And I knew that my mother wanted that deciding seventh game just as much as I did. However, I knew she wouldn't get it. I figured Mantle and company had lost a few games to keep this thing exciting. Of course I would have preferred for them to whack out the Pirates in four straight. But if they wanted to win in seven games, for ultimate suspense, I could accept it.

The next afternoon I was daydreaming in class about how the Yankees were down in Pittsburgh knocking balls all over the field and into the stands. I had them leading 18–0 after seven innings, humiliating the entire town. I imagined I had become a grown man while my mother had become a little eight-year-old girl. I'm not sure whether she was my daughter or not. We were watching the game on television, and she was frightfully upset because the Pirates were losing so badly. I patted her on the head and whispered softly, "Don't cry little Margie. It's only a game. Maybe your team can win the World Series next year." I didn't tease this little girl.

I went into shock after school when I heard on Michael Stein's transistor radio that the Pirates had just rallied for five runs off of Bobby Shantz and Jim Coates in the bottom of the eighth to go ahead 9–7 and that Tony Kubek, whom I thought invented the shortstop position, had been forced out of the game when Bill Virdon's grounder hit a stone and hit him in the throat.

"Don't worry Raymond," Michael said gravely. "We'll catch up."

I sped home to watch it happen.

Moms was already enjoying herself when I came in. "It's bop bop bop just like I told you it would be. Come on in here and see those Yankees of yours get beat." I was silent, sank limply into a chair, and prayed.

Bobby Richardson looped a single to left-center and Dale Long followed with a hit to right, sending Richardson to third base. Gil McDougald came in to run for Long. The manager yanked Bob Friend and brought in Harvey Haddix to pitch. Maris, Mantle, and Yogi Berra were coming to bat. It definitely looked like a big inning was blooming.

"All right Harvey, let's strike them out. Be hard on em sugar. Be hard." I silently opposed her. Come on Roger. Pleeezzz. My legs were shaking now and I was clutching the arms of the chair with my clammy fingers. Pleeezzzzz!

Maris popped out, runners holding the bases, and up came the magnificent Mantle.

"Here's an easy one, Harvey darling. Just throw it through the hole in his bat. Watch your big shot now, Keith. Watch him."

Mantle ripped a single to right scoring Richardson to make it 9–8 and sending McDougald around to third base and me up out of my seat. "Yeah we gon git em now. We gon git em now. Here comes Yogi."

"That don't mean nothin. He'll either strike out or hit into a double play."

"No he ain't, Ma." I couldn't be any more rebellious vocally but I figured my mother had to be off her rocker if she thought Yogi would strike out or hit into a double play. All of New York knew that there wasn't a better hitter in the clutch than old Yogi.

But Berra wasn't too spectacular this time. He smashed a drive toward first, which Rocky Nelson fielded before stepping on the bag. Two outs. He whirled to try to nail Mantle at second base to end the game, but Mickey was sneaking back to first and, though their bodies collided, Mickey beat the tag. McDougald crossed the plate and the score was tied.

"Yay Mickey. I knew we could catch up."

"Aw boy, now they playin dirty. You see how he tripped that man to get back to the base? He cheatin, but it won't get him too far."

"He didn't trip him. They just fell together."

"He tripped him plain as day. Ain't you got eyes?"

Moose Skowron grounded out to end the inning but I wasn't overly worried. I was sure Ralph Terry could hold the Pirates until we could get another turn at the plate. But he failed! Mazeroski smacked the second pitch over the left field wall and the game was over. Merry fans swarmed the field as Mazeroski rounded the bases with his arm swirling, hat in hand. My throat grew lumpy and tears began rolling down my cheeks. Moms was very happily into one of her bop bop bop routines.

"Here's how he did it. He just closed his eyes and went bop."

"He did not close his eyes!" The tears were coming heavy now, and I was sniffling.

"Yes he did, boy. He closed his eyes and knocked it over the wall. What? Are you crying over this game? Don't be so silly. You shouldn't have been rooting for those stupid Yankees in the first place. Now they got you cryin. Look at Yogi. He cryin. Your great Mickey, he'll be cryin too. They'll know better next time they fool around with these Pittsburgh Pirates. And here you cryin over a little old ball game."

The tears kept flowing. How could God twist the Series so badly? The Yankees outscored the Pirates 55–27 and still lost the Series. In the locker room afterward, Mickey stated, "This is the first time that we lost a Series when I know we should have won." Yeah Mick. I know what you mean.

I was too often too sensitive around the house I suppose, but it certainly wasn't all tears. There was the pure joy of watching Debra Lynn grow and learn to make mud pies, of secretly outracing the bees to the white and gold honeysuckles in our neighbor's forbidden yard, of helping Judy master the first grade, of twisting with Sherry and Chubby Checker, of staying up to help Guy Lombardo bring in the new year, running outside with Sherry and Judy and waving west, toward Manhattan, and yelling with all our might, "Good-bye 1960. Good-bye."

It's about this time that my father comes front and center. I remember studying him very closely. Saw the annoyance on his face when I ripped yet another pair of pants at the knee. Saw the pride when I solved yet another math problem. Saw the determination in his stride as he went up the block to recover my baseball glove, which had been stolen because I hadn't kept close enough watch on it in the schoolyard. I would have fought the boy if I was sure he had the glove. But he kept denying he had it—until my father showed up. And when our family went out to Coney Island I watched Pops swim boldly out into the ocean, left us wading near the shore. He went out so far we could barely see him, out farther than anyone else. Sherry became nervous.

"He might drown all the way out there."

"Nah, he ain gon drown out there. He can swim all the way to Spain if he wants to. He can swim!"

And he could make you laugh also. He'd sit at the kitchen table and yawn loud and long like a siren. Then he might burst out singing the food song, matching meals to the days of the week. I'd get confused sometimes about which day to link up with the roast beef, but I'd be right with him by the time we hit the weekend:

Today is Friday, today is Friday
Friday's fi-ish
Is everybody happy?
Oh I should say.

Maybe not. Pops was showing up in my bed at night quite regularly. I really didn't know anything was wrong because I had a notion that it was all right for fathers to hang out that way with their little sons. Only when he moved upstairs into a room set off from the rest of the apartment up there did I recognize the separation for what it was. I didn't ask many questions about it and didn't receive much of an explanation. I still didn't know about slow horses and fast women.

My mother went to a parent-teacher conference that spring. I was glad she attended because I had a couple of compositions up on the bulletin board. When she returned home, she immediately began beating me across my back with the ironing cord. I had no time to concoct a defense. Hell, I didn't even know what the charge was. Only when she fell into her groove was the meaning of her action revealed.

"So you fightin people in school hunh?"

"No Ma, no, ooch ooch owww. . . ."

"Don't lie to me boy. You know you punched that girl Susan in her eye."

"Ouch ouch . . . but . . . but ouch. . . ."

It was going to be my worst beating yet. I wanted to annihilate Mrs. Rosen, who I figured had spilled the beans.

Hung around a lot with Lonnie Blair that summer. Got better at stickball and fighting. Watched Mantle and Maris chase Babe Ruth's home run record, and kept an eye on Frank Robinson and the

Cincinnati Reds, who appeared as if they would win the National League pennant and provide the October opposition for the Yankees. And I was especially mindful of Virgil Ivan Grissom's flight aboard the Liberty Bell 7, you know, had to keep Raymond sharp for another one class.

5

Getting Over the Hump

In the memoirs and/or case studies of Jonathan Kozol (1968), Gerald Levy (1970), and Daniel Fader (1971), the third grade is cited as a critical juncture in the elementary school education of African-American, urban, public school students. Each of these writers believes that these children for the most part enter public school with normal to high levels of self-esteem and a matching eagerness to learn, but typically fall behind academically by the end of the third grade, as they have found academic pursuit unfulfilling and have begun to retreat from the process. This perception has been confirmed many times in the literature (give or take a grade). The obvious conclusion to draw from such consensus is that African-American students will indeed develop the academic ability to succeed throughout public school if they can but weather the early years, can but get over the hump.

In this chapter I will assess my own school pilgrimage through that apparently crucial third grade, analyzing the factors that allowed me to negotiate the passage in fairly good academic shape. However, I must first consider why so many researchers feel that it is such a formidable task for a Black child to complete four years of public schooling—and actually enjoy doing it. Toward this end I will provide a historical sketch of the general nature of public schools and describe how Blacks from backgrounds similar to mine have fared in such institutions. I will also explore some of the pedagogical implications of both their experiences and mine.

The Hump

The public school system I entered in 1957 was a de facto segregated system, one that wasn't working well for Blacks as a whole then and, in fact, one that never had. Consider the following description by Colin Greer (1976):

> The report of the Superintendent of Schools for 1957 showed a drop of 20,000 in the number of white pupils. Negroes then formed a highly concentrated 20.1 percent of the school population. As many as 455 of 704 schools in the city were "homogenous" with less than 10 percent blacks in white schools and vice versa. In 1954 Kenneth Clark argued that the Brown decision be applied to the schools of the North that were segregated by the effects of a combination of neighborhood concentration of Negroes, and neighborhood school zoning. The Board of Education requested the Public Education Association to examine the problem. One year later it reported that in schools of high non-white concentration the children scored below children of other schools in various achievement tests. The school buildings in these districts were older and the proportion of substitute teachers highest.
>
> In 1957 the Board of Education began to keep meticulous ethnic—"black, white, and other"—records on the racial composition of its schools. By this time blacks constituted 25 percent of elementary school pupils and 20 percent of both junior high and vocational high school student bodies. Only 5 percent of the academic high school population was black. Six years later State Commissioner Allen's study of school segregation found the rate of segregation and poor black performance increasing and projected the continuation of the trend. Segregation was virtually synonymous with urban school inadequacy. (pp. 149–50)

That such a system failed Blacks so miserably comes as no surprise to Greer, though he argues that segregation is a reflection of other evils in society, not a cause in and of itself of Black failure in school. Greer's overarching contention is that Blacks are but one in a long line of minority groups that have been denied success within the urban public school community. The treatment they have received has been particularly harsh, but not unique. For the actual social purpose of the public school has long been, Greer states, to fail up to 40 percent of its students. In this view of American educational history the public school is not seen to be a magnificent vehicle for upward mobility, as is the traditional notion; it is viewed instead as a machine that exists to disable students, to remove them from the running for middle-class status, thereby ensuring the maintenance of exploitative social structures. Greer wants us to understand that school identifies those who can accept a strict routinizing of their lives, points out those who can be expected to perform, to know their places. It is seen as a giant sorting operation that helps define for America those students for whom the promise of "getting ahead" will be fulfilled. Those who are slated to live lower-class lives are conditioned to accept their fate and taught how to function in their prescribed roles.

Revisionist historians such as Greer do not claim that this general failure is the result of any personal conspiracy; the assertion, to the contrary, is that it is the product of the social organization of public schools, a network of relations that has inexorably achieved the political task described above regardless of personnel changes. Naturally one may quarrel with Greer's conceptualization. I, for one, favor a more transactional analysis, a focus on the choices certain individuals make when confronted with certain circumstances. Such an approach seems richer to me than the strictly deterministic notion Greer sets forth. Consequently, when assessing school communities I am more apt to speak of their nature than their purpose. But I must admit that whichever lens is used, in this case the object looks pretty much the same: Masses and masses of minority students have been unable to use the public school system as a ladder of upward mobility. It is clear that whatever benefits the school can claim to have offered can be matched, if not overshadowed, by a legacy of default.

Levy, a sociologist, conducted perhaps the most interesting study (1970) relevant to this particular line of thinking. During the 1967–68 school year, he went "underground" by taking a teaching job in a ghetto elementary school, fictitiously called Midway, which had an overwhelming Black and Puerto Rican student population. Because Levy was a "floater" (a teacher without regular assignment), he had no trouble conducting the wide range of observations that are summarized below.

The older teachers ("chronic" teachers in Levy's terms) firmly believed that "control must precede education" (p. 25). They spent the great majority of their time and energy as teachers attempting to master the technology of control, a system of devices including bribery, work routines, and even physical violence. In actuality, for the chronic teacher, control did not simply precede education but was education itself. The younger, more idealistic teachers (the "acute" ones) went to the school feeling that they were morally above such practice and posture. However, when their humanistic overtures were rebuffed, when they were psychologically destroyed by openly rebellious and "disrespectful" students, then they all too happily embraced the chronic teachers' methods and thereby served, too, as agents of control. Many of the acute teachers went to Midway to avoid Vietnam, but the militaristic rigidness they soon adopted would certainly have served them well as soldiers. They paid a high price, however, with their own psychic ambivalence.

While the teachers and students were destroying each other, the students were learning something very crucial: how not to remain eligible for middle-class life. They learned very well how to play their roles as lower-class citizens. Through contact with their White teachers, virtually their only contact with mainstream America, they learned in what terms they would be viewed by the larger society. Or as Levy phrases it: "By the end of the third year, in many classes, education has hardened into open class struggle between teachers and children" (p. 86).

Drawn into this fray were pass-the-buck administrators, thoroughly frustrated and angry parents, and a small number of Black teachers, who experienced the conflicting demands of race and profession. They were most trusted by the students and were thus in a position to betray them most effectively—which they did.

So the ingredients at Midway formed an explosive mix. But as long as the explosions that did occur were contained, the school functioned to, in fact, further suppress. Such a state of affairs led Levy to conclude that "with class politics cloaked in the language of social amelioration, Midway illustrates the contradictions of a society committed to the American dream in a period when that dream is becoming less and less realizable" (p. 176).

For those concerned particularly with language arts instruction, perhaps the most fruitful aspect of the analysis presented by the likes of Greer and Levy is, ironically, that it has nothing at all to say about linguistic or cognitive abilities or disabilities. As mentioned earlier, theirs is a straightforward, materialist conception based on the scarcity of resources made available to the masses as a whole; the historical role of Black folks in urban America as a reserve, contingency, or marginal labor force; and the maneuvers of certain interest groups that wish to preserve the status quo. This is important to bear in mind when one hears arguments citing Black language or the inability of Blacks to master Standard English as the major cause of their lack of success in school. One should realize, given the nature of school as it has evolved, that despite any method of instruction per se, the odds have been greatly stacked against many of the Black children who, at the age of five or six, have so optimistically crossed the threshold of public school. It is little wonder that researchers have perceived these children to be entering an educational death trap that in just three or four years practically forces them to abandon their initial enthusiasm for school-based educational life.

Gittin Ovuh, Getting Over

In the city's segregated school system, P.S. 90 on 148th Street was a typical "Black unit," an overwhelmingly Black student population housed in a substandard physical plant staffed by White professionals who, I am sure, would not have minded working somewhere else. Nevertheless, I entered school with little trepidation—certainly none, as the preceding chapter indicates, with respect to my language abilities. Largely through my encounters within the home, I possessed the self-esteem and linguistic skill to participate in a spontaneous, unselfconscious manner among my peers and to feel unintimidated by the mere presence of a White teacher. My first rating on the personality scale used by the Board of Education (see Table 2 in Appendix) included a positive mark in Relationship to Other Children and high marks in Leadership, Self-Confidence, and Initiative. I was also labeled "moderately aggressive" and characterized as one who "occasionally resents group control." Nothing in that personality description of me as a kindergartener predicts any serious problems.

I received virtually the same character assessment for the two months I spent in the first grade at P.S. 90; the only difference was that I was then rated as "responding well to group control." Again, there was no cause for anyone who possessed faith in school to become alarmed. At the age of six I did not feel betrayed by school, had not perceived any hostility being directed at me. I felt, quite to the contrary, very excited about getting on with scientific endeavors.

I landed in school just one month before the Russians launched Sputnik and the space race began in earnest. My fascination with this contest for technological supremacy, an interest no doubt spurred on by the government-induced commitment of the school vigorously to promote science and mathematics teaching (see Perkinson 1977), is another theme evident throughout the narrative. As the story indicates, my base of operations was shifted from Harlem to Queens in November 1958. The most noteworthy aspect of that move for me in education was that the specific nature of the much-postulated hump I would have to try to climb changed radically. Rather than having to endure as a Black student in a segregated Black school, I was going to have to make it as a "minority" student in a predominantly White institution.

Aside from the obvious culture shock I experienced, the major problem I confronted was the opinion that had been formed of me by school officials. I was assigned to 1-4 class as opposed to the 1-1 class that I had been in at P.S. 90. This move was very important inasmuch as the public schools were operating under a multitrack system by that time. In most instances, students in the *one*-level classes were considered the most capable learners; those in *four* or *five* classes were viewed as relatively slow. Perkinson claims that such a multitrack arrangement "often proved to be a 'cover-up' of a highly segregated educational program" (p. 60). I am not saying that because I was a kid fresh out of Harlem, someone decided that I was automatically supposed to be slow. What I do know, in retrospect, is that at some point I had to make it to the one-level class to have my best chance of academic success at P.S. 149.

Of course we know that I made it. After spending less than two months in 1-4, I was transferred to 1-3, and I was in 2-1 the following September. This account differs from the one given in "Semivoices." In my recollection I saw myself as always being in the one-level class. But despite this discrepancy, the essential import of "Semivoices" remains the same. From the outset of my career at P.S. 149, I displayed enough qualities having to do with being adept at struggle, with being a confident, moderately aggressive but cagey competitor.

But the stress of trying to get over the hump at P.S. 149 found some expression on the personality scale. Several of the ratings I received during my first three years at the Queens school contrast sharply with the way I was perceived in Harlem. Although my self-confidence and initiative were never questioned, my ratings plunged relative to leadership ability and my relationship with other children. I cannot imagine that I would have received such marks back up at P.S. 90, not among those with whom I had so much more in common. I was said not to get along with other students even *before* I punched the girl in the eye. My teachers in Queens could not appreciate just how hard I worked to fit in socially or how effective I actually was at finding a niche that would be acceptable to the class as a whole.

By the end of third grade, in addition to the marks indicated above, my occasional resentment of group control and my occasional evading of responsibility had become constants. Also, that my relationship with my parents seemed disturbed was duly noted. I guess my teachers were more accurate in those assessments. Unfortunately, the only conclusion they drew from them was that I needed "supervision." They were nowhere near the whole truth about me, which was, in short, that I was showing some cracks under the strain of all the various role-playing I was engaged in. Nonetheless, I held myself together enough emotionally to handle the academic requirements of those one-level classes.

At the close of my third term at P.S. 149, I was classified as satisfactory in reading, writing, and oral communication. That was no spectacular accomplishment per se, but the way in which it was achieved is what is most worth considering. It took great social acumen to go from 146th Street in Harlem to a roughly 97 percent White environment in a classroom in Queens and be judged, at the age of nine, as satisfactory in language use. I will examine this movement from a broader perspective.

A Transactional View

My getting over the hump is attributable above all else to the fact that I was able to participate in a series of social deals or transactions that benefited me. There is no way to recount them all, but "Semivoices" indicates the most outstanding and suggests the range these transactions covered.

Relations in the home once again become a point of interest. I argued earlier that it was largely through the supportiveness of my mother and older sister that my language abilities began to flourish and that such support was the chief reason I entered school expecting to succeed. It is clear in "Semivoices" that my father was also a key member of my booster club. Having been deprived of formal educational opportunity, he had extra motive for wishing me only the best in school. Naturally my frantic need to show off on parents' observation day was a way of reassuring him that the best was indeed taking place.

For the same reason I was glad my mother went to that parent-teacher conference. I knew she would see displays of my work. Unfortunately, she was told about my display of temper. Because she heard about the incident long after it occurred, I think my mother's strong reaction to the news was one of fear more than anger. She was afraid I would jeopardize my chances by becoming too great a problem, and she let me know in the best way she knew how that she couldn't allow that to happen.

Despite my mother's obvious concern with my education, she proved to be frequently inaccessible for my direct questioning, no doubt because of the weight of other problems upon her. But I resolved that difficulty fairly well as evidenced by the scene of my moon-sun confusion in which I used my sister to mediate the learning experience. And I kept on stepping. On balance, my familial relations, which I helped establish to some degree, continued to give me the self-confidence in my ability that was noted by every one of my teachers.

The second outstanding deal I was able to strike was with my peers in the classroom. Notwithstanding the black eye fiasco, and partly due to it, I was in good standing in that circle by the close of the third grade and eventually became a frequent and most welcome visitor in several of my classmate's homes. We already know that I went to P.S. 149 armed with some sense of the benefits of code-switching, as my name-switching technique illustrates. But as a result of trying to land and then landing such a key position among my classmates, I greatly enhanced that set of skills.

Hudson (1980) provides further insight:

> If we think of a child in an area where there are two groups of children of roughly his age, and he belongs clearly to one of them, then he will most probably model his speech largely on that of others in the group he has *chosen*. In other words, at each act of utterance his speech can be seen as an ACT OF IDENTITY in a multi-dimensional space. (p. 14)

My classmates had Raymond's allegiance, and he could communicate much like them. He could not exactly speak like the child of middle-class Jewish parents, but he certainly could avoid sounding like the average kid from Harlem.

The deal I cut with the principal is arguably the highlight of "Semivoices." My skills of impression management were put to, and passed, their stiffest test to that point. I had to appear, as the story depicts, most remorseful, but I couldn't lay the remorse on so thickly that my performance appeared to be too much con. Mr. Price quite naturally could lay a little con himself. I traded him renewed commitment to an agenda for dedication to an image.

My teachers and I hammered out a similar agreement. Although they habitually complained about my talkativeness, I never became a serious acting-out problem, a fact the personality scale is testimony to. And because I handled the curriculum so well, they just about had to put up with me in the one class and expect the same level of achievement from me anticipated of all one-level students. Consequently, I profited from what popularly has been termed the Pygmalion effect, an expectancy process in which the teacher sets high achievement as the "occasion" and the student "rises" to it.

In the original Pygmalion study conducted by Rosenthal and Jacobson (1968), children at a California school, referred to as Oak School, were given a learning ability test. The twenty teachers included in the study were then told that a certain percentage of their students had been identified as "bloomers," children who would show marked improvement during the course of the school year. In reality, no such identification had been made, and the so-called bloomers had been selected at random. Nonetheless, after retesting, the bloomers between ages six and eight showed significant gains in IQ. The notion of the self-fulfilling prophecy had empirical substantiation.

Much controversy has been generated by the Rosenthal and Jacobson study, responses ranging from harsh criticism to an acceptance far more rigid than the data suggest. Subsequent research efforts, possibly because of weaknesses in design, have failed to confirm the effect. Even the original study failed to show this dynamic operative in a majority of cases. However, Colin Rogers (1982), who has specialized in the study of expectancy processes in schools, seems to have approached the matter sensibly.

> It ought to by now be clear that any straightforward conclusion regarding the existence and nature of the teacher-expectancy effect is unlikely to be forthcoming. The studies directly concerned with examining the presence or absence of the effect and those concerned with some

> of the central aspects of the teacher-expectancy effect show that it is not an all-pervasive phenomenon. It is unlikely to be found in every classroom in every school. By no means could the available data be interpreted so as to suggest that every school-child and every teacher will be directly affected by the operation of a self-fulfilling prophecy. However, it would be reasonable to conclude that every child and every teacher is potentially "at risk." The teacher-expectancy effect is potentially omnipresent if not actually so. This conclusion is sufficient to justify continued examination of the self-fulfilling prophecy within the schools. Furthermore, such future research should no longer continue to attempt to demonstrate the actual existence of the effect. There is now sufficient evidence to show that some pupils at some times will be the victims or beneficiaries of the biasing effects of their teachers' expectations. (p. 167)

Given the environment I was in, I think it is extremely naive to believe that I did not have to conquer some measure of malevolent prejudice, and by doing so I profited from a benevolent type.

A fifth vitally important transaction, one that won't be considered at length just yet, was worked out with the community, particularly my blood brother. No matter what aspirations I held and achieved along with Whites, I can honestly say that I never had any conscious longing to *be* White. I never wished to trade my background or culture. Remember, I was a lover of Eighth Avenue. My blood brother could understand all the Black things about me and share with me a special camaraderie. Both he and the community at large have had their say in how this entire work has taken shape.

I hope by this point to have dispelled all conceptions that early elementary school progress is most appropriately explained as the maturation of some genetic gift or exposure to some success-stamping curriculum. Genetic predispositions are little understood, but what is certain is that, whatever they are, they must be expressed in a social world, a world of negotiation. Exploring the scope of social relations in an educational world will yield the most veridical understanding of educational progress. As for the curriculum referred to here, it was the same as that in place, with mixed results, all over the city. There was no magic in it.

Looking back at the early years, I find it impossible to recommend that African-American students be asked to follow in my footsteps, to leave the onus almost entirely on them to fit in, to hope they can pull together a similar but just as improbable combination of pacts in order to accomplish the task of language learning in school. As mentioned previously, even with the success I was achieving, my complex juggling act was a tremendous strain on me. And although it is correct to view third grade as a critical juncture, we will see that there were major hurdles yet to face. So if I criticize elements of the school system, let it not be said that I am being ungrateful. I learned a lot, but I had to foot the psychic bill for any success I managed to attain. Surely, in one sense, the consumer is always right.

Eradicationism, Pluralism, and Bidialectalism

The situation of most African-American students concerning formal language instruction can be analyzed in terms of eradicationism, pluralism, or bidialectalism expressed in institutional policy and/or the actions of individual teachers. When pondering the best approach to instructing these students, it is important, therefore, to consider the relative merits of these views.

Eradicationists believe that Standard English is the only language variety that has a legitimate function within the school. In their judgment Black English is not only inappropriate but indicative of minimal intelligence or cognitive deficiency. They may cite researchers such as Bereiter and Engelmann (1966) and Jensen (1969) to back their claims. From their outlook, poor reading and writing scores by Black English speakers are understood to be the direct result of these students' inability to abandon their own delimiting dialect. Some eradicationists want these students to receive instruction before they even show up at school. As erasing Black dialect is a worthwhile aim, the reasoning goes, the earlier such treatment is initiated, the better off the speaker of that dialect will be. After all, they ask, since other minorities (usually meaning European immigrants) readily took to Standard English and subsequently progressed, why shouldn't Blacks be expected to do the same thing? Some eradicationists even contend that other elements of Black culture should be discarded as well—all, of course always, for the students' benefit.

Kozol ran headlong into eradicationism in process within the Boston public school system. The repression, frustration, and anger he encountered are not untypical of how such a concept is manifested in reality. Among other abuses, including strict control over whatever writing they managed to squeeze out, the students were exposed to a most uninspiring reading program, expected to wrestle with books they could neither relate to nor enjoy. Kozol describes the predicament:

> For nothing could better typify the image of the crumbling school structure than the dry and deadly basic reading textbooks that were in use within my school. . . . The volume aimed at Third Graders, used for slow Fourth Graders at my school, was called *New Streets and Roads*. No title could have been farther from the mark. Every cliche of bad American children's literature seemed to have been contained within this book. The names of the characters describe the flavor of the stories: Betty Jane Burns and Sarah Best and Miss Molly and Fluffy Tail and Miss Valentine of Maple Grove School. . . . The children in my class had been hearing already for several years about Birmingham and Selma and tear-gas and cattle-prods and night-courts and slumlords—and jazz. To expect these children to care about books which even very comfortable suburban children would probably have found irrelevant and boring seemed to be futile. (p. 79)

Kozol introduced material the children found relevant and stimulating. But he was eventually terminated for this action, specifically for teaching Langston Hughes's "Ballad of the Landlord." The following is Kozol's account of a statement by the Deputy Superintendent.

> Miss Sullivan's statement on my dismissal was much the same as Mr. Ohrenberger's [the Superintendent's], adding, however, a general admonition about the dangers of reading to Negro children poems written in bad grammar. Although Langston Hughes "has written much beautiful poetry," she said, "we cannot give directives to the teachers to use literature written in native dialects." It was at this time that she made the statement to which I have alluded earlier: "We are trying to break the speech patterns of these children, trying to get them to speak properly. This poem does not present correct

> grammatical expression and would just entrench the speech patterns we want to break." (p. 204)

Such a supercilious commitment to eradicationism ignored the facts that (a) children generally do not talk like poems, (b) the dialect was already entrenched, and (c) teaching the poem was a real educational success. To hear from Kozol once again:

> I also think it ought to be taken seriously by a teacher when a group of young children come in to him one morning and announce that they have liked something so much that they have memorized it voluntarily. It surprised me and impressed me when that happened. It was all I needed to know to confirm for me the value of reading that poem and the value of reading many other poems to children which will build upon, and not attempt to break down, the most important observations and very deepest foundations of their lives. (p. 165)

Although the events reported above epitomize "Black units" in Boston's de facto segregated school system circa 1965, there is much evidence that eradicationist practices have always been on display in numerous institutions attended by Blacks, regardless of racial distribution. Legal action in the celebrated King case, for example, was initiated on behalf of fifteen children who attended a school at which only 13 percent of the students were Black. It is interesting to note that the furor generated by the case along with the subsequent criticism of Judge Joiner's decision demonstrate that the eradicationist impulse in the nation is still strong. A clear example of this is "What's Wrong with Black English," an article by Rachel Jones (1982).

The best thing I can say about eradicationism is that it is definitely wrong and has never actually worked. Certainly nothing in the modern body of sociolinguistic theory gives even the slightest credence to the strategy. Trudgill (1974) informs us that

> linguists, and many others, believe this approach to be wrong, for several reasons. First, it is wrong *psychologically*. Language, as we have seen, is not simply a means of communicating messages. It is also very important as a symbol of identity and group membership. To suggest

> to a child that his language, and that of those with whom he identifies, is inferior in some way is to imply that *he* is inferior. This, in turn, is likely to lead either to alienation from the school and school values, or to a rejection of the group to which he belongs. It is also *socially* wrong in that it may appear to imply that particular social groups are less valuable than others. This is particularly undesirable when the language being stigmatized is that of lower-class black children and the one which is being extolled is that of white middle-class adult teachers. Finally, and perhaps most importantly, it is *practically* wrong: it is wrong because it does not and will not work. . . . The fact must also be faced that, in very many cases, speakers will not *want* to change their language—even if it were possible. (pp. 80–81)

Pluralists insist that the language of Blacks be left alone since it is as good as any other. While it is true, these critics assert, that Black English speakers suffer setbacks in the society at large, such setbacks are due to who they are—not what they speak. As Sledd (1973) opines, "But in job-hunting in America, pigmentation is more important than pronunciation" (p. 212).

An experiment by Frederick Williams (1973) fuels the argument that racial prejudice overrides concerns of linguistic output. Separate videotapes were made of three children: Black, White, and Mexican-American. Enough of the children was visible so that racial characteristics were apparent, but the children had been filmed at such an angle that a viewer could not see the movement of their mouths as they spoke. The same voice-over was then dubbed onto all the tapes. Nonetheless, when student teachers were asked to rate the children's speech for standardness and fluency, the White child's speech was rated superior. It seems foolish to dispute the belief of Burling (1973) that "when we are contemptuous of a people, we tend to be contemptuous of their language" (p. 20), even if what they are speaking is really our own.

Pluralists may compliment the sociolinguistic sophistication of Switzerland, where quadrilingualism is officially established; they may praise the sensitivity of the German public school system for its adroit handling of dialect differences (see Fishman and Leuders-Salmon 1972). Or they may vigorously denounce American education, forging, in essence, a language-oriented extension of the Greer-Levy critique. O'Neil (1973) pursues that line of thought:

> How then does language education—without, remember, worrying about the motivations of individual teachers, school administrators, or textbook makers—fit into this analysis? On this analysis it follows that the enterprise of making lower-class speakers over into middle-class speakers is simply a piece of the educational emptiness that helps maintain the present distribution of power in society. For wasting time there, on a thing that is bound to fail, serves to render school children skilled enough to be exploited but finally uneducated, used to failure, and alienated enough not to oppose exploitation; thus for them to continue to agree that they had their chances to succeed in a free and open society but that they failed. No one's fault but their own. (pp. 189–90)

Concerning the immigrant-success fallacy, a favorite one among eradicationists, pluralists will agree that the means by which any progress was achieved is unlikely to appeal to the majority of Black children. They concur with Fader:

> Children of white immigrants knew they had only to assume the clothing of the dominant group—in large part, its language—and they could live undetected in its midst. Knowing that lifelong masquerade to be beyond them—being so informed by the shape of everything from the obelisk of the Washington monument to the rectangle of a television box—black and brown children see no reason for wearing clothes that give them neither warmth nor camouflage. (pp. 116–17)

To the pluralist the crucial work involving language education is to develop a school system (and of course a society) in which language differences fail to have deleterious consequences for those whose language has been traditionally frowned upon. The proposal is not to ignore Standard English. One would certainly teach all children to read it. But beyond that the feeling is that in a more equitable societal arrangement or in a subenvironment pursuing that goal, Black students will be not only more inclined to see the value of expanding their productive communicative repertoires, but prove rather skillful at accomplishing the task.

Bidialectalists postulate that Black English is equal to Standard English but not quite equal enough. They acknowledge that the language variety is not inferior linguistically or conceptually but, claiming to be pragmatic, they feel that Standard English must be mastered by Black children in the schools so that these children can keep the possibility of upward mobility alive. Bidialectalists would rally around the argument of Baratz (1969) that "since standard English is the language of the mainstream it seems clear that knowledge of the mainstream system increases the likelihood of success in the mainstream culture" (p. 76). Beyond such general assent, however, the bidialectalists defy stereotyping. They range from thinly disguised eradicationists to would-be pluralists blocked by a lack of commitment. But pluralists, who view a policy of bidialectalism, like eradicationism, as a tool of subjugation, are uncompromisingly critical of even those at the latter end of the continuum. As Smitherman espouses, "Teaching strategies which seek only to put white middle-class English into the mouths of black speakers ain did nothin to inculcate the black perspective necessary to address the crises in the black community" (p. 209).

The concepts of eradicationism, pluralism, and bidialectalism undoubtedly will be tossed around and debated for some time to come, with sparks flying. It should be obvious, however, that the pluralist notion is correct and is the only one in this day and age to which the majority of Black children are likely to subscribe. Eradicationism is surely wrong and at any rate impossible unless the children themselves are eliminated. Being bidialectal can certainly be a valuable skill. But people don't become bidialectal just because someone thinks it's a good idea. They mostly sell themselves on the need to be bidialectal. It's a matter beyond curriculum.

Social relations are a far more vital factor for Black students in school than differences of language variety. Black children, like all people, make decisions based on vested interests. If they were to perceive that the social dialectic were in their favor, learning another dialect could not be a major problem. In fact it would be extremely difficult to *prevent* them from learning Standard English. For most Blacks in school such perception can form only within a setting in which teachers genuinely accept them as they come and respect them enough not to sell them myths of simple assimilation. The worst thing any of us can do, who have bought such myths for however long, is to pretend the package was always an easy one to carry home.

6

Big Fame and Other Games

I

One of the first things Mrs. Kaufmann wanted to know was how her class of nine year olds was responding to the era of space exploration. She wanted poems for the bulletin board on this theme. I had never tried writing any poetry before, but I figured I could do it if I wanted to. So after a brief moment of thought and deciding on the rather unimaginative title "Space Poem," I hacked out my first stanza:

A trip to Mars
Is like one to the stars,
A place to go
And a place you don't know.

Dumb, sure, but I was in step. And I took my reader on a wondrous tour of the galaxy before winding down with:

But no matter how far I roam
I'll always want to come back home,
Where the atmosphere is always glad
With my three sisters and Mom and Dad.

I was satisfied with the effort; there was no problem with rhyming; I felt I had a decent poem. Mrs. Kaufmann agreed. I was standing at her desk as she removed her glasses and cast her long black hair over her shoulders.

"This is good work Raymond," she said softly. "I'm going to use it for the bulletin board."

"Thank you Mrs. Kaufmann." I couldn't think of anything further to say.

"You have a fine rhythmic sense. Did you know that?"

"No Mrs. Kaufmann. I don't think rhyming words is all that hard."

"Rhyme is something altogether different," she smiled. "I'm speaking now of rhythm, of the flow of words, of the syllable count, the stresses, the beat. I'm talking about the beat. Do you understand what I'm saying?"

"Yes. I think I do. More or less."

"Do you count the syllables Raymond?"

"No Mrs. Kaufmann, I just go by how it sounds. If it sounds all right I leave it. If it doesn't, then maybe I'll change a word or two."

"Weren't you aware of the fact that you were groping for rhythm?"

"No. Not really. Like I said, I just go by how it sounds." She put her glasses back on and fidgeted with them until they were just right. Kept a constant eye on me.

"Do you like poetry Raymond?"

"It's OK I guess. I never tried writing any before."

"Well maybe you can develop your ability. You should practice more. And read more too. Do you have a library card?"

"Yes I have one. I've had one for a long time."

"That's good. . . . On your next trip to the library be sure to look up Langston Hughes and Ogden Nash. You might like them. Should I write the names down, or can you remember?"

Langston and Ogden, how could I forget? And I found that Ogden could keep me laughing with his zany rhymes as he satirized everything from nicknames to advertising slogans. Langston made me laugh also as he satirized everything from funerals to freedom. But Langston would slip in some somber thoughts about funerals and freedom that I didn't fully understand. So I figured I had to keep laughing with him for the time being and catch on to the other stuff further on down the line, when I got big.

I thought poetry writing might be a good hobby, maybe even as good as space study itself. But by then, both had to take a back seat to athletics. That became the undying compulsion and I played and observed all I possibly could. The moments were unfolding that would become the central core of my sports memory, visions I can recall more readily and with more exactness than many events of far more recent times. Naturally there were the boys in pinstripes. And Mickey, who might have been the greatest if he could have kept his legs off the operating table. Well there were all sorts of injuries, really, and there was blood oozing from a wound in his butt, blood staining the seat of his uniform as he lashed a wicked liner off the scoreboard in Crosley Field and limped to first base. There was Wilt the Stilt averaging 50.4 points per game and tossing in 100 one night against the Knicks. And Elgin Baylor, the greatest forward of them all. There were men called Katcavage, Robustelli, Webster, Rote, Gifford, Barnes, and Y. A. Tittle rolling up big victories on Sundays. And there was Del Shofner, on a bitterly cold day at Soldier Field, dropping a sure touchdown pass in the end zone as the Giants blew the title to the Bears. There were Sugar Ray Robinson and Gene Fullmer and my biggest childhood hero of them all—Sonny Liston.

Sonny would bring those massive fourteen-inch fists directly to the center of the ring, fix his menacing scowl just right, and then swat his opponent down. And I loved it. Lots of people talked bad about Sonny in an attempt to discourage my admiration, but this only strengthened my adulation. Sure I knew Sonny was considered a thug and all, but I also knew he could knock out three guards at one time in the jailhouse. You see, Sonny had what most men wanted: a big reputation. That was important.

When he bombed Patterson in the first round in Chicago to gain the crown and then bombed him again in the first round in Las Vegas to retain it, I was simply overjoyed. But Floyd was so embarrassed that he began sneaking around in phony mustaches and disguises like that, which was something I couldn't understand. Floyd had done his best so, according to my father, he had nothing to be ashamed of. I didn't think an athlete, a hero, should have to wear a mask.

For a time I belonged almost exclusively to 149 playground. Had to put down Junction Park because it was too small for football and softball and only had two hoops. Lonnie Blair played sports in spots, mostly handball. He stayed around Junction Park or up at 92. He thought I was foolish for wanting to play it all. I thought he was foolish for wanting to miss any, a single odd roll of the football. I had to have it all, and it became a problem.

One day in early December I persuaded several of my classmates to join me in challenging a group of fifth and sixth graders to a game of two-handed touch after school. When our challenge was accepted I was excited because it meant a rare chance for me to get some real competition. My classmates were fun, but things had already reached the point where I had to coast when playing against them in order to keep our games interesting. There wasn't a single one of them who could get two hands on me in the open field, and there wasn't one I couldn't track down with ease. My side always had a sure win, but I kept it close. No need, however, to coast against the older boys. I had been watching them play regularly and knew we didn't have much of a chance. Which meant it would be up to me to create one.

At dismissal time I was so eager I quickly vaulted from my seat, only to bang my right knee hard against the side railing. It wasn't the first time I had done it but it was certainly the worst time. I must have banged that knee at the worst possible angle or something, just couldn't shake the pain. We got slaughtered in the game. And there was this guy named Bennett who put the tag on me at every turn. Whenever I got the ball, grimaced, and tried one of my Ernie Davis moves, he slapped on the tag easily and laughed tauntingly, "Ha. I thought you were supposed to be so good."

After the game I limped home and began rubbing alcohol on the painful joint. It was so swollen it alarmed the usually placid Sherry.

"That thing looks terrible . . . nasty. A whole sea of alcohol wouldn't help that knee."

"You don't know what a sea would do," I snapped. "All we got is this bottle. It'll be good enough."

"Hmph. That's what you think. You wait."

Sherry was right. I used the whole bottle and didn't feel any better. I decided to try to catch Pops upstairs. Luckily he was in, and I hobbled into his room with my pants leg rolled up.

"I need some money for some alcohol for my knee." He looked at the joint and winced as though it hurt him also.

"You been walkin around on that? What happened?"

"I banged it on the desk in school."

"Runnin and actin wild I bet. I'll lay odds on that." Then he asked sternly, "Were you?"

"No," I answered sharply. "I was just getting out of my seat and it just happened. I wasn't fooling around or anything like that."

"That knee looks too bad to have just happened." But he didn't press the issue, merely stated calmly, "Well you sure don't need no alcohol. We need to check this thing out at a hospital."

It was found that I had a multiple fracture of the patella. In other words, a cracked kneecap. I thought this would get me a cast similar to the one Michael Stein had when he broke his leg skiing. But instead a nurse wheeled me upstairs and dumped me in a bed.

"But where's my cast?" I asked my father in protest.

"I don't know about no cast. I guess you won't be gettin one."

"Well what are they gonna do to me? They have to do something."

"Oh they'll do somethin all right."

"But what?"

"Make you feel better."

"How?"

"By takin care of that knee for you."

"Yeah but they're supposed to put a cast on it and they're not."

"Maybe they don't need to in this case. They might have to figure out somethin else."

"But WHAT?" I was just about at the panic stage.

"Can't tell you that son. You being a patient all of a sudden don't make me no doctor all of a sudden. They'll get everything straight. Just relax. Take it easy."

Turned out the doctors weren't too sure about what to do themselves. I heard something about a possible operation, something else about a possible draining of fluids. All I knew for sure, however, was that I was lying with my leg in traction virtually all day and night, running a hell of a fever, and taking plenty of needles in tender places.

My mother showed up nearly every day after work with the newspaper, maybe some magazines, and more fruit than I could ever handle. She would finger the knee ever so gingerly and relate stories from home. I always asked first about Debra Lynn.

My father would show up, at other times of course, with sports magazines and even more fruit. We talked mainly about football. It was almost time for him to slip down the stairs and out the door for good.

I spent most of my time in the hospital gazing out of the window, often counting bricks on the adjacent wing. Sometimes demolishing the building with my imagination. Sometimes reconstructing it. Sometimes modifying it, making it slightly taller but narrower or shorter but wider.

I worried about my mother a lot. Wondered if she could stay so solid. She had super moments, but she was no superwoman type. Couldn't handle every big thing and every little thing too. Even back then she would load me, specifically, with responsibility, expect much of me. No overprotection. No simple matriarchal stuff with me. Naturally we had our battles over priorities, over power. But overall, she was a pretty good designer of futures.

The nurses were nice, but I felt overly self-conscious about using the bedpan. Just figured no nurse really wanted to do that job. I would withstand severe stomach cramps far longer than I should have, repeatedly denying the need for the pan, until I would finally break down and request it. And I would read off and on, no real concentration, and give away most of my fruit to other patients who stopped by to visit. I read the card from my classmates over and over again and it always said the same thing: You are sorely missed. Of course I already knew that I was sore, but missed, well, that was nice to hear. And then on the 23rd, as my fear of being confined on Christmas was peaking, I was allowed to go home.

I was preparing to hop down from the bed when my father's voice caused me to hesitate. "Wait Keith. They're gonna take you down in a wheelchair."

"A wheelchair? Not me. I don't need no wheelchair." I hopped to my feet and promptly collapsed, would have hit the floor hard if not for my father's quick reflexes.

"Ain't no need to get hardheaded now boy."

"You mean I really can't walk?" I asked incredulously.

"You'll be all right in a little while. Just have to get your balance back. Can't stay off your feet for weeks and just hop up and scoot around. Takes a few minutes. Gotta get readjusted."

I went home to learn to walk for the second time in my life, and Sherry spoiled Christmas in a way by telling me she knew she was getting a radio. I suspected I would get one also since we both had received watches the year before. My guess was correct and, though there was no moment of surprise, there was a moment of happiness as the holidays rolled on and we kicked out another year on the front steps.

I closed out the school year in pretty decent fashion. Only major problem had been that I had left most of my language arts workbook blank. Mrs. Kaufmann didn't check them regularly, and it was easy to take liberties. Whenever my turn came during class review, I simply read aloud the answer I would have written if I had bothered to do the exercise. One day, however, Mrs. Kaufmann did decide to check. I can't remember if it was just on general principle or whether she had caught someone else faking it. That part is a little fuzzy, but it's clear what happened to me. I was run over quickly by the Kaufmann-to-Sherry-to-Moms express. Had to shake the pain off, drag myself back together, and spend an entire evening confined to my room as I made up the work. The only consolation was that I secretly caught a Yankees game on the radio.

I had written a poem about my latest heroes, John Glenn and Scott Carpenter, and received my standard report card, mostly "goods" and "excellents." But although Mrs. Kaufmann could appreciate my poetry, she didn't enjoy my chattering, which had heightened considerably, and she gave me only a "fair" in conduct. She scribbled in red ink that "Raymond could use more self-control."

My mother said my behavior had better improve the next term. Actually, the threat she made was rather emphatic. I began thinking that I would absolutely and positively improve. But I knew I wouldn't.

II

In September, school started smoothly for me but not for James Meredith. Outside of my family, no one was too concerned that I was in 5-1, but there were many people upset over the fact that Meredith wished to become the first Negro to enroll in the University of Mississippi. Marches and demonstrations by White folks. Countermarches and counterdemonstrations by Negroes. Shotgun ambushes by White folks. Marches and demonstrations by Negroes.

"Wouldn't hafta go that far to keep me from goin to school," commented Lonnie Blair, who was moving from four class to four class. "All they'd hafta do is ask. Would you go Keith?"

"Nah, not me Lonnie. Even *I* don't like school that much."

"Good thing you don't. Cause if you did you'd be kinda dumb."

"I know. Still, those people shouldn't be prejudiced down there."

"Yeah but you know how it is. That's how they be."

That's all the moral support Meredith could get from us two ten year olds. But a few weeks later I was able to get a striking adult view of this and other situations when I was ordered to the barbershop.

As I reluctantly came through the door, Mr. Horton waved me up into his chair. "How you son? Your father said you was comin by today. I see you done let it git nappy enough, don't you think?"

"Yeah I guess so. . . . How's business in general Mr. Horton?" My father always asked him that question.

"Slow Tuesday son, that's all, slow Tuesday." He tied the apron around me and reached for a comb. A man in a suit rose, with the help of a cane, from the other chair. He brushed loose hairs away with his left hand, and as he extended to his full height I could see that his right leg was several inches shorter than the other. Besides that he seemed to be in real good shape. He pulled a bill from his pocket, turned it over to Boone, and told him to keep the change. Boone looked as if he was trying to save up for a haircut of his own. I mean I had never seen a barber as sloppy about his hair as he was. He wore the first and wildest afro I ever saw. Had a scraggly beard and sideburns. He certainly wasn't such a good advertisement but was, in fact, a good barber. Lots of people asked for Boone. Boone or Horton, didn't make me any difference. Not for the close shave I had to get. Just be fast.

Boone began brushing his customer's clothes with the whisk broom. Then he added, "Thank you Shortside. Appreciate it."

"Ain't nothin Boone, my good man. You know it ain't nothin but a drop." He stretched his left arm out to the side as he started to yawn. When he composed himself again he announced his leave. "Well I got my haircut now. Let me go on and finish sprucin up for the evenin."

"You do that," said Boone. "You take care."

"Yes Mr. Shortside," intruded Mr. Horton. "You watch out for them women."

"Watch out for em? Now Horton, you know I can handle the young ladies. Man, you shoulda seen me the other night." Mr. Shortside had come alive with agitation. "Man, I had this sweet young thing up in the apartment. We naked and she done got me all worked up and everything and then she wants to sit on the edge of the bed and all of a sudden play shy. She was wonderin if she could play for some big money I guess. Says she wanna discuss matters. Can you dig that? 'Discuss matters.' I git a little mad but I don't let on, you know. Can't let the chick have the satisfaction of thinkin she can git next to me like that. I just puts the intelligence in my head. I carries it around in my socks, only got a little bit and I needs to save it like that. So anyway I puts it in my head and then I realize that all I gotta do is keep my cool and use a little indifference myself, you know, like I could take it or leave it myself. And let me tell you somethin. It wasn't long before her mind got off the discussin and back to the bustin. Oh she had a little somethin to say about lookin for real love and all that. But I convinced her that the real love couldn't start until she shut her damn mouth. And I layed it on her too. I ain't got no handicap like that." Mr. Shortside paused briefly to savor whatever the memory was, then switched his tone to one of mock complaint. "Now I can't git rid of the chick. It done even got to where I'm actually duckin her now. Girl trying to be on me tight as a orange peel be on a orange. She gittin peeled though, better believe that."

Boone had been simmering with laughter. Now he boiled. Mr. Horton uttered a restrained "heh heh heh" and continued to comb my hair, me amused all the while. Mr. Shortside grinned, having played his audience well. He then directed his attention my way.

"You a handsome nuff boy, be able to git on it one day like ol Shortside. Can't promise you'll be good as me, but you bound to have just as much fun anyway."

"This Gil's boy here," cut in Mr. Horton. "You know the tall fella be in here, crazy about the Giants like us?"

"Yeah yeah yeah. I know him. Good man. . . . You know, I was kinda thinkin this here boy reminded me of somebody I knew. Gil, hunh? This the boy got to be crazy about those Yankees then? Is that so young fella?"

"Uh hunh."

"Well you really don't think they can take this World Series, do you?"

"Uh hunh. I do. They'll beat San Francisco." That answer didn't sit well with Mr. Shortside, so he dismissed it.

"Well every fella got his own weakness, ain't he Horton?"

"You're right about that Shortside. But he's just a kid. He can't remember anything about when the Giants were here in New York." Mr. Shortside studied my face, like it was hard to figure I was only nine or ten.

"I reckon you're right about that Horton. But tell me somethin young fella, you do know about prejudice, don't you?"

"Uh hunh. I know about it." I was ready to listen to an anti-Yankees speech such as the ones my mother gave, but Mr. Shortside came from another direction.

"Well what is it then?" he demanded.

"It's, um, it's, uh, I mean it's like when they didn't want that man in Mississippi to go to school."

"Why it sure is," he responded with surprise. "Gil say he ain't got no dumb boy, and he ain't either. Hey Boone, before I go why don't you tell me and the kid all about the University of Mississippi? Is it truly the University OF Mississippi or not?"

"Aw go on Shortside," Boone laughed. "Why you wanna go back into that? I thought you was talkin baseball."

"Well baseball ain't the whole ball game, if you dig what I'm sayin. So come on and philosophize for me and the kid." Then he turned to ask me another question. "You didn't know Boone was a philosopher, did you?"

Actually I did. But his main topic on the Saturday mornings when I was usually around was the women who had made him angry.

Boone sat in the barber's chair and propped his feet up on the metal footrest. Stuck his hands into the large pockets of his light blue shirt-jacket. "Well I'll tell ya," he began. "It's OF Mississippi because Negroes are now included in the chance to go there, but it's OF Mississippi because they gonna catch all kinds of hell for really tryin to do it. So it's OF Mississippi and it's good, and it's OF Mississippi and it's bad. And then you can say that it ain't really the University OF Mississippi at all because a Negro might can use that school to get a job opportunity just like a White boy, and that definitely wouldn't represent what Mississippi is all about. So it is and it is and it ain't. All depends on how you look at it."

"Hear that son?" Mr. Shortside would not allow a lull. "Wanna know what all that philosophizin means?"

I certainly did. Up to that point I had only thought that the name of a school was the name of a school. That's all.

"Well do you?"

"Yes I do."

"Then I'll tell you. It means the stuff is so screwed up. Usually when you hear a whole buncha jumbled up philosophy, it means somethin real screwed up is goin on. You git halfway confused tryin to explain the shit. Ain't that right Boone?"

"Yeah Shortside. You ain't far off base puttin it like that. There's always something wrong when those funny explanations come up. Like some folks say he shoulda went wherever he was wanted, while other folks say he shoulda been wanted wherever he went."

"That's right son," beamed Mr. Shortside. "And let me tell you, course you gotta 'cuse my French, that what it all comes down to is that a muthafuckin cracker just don't mean a nigguh no good. It's in the skin, son. It's definitely in the skin. Don't let nobody never tell you that it *ain't* in the skin. And it's the same thing South or North. Ain't a whole lotta difference. Just like I see Kennedy done got this fair housing bill passed, but it don't mean nothin to the people right over here down the street in Honkieville. The bill shoulda been written on toilet tissue cause that's the amount of respect the average cracker gonna give it. Ain't it like that Horton?" Mr. Shortside was pacing now. Handling his cane very well. Moving far swifter than I had thought him capable.

"I think you're right on it," replied Horton.

"Yeah I knows I am. Man with smark socks can't be no all the time fool. Helluva a situation we in, ain't it Boone?"

"Sure is. This a funny country we tryin to call our own."

"Damn right. Helluva funny country. I wouldn't care if Uncle Sam and Baldy Red blowed this whole mother up as long as they let me and a few of those pretty young gals live."

"Now sir," Mr. Horton began laughingly. "Is that all you want from the whole deal?"

"Yeah Horton. Why not? Ain't nothin better to live for. Not how I'm lookin at it now."

Mr. Shortside and Boone became very special in my eyes. They gave the current events much better than Mrs. Holtzman did. More analysis and fervor. My teacher stayed more on the side of soft regret and subdued hope. Whereas she was detached, they had definite points of view.

There hadn't been much spoken about race relations in our home. Only when Moms spoke out against the Yankees. We were never taught to hate White people as a whole. Of course I had always managed to hate them enough for Lonnie Blair. Now I had to ponder whether or not I could despise them enough for my newest mentors, who were taking matters to a new level.

I studied my classmates even more closely. Particularly zoomed in on Michael Stein as we had become pretty solid companions ever since the treaty fiasco back in '60. He and I would recruit other classmates to his home for games of Monopoly and Stratego. Because I had the latest curfew, I could always stay later than any of the others. Many times I would be on hand to greet his parents, who always seemed glad to see me, as they came in from work. And Marcia Stein, Michael's seventeen-year-old sister, seemed especially fond of me, always laughing when I beat Michael at Monopoly and asking me questions about the one class. She usually wanted me to stick around for dinner, even said she was insisting. But I wouldn't. Whenever she popped the question I would glance at my watch and announce that I had to hurry home. I wasn't comfortable enough to sit at their table yet. Besides, I felt my pace was steady enough.

Then there was Marty Rosenberger. He was a real underdog at times, a clumsy sort who could barely walk and hold his pants up at the same time. But he was highly spirited and hustled hard in every sport we played. I always chose him for my team, always bolstered his self-confidence in order to combat his clumsiness, and we got along fine.

The first time I made a prolonged visit to his home was on a Saturday. We were going to watch the basketball game featuring Providence College and Jimmy Walker, who they were billing as the next Oscar Robertson. I raced up to the Southridge Co-ops, excited about his game and mine. As I came off the elevator, Marty was coming out into the hall carrying a bag of garbage. He let the door slam behind him.

"The lock is off Raymond. You can go on in. We have free run of the place."

"All right Marty, game is just about on, isn't it?"

"They're introducing the lineups. Go ahead. Just take your sneakers off before you step on the carpet. It was just done."

His words stunned me for a moment because I had on some air-conditioned socks. You know the style. They weren't all that bad as ragged socks go. Lonnie Blair wouldn't have given them a second thought. But I needed a perfect pair for Marty Rosenberger.

I shot a quick look at Marty nearing the incinerator. Fortunately it was toward the other end of the hall. Slow and clumsy as Marty was, I knew I had a chance. I hurried inside, took my sneakers off without bothering with the laces, and dashed wildly into Marty's room. The second dresser drawer I opened was the correct one, and I changed into a perfect pair of white sweat socks about as quickly as it can be done. The fit was pretty good. I stuffed my own socks into a pocket of my jacket and bolted out into the living room, beating Marty by several seconds. This wasn't quite what Mr. Shortside meant by "smart socks." But in my own way I was learning.

I accepted invitations to their birthday parties, joined the Cub Scouts with them, pack 325. Anything to observe. I watched them in the library down on 82nd Street. While I would delve more into my poets and sports heroes like Joe Louis and Jim Thorpe, they would be more into Anne Frank, thereby influencing my own future reading list. Anything to stay on top of the situation.

One afternoon after a touch football game Michael, Marty, and I were left sitting on a park bench.

"I think I'm getting better now," Marty asserted.

"You are better," I instantly assured him. "You hang on to the ball better now and you're not afraid of the hard passes. Keep it up and you'll be better than me one day."

"I doubt it Raymond." So did I. But like I said, I always did this sort of thing with Marty.

"Don't doubt it Marty. Practice makes perfect and that's all you have to do. You too Michael. You can get a whole lot better also."

"I guess so. But it's only football. My dad says brains are better than brawn."

"Brains *are* better than brawn," I promptly retorted. It was an old debate for us and I was ready to win it convincingly this time. "But that's only if you have to choose one over the other. Having brains *and* brawn is the best you can do. And anyway, catching passes isn't brawn; it's skill. Brawn and skill are different."

"Yeah? Well my dad says that school is more important than all of that. He wants me to do exceptionally well so I can make it all the way to medical school. I know I'll be a doctor. I just don't know my specialty yet. What about you Marty?"

"I think I'll be an accountant or something. As long as the money is good. I won't accept anything under $200 a week. My dad says that's the least he would work for."

This was back when a yearly salary of $10,000 was a very big deal. I knew my father wasn't even halfway to that figure. Not toiling in that machine shop.

"What about you Raymond?" asked Michael abruptly. "What are you going to do?"

"Well I haven't really decided yet," I countered without hesitation. "I can be a lot of things. I might be a football player, a smart one. Or I might be some kind of scientist, or engineer. Or a doctor or an accountant also. No telling what I might end up doing. World may blow up before we get to be adults anyway. You know how they keep talking about World War III."

"Don't say that Raymond."

"Aw I'm just kidding around Michael. Don't be so scary. It won't happen."

"I hope not. But it is possible, isn't it? My dad says Krushchev is a very dangerous man. Calls him the Red Hitler."

"He is bad," Marty cut in. "But nobody's quite as bad as Hitler. There's nobody as bad as somebody who exterminated six million people. That's like killing most of this whole city. If Germany had won the war, Michael, we'd be in concentration camps right now. We might even be dead. He probably wouldn't bother you Raymond. You'd be sorta lucky to be a Negro."

"Man are you crazy? He hated Negroes too."

"You sure about that?"

"Of course I'm sure. Don't be so dumb Marty. I know he hated Jesse Owens for winning all those gold medals at the 1936 Olympics. And I know he hated Joe Louis for knocking the hell out of Max Schmeling. Tell him Michael. Ask your dad about all that. He hated Negroes just as much as he hated Jews."

"I have to check on that," Michael said cautiously. "Maybe he did hate Negroes also, but it must have been a little different from how he hated Jews. He would get us first for sure. Right Marty?"

Naturally Marty agreed with him. I never would, though it wasn't an argument I would press. I knew Jews caught plenty hell. But of course I knew Black folks caught plenty hell too. Some of it from Jews.

We had one of our standard games going on, and Leonard Landau, Barry Weinstein, Mark Greenberg, Marty, and I were one touchdown up on Michael, John Levy, Barry Goldberg, Mark Friedman, and Jerry Weissman. Jerry was running out to catch a pass and I was right with him. Our bodies bumped together slightly, and as I stumbled a bit Jerry made the catch and started sprinting down the sideline toward a score. As I was recovering my stride I was thinking about whether I should let him go on and tie the game. A tie was always interesting. Made everything seem more heroic. But I decided not to let Jerry do it. He was the kind of guy who would brag too much if he scored a touchdown on me. I was aware that he resented me a lot because he realized he would have been the best if I weren't around. No, I couldn't allow him to score on me. Michael or

Marty, yes, but definitely not Jerry. So I tracked him down and put a firm two-handed tag on his back just as he was cutting back to the inside. But instead of stopping, he kept running at full speed, and when he crossed the goal line he started jumping up and down and waving the football about over his head. His teammates, who actually weren't in position to see the tag clearly, were running up to congratulate him. Marty, appearing puzzled, drew alongside of me.

"Looked to me like you got him."

"Yeah I got him. When don't I get him? . . . I guess nobody else saw it. He knows I tagged him."

"Maybe he didn't feel it."

"He felt it. He's just trying to get away with something."

"No way," Marty vowed, and he ran up ahead shouting, "Raymond got him. Raymond got him back there. Come back and play it from back here. He was tagged."

"Get out of here," screamed Jerry. "I got a touchdown."

"No you didn't. Raymond tagged you back here."

"He did not!"

"Did so!"

"Oh get the hell outa here. He did not."

"I did so," I shouted back, drawing closer. "You know I tagged you. You're just trying to be some kind of hotshot, that's all."

"Ah you get lost too, Raymond."

"No! You don't tell me to get lost."

"I can tell you all I want. You're just mad I beat you for the touchdown."

"You didn't beat me for any touchdown."

"I did so! I beat you!"

"You did not. If I didn't tag you, then why did I stop running?"

"You just couldn't catch me."

"Aw come on. You know I can beat you by a mile."

"You can not!"

"Can so Jerry. I'll race you right now and prove it."

"That has nothing to do with this. I got a touchdown."

"But I tagged you."

"You did not! I didn't feel any tag. Did anybody see him tag me?" A couple of players from both sides ventured that it looked like I might have tagged him. No one was definite, however, except Marty.

"I saw him tag you. It was clear to me."

"Ah go to hell Marty. You're just brainwashed."

"I am not."

"You are so. Look, I got the touchdown already so let's get the game moving."

"We'll get it moving," I interjected, "as soon as we bring the ball back to where it belongs."

"But it belongs up here! I got a touchdown!" He was so frantically persistent I began wondering if he was sincere about not feeling the tag. But then I dismissed the thought. I mean I just knew the tag had been firm enough. However, in the face of his steadfastness I was willing to settle for a traditional schoolyard compromise: choosing for it. It was a suggestion thoroughly acceptable to everyone except Jerry.

"No way! I got a touchdown!"

"You did not. I tagged you. I'm giving you a chance to choose for it. Or we can even do the whole play over again. One or the other. But you just can't take a touchdown like that."

"And you just can't take one away either."

"Well let's choose then. You know how they say, cheating shows, never goes."

"Why don't you choose him?" Michael asked. "We're wasting time."

"No! I won't choose him. I got a touchdown!" He became even more worked up, teeth clenched, head shaking vehemently, sandy hair flopping about. I was thinking about conceding the touchdown and then embarrassing him with my skill throughout the remainder of the game. I was thinking about this real hard until he said, "You're just a filthy cheatin nigger, that's all. Just a cheatin nigger and that's all you know how to do."

Well my head just exploded inside as the world around me came to a complete standstill. After a moment I could hear my thoughts real good. *Nigger? Me? Now Jerry Weissman got more sense than that. Well ain't he? I knows he don' think he that bad. Do he? Just because he a little bigger than me now, so what.* My palms turned clammy and I cocked my right hand to bust him straight in the mouth. He reeled backward and I bloodied his nose with another right and followed that with a jump-kick to his stomach. He fell to the ground and I pounced on him and straddled his chest. I yanked him by the collar and peered down into his trembling blue eyes.

"I wish I had a knife," I declared without waver. "I'd stab you straight through the top of your head and kill you. You hear me?" I could tell he believed me. Momentarily, I believed myself. I started shaking him with all of my might. He surged to resist, but he couldn't get loose from my grasp until I finally let him.

Jerry scrambled to his feet. Tears streamed down his cheeks, tears ran into smeared blood. He scooped up the football, you just know it had to be his, and he broke out running. As he passed Marty, Marty punched him on the side of the face with a pretty good left hand. Surprised me by how well he threw it, how coordinated. Jerry staggered forward and I rushed up to boot him in the rear to get him going full tilt again. He hollered back over his shoulder, "I'll get both of you. You wait and see, you filthy cheaters."

The crowd dispersed uneasily and I walked out of the schoolyard behind Marty. He was genuinely as upset as I was.

"Wonder what he's got up his sleeve, Raymond."

"Better be nothing. Best thing for him to do is leave us on alone. I'm not even worried about it."

Jerry apologized the very next day. He still insisted he was right about the game, but admitted he was way out of bounds with the name-calling. He said his own parents told him that he was wrong. I shook hands with him and forgave him verbally—but not inside.

Lonnie Blair was amused by the incident. He couldn't stop laughing and rolling all over his bedroom floor.

"You sure showed that Jewboy something, didn't you?"

"Yeah man. I rocked his chops pretty good. Shook his mind up too."

"You did the right thing. Just because you nice enough to play football with them don't give them Jewboys no right to think they can jig over you. That's just like a Jew too, you know, tryin ta take advantage of somebody. You know I'd like to crack me a few of them Jewboys myself. I'm surprised they didn't all jump you. They're good for something like that."

"Well I know they probably wanted to, but I was ready for em. I woulda grabbed somebody and choked him until they all backed off. That's the way you do that you know."

"I know."

I didn't tell Lonnie about the loyalty of Marty Rosenberger, or even about how much a friend Marty always was. Lonnie would never have understood.

III

I knew a little all-purpose chemistry by the end of the fifth grade, knew that lack of mortgage payments was a surefire formula for foreclosure and eviction. And as a result of this uncompromising bit of science (brought about by slow horses and fast women again), we moved into an apartment about a half mile deeper into Corona, into the heart of what many were calling a two-story slum. Couldn't even get a glimpse of Jackson Heights. Northern Boulevard, as it cut through our neighborhood one block to the south, looked a lot like that old Eighth Avenue. As a matter of fact our neighborhood was often dubbed "Little Harlem."

Old adjustable me tried to fit right in. On my block there was a bunch of Lonnie Blairs to befriend. Of course I would reveal to this group only those parts of me I felt they could best understand, as they did in turn, as we cemented our bonds.

"I'm gon be a major leaguer."

"Aw man Junior, you ain gon be no goddamn major leaguer. Yo fat ass too slow, man. You knock a ball all the way off the center field fence and the man still got time to chase the ball down, stop once or twice to pee, and still throw you out at first base."

"I ain't that damn slow, P.J."

"Aw nigguh, you slower than that. I'll dust you man. I'll give you half a block on a two block race and still dust you. We can go now. I'll show you how slow yo fat ass is."

"Naw man. You got it."

"Yeah I know. I'll pass yo ass so fast you'll think you goin backwards."

"So what man. At least I can hit. Now tell me I can't hit."

"Hell yeah you can hit. Everybody know you goddamn sure can hit. But so what? I can learn to hit like that too. But yo chubby ass ain never gon move no faster. So if any major leaguer gon come outa this here block, it's gotta be me. Ain't that right Robbie Bo?"

"I don't know about that P.J. Maybe Keith can be one too. I mean he good as hell with that glove and handles the rest of the game none too bad."

"Well maybe he'll come after me. I don't care. As long as I'm the first famous nigguh off this block. All right Keith?"

"Don't make me no difference."

"I'll come see yall in every city yall play in," declared Butchie. "I'll be a big time gangster or somethin by then and have mucho money."

"Aw man, you scared to be a gangster."

"What you mean Wallace? I ain't scared."

"Would you kill somebody?"

"Damn right I would. I'll Al Capone a nigguh in a minute. Half a minute if it's a White boy."

While it was mandatory to hate the Whites, we couldn't stand being called Black. That was an automatic fight. Most other jibes were tolerated if done in customary taste, or if the target of the insult was in a decent mood. But of course, you could never count on either.

"Hey Butchie, yo momma wear combat boots." (An old standard lead.)

"So yo momma don't wear nothin. Most bitches don't when they out hoin' all over town." (Definitely a nonstandard reply.)

Time out for Butchie and P.J.

"Hey Keith, where yo Pops at man?" (Usually fair game.)

"He in his skin nigguh. Where you think he at?" (Not in the mood.)

"Mine's home with me every night dummy." (Pushing the issue.)

"Man, you don't know if that's your real father or not." (Last chance to back off.)

"What the hell you mean I don't?" (Dare you.)

"You know how they say, Wallace. Momma's baby. Daddy's maybe." (Ready.)

"So what you sayin?" (Stall.)

"That there's one more triflin bitch in this world than you thought there was." (Stop stalling.)

Time out for Wallace Jones and Keith Gilyard.

I tried to stay up on my current events and was rewarded by having my senses brutalized by the outrageous happenings in the South. Events like the Meredith affair were occurring steadily. Although it was less than a year since I had been relatively detached concerning Meredith's suffering, I was, nevertheless, quite indignant at the latest outbreaks of bigotry. Negroes were doing simple things like registering to vote and were being greeted by bombs and bullets and cattle prods and rubber hoses and police dogs. Emblazoning my memory. I couldn't believe that the response of most of those Negroes was to continue marching and demonstrating and trying to register. My youthly instinct and vision required that a full-scale war be conducted in the South, not merely a one-sided blitz. I mean if you get hit you got to hit back, right? It seemed simple enough to me. Hell, I felt those Negroes down South didn't have to worry about Krushchev and the Russians. Those Negroes were going to be wiped out by the Ku Klux Klan before then.

For an adult view of the situation I had to go down to the barbershop. Boone told me the issue wasn't as clear cut as it seemed. Mr. Horton, who had grown up in the South, told me I was really too young to worry about vengeance. When I ran into Mr. Shortside, who also had grown up in the South, he told me that the Negroes down there were plum loco if they didn't have better sense than to offer to line up to get billy-clubbed. Shorty was my man. But I knew that Boone and Horton were no fools. And certainly Martin Luther King Jr. was not. I mean he spoke so well. I began to form the uneasy impression that there was something about this whole problem that I wasn't quite grasping yet.

So I was a puzzled spectator that summer. I was immensely proud as I saw more than 250,000 people jam the streets of the nation's capital during the March on Washington. Felt proud as I listened to Martin's speech of ideal integration. I knew Martin had a beautiful dream. And with all those people rallying around the Lincoln Monument, on television they seemed like damn near all the folks in the world, I thought there was enough strength available to make King's dream come to life. Wasn't any way that glorious day was supposed to be followed by the bombing of a Negro church in Birmingham, Alabama. Four more Black casualties. Young girls. Like Sherry and Judy and Debra Lynn.

"Hey Keith, my grandma lives down there in Alabama."

"That ain't nothin Robbie Bo. Mine's too."

"Yeah? Well they better not start no stuff like that in my grandma's town."

"They better not do it in my grandma's town neither."

"And you know these honkies up here better not start no stuff like that. We'd really have to take care of them then."

"You right Robbie Bo. We'd have to."

My biggest hero that summer was Sherry. She was on her way to junior high school in the fall and a place in a Special Progress class, the only Black I knew who had made one. She didn't make it from the one class; she had been in 6-2, which should have tipped me off, but her marks on all the standardized exams were so high that she was included anyway. Now she had a chance to do the seventh and eighth grades in one year. That two-year program was rough. The three-year program was enriched, but you didn't skip any time. It was more prestige than pressure.

I was permitted to remain at 149 for my final year of elementary school and I started the term with great zeal. Naturally. I couldn't wait to make S.P. myself. Fortunately I was up to the task because 6-1 was the most competitive class I had ever been in. Whenever I went up to Mrs. Kessler's desk to pick up a test, I was mugged by someone anxious to see what grade I had received. Everyone in the class had the news before I even reached my seat. Our 100s were waved about jubilantly like flags and our 70s somehow managed to get lost. I had my share of flags and wasn't worried.

Sherry asked out of S.P. after only one marking period. It had been too much cramming for her, too much emphasis on fierce competition. She was too introverted to handle the pressure cooker. They couldn't take away her intelligence, but they couldn't make her knock heads either. She really wanted no part of special progress at all. Not in a one class or an S.P. class. She was transferred to one of the average classes and she flourished.

I wasn't too disappointed in Sherry. Even then I could understand that she had been more victim than failure. I just wished I could have lent her my guile, spirit, and ability to hang tough.

Judy and Debra Lynn, who was beginning kindergarten, were over at 92, the midget reformatory. I just hoped they didn't have to fight.

The Negro got himself into further trouble, if you can imagine that, when Kennedy was assassinated. At least that's what some of the older folks in the neighborhood were saying. Said he was the Negro's best friend and that the Negro would be at a great disadvantage without him around. I had nothing personal against Kennedy, but I didn't think he and the Negro were ever quite like Lonnie Blair and me. Lonnie would never watch anybody harm me.

What shook me the most that year was the controversy that stemmed from the announcement by the Board of Education that a plan was under consideration to "pair" 92 and 149 in order to desegregate both facilities. Like most residents of Corona, I was in favor of the idea. Of course I would be out of elementary school by the time the plan was implemented, but I thought the plan would make school better for Judy and Debra Lynn, give them a better opportunity to learn. And these two schools were so close together that busing wasn't even part of the issue.

Regardless, most of the people in Jackson Heights were dead set against the plan. There were numerous threats and lawsuits on their behalf. A series of articles was run in the *New York Times* exploring this and other aspects of Northern White Prejudice. Boone saved the paper for me each day and I devoured the accounts. Paid particular attention to how White folks, while allowing themselves to be quoted only anonymously, were trying to justify their ways of thinking. Lame reasoning such as:

> I feel that every group should have their equal rights. But I look at this thing as the other side trying to obtain their equal rights by taking over mine. . . .

and

> I wish there was some way for everything to be integrated peacefully—you know, there could be one or two colored at first and maybe more later, and nobody would mind—I know that nobody would mind. It's just the large number that I'm afraid of. And that's what everybody else is afraid of too. Not just in housing, but in the schools, too. . . .

and

> Look, it's not just me. Everybody does this. You tell your friend that there are plenty of places he can find an apartment, across Junction Boulevard. . . .

and

> The educated get along pretty well. At the United Nations they sit and talk together all day, and talk together all night, and they eat dinner together and go to each other's houses, and they get along. But the lower classes never can get along. They'll always be fighting with each other. Now, right now, the colored is in the lower class. . . .

Langston Hughes and Mr. Shortside had always contended that a thick vein of prejudice was all around us up here, and I had come to believe them. But now I had it all in print. Positive proof straight from Whitey's own mouth. And what unsettled me so much was that I began wondering if I actually knew any of the people quoted in the newspapers. Had I been in any of their homes? Had I played with their children? Did Michael Stein's mother really hate me and only pretend to be fond of me?

It became easier to forgo the usual activities in the playground and either join Lonnie in Junction Park or take an early hike up to the block. When I did play with my classmates I didn't coast any more. Played hard.

I wrote a stinging attack on White Backlash that brought acclaim from my classmates, teacher, principal, and other schoolmates. I basically argued that the only way to correct injustice is all at once. Anything short of that is but more injustice. The logic was simple. And in addition to my general argument, with the *Times* as my evidence, I made reference to what was happening right in Jackson Heights.

The essay stayed on the bulletin board through two "marquee" changes. Of course I doubted the sincerity of all the approval I received, all except that of my Black schoolmates. They were the only ones in that environment who possessed a fervently expressed indignation to match mine over the nerve of some White folks to demonstrate or insinuate by word or deed that Blacks wanted too much too soon.

Lonnie Blair, unlike Mrs. Kessler and Mr. Price, knew what restraint went into that piece of writing. Lonnie knew I had really just highlighted the basic issues, hadn't told them about all the stuff we had been hearing from this new guy named Malcolm.

The term dragged to its final day and I wound up with a long string of "excellents" on my report card, bagged that S.P. spot easily. I wouldn't be going to junior high school in Jackson Heights with the others. I was out of the zone. The fact that my own sister was already enrolled in the school didn't seem to make any difference to anyone in charge. She could remain, but I wasn't welcome. Michael wondered if I would ever come to see him. I said I probably would.

That same afternoon we had a softball game going in the park. I had just hustled into third base with a triple when I happened to look up and see Lonnie Blair, along with a group of his friends from 92, climbing through the hole in the right field fence. As they all bopped in from the outfield I knew trouble was coming.

James Bishop, a sturdy kid, started hassling Leonard Landau in the batter's box. "Lemme git a hit."

"But we're playing a game. You're not supposed to interrupt a game just like that."

"Aw gimme the bat you White asshole. I know what I'm suppose to do." James snatched the bat away, shoved Leonard aside, and assumed a batting stance. "Come on Blondie," he called out to the pitcher, Mark Greenberg. "Come on and throw the ball."

Mark held the ball in his glove and didn't say anything. This was the opening James was looking for.

"Oh, so you think you bad, hunh?" He dropped the bat and headed slowly toward the mound. By this time Lonnie was standing at third base with me. His presence had caused Barry Weinstein, the third baseman, to ease over next to Barry Goldberg at shortstop.

"That boy gon git his ass beat now," Lonnie said matter-of-factly.

"He shoulda thrown the ball," I replied.

"Yeah, maybe so. But somebody gotta git their ass beat down here. Maybe everybody. 'Cept you know ain nobody gon mess with you."

"I know ain't nobody messin with me. It's these gray boys that's in trouble and I don't care nothin bout that. I'll even git down myself if you want me to."

"Nah Keith, you don't hafta do that. We don't need no extra help for this, probably won't bust them up that much anyhow. All depends on how bad they jump. I'm just gon try to git somebody to hit me first or call me a nigger or somethin so I can stomp him. Won't nobody be able to blame me neither. School's over now."

"Yeah Lonnie," I said, slapping him five and grinning. "School's really over now."

James kept pushing Mark around pretty hard but wouldn't tee off and really nail him. Like Lonnie, he was waiting to be offended. But Mark simply kept collecting himself long enough to ask "Why don't you stop it?" before getting pushed all over again. The spectators were laughing and the ballplayers were terrified. All except Marty Rosenberger. I saw his face redden as he sat on the edge of the dugout bench next to John Levy. I could picture him running out to take up for Mark Greenberg and getting thoroughly thrashed, a classic case of will without skill. Even as I stood with Lonnie Blair beside me, I knew that I could not allow Marty to get hurt.

Mark got pushed again, and he looked over at me as if he thought I could do a little negotiating. I became aware that most of the other ballplayers were casting glances at me also, wishing I could be their champion, their general. They had to be crazy. Number one, I didn't want to bail them out. Number two, it wasn't possible anyway.

James shoved Mark to the ground and headed over toward the shortstop position. The other Black kids fanned out to enact their own scenes of harassment, of baiting.

Lonnie Blair focused on the dugout. "Guess I'll jig with somebody in there."

"Me too Lonnie."

"Nah man, you don't have to."

"But I want to. These gray boys been gittin on my nerves too much anyway." I ran over ahead of Lonnie, ferociously shoved Marty Rosenberger to the ground and pinned him there by sitting on his chest, using the dugout fence to brace myself.

"Hey get off me," Marty protested. "What the hell do you think you're doing?"

"Shut up you little Jewish punk bitch before I get up and stomp your ass."

John Levy was horrified by my words, but Lonnie Blair roared approvingly. Then he grabbed John's bat and began swinging it wildly (though really with control as he was careful not to hit John). But John, unable to read the action correctly, fled the dugout in panic, his perceived attacker right on his heels.

"Get off of me Raymond," Marty balked. "What the hell are you pulling?" He struggled to get loose but I easily held my position.

"Take it easy," I whispered. "I'm trying to keep you from getting hurt. I know you Marty. You'll get out there running your mouth and get yourself hurt."

"But look Raymond, I'm not scared." Now his whisper equaled mine.

"I know you're not scared, but everybody else is."

"That's their problem."

"No it's your problem because you'll be the one on the spot. Believe me. I know what I'm talking about."

"But those guys are just bullying people. It's not fair."

"But it's fair what I'm doing. And if you don't think so then maybe we can get up and fight for real. I'll kick your ass myself. I'll be just like them."

"But I know you're not."

"Look Marty, you don't know anything. So just relax and shut up."

Marty only put up a token struggle after that and from our peculiar entanglement we saw the action draw to a close. We saw that no one put up enough resistance to get roughed up very much, and we saw James snatch the gloves of both Barrys and sprint away. A couple of his partners took gloves also, and then all of them began to speed away. Lonnie held up his new bat like a torch and followed, calling back over his shoulder, "Hey Keith we gotta split man. Come on."

"Yeah man. Hold up." I hopped up, offered Marty a weak "Take care" and dashed out toward right field, past the blurred white faces, running straight for that hole in the fence.

There would be no coming back in the years to come. I never knew how Marty eventually explained me to the boys in the past. I never knew how this final scene of this six-year drama affected them as a group.

My fellows up ahead, well, they had hate on their backs but not really in their hearts. They had a lot of toughening up to do.

As for me, oh the deep me, if I could just reach high and far. . . .

IV

Summer 1964. President Johnson pushed another Civil Rights Act through Congress. It was supposedly a guarantee for the desegregation of public facilities as well as an assurance that a policy of affirmative action would be widely implemented. What it actually was, in the esteemed opinion of Mr. Shortside, was just another piece of toilet tissue legislation.

A White cop in Harlem shot a fifteen-year-old Black boy, an event that set off a series of riots up in the old home town. Johnson speculated that communist forces had instigated the riots and he sent in the FBI to investigate.

It was "Freedom Summer" in the South. The key object was to increase the registration of Negro voters. But the Klansmen kicked off the drive by murdering Chaney, Goodman, and Schwerner and dramatically reaffirming that they would just as soon kill a White sympathizer, especially a Jew, as kill a Negro himself. Boone said he had seen it coming.

I suggested to Mr. Horton that maybe Johnson should evacuate everyone from Mississippi except the Klan and then drop the atom bomb on Mississippi just as Truman dropped it on Hiroshima. Mr. Horton suggested once again that I could get a little too serious-minded at times.

Perhaps Mr. Horton had a point. After all, I was almost a teenager. Wasn't it time to stop worrying about these weighty matters? I mean the outline of my life was fairly clear. All I had to do was protect my own self, finish growing up, and grab my piece of the glory. Relax as much as possible for now, you know, cool out with my friends and enjoy my surroundings. Stop worrying about such great conquests. Spend the summer being as much kid as I could be. And the main battle a kid had in the summer was to beat the heat.

The World's Fair was a major outlet, and I considered it the greatest exposition ever created. Coney Island or the circus or the Museum of Natural History didn't even come close. We residents of Corona were the luckiest of people because the fairgrounds were like a local park for us. Visitors were streaming in by the thousands from all over the world to reach the same place we could reach with a twenty-minute walk. We had the most time to see everything the fair had to offer, from the Unisphere to the Watusi dancers in loin cloths and Converse sneakers. We had more chances than anyone else to run around all the pavilions and witness just how diverse and brilliant humans could be.

We were elated at how the whiz kids at General Motors, Chrysler, and American Telephone and Telegraph were going to make the future such an easy and convenient place in which to live. As resourceful as they were, they had us believing we would all own a telephone with a video screen and a flying car like George Jetson by the time we were thirty. I thought the folks at National Cash Register were superbly ingenious as they had developed a transparent slide, which wasn't much bigger than a book of matches, on which the entire *Bible* was reproduced. And I must have watched the display of nuclear fusion in the General Electric Pavilion at least fifty times. It was a fresh thrill each time they heated the chamber of deuterium to forty million degrees to produce that thunder and lightning effect in the exhibit hall. It was as if I, myself, had made a discovery. And you know I had to check out the rockets, those magnificent missiles. They had one rocket so massive they couldn't even assemble the whole thing for display and that, naturally, made it seem all the more awesome. Only thing that spoiled the attraction was that it kept me wondering about what the Soviet Union had. But the Russians, of course, weren't represented.

So we roamed the fair at will, the nappy-headed boys of curiosity. First we'd see the exhibits that were free and then we'd sneak or beg or pay our way into the others. We put in a good share of our time on the rides, mostly the monorail and the Pepsi Cola Tour of the Globe. We came to know the fair so well that by the time our parents got around to taking us we were qualified to give them a guided tour. Most of us didn't actively assume the guide role though; we let our parents think they were introducing us to the fun.

One morning Wallace Jones and I had romped about the fairgrounds so much that our feet were sore. We were hungry also since our money had been on the low side that day, and that made us especially anxious to head for home. Gingerly we stepped out onto Roosevelt Avenue beneath the El train roaring by overhead. They had all new cars on the line for the fair. I watched sparks jump from the rails. Wallace pointed across the road to deserted Shea Stadium.

"Look Keith, the Mets act like they never wanna come back home. What the hell is wrong with them?"

"Ain't nothin wrong. That's just the way the schedule runnin. They'll be back next week. Milwaukee Braves comin in too."

"Good. I been waitin to check out Hank Aaron. I wish they was over there now so we could sneak on in."

"I don't know Wallace. I'm so tired all I wanna do is git home. But after I rest up I'm goin hustlin. You still goin, right?"

I couldn't get an answer just then. Wallace had spotted two White boys pedaling our way, heading toward Flushing. You could often catch White boys cycling down Roosevelt that way, skirting along the back edge of dark town. As they drew close we could see that they were about our own age. Maybe one was a year or two younger. Both sported a carrot top, a freckled face, and a set of big ears. Unmistakably brothers.

"Let's scare em up," Wallace suggested.

"I'm down," I promptly responded.

Wallace rushed out into the street to become a human roadblock, and before I joined him I sucked in a good long breath to summon vitality back into my frame. I was stretching past five feet by then, like Wallace, with almost ninety pounds to push somebody around with.

The older boy reacted first. He tried to steer his sleek ten speed wide of Wallace, but he wasn't lucky enough to catch any traffic coming to run interference for him and Wallace ran him down easily. Pinned him in against the opposite curb. The younger brother panicked and almost fell from his gold-colored ten speed. When I grabbed hold of his handlebars I actually steadied his bike and prevented him from toppling over.

"Hey what's wrong with you?" he squealed.

"Ain't nothin wrong with me, stupid. What's wrong with you? That's what you should be tryin to figure out. You're the one with the problem."

"I don't have any problem."

"Don't think so hunh? Well maybe you can figure it out next time you look in the mirror. It ain't Howdy Doody Time out here you know, you little freckle-faced punk."

He looked fretfully over to the other side of the road and my eyes followed him, just in time to see Wallace haul off and punch this other poor guy right upside the head. The carrot top was no timid fellow though; he took a clumsy swipe at my friend but missed as Wallace danced back out of range. The boy was more than willing to tangle, however, and he climbed off of his bike to mix it up. They exchanged a few quick and solid blows, but then Wallace got shrewd and delivered a powerful kick to the groin. It was a favorite maneuver from a type of kickboxing we referred to as Stato, and Wallace had definitely statoed his opponent good. The boy slumped to the ground and Wallace ran around him to grab his bike.

My own carrot top became hysterical and left me holding his bicycle as he hopped off and dashed wildly toward his fallen brother. And just then a beat-in green Chevy screeched and slanted in toward Wallace. A stout man with long black hair and a taped-up stick scrambled from the car to give chase. He was waving his weapon and yelling menacingly, "Hey you fucking black nigger. Get your ass back here. I'll break your fucking nigger neck if I catch you, you black nigger you."

The man was surprisingly fast, but not nearly fast enough to catch the speeding Wallace Jones, who was pedaling furiously. The man hurled his club viciously, aimed it straight at the back of Wallace's head. As it fell wide of the mark he cried out in anguish. "I'd like to break your freaking ass for you, you lousy black dog."

As I watched this man perform it became immediately obvious to me what I had to do, so I mounted that shiny gold-colored ten speed and took off in the opposite direction just as swiftly as I could. My first major theft. And I didn't even have to give it much thought.

My fear was barely under control as I started a careful but speedy zigzag pattern, turning at every corner, ever watchful for the wrathful Samaritan propelling the green Chevrolet. I told myself I was angry at Wallace for forcing my hand, but I was unconvincing, and with each ensuing pedal the realization grew within me that I would gladly have volunteered had I known this adventure would feel so great. It was a sensation that outweighed any sense of guilt and, predictably, I was quick to rationalize.

Sure I had a bicycle at home, a decent secondhand three speed. But it was broken now, a problem with the back sprocket, and a new back wheel would cost more than the whole bike did. Forget it. I deserved a nice shiny ten speed and figured the White boy could get a replacement far faster than I would have been given an original. So this was like a Robin Hood thing. Besides, didn't I have to take this bicycle or get killed by a maniac?

The bicycle caper made us heroes on the block. Big Rob (who used to be Robbie Bo) was immensely pleased. He was fourteen now, involved with street gangs, and suddenly too old to hang around with us. But he still served as a role model and commended us for having heart. Other guys more our age were quite willing to have heart also, and a bike stealing boom was set off.

We doubled up on the bikes we already had and went scouting out in White neighborhoods. When we spotted a prospect we dropped off one of the piggyback riders. He knew that if he backed out he would be stranded, so he always snipped the chain, raided the yard, threw the punch, or did whatever else was necessary. In brief order we each had a handsome ten speed. Then we argued about who had the handsomest and began stealing all over again. Sometimes we simply traded in a good bike for a better one, you know, left the victim something to get by OK.

The backyard of Wallace and P.J. became our workshop. Their father didn't pay us much attention, and we were constantly filing off serial numbers, painting frames, and switching parts. Whenever we surfaced on one of our creations we'd tell our parents we had borrowed a bike from a friend. It was a rather thin line but they didn't question it much. And the bikes kept rolling in. We found allies on surrounding blocks and things eventually reached the point where stolen bike reports were flooding the 109th, the 110th, and the 114th precincts. The *Long Island Press* even ran a story about a suspected organized bike ring in the area. We all had to laugh about that one. We had been organized largely by impetuosity, and our only real profit was our own excitement.

Every now and then, however, we had to let the bicycles rest. Wallace was almost caught by the police before he could make it back to the workshop. The squad car, with the little White boy in the back seat, circled the block about six times before we were left alone. But we knew they were too suspicious. Time to cool out for a spell. Little matter, there were other activities that had to be squeezed into our days, and we didn't have to be pedaling to do them.

We had to keep trying our hand at sports, although maybe not with the best of sportsmanship. I mean we had a baseball team that would have scared the Bad News Bears off the field. And we had to jog the few blocks on down to Flushing Bay. Didn't care if the tide was out; the resulting stench never bothered us all that much. The usual challenges down there were to see who could be the ones to catch the first polluted eel, stone a rat to death, or skip a pebble across the water better than anyone else.

Sometimes we would just sit on the benches and watch the airplanes take off and land at LaGuardia, which was at the western end of the bay. For some reason, one of us invariably wanted to fly to Mexico. A more reachable fantasy was found down toward the eastern end of the bay, at the marina, where we could actually sneak on the boats that were anchored there. We couldn't figure out a way to sail anywhere, but despite that small inconvenience the marina was one of the greatest locations for dreaming.

We each usually picked our own private boat to relax in. The tan and olive *Betsy's Delight* was my personal favorite, and I figured I wouldn't mind meeting Betsy herself one day. Our tastes were so similar. But alas, I covered my tracks so well I was positive that Betsy didn't even know I existed. In fact, we all had the utmost respect for our boats; I mean they had such a soothing effect on us. We would bring hooks and sinkers and strings, and fish lazily for eels that we usually tossed back into the water. Or maybe find a mellow station on our portable radios and watch the sun droop to the tune of "Girl from Ipanema." Or maybe just lie back and close our eyes and listen to the waves ripple and dash up against the sides of our floating paradises.

One evening we went to the marina to find that an unconquerable barbed wire fence had been erected to keep us out. We later learned that this action had been taken because a group of vandals had used our boats for graffiti practice. So that canceled out our evenings of tranquility at the bay, but at least we still had lover's lane. We generally saw a pretty decent show of foreplay before being chased, so we didn't much mind being run off from the cars, but we would have paid anything to see what was going on inside those Volkswagen vans that were popular that summer. And it was near where they had been parked that we often found used prophylactics, which one of us would manage to nudge onto the edge of a stick and chase everyone with. I ran some of my fastest sprints to avoid getting tagged by a used rubber.

We were acquiring all types of sexual knowledge, and naturally we had to share as much of it as possible with the girls, or was it the other way around? Whatever. The boys with skinned knees had become afflicted with that biggest of curiosities, and the girls, with their hair flying every-which-a-way, had bodies that promised to charm up more trouble than they were prepared to handle. We spent hours playing Spin the Bottle or indulging in a stimulating little game known as Truth? Dare? Consequences? Promise? or Repeat? We should have just called the game "Dare" because that's the only option anyone ever selected, and that's how most of us obtained our first passionate caresses and long soulful tongue kisses, in other words, that's how we first "macked out." White folks "made out," so I guess we had no choice but to call what we did something different. And there was an all-the-way dare, but I never saw it accepted in public. A lot of behind-the-scenes daring was also going on, however, and when discussing this activity it was difficult, as you would imagine, to distinguish fact from fantasy.

And there were still other things to squeeze in. The price of many of our favorite sodas jumped from thirteen cents to fifteen cents down at Mr. Jordan's that summer and we couldn't appreciate it at all, so we formed a syndicate to protest, or rather, to threaten. We cut print from the newspaper (so detectives couldn't trace our handwriting, a Dick Tracy idea) and we composed a message to slip under Mr. Jordan's door warning him to roll back prices or else. Of course Mr. Jordan chose to settle for the "else" and we proceeded to sneak out far more things in our clothes than we ever paid for. We probably wanted to do it anyway. But since he was a feeble old Black man I guess we needed that sense of justification. I know it helped me a lot. And about the only time we gave Mr. Jordan a break was when one of the delivery trucks came around. Then we concentrated on raiding the truck.

Now we were so close to home that those truck raids were something we shouldn't have been able to carry out regularly without someone informing our parents. But as I look back I realize our success was due largely to the disintegration of an important community concept. The old practice of "he's a child of the neighborhood so I'll straighten him out first and then take him home to get straightened out some more" had virtually faded out. The code of "we had better mind our business" was prevalent. And we took full advantage.

Even more things to squeeze in. Watching Yogi take a fling as manager. Watching the Phillies blow the best chance they ever had. Winning a marbles championship, becoming superior at jacks, trying to make a spinning top spin for an eternity. Building a go-cart for the races, taking a shot at raising pigeons. A skateboard, a pair of skates, a yo-yo, a unicycle, a bo-lo paddle, boxing gloves, a limbo stick, a jump rope (just to be near the girls). And always moving to the music, always being the music. We had to dance all over the street, just as the record said, and there were so many steps to learn.

7

The Self, Advancing Literacy, and Sidewalk University

Purkey (1970) describes the self as a "complex and dynamic system of beliefs which an individual holds true about himself, each with a corresponding value" (p. 7). With this concept in mind, I will reflect in this chapter on the self that emerged in "Big Fame." Of primary concern is the manner in which my linguistic abilities grew relative to this network of constructs. Naturally, since I view discussions of the self and linguistic growth as woefully incomplete without some attention to aspects of the social transactions affecting both, such perspective, as was the case in earlier chapters, will be provided. Furthermore, I will examine selected experiences of other children.

A belief I held very dearly throughout the elementary school years, one that reverberates throughout the narrative, is that I was destined to become someone important in mainstream society. As a consequence I also placed a high value on possessing a well-developed set of language skills. Such skills were a synonym for the academic progress in school that I believed would secure my inevitable recognition. My advancing language skills, in turn, because they were a measure of how well I could do in my "training ground," served to further solidify my belief in my eventual prominence. My proficiency in language use, therefore, was inextricably bound up with my emerging self. Or as Britton (1982) puts it, "we master language by using it to make the most of our lives" (p. 205).

An Advanced Literacy Set

At the close of my elementary school career I was rated excellent in reading, written communication, spelling, handwriting, and oral communication (see Table 3 in Appendix). I had earned admittance to a special progress class. In the Outstanding Abilities section of the Guidance Data column, I was described as "an eloquent speaker and very much interested in social studies." I was also judged to be a fine athlete. Moreover, my performance in school had previously solicited the remark from my fifth-grade teacher that "poetry-creative writing" was my outstanding interest. Also, not coincidentally, in grades five and six I was recognized by my teachers, for the first time since I left Harlem, as a good leader. All these evaluations are consonant with information given in "Big Fame." However, what may not be so apparent is how directly related these comments are to the specific manner in which I constructed my advanced literacy set (to expand on Holdaway's term). I will endeavor to make the connection clearer.

During the latter half of elementary school my writing ability came to the fore; at least that is how my memory informs me. As mentioned in earlier portions of the narrative, I have some vague notion of earlier writing activities such as handwriting drills, spelling tests, compositions, and book reports. But aside from that, there are no memories from the period prior to fourth grade comparable to the sharp recall expressed earlier about my initial reading experiences. In fact, when I began the essay portions of this book, I was somewhat alarmed that no such recollections were evidenced in the narrative. Unable to imagine that the one ability around which the whole project most revolved should receive such little mention, I viewed the lack of anecdotes about writing development as a flaw. However, I came to realize there would be no reason for my earliest attempts at writing to stand out since they were not accompanied by any difficulty or trauma (such as the bloodshed that underscored my initial tries at reading). Only a writing event of great magnitude, which I viewed my venture into poetry writing to be, would leave the indelible impression later capturable in autobiography.

Another way of framing this is to say that writing only appeared significant to me when I could use it as a means of expressing myself. My experience was similar to what Bissex observed. "The development of writing . . . was part of the development of the person rather than the product of an instructional skills sequence" (p. 108). In my case, writing development was so little a part of a skills sequence that I even curtailed my participation in such instruction. As revealed in the text, the most severe reprimand I received from my teacher in the fourth grade was for not keeping my language arts workbook up to date. It didn't seem to matter to her that my writing ability was up to date. The teacher, in fact, was caught up in contradiction, for in encouraging my creativity by exposing me to more and more poetry, she effectively helped to stifle my patience with workbooks, especially since doing fill-ins neither aided my expressive ability nor taught me anything new about grammar. The last reality was made ostensible by the fact I could run through an entire workbook in one day. So despite her chastisement and that of subsequent teachers for not doing language arts homework, the bottom line for me was that I was becoming the poet-essayist I wished to become. This would always get me judged on the personality scale as "evading responsibility"—though I was being totally responsible to my emerging self.

I don't recall much poetry other than "Space Poem." There was a poem about Clupzitzobop that several classmates enjoyed. And besides the essay on White Backlash, which received so much attention, I vaguely remember doing a piece about automation. I wasn't a prolific writer, nor am I now. I treat writing much as I treat old friends. I don't visit as much as I should, but I'll not hesitate to burden it with my greatest problems. In a time of crisis, which essentially means I need to reweave or perhaps just repair or maybe attach a sleeve to the basic fabric of the self, such as how to value impending fatherhood, I can get very busy with a pen.

It is useful to conceive of my writing ability as having been funded by my reading and oral skills. The narrative informs us that my teacher helped to promote my early poetry experiments by urging me to read Nash and Hughes. (Kozol would have been proud of her.) What is not mentioned in the text, but is implied, is that we had been exposed to poetry in class prior to our own attempts to write some. Certainly by then I had read the full offering of books by Dr. Seuss. And as I look back again at "Space Poem" it is clear to me that my rhythmic and rhyming patterns owed much to that exposure. So here is a rather simple case of reading funding writing.

Of course poetry wasn't all I read. There were the science fiction books, the comic books, the child-detective and adventure books, the encyclopedia my mother insisted we have despite its cost. We got her money's worth.

My interest in sports made reading about sports necessary. I collected a large number of sports magazines and established my usually still enforced sports-pages-first policy of reading the daily newspapers.

But I did get around to the front sections. As my teacher noted, I was keenly interested in social studies. I had to keep up with the space race and the KKK.

With the reading program I had underway, which was critical in developing that skill itself, my writing was bound to flourish also. This dynamic is described further by Mayher, Lester, and Pradl (1983):

> In all, the written material provides ideas, sources, points of view, and sometimes models for students to use in their own writing. Another, less explicit, benefit is that the more reading our students do, the more possible it is for them to develop an "ear" for the written language.
>
> That's a strange analogy, in one sense, since we're talking about reading, not listening. How *does* reading develop your "ear" for language? We're often confronted with questions about how students learn to write complete sentences; how they learn about organization and coherence; how they learn all these things if they're not directly taught. Much of this is learned through talk, but some of the unique characteristics of the written language can only be learned through reading and writing. By providing students with a wide range of reading material—from poems to editorials to technical reports—we're giving them examples of writing that employ the features we wish them to use. The more they read this material, the better they'll become attuned to acceptable standard written English. (p. 109)

My oral skills were an equally important source of funding for my developing writing. It was largely through conversation that I was able to gauge how the self I expressed in writing was being received by others, thus enabling me to adjust my self-concept in ways I deemed appropriate, in essence, to create the self I would express in subsequent writing.

I was bombarded with so many contradictory stimuli that I had to be a garrulous child in order to organize it all. I was delving into the lives of my classmates, gaining a more highly developed sense of how individuals belonging to other segments of society lived. I was also more deeply concerned with racial discrimination in America and with modifying my stance toward the larger society while keeping a range of community sentiments in mind. I had a lot of mental synthesizing to do, and I decided to do much of it during those large, six-hour chunks of time spent in school. I would sneakily chatter as much as I could but, unlike some of my classmates, I was never afraid to ramble on for the general public. I spoke when called on, actually campaigned to be called on, volunteered to give speeches—and still was a disruptive chatterer.

Perpetual talking was the reason I would never receive an "excellent" in Social Living, though I was apparently socializing very well. After all, I wasn't talking to myself. But I always received a "fair." Even the G given to me at the end of sixth grade (see Table 3 in Appendix) was superimposed over an F, which shows there was maybe some hesitancy over the matter. Again, as with the admonition for lagging behind in the workbook, my teachers didn't realize how the deviance made the normative behavior possible. For I never talked when writing was assigned, though my talk was indeed an important prelude to those occasions. While it cannot be denied that I experienced certain value conflicts that militated against my ever being very "disciplined" in school, and this is especially true in the later years, I suspect, nevertheless, that I would have been less of a "behavior problem" and maybe even a better writer if my teachers had exhibited an understanding similar to that found in the work of Martin et al. (1976):

> We think a school could be, and should be, an environment in which all kinds of talk do—in fact—happen; where children can talk to adults in both formal and informal situations, where purposive, or directed talk goes on—as it always has—and where undirected and unconstrained conversations are also seen as part of the educative process. (p. 17)

There was a strong collective desire to talk informally in those classrooms. As stated earlier, I could always find various partners for conversation. This was true even though none of them as individuals would dare chatter for any lengthy stretch. I had more nerve than the rest of the class, but I can hardly prove I had more need. Who knows what frustration lingered at the base of their relative conformity?

What *I* am most positive of is that because of the ability I possessed in reading, writing, and speaking, much of which developed despite the constricting nature of some aspects of schooling, I departed from elementary school as a confident user of a language accepted in the mainstream. By remaining my own best guardian of the self, I had realized a great deal of the communicative potential I had first brought to school.

The Bent-but-Not-Broken Home

At this point I will address more directly the concept of the "broken home." Along with the eradicationist spiel, this concept has long been used by educators to generate pat explanations for many problems exhibited by African-American students in school. Because the closing section of "Big Fame" shows that I was primed to "act out," it is imperative that the relationship between my home life and school progress receive a bit more discussion.

School records indicate that my outstanding disability was "father not living with family" (see Table 1 in Appendix). It was not enough "disability," however, to keep either me or my sister from going to special progress classes in junior high school. That would have been an observation worth recording, for such remarks would at least have highlighted how much emphasis was put on education in our home. But it's always been especially difficult for teachers to break molds. The most thoughtful (and mold-breaking) comments made by any of mine relative to the issue were the question mark offered by my fifth-grade teacher and the blank spot left by my sixth-grade teacher when asked to evaluate my relationship to my parents (see Table 2 in Appendix). They wouldn't even pretend to understand it.

Nor am I the ultimate authority. But I will state unequivocally that the consistent belief in my ability shown by both of my parents was a major reason I was always, for one thing, in better shape than the school system itself.

Sure there were family difficulties, but the contention that they were directly translated into school problems is ludicrous. To label my "broken home" a learning disability represents, among other things, a failure to view me as an active participant in my own reality and a refusal to see that I had to wrestle with the clash between public school values and the values of the street school, often referred to in the streets as Sidewalk University. The narrative clearly illustrates the conflict, which was the crucial tension I had to deal with, a tension largely produced by knowledge of some of the contradictions inherent in the mainstream world of which I longed to be a part. It wasn't my father who persecuted James Meredith.

The most dramatic impact my father could have had on altering the course of my life after elementary school would have been to keep me out of Sidewalk University. Whether he could have done that is, I think, unlikely; it is definitely unknowable. We do know that I enrolled.

Sidewalk U

The one belief I held above all others, including the one of "destiny," was that I should fit in with my community peers, which meant adopting their value system and, in fact, helping to develop it. Even the hope for success expressed at the close of the schoolyard scene was done in the context of running with the "crew." The contradiction was powerful. Up to that point, due to adroit impression management, I had been able to give convincing performances before both school and street audiences. But it was inevitable that my act before one group would suffer, lending strength to my presentation before the other. In refusing to jeopardize my peer ties in the community, I made a decision well understood by Eugene Perkins (1975):

> If he chooses to withdraw, and few do, then he will find himself being the scapegoat of his community. The exclusion from the dominant culture patterns of the community could also cause him great anxieties and possibly serious psychological problems. The norm for social deviancy is often different in the black ghetcolony, and sometimes the child who tries to emulate so-called conventional behavior is seen as being more deviant than one who openly violates certain conventional standards. (p. 29)

I became very active, and in many ways a leader, in a cultural system in which taking from Whites was congratulated and a militant political orientation was favored over the moderate stance the school system, and the home for that matter, would have me assume. In our group, moderation concerning issues of race relations was defined as backwardness. We felt that Black political activists should receive all they demanded right then and there.

Perkins, whose work has been much too underpublicized, offers a taxonomy of character types usually found among the youth of the Black community. Although there is no precise one-to-one correspondence between the traits I possessed and any of the types he presents, my increased involvement in the Street Institution, as he calls it, can accurately be understood, nonetheless, as my movement from being a "Regular" to becoming a "Cool Cat."

> The Regular is an accepted member in the Street Institution although he is not bound to all of its norms. He is the youngster who gets along with almost everyone without compromising his own value system. His ability to interact with his peers, and not be totally influenced by them, is a tribute to his uniqueness.
>
> He is "one of the boys" and again he is not. The Regular is able to vacillate roles because he has never made a full commitment to the Street Institution. Actually his primary values are closer to white middle class values than those of his peers. He is usually a good student, conforms to most conventional laws, has close family ties and rarely belongs to a gang. Yet, despite this allegiance to white middle class norms, he knows enough about the Street Institution to function within it without undue stress. Because his coping posture is more flexible than his peers, he is able to "free enterprise" and engage in only those activities which he feels are relatively safe. (pp. 41–42)

As a Regular I could both entertain and withstand my blood brother, adjust to new surroundings, and keep Shorty's information from directly fueling drastic behavior. As a Cool Cat, however, I was expected to provide certain guidance for my community peers. Clarity of position was required concerning fundamental matters such as the plight of Blacks. And although I didn't have to be flamboyant, which could even be a negative trait, my identification with the group had to be firm. If it hadn't been, I could not have become a Cool Cat in the first place. Perkins describes my role well:

> The Cool Cat is probably the most imitated of the lot. Being cool is very important in the ghetcolony. When things go down in the ghetcolony, such as intense police harassment, it is advantageous to be cool. When situations become "uptight," being cool is a trademark of street sophistication. Black children learn how to be cool under the most extenuating circumstances. Being cool implies that one is "hip," "together," and is able to function under considerable pressure. It becomes a stabilizer

> that allows one to minimize threatening situations and ignore others which he cannot effectively deal with. It also accompanies a lifestyle that is personified by a neat appearance, skill in verbal manipulation and an uncanny ability to stay out of serious trouble.
>
> The Cool Cat often appears indifferent to the problems around him, as though he is insensitive to pain, frustration or death. He rarely allows his real inner feelings to surface, because they may reveal that he is more sensitive to other people. The lifting of his protective shield would make him appear timid, and therefore dilute his image. The Street Institution has trained him to act in this manner, to be cool, stern, impersonal in the face of all kinds of adversities. (p. 40)

Of course the transition from Regular to Cool Cat was neither as sudden nor absolute as described above. The description was intended as a thumbnail sketch roughly explaining the major shift in orientation recounted at the close of "Big Fame." It was not offered as an oil masterpiece depicting the full range of shades and hues accompanying the overall transformation. The interplay of school culture and street mores would continue to be a drama of rather intense ambivalence for me, as will be reported later. More important at this juncture is to develop a further sense of how this type of tension may guide the actions of other student-citizens and, consequently, those of people who propose to teach them in school.

Marva's Way

In 1975, after resigning from the Chicago school system, Marva Collins founded a school that since has been the object of much national attention. The school, Westside Prep, was featured on *60 Minutes* and was the subject of a television docudrama. Fortunately, a book has followed (Collins and Tamarkin 1982), which both focuses on Collins's pedagogy and serves as a valuable field study of a Black educational community. Many of the plaudits Collins has received are no doubt well deserved. Nonetheless, I do have reservations about what goes on in that unique educational environment.

One cannot seriously question the academic achievement per se that has taken place at Westside. When the students were tested in 1979 by an outside administrator, they scored higher and had progressed more than any other group tested. And tests alone, of course, could not tell the whole story. Gains in general awareness, confidence, and pride were also in evidence. By reading the myths, the fables, the Washington Irving, the Dostoyevsky, the especially beloved Shakespeare—in short, all the *literature* Collins had insisted they all read—the children had experienced remarkable academic and intellectual growth, had become able and, most importantly, *willing* to express opinions in formal settings. But the testing program could give no clue as to how much of themselves (or their *selves*) they chose not to reveal or how those decisions affected them. Such was not the purpose of the testing. However, one might expect Collins herself, as a self-proclaimed progressive educator, to be extremely concerned about a possible clash of value systems. But such does not appear to be the case.

While it is demanded of these children that they become avid readers of the classics, they are not, strangely enough, encouraged to read Black classics. Collins fails to include any on the official reading lists. Dickens is all right. And Tennyson is "in" along with Spenser, Aristophanes, and Thoreau. But there is no mention of Zora Neale Hurston, Ralph Ellison, Toni Morrison, Gwendolyn Brooks, or Richard Wright. Collins specifically ridicules Wright's *Black Boy* (1945 [1966]), recognized widely as a masterpiece. She claims it is too violent (though it's not as explicitly so as the *Macbeth* she cherishes) and that her students already have been exposed to enough of that type of writing. In discussing a passage from *Black Boy* along with other curriculum materials, Collins asserts that "all that 'relevance' undermines the very purpose of an education" (p. 156).

It remains beyond my comprehension how anyone's education can be undermined by exposure to Wright's autobiography, which shows a character so thirsty for book knowledge he seeks to devise a way to sneak volumes from the library. Wright phrases his predicament clearly:

> There was a huge library near the riverfront, but I knew that Negroes were not allowed to patronize its shelves any more than they were the parks and playgrounds of the city. I had gone into this library several times to get books for the white men on the job. Which of them would now help me to get books? And how could I read them without causing concern to the white men with whom I worked? I had so far been

> successful in hiding my thoughts and feelings from them, but I knew that I would create hostility if I went about this business of reading in a clumsy way. (pp. 267–68)

One might expect that the conservatism voiced by the strong disapproval of some of the very best in Black literature would also be expressed by a policy of eradicationism with respect to Black English. Collins is indeed consistent in this regard. As she addresses the class one day: "Children, listen to me for a moment. To succeed in this world, you must speak correctly. I don't want to hear any jive talk in here or any of this stuff about black English. You must not think of yourselves as black children or ghetto children. You must become citizens of the world, like Socrates" (p. 30). Obviously she didn't point out that there isn't any such language called worldcitizenese. Collins later offers a further explanation of her beliefs about language instruction: "The experts claim that correcting an inner-city child's grammar will damage his or her identity. I believe that not correcting grammar will damage that child's whole life. While others lowered their standards for inner-city students, I made mine higher" (p. 185).

There are at least four conceptual weaknesses evident in this passage. First, to make light of how bound up language is with identity represents a definite shortsightedness. That much should be clear by now. Second, one should know that despite attempts to "correct" children's grammar, children themselves for the most part *choose* which language varieties they will speak. Third, choosing to speak Standard English has been no guarantee that one would not be "damaged." The emptiness of the eradicationists' argument is revealed by the reality that (a) generations of Black English speakers have been subjected to "correction" programs that haven't worked and (b) their contemporaries who have mastered Standard English still have faced inordinate struggle in trying to "succeed." And fourth, it is misleading to explain the achievement at Westside as the result of standards set as opposed to standards negotiated. Such explanation begs the question of active student compromise.

Perhaps the sternest test of Collins's approach came when she ran a city-sponsored summer program for elementary school students (relatively unpromising ones) from Chicago's notorious Cabrini-Green housing projects. Of the 140 children who began the program, 87 finished, and in the process they demonstrated significant gains in language skills. On the other hand, 53 students (38 percent) dropped out of the program. These are the mixed results some observers would anticipate from a public program in which Horatio Alger and universalist mythologies are heavily pushed. Many students will buy into them, but a large number, recoiling from value conflicts, will not. Note how close the 38 percent drop-out rate is to the 40 percent failure rate Colin Greer (1976) claims is a built-in feature of most public educational programs.

This is not to say that Marva Collins is no better than the average public school teacher. After all, she specifically requested Cabrini-Green's "worst" and did, in my estimation, a more than creditable job. She's no miracle worker, a tag the media have often given her, but she is a fine teacher. She would be an even better one and would reach even more students if she toned down the proselytizing a bit and allowed more of the children's street experiences, particularly their language, to have legitimate functions in the classroom. Such experiences could be a starting point for crucial and truly enriching discussions, as opposed to superficial teacher-dominated ones, of relationships among language, knowledge, culture, identity, politics—in brief, many of the connections Black children often ponder. If her students can read Shakespeare and toss about polysyllabic words for effect, then they can participate in such a forum.

With all the skill, dedication, and commitment to Black people that Collins possesses, it seems a sad irony that she doesn't realize that it is the sum of her loving and her Blackness that allows her to spout convincing universalist rhetoric to those children she does reach. They trust her. However, her pedagogy is not one to put in the hands of those who won't work as hard, won't love as much, or can't be as Black. I feel safer recommending that teachers wishing to turn young Blacks into mimics and scholars of Shakespeare should be prepared to engage in a more far-ranging than usual discussion of Ferdinand's assertion: "I am the best of them that speak this speech / Were I but where 'tis spoken" (*The Tempest*, act 1, sc. 2).

Thirty-Seven Learners

The memoirs of Herbert Kohl (1968) also provide an important outlook concerning the education of inner-city Blacks. Kohl describes his work with a sixth-grade class in Harlem during the 1962–63 academic year, the same year I would have been a fifth grader in Harlem if my family hadn't moved. I missed exposure to the stern suppression and harmful neglect that Kohl understood to be characteristic of the system there. His thirty-six pupils understood it too:

> I took the children to the Teachers College cafeteria where we sat and had lunch. Not that people didn't stare and sit uncomfortably next to us. Marie sat down next to me and asked: "Who they think they are anyway, rolling their eyes at us?" I explained to her that the people she saw were training to become teachers. She smiled and nodded. That explained the hostility and coldness. (p. 121)

But although the Harlem school system generally was in no better shape than the one Kozol encountered in Boston, it wasn't nearly as restrictive with respect to the actions of individual teachers. One could be as creative as one dared to be. Given such autonomy, Kohl and his students conducted a workshop in humanistic education.

Kohl stresses throughout his book the importance of the teacher as receptor and, most important, how he took his own advice. He entertained matters of concern to the students, matters like their ghetto habitat and their peculiar problems. He listened, without prescribing a particular manner of speaking, to the stories of their lives. Even though there is little one teacher can do substantially to change many lives, there is, as I hope to have made clear so far, great value in encouraging the discussion of community experiences within academic environs. As Kohl explains in his own words: "I could do nothing about the facts, therefore my words were useless. But through listening, the facts remained open and therefore placed school in the context of the children's real world" (p. 45).

Once the children gained full confidence that the classroom was a place where much of what perplexed them could at least be aired, if not ironed out, they became tremendously enthusiastic about school. They read voraciously as Kohl made available plenty of literature, myths, and other items of personal interest. And as in my own case, all this reading enhanced their productive language capacities. Particularly impressive was their writing: deep, provocative, sometimes humorous. Many of them wrote prolifically, often producing texts in excess of three thousand words. Set in the context of what some of them were accomplishing, my own poetry and essay experiments were nothing at all unusual—or remarkable.

During the course of the term the students as a whole demonstrated significant gains on standardized IQ tests and seemingly miraculous gains on standardized reading tests, though they viewed the exams as necessary evils. Both the thirty-six students and Kohl knew that the crucial work had taken place within the classroom environment, which all thirty-seven of them had worked vigorously to endow with meaning. Kohl summarizes the experience:

> The children learned that they could do unpleasant but necessary work; they also knew that the test preparation was not all there was to education, that the substance of their work, the novels and stories, the poems and projects they created, were the essential thing no matter how the external world chose to judge them. They were proud of their work and themselves. I felt thrilled and privileged to teach them and witness them create. I offered what I could to them; they offered much in return. I am grateful that over the course of the year I could cease to be afraid and therefore respond to what the children had to teach me of myself, of themselves and the world they lived in and we shared as human beings. (p. 178)

Unfortunately, one year's experience could not ensure further progress for these students in formal education. For as they went forward into junior high school they once again entered classrooms in which their lives were not regarded seriously, where their language once again was subjected to attempts at eradication. Some of the students who ventured into predominantly White schools outside of Harlem soon expressed a desire to leave those institutions. They had not enjoyed the intense competition.

In certain ways the most interesting graduate of Kohl's class was Grace, who had been the most academically advanced by far. Grace, one who could relish the competition, was the only one of the thirty-six children to make a special progress class. She subsequently did so well that upon graduation from junior high school, she was in a position to turn down her acceptance at the prestigious Bronx High School of Science, opting instead, as beneficiary of a hefty scholarship, for an exclusive prep school in New England. Her letters to Kohl, which spanned a period of several years, were little more than straightforward progress reports of her success. Kohl was thus prompted to remark:

> Now Grace is in her second year in a New England Prep School. She fits wholly neither there nor at home in Harlem. She is one of the "school Negroes," a gifted one but still an anomaly. The other students are as open as possible, and she has made several sincere friends. Yet to live simultaneously in two worlds, a rich white one and a poor black one, is to be fully part of neither. Grace has become alienated from Harlem, her home, her friends, her very self, in attempting to be a part of the prep school world. But she can't fully participate there; she's too poor, too lonely, too much of a special case. It is hard to know what will come of her alienation, whether it will pull her apart or whether she will transcend it and show us adults a way to synthesize the contradictions we make and allow in our society. (p. 223)

Grace's dilemma was very similar to the one I encountered and to that faced by Richard Rodriguez (1983). I wonder if eventually she became rebellious (more like myself) or continued to chase the Dream (more like Rodriguez). Phrased another way, in sociolinguistic terms, it is a question of whether she has used her pain to criticize eradicationist policy or to affirm it.

While there are many other closely related studies that can be cited along with those above, I think the educational experiments I have chosen to report here fairly well represent the range of classroom situations in which Black students find themselves; that is, despite adjustments for the ethnicity and gender of the instructor, virtually all classrooms can be imagined as functioning somewhere between the open approach used by Kohl and the rigid method employed by Collins. Approaches strongly resembling Kohl's certainly seem superior.

Reconsidering Labov's Lames

Before closing this chapter I will quickly shift focus from classroom practices to field research in order to examine briefly some aspects of the research Labov (1972) reported under the title of "The Linguistic Consequences of Being a Lame." Such examination will underscore the major themes I have so far brought to the surface—namely, the self as a dynamic system, the linguistics of selfhood, and the interrelationships among school and street cultures. In addition, analyzing Labov's work serves as a good lead-in to the final segment of the narrative, which will even further highlight these issues.

Labov generally has conducted outstanding research with respect to Black English, having provided arguably the finest linguistic descriptions of the dialect, given cogent explanations of the vernacular relative to reading and oral skills, and exhibited an understanding of the cultural and political tensions that help divert the interest of Black English speakers from the schools to the streets. However, his explication of the transactions occurring in the street environment itself leaves much to be desired, mostly because he makes too direct a connection between "hipness" and the level and frequency of Black English contained in one's speech. Having worked among a few select gangs in Harlem, who as a whole often spoke the lowest-prestige form of Black English, Labov concludes that these youngsters were more streetwise or "down" than a group of kids he identified as squares or, in the vernacular, lames. But since he made no detailed observations of these so-called lames, one is left to wonder why he draws this conclusion with so much conviction.

Labov, being a lame himself, was susceptible to being fooled by any Regular or Cool Cat who wished to entertain him, especially when his method of study was suspect to begin with. He has usually insisted that language is studied most validly if one has access to normal social discourse. Witness his own comments:

> We focus upon natural groups as the best possible solution to the *observer's paradox*: the problem of observing how people speak when they are not being observed. The natural interaction of peers can overshadow the effects of observation and helps us approach the goal of capturing the vernacular of everyday life in which the minimum amount of attention is paid to speech: this is the most systematic level of linguistic behavior and of greatest interest to the linguist who wants to explain the structure and evolution of language.
>
> But there is a second even more compelling reason for us to select natural groups of speakers rather than isolated individuals. The vernacular is the property of the group, not the individual. (p. 256)

Labov indeed followed his own prescription when he studied the gangs, but he studied the so-called lames by use of the formal interviewing technique he otherwise eschews. So while he speaks of the linguistic consequences of being a lame, and such consequences certainly are that many lames speak fairly standard English, we don't know if *his* analysis is based on the output of any real lames at all. He hasn't observed these youngsters well enough to make such a claim legitimately. He can only resort to making the case by definition, and as the description below shows, he has enough trouble trying to accomplish that. "They are less open to social pressures to fight, to steal, or take drugs. Of course some lames steal, shoot up, and drop out; but as a group they have a better record" (p. 285). Uncertain about what a lame really is, Labov is reduced to offering group comparisons, which, besides being contradictory, still can't tell us how *he knows* who specifically is or is not a lame.

The chance that Labov was put on to a great extent is very real. He left himself open to the possibility by failing to be as diligent of method as he probably desired to be. There were shrewd youngsters out there who were not in traditional gangs but were, nonetheless, fashioning and reinforcing and projecting intricate selves through complex manipulations of Black English and Standard English. By overromanticizing the basilect often heard in the street clubs and viewing the language of the so-called lames as diametrically opposed to that of the gang members, Labov may have missed an opportunity to describe those intriguing processes. If he understands the game of the streets half as much as he professes to, he must know that in streetball, as in basketball or football, the ability to fake deftly to the right and then go left is a much-valued skill. It allows a person to choose to a large degree how predictable he or she is. It makes one difficult to judge.

8

Valedictory

I

Regardless of the fact that I had qualified for an S.P. class, school officials had me ticketed for Junior High School 16 in Corona, which didn't even have such a class. But my mother wasn't going for that move and she freed me before the end of the first week. Getting out was the easy part. The main problem was where to go from there. Following my sister was the most appealing choice to me. No such luck. I was shipped down to William Cowper Junior High School in Maspeth. I was among the first wave of Black students sent to that school and, through the same zoning maneuver, so was the other half of the new dynamic duo, Wallace Jones.

My mother's brother, Uncle Howard, came through for me big. He had managed to gain a pretty steady hand in the real estate business by then and was intent on seeing to it that his nephew began junior high school on a fashionable note. He bought me a pair of Italian shoes, a mandatory fashion item; a pair of black ripple-soles, which were worthy of added compliment; and a pair of brown suede crepe soles, a definite eyebrow raiser. And I received a good supply of pants, shirts, socks, underwear, and handkerchiefs. I would have liked a couple of expensive, status-symbol knit sweaters, but I was never one to overload a gift horse's back.

Moms didn't appear overly grateful for what her brother had done, but I certainly was—had a great start toward a better-than-average wardrobe. That was important for a soul brother, a name a lot of us were beginning to call ourselves. You could obtain respect simply by dressing well. In other words, you could get over better if you "vined." Get more attention from the soul sisters. Avoid some types of initiation. Evade becoming a laughingstock. Of course if you were just a plain bad MF you could get respect also. I preferred to try to earn it with style.

The classroom situation wasn't anything to worry about. When I arrived at Cowper, the two-year S.P. class was reportedly full and I was assigned to a three-year class. My mother had an urge to protest this move also, but then decided, with me in agreement, that the three-year program wouldn't be so bad after all. She probably recalled Sherry's misadventure. As for myself, I wasn't too keen on the idea of making up a grade on my sister anyway. I didn't want to become an embarrassment for her, you know, let her keep her place.

A 65 was generally the minimum passing grade in school, but in S.P. we were told that our minimum passing grade was 85. Marks below 85 on our report card would be circled with red ink as a reminder that they were below expectation. Consistent scoring below 85 was grounds for termination. I wasn't frightened in the least by such requirements. I felt I could score as highly as I wanted.

I had a soul brother and sister in the class. First Blacks that sat in a classroom with me since the first grade. Karen Owens was so cute I couldn't drum up enough nerve to speak to her much, though she was always nice enough. Danny Baylor and I clicked right away. He was from near the home neighborhood, down in East Elmhurst, and liked to talk as much as I did. He vined pretty well, even had a few knits. He was a little short on street savvy, but I had lots to give. And he could take or leave the White boys just as I could. So we were cool, would sit around and poke fun at our classmates who wore highwater pants, Beatles boots, Nehru shirts, and saturated their hair with Brylcreem; or others who followed the school regulation of wearing a tie every day and ran the same pair of cheap charlie pants for a week. It was a major offense for a brother to run a pair of pants, but it seemed standard procedure for several of our classmates. Danny and I didn't realize that some of their parents had already socked away plenty toward college tuition.

I started the term well but began to falter after only a few weeks. I couldn't keep my mind functioning right, wouldn't concentrate, didn't seem interested. Wouldn't raise my hand much, wouldn't do my work thoroughly. All the ability I had to play the school game was failing to manifest itself.

Only Math seemed to motivate me. That algebra Mrs. Friedman was teaching us posed puzzles that never failed to seduce. Other classes were very boring by comparison. Even Science, with the experiments with magnets; even Spanish, which was new and should have captivated. A danger was near. I could feel it but just couldn't define it, couldn't get the tangled web of personality and environment to unravel into anything comfortable and clear.

One thing that was clear, but uncomfortable, was that there were too many rules. Those ties every day, baggy blouses for the girls, no turtlenecks for the guys, walk to the right of the thick red line in the hall, never intersect the thick red line in the hall, use the up staircase for going up, the down staircase for going down, line up in the yard, line up in the hall, sit tight in the auditorium, stay confined during lunch period. This brand of regimentation had no redeeming value I could see, so I viewed those rules as simply something to break, a decision that introduced me to a variety of disciplinary methods. If you didn't wear a tie, for example, which I hardly ever did, you had to print the word "tie" on a piece of paper and fasten this paper tie to a button of your shirt. I saw some guys use more paper on ties than they used on homework. I was almost in that category myself.

But even such nonsense as this wasn't supposed to affect me inside the classroom itself. I could always handle a classroom even when I could handle nothing else. I could excel beyond all interference. I hoped I was experiencing a temporary case of listlessness, that's all.

On the first report card my marks hovered in the 80s, with the exception of a 92 in Math and a 95 in Gym. That I had to improve was simple enough to see. Wallace Jones, however, was perplexed. Holding a nifty collection of mostly 65s in his hand, it was hard for him to accept someone drawing a bold red circle around so admirable a mark as an 80. I didn't bother to explain that I should have been getting at least 90 in every subject. Not after he said he was glad he only failed one thing.

Moms had a perplexing moment also. The smooth brow became wrinkled as she scanned the report. She squinted at each unexpected grade. But her only words were a flat "you can do better." Certainly I could. I just didn't.

One morning in late November I was leaving the bakery across Grand Avenue after stocking up on some beloved crumb buns. I would hide these in my desk and sneak munches during my early classes. Wallace was running over from the soda shop, dodging cars along the way, with a piece of news fresh off the grapevine.

"Hey Keith, I got a dynamite jump off. Hooky party, man."

"Yeah?" I was immediately interested. I had a couple of rounds of hooky under my belt by then. But only light stuff, you know, like hopping the 7 train into Manhattan to explore Times Square. Hooky parties, from what I heard, were the big leagues.

"Yeah man," Wallace continued. "This dude Benjamin I know is givin it. Be some older people there, ninth graders and stuff. Be a good chance to git your thing wet."

That was definitely a worthwhile concern. Wallace said there were only dry guys and wet guys. The wetter the better. And he was super eager to be among the best. I knew my good friend Mr. Shortside would be very fond of Wallace Jones. I had my own bashfulness to contend with of course, but I knew I had to try to beat it as soon as possible.

"Well I'll tell you Wallace, that does sound pretty dyno to me."

"Damn right it's dyno. That means you ready then, hunh?"

"I'm ever ready, just like the battery. Where is this party? Let's go."

"We gotta go back out the way, man. Down on 35th Avenue. Benjamin got a nice crib. Got upstairs and downstairs and a finished basement. It's perfect for partyin. How a day in school sound up against that?"

"Sounds like nothin to me. What you think it gon sound like? I said I'm down."

"Yeah OK. But there's one thing you have to do first before you can git all the way down."

"Oh yeah? What's that?"

"Give up halfa dem crumb buns."

I tossed him the bag and we took off for the bus stop. Had the old blood racing again. A chill wind pinned my ears back and momentarily cloaked me in a shiver.

The set at Benjamin's was cool, just as Wallace had kept forecasting. As soon as I got there I knew I had indeed reached the big time. The voices of Smokey Robinson and Little Anthony spun out from the hi-fi. A couple rubbed together passionately in the most basic of dances. The aroma of pancakes shared the air with the smell of marijuana. Bacon shriveled up in sharp contrast to expanding natures. Sugar was passed along with sugar, and lemons were squeezed along with fresh young girls. The grits were thick like my throat.

Wallace hadn't told me that he had a buck-toothed beauty named Shirley awaiting his arrival, that the information about the party had actually been relayed to him as a message from her. After she was introduced to me, she was tugged by Wallace over to the sofa. I retreated to the hi-fi to thumb through the stack of 45s and pull off one of the classic maneuvers of an overly self-conscious young fellow. I became the disc jockey.

After awhile, after everyone had played their openings, the great Benjamin himself assumed center stage. He was a highschooler already, hot on the trail of some wild eighth grader. He was clad in slippers and a robe, endowed with authority.

"Yo everybody," he boomed. "I got too many here. I don't wanna bust no bubbles or nuffin but some of yall gotta go. And like I don't really wanna be kickin out nobody, but like I really didn't do all this invitin myself from the git, you know. We fixin to have like a serious thing here, like a couples thing. This ain't no babysittin operation or no place for no lames. So I ain't really pointin out nobody, but some of yall know yall ain't qualified to hang out here. So dig, rather than to hafta be peepin hole cards, I'm gonna let yall go on and tip easy, you know. Like I said, I really don't wanna hafta be peepin no hole cards."

Wallace came over to tell me something I had already figured out, that I wasn't going to be able to disc jockey my way through this affair.

"Hey Keith, you gotta crack on one of them dames so you can hang on out."

"I would man. But I don't see nobody all that fly."

"That ain't nothin man. Who said they had to be fly? Shirley ain't all that fly, but what it mean?"

"Yeah Wallace, but a lot of these broads probably ain't droppin no drawers yet anyway."

"Yeah well that's what you're here for, to git em started. Don't be scared Keith. All you hafta do is pull one off to the side and explain how you diggin her. Your style is hip enough you know."

"I know man, but see it's a th—"

"Who you with man?" Benjamin had cut me off.

"I came here with Wallace."

"No little man, not like that. Is you got a squeeze or what? You know we ain't havin no deadbeats here. Not no nigguhs. Maybe you'll see a sister git away with it cause it might be the only way to keep another broad around. But ain't no nigguhs can git away with it."

I started to tell him that I hadn't really planned on staying, you know, that I was only killing a few minutes before I had to go take care of some other more serious business. Wallace's tongue, however, was quicker than mine.

"But check it out Benjamin, like this is my cousin Keith and he's kinda new around here and don't really know that many people yet. But my brother, see, he say he wanna see Keith git in the groove, you know. And he say you a good man to see about that. You know how you and P.J. is."

"Oh yeah. Me and P.J. is boss." He stepped back to look me over. "So you a cuz of P.J. hunh? Me and him is pretty tight. Done a lotta solids for each other. So tell P.J. not to worry about your H.O. card no more. I'm gon make you a lil tiger just like Wallace. But first you gotta start off right by gittin your head right and then you can go from there."

He yanked a nickel bag of reefer and a pack of Bambu from a pocket of his robe. I put down the records I was holding and accepted the gift casually.

"Bust it all the way down if you wanna," he advised. "You my man." He turned and walked away. Wallace was elated.

"Benjamin's gon be all right with you now Keith. You gittin reefer like this. You never had none before, did you?"

"Naw man. I missed that time Big Rob was turnin everybody on. I know I can handle it though."

"Probably can. Ain't no big thing nohow. I'd git down with you but Shirley got some herself. I don't know. I'll still come check you out later."

"Yeah all right, if I'm not hooked up into something else."

When Benjamin was satisfied there weren't any more hole cards that needed to be peeped, he directed the remaining couples, only six, to various love nests about the house. I was stranded in the living room of course, but there were two sisters stranded with me. They were sitting on the sofa appearing decent to the eye and truly provocative to the mind. And with the marijuana as my crutch and possible advantage, I embarked on confused pursuit. I sank into the matching chair and set the reefer and Bambu down on the table before me.

"I know you sisters down with this, ain't yall?"

"Yeah we smoke," answered the "healthy" one with hair that fell down her back in a single long braid. Even though she was seated I could tell she already had hips her parents couldn't trust.

"That's good then. We can all smoke together. What's yall's names?"

"Mine is Chrystal."

"Helen." She was dark and had long unstraightened hair that fell loosely over her shoulders. She wasn't quite as jock as Chrystal, but I considered her prettier. She had a small, distinct face. Bright eyes. Didn't seem to belong there.

"What's your name?" asked Chrystal.

"Well everyone calls me just plain old Keith. That's my proper name."

We all beamed. I didn't figure to make any errors with the small talk; I just had to solve the problem of the reefer. Not the smoking part, I knew I would eventually get around to that. The rolling up of the joints was what I was most worried about, you know, how to get the girls to do it without me losing face. I had an idea how it was supposed to go but was sure my attempt would come up clumsy and expose me for the rank amateur I was. I didn't know there were plenty potheads who were lousy rollers.

"I don't want to trouble you sisters, but I jammed my finger playing basketball in the gym yesterday. If one of you knows how to roll, you can help me out a lot."

"Ah shucks, that ain't no problem," Chrystal assured me. "Both of us know how to roll good."

The girls expertly rolled up three quick joints; Helen produced a sporty chrome lighter and we began to get high. I inhaled too much at first and coughed violently. I told the girls I had a cold and made a pact with myself to be smoother. And as I got my technique down pat, more of a soft swallow, I expected my head to feel funny, you know, experience some kind of floating sensation. What I got instead was an invisible hand vigorously tickling my ribs causing a giddiness that was threatening to blow my cool. I managed to keep my jaws tight though, and kept on puffing, concentrating on my rap, adding a year or two to my age and a couple of female admirers to my past. We also talked of the relative demerits of our schools, and we identified a number of common acquaintances, yet avoided the reason everyone was supposed to be there at the party. We compared opinions on all the popular songs and singers and of course I kept the music spinning all the while. I was feeling really comfortable for the first time since Wallace had tracked me down that morning, didn't even mind if Chrystal and Helen caught me staring at them, didn't shy away when our eyes met. Everything was mellow. And I was on my third joint when the big break came.

Helen decided to go to the store. Reefer and I instantly interpreted the move as a seductive ploy by Chrystal. Figured this was how they worked their show, so when Helen left we immediately accepted the invitation.

"So come on," Reefer and I said as we sat next to her on the sofa and tried to embrace her.

"What's wrong with you boy?" she shot back, eluding our attempt and springing up from the couch.

"What you mean Chrystal? Ain't nothin wrong. I just well, I mean, well, uh, you know the scoop."

"Boy, ain't no scoop here! What, are you crazy or somethin?"

"No I'm not crazy. You know you really wanna git down, don't you?"

"Hell no nigguh! What makes you think I came here for that? Who you been talkin to?"

"Nobody. It's just—"

"Just nothin. You better leave me alone. That's what you better do. . . . What makes you think I like you anyway?"

"Nothin. Nothin." Reefer and I were wondering why such tantalizing breasts would change their mind. But though we were bewildered, we knew better than to press the issue and cause a ruckus that undoubtedly would lead to our ultimate embarrassment. We had little choice but to accept the setback. There was, however, some measure of consolation. I could at least prove to Wallace that I tried. And I later found out, though he hid the truth for a while, that mere trying was as far as Wallace had gotten with his girl. He finally admitted that she had come up lame on him.

II

I spent the Christmas recess at Uncle Howard's house out in Cambria Heights, tucked in near the Nassau County line, a couple of rungs up the ladder of aspiration from Corona. Uncle Howard's place was a good visit for me, especially when I got to go alone. Then he and Aunt Ruby and my twelve-year-old cousin, Stephanie, could direct all their attention my way. Aunt Ruby even let me set the dinner menu most evenings, and I was able to achieve the exhilaration of watching someone prepare meat loaf rather than chicken for the simple reason that I decided they would do so.

Stephanie had a taste for adventure and mystery. She was a natural freak for Nancy Drew and Huck Finn and Alfred Hitchcock. But her favorite was me. So after she was sworn to secrecy and properly warned not to get any ideas, I would fill her head with embellished accounts of my latest exploits and observations. Stephanie would sit amazed, soaking in everything forever.

Her life was bland, which was fine with me as I thought the bland life was ideal for her. I was happy to see that Uncle Howard and Aunt Ruby were very particular about the types of kids she hung around with. All squares. There was this brother in the other three-year class, Donald Anderson, who was treated that way. He didn't vine too well and usually sat off by himself in the cafeteria, like maybe he was a little uppity. I was the only one of the "in crowd" who ever approached him, and I immediately discovered that there wasn't anything snobbish about him at all. As cousin Stephanie did, he had to live inside a square. And I figured the square was enabling him to excel in class.

I would fantasize, then, about being like Donald Anderson and cousin Stephanie. It would never last too long, though, before I snapped to my senses and realized all over again that a square's life just wouldn't do. I remained grateful for the relative freedom with which I was entrusted, even wanted more.

One night during my visit, after Stephanie had finally put me down in favor of bed, I was in the kitchen reading a magazine article about Martin Luther King Jr., who had just that month received the Nobel Peace Prize. He was the youngest man ever to win that award and that seemed quite a feat to me. Naturally I had to find out all I could about how he had become so respected so quickly.

Uncle Howard came in for some ice. According to him, late television and sipping scotch, lightly sipping scotch, was a great combination. His eyes twinkled and he flashed his amusing grin. He had the manly version of the face my mother wore when she was happy.

"Hey Keith, what are you reading about now?"

"Oh this is only a little article about King winning that Nobel Peace Prize."

"Yeah isn't that something Keith? Just goes to prove what I tell folks all the time. The man is a great leader. This is something for the soul brothers to be proud of, don't you think?"

"I guess so Uncle Howard. He must really be something to get a prize like that." I was far more concerned with King's fame than I was with his politics, but I liked to admire him the right way for my uncle.

"He is that," my uncle replied. "He's doing a good job getting the brothers and sisters their rights."

"Yeah, a lot of people think he's loquacious just for show. But that's not how it is."

"Loquacious hunh? Runnin off at the mouth. I like that. That's your word already or you just picked it out of the magazine? I know it's probably yours."

"Yeah I already knew it, but it's not really that big a word. It really ain't no big thing."

"Yes it is too. You got a good head for the books. Stephanie's like that. She's pretty good. But not as good as you. Not quite. You can be about the best, that is, if you want to be."

"Yeah? Well I always want to do well."

"Oh I'm not so sure about that now. I used to be, but I don't know now . . . and I've been meaning to talk to you about it anyway."

Uncle Howard finished plunking cubes into his glass. He returned the tray to the freezer and sat opposite me at the table. He spoke slowly. "Well Mr. Keith, your mother says you aren't doing as well in school as you might."

"When did she say all that?"

"One night on the telephone. It wasn't any big production. I was just asking about you and your sisters and she said you could be doing better than you were."

"What, she said I was doing bad?"

"No she didn't say all that, only that you should be doing better. New school isn't too rough for you, is it?"

"No it's not all that rough. I didn't get such a hot report card but I'm doing a whole lot better right now. You'll see."

He jumped up from the table, sipped the excess water from his glass. "You know Keith, it's your world baby. Stick with those books and they'll take you places. You and Sherry and Stephanie, all yall. That's a big break too because when I was comin up there wasn't any guarantee we could attend school. Man, I had to miss two whole years to work and help your grandmother. By the time I got back I was in the same class as your mother. I must admit it was a blessing though. Your mother's the one who pulled me through. She was the sharp one. That's why, uh, well, uh, well forget that. Just look. I don't have a lot of brains but I got a lot of hustle. I'm merely out here try in to do as well as the next man. I think I'm doing all right, don't you?"

"Yeah Uncle Howard. You're doing real well."

"Well you gonna do even better. You keep at those books like you're supposed to and you keep your spirits up. Don't get caught up in the wrong crowd out there. It's like driving, keep your eyes on where you have to go. I understand that it's a little rough over that way, and there's a lot of guys you probably see who aren't as interested in the right things as you are. But don't be a follower or anything like that. Go for yourself. I know you. You see things pretty quick to be so young. So keep seeing good and go for yourself." He jingled his glass of ice and drank off the excess water again. "Hey Keith," he resumed. "Remember baby, it's gonna be your world."

"Yeah. I'll remember that."

"OK then. Let me go on up and sip this scotch. Not to get intoxicated you must understand. I just like to sip. See you in the morning."

Uncle Howard, as it turned out, had a notion about seeing me every morning, you know, like a permanent custody thing. Moms wouldn't even entertain the idea. I didn't catch the conversation, but whatever was said put a strain on their relationship for a while. Plus Moms said that Uncle Howard was a drunken fool.

Malcolm went down in a hail of bullets right about then. I really didn't think they would get him. When they bombed his home, Wallace and I walked over to survey the damage. I thought some people were simply putting the scare on him. I had a hunch, obviously a poor one, that they wouldn't close him all the way out.

I took this news harder than I had taken the Kennedy tragedy fifteen months earlier, although this was opposite the general reaction in Malcolm's own neighborhood. The heads were really hanging low after Kennedy's death, but Malcolm's demise didn't produce half as much grief. It was a hot topic for talk, however, and I heard enough opinions to be totally confused. I heard the communists were behind the assassination. I heard it was the CIA. Others said it was some dope dealers because Malcolm had been fighting drug traffic up in Harlem. And of course folks were talking about the Muslims. The mosque uptown was set afire, and the one in Corona, which was only one block from my home, was being watched by a special police patrol.

Wallace Jones didn't seem to give much thought to the situation, was nowhere near as frightened or reflective or angry as I was. Maybe Uncle Howard had something there about quick eyes. Nonetheless, my feet were never any faster than Wallace's and we kept racking up adventures in tandem. Even had special ones for school.

They held an after school center in the boys' gymnasium. Wallace and I would shoot a few hoops, give things a chance to settle down, then slip from the gym to roam the rest of the school. Our favorite stop was the Home Economics classroom, where we often found a stash of cookies and fruit juices. Many of the cookies would be inedible, so we had a fierce scramble to see who could grab the majority of the edible ones. We saved the brick-hard ones for our own little discus throw competition.

We never found enough supplies to try to make our own batch, and Wallace said he was going to be the first male to enroll in Home Economics. I said if he made it I would follow. But both of us eventually had to content ourselves with Woodworking Shop.

Our most intense adventure that term was not planned, though it was more or less expected as White boy trouble was inevitable. The situation inside the school was calm enough, but the community at large was hostile and some of the older adolescents in the area were the ones who would transform this general hostility into specific physical incidents. There had been a few clashes up by the train station and on the bus, but Wallace and I had missed those gatherings. We had to face our encounter alone.

We were almost two hours late for school that morning because a hooky party had been canceled on us. Wallace had the crumb bun money, and after we got them, not being in any hurry at all, we crossed over to the soda shop and hoisted a couple of egg creams. When we emerged from the soda shop, four guys who looked like third-rate imitation Hell's Angels were at the bus stop apparently waiting for the bus to Ridgewood. I figured they were from Grover Cleveland High School, if they went to school at all. Wallace and I tried to ease by invisibly but didn't succeed. One of the boys casually ripped off a car antenna.

"Hey, you niggers got lotsa balls to be stragglin in like this. Ain't nobody to save your black asses. You know niggers need protection."

We quickened our step, poised to run. All we needed was the starter's pistol, and Wallace fired it himself in the form of words.

"Yeah? So who protects yo momma then?" And we were off.

The White boys were just as ready to sprint as we were, but it was a simple case of the fox running for dinner while the rabbits were running for their lives. In a footrace such as this, Wallace and I simply could not be caught.

"Which gate Wallace?" I cried out as I was moving at top speed. Even with a few books in my arm I stayed right with him.

"Side one. First one." Wallace surged in front by half a step. We turned into the gate entrance and sped up the walkway to the door. It was locked. We tugged frantically at the handles and banged furiously on the heavy brown door until we were out of time. As we hit the gate entrance again our pursuers were just about there. Wallace pivoted better than Gale Sayers, hardly breaking stride as he turned down the block. I stumbled slightly and heard the whoosh of the antenna as it split the air just a fraction of a second behind my neck. Fear, fortunately, pulled me together rather than ripped me apart and I became a too-swift rabbit once again.

We almost ran through the next door before we even had time to stop to open it. We paused in the doorway, panting, watching their approach. They stopped short of the gate. Winded.

"Better hope we never catch you," gasped the bearer of the steel whip. "Whooo, a scared nigger sure knows how to run."

"So what sucker," I countered. "I see a punk ass honkie sure knows when to stop too."

"Oh yeah? We'll come in there and beat your asses for you."

"Oh yeah Joey?" cut in Wallace with his White boy imitation. "Beat my meat is what you'll do, you greasy pimple-faced bastard."

"Oh just listen to the wise asses now. Big talk on the run. We'll see if you make so heavy with the cracks this afternoon."

"Ah go suck an egg Joey. You ain't got the nerve."

"Oh no shitface?"

"Shitface? Hey be nice Joey. That ain't what your mother called me last night."

"Joey" started for the door. It was only a bluff but it was enough to send us deep into the shelter of the school and into the fortress of our own laughter.

Turned out their rumblings about that afternoon were mere bluff also. Too bad. There was about a score of young brothers out there hoping they were for real. Crowds had heart. Individuals had to be ever alert and speedy.

III

NASA was emerging from a lull. Astronauts were being sent up in pairs that spring. The second duo, McDivitt and White, was good for sixty-two orbits. Impressive. It felt good to relate to an old value.

School certainly wasn't getting my loyalty. I was mired in mediocrity, fortunate not to be doing much worse. Uncle Howard blamed my friends, my "bad influences." He said I was becoming too much of a follower. I didn't argue the charge, partly because I knew his mind was made up already. But I knew Uncle Howard didn't understand everything about following and leading, definitely didn't know how I handled Marty Rosenberger by myself.

When the term ended, Wallace once again praised my marks. He was especially impressed by my reading score, which was at a so-called eleventh-grade level, a full five grades above his.

My problem in school, to my teachers, was a lack of effort on my part. My problem, to me, was that I had simply had an off year. All people, even Mays and Mantle, were entitled to one.

That summer we played all the old fun back. Only major change in the format was the addition of a little Colt 45 malt liquor, a little Bacardi rum, a little Bali Hai wine, and a little herb. I now had marijuana and the General Electric Pavilion at the World's Fair joined together. I felt you would have to go a long way to top that. Oddly enough though, my personal highlight of the summer came when I was perfectly sober.

It was about as calm a Saturday afternoon as we could possibly have going. Just a little stickball game in the street. Without even any arguments. The sheer pleasure of guiding a bat powerfully and gracefully into the back of a rubber ball.

Everything was fine until I was summoned to the house to mop the kitchen floor. Now I never saw anything wrong with swinging a mop. It was even pleasurable at times, but during the middle of a totally serene game was not one of them. I was upset, so I became somewhat illogical.

Instead of knocking out the task promptly as I usually did, I decided to sulk and procrastinate and generally get on my mother's nerves. I stood in the middle of the living room shuffling a deck of playing cards and introducing myself to some new boyfriend of Sherry's and trying to sound as hip as I could. I knew it wouldn't be long before my mother reacted.

"Boy, stop messin around and git in there and do that floor like I told you to." Objectively speaking, that was a reasonable command.

"Don't rush me," I dared to respond. "I'll do it when I get ready."

"What did you say?"

Now you hear many people ask this question rhetorically, you know, when they had indeed heard what had been said. In this case, however, I was sure my mother thought she was hallucinating. She needed reassurance, and I provided it with a voice that was strong and bold and unmistakably real.

"I said don't you rush me. That's all. I'll mop when I get good and ready to mop."

Moms trembled with anger and I winced mentally. She was going to come with her best—an old severed ironing cord.

The pain cut through my T-shirt like fire, covered my whole back and then flamed out to my arms. I squeezed my hands into the tightest fists I could possibly make, bracing to endure the assault without even the slightest whimper. With my own defiant inspiration and the pressure of Sherry's friend looking on, I figured to have enough resolve to get through. Moms continued lashing away with that cord, trying to break me. Sherry's friend could only admire my toughness. Then as my mother went to lash at my arms now folded up against my chest, her eyes met mine. Whatever she saw made her lashing lose its steam. She hit me a few relatively painless licks and stomped off into her bedroom and slammed the door. I couldn't bank on it, but I could sense she would never try to whip me again. I knew she could never make me cry again and, after all, what good is a beating without yells and screams and promises to do better?

"See. You really upset Ma now," Sherry accused. I thought she might be sympathetic toward me, but I should have known better.

"I didn't upset anybody," I snarled.

"You did!"

"I did not! Let me beat you with that ironing cord and then let's see who's the one that's upset."

"I'm not talkin about like that."

"I know you're not. And that's your main damn problem. You can't ever talk about nothin mean a goddamn."

I stormed off into the bathroom and latched the door behind me, leaned back against it. Sore, but wanting to howl with joy. I had a victory so immense and dangerous it couldn't all sink in just then. I moved to the mirror and proudly inspected my whelps. And naturally I had to check out those wonderful eyes. What was there besides plain old brown? I couldn't get it. I stretched them, squinted them, tried all the variations of my Sonny Liston glare. But I didn't see anything in them that would have startled or frightened or defeated me. It would have to come to me later. I had a floor to mop and I was determined to do a good job.

So that was the outstanding event that summer until a Black man who was drunk and driving was arrested by a White highway patrolman for drunken driving and the entire Watts district of Los Angeles exploded. Snipers and blazes and twenty thousand government troops and looting and machine guns and tear gas and bayonets and curfews. Thirty-four dead. Over one thousand injured. Over three thousand arrested. The most shocking incident I had seen on television yet. Even more shocking than the Harlem riots and the death of Oswald. It was, when I least needed it, another fiery decoration for my memory.

President Johnson denounced the Black rioters and said that just like the Ku Klux Klan they were destroyers of a free America. But President Johnson never sent twenty thousand troops against the Klan. He might occasionally restrain but he would never attack. You would never see three thousand Klansmen arrested. I felt that President Johnson shouldn't talk us into the same boat as the Klan if he never were actually going to put the Klan in the same boat with us. Wallace had it figured exactly the same way. We felt it was something any thirteen year old should understand.

IV

My off year was quickly becoming an off two years. I couldn't get my all-around academic game going, and early in the term I had a feeling, a rather indifferent one, that my time in S.P. was almost at an end. No one in my class thought I was dumb, however. They knew, as I did, that I simply didn't give as much of a damn as I should have. And since we all knew I could hang out with the "smart crowd" if I wanted to, proving myself to them was not important.

Danny Baylor was slipping badly also but wasn't any more concerned than I was, said he could take S.P. or leave it. And there were several White boys, such as David Greene and John Stark, who said they felt the same way. We were the rebels, the ones who had to be threatened with zeros three or four times before we would at least temporarily simmer down. We were nowhere near as defiant and antischool as Wallace Jones and some of my other friends, who couldn't be intimidated with subfreezing marks, but we were a lot tougher to handle than, say, a John Sabo, who would blush with embarrassment if he were caught for so trivial an offense as gazing out of the window instead of focusing on the blackboard.

My math was still pretty decent, but English became my favorite class that year, partly because of the way we were challenged by Mrs. Applebaum. A model of confidence and class, she claimed she wasn't at all impressed by how intelligent we were alleged to be, would tell us, in fact, that we were vastly overrated. I felt personally offended. I mean teachers were always after me about discipline and effort, but none of them had ever directly questioned my capability—at least not convincingly. But Mrs. Applebaum had me on the ball for a while, you know, for the sport of it. And though I didn't produce all she thought I should have, I absorbed more than she'll ever know. Gained my greatest understanding of the short story in general, of "unity of purpose." Enjoyed some particular stories such as "The Gift of the Magi." Although I fully understood how the story was viewed popularly as a tale of great love and selflessness, I also saw the work as confirmation of a dictum I had once heard my mother express: Love is an understanding between two fools. Mrs. Applebaum laughed and said that both my mother and I might make good literary critics.

I even let Mrs. Applebaum talk me into entering the oral recitation contest. I had read parts of "The Highwayman" so well in class that she thought I had an excellent chance to win the medal. She even volunteered to coach me after school. We would get the whole enchanting, beautifully lyrical poem to sound just perfect.

When I went to sign up for the contest I discovered that the selections had to be by American authors. No "Highwayman." I instantly decided not to compete but was later persuaded otherwise by Mrs. A. I wound up choosing some long patriotic poem by William Cullen Bryant, can't even remember the name of it, and in the contest I was totally outclassed by this girl named Vivian. She was definitely talented, no doubt about that. I mean she had even taken formal drama lessons and I wouldn't be surprised if she showed up on a Broadway stage one day. But I still feel I would have had a real good shot at that medal with "The Highwayman."

Mrs. Applebaum said she was proud of me because I had managed to come up with a good effort. Wallace Jones and company thought the contest was fixed. They were sure I had given the best "speech." But I knew better. Vivian truly deserved to win that award. But I didn't feel as though I had lost anything at all.

I guess that was the high point on the calm side that year. The wild side only grew wilder. Along with several other hustles, I mastered the art of "roughing off" money from some of the other kids—that is, obtaining cash through intimidation without the use of physical force. The key was to avoid actually "taking" the money to avoid ever being accused of theft. This was surely not a hustle for everyone. To be successful at the rough off game required great judgment (to pick the right mark), personality (to sell the bluff smoothly), and cunning (to leave the victim either feeling he had done you a favor of his own will or just plain afraid to tell). If you fumbled a rough off attempt you had to back off, fight, or maybe commit an out-and-out robbery. I may have backed off once or twice but on the whole I was as good as any artist in the school. I could have won a prize.

V

The guidance counselor for the eighth grade, Mrs. Gold, hopped on the bandwagon of those who would speak to me about my wasting good potential. But whenever I talked with her, her wording or logic or both seemed clumsy and she turned me off. There wasn't much guiding she could do for me.

Wallace got into a fight down in the cafeteria and my name became prominent during the ensuing investigation. I was summoned to Mrs. Gold's office—but not to give my account of matters. She was using the opportunity instead to sound off, to counsel, once again. She annoyed me immediately.

"Tell me something Raymond. Why do you hang around, let me say, with Wallace Jones?"

"Because he's my friend and next-door neighbor. I need more reasons than those?"

"No. No, those are good enough reasons I suppose. But why the others? Are they friends also?"

"You mean like Harry Jenkins and Thomas Warren? Yeah, they're my friends too."

"But why would you choose friends like that? You're not the same type of kid that they are. Just look, you're gifted enough to be an S.P. student and all. Doesn't that say something to you about the kinds of friends you should have?"

"Not really. I understand what you're saying, but I make friends with the people I like. And I don't think any of my friends are better than me and I don't think I'm better than any of them. Maybe you don't think they're ideal for me but, uh, but I'm not gonna worry myself too much about what you think anyway."

"Now relax Raymond. Just relax. I don't mean to upset you. I'm just concerned about your future. You can go a long way in life if you don't let anyone hold you back. I believe you are multi-talented and that there are all sorts of opportunities that can open up for you. Wouldn't your mother like to see you make something of yourself, become somebody special?"

"Of course she would, I guess."

"Well you can do it. But, like with anything important, it will take a fair amount of responsible effort."

"Yeah I know that. Can't expect to get something for nothing." I eased up on the counselor a little, gave her a little of what she wanted to hear.

"That's more or less it. And you have to have your mind set on the proper things, proper values. You know Raymond, and I don't mean to sound too ominous, but have you ever thought that a psychiatrist could help you?"

"Help me do what?" I replied while remaining cool.

"Help you solve some of your emotional problems. Again, excuse me if I sound ominous; I don't mean to imply that anything's terribly wrong with you. You're not crazy of course, but everyone has little problems from time to time. Don't you think so?"

"Yes, I imagine so. I know I have problems but I think I'll just solve mine by myself."

"If you can."

"Yeah, if I can. Even if I can't I'm not gonna worry too much about it now because really my main problem is becoming an adult. Once I get older, old enough, you know what I mean, then I'll be OK."

"I see. Would you be afraid to see a psychiatrist if I could arrange it? Naturally your mother would have to approve." I knew right then I would never have to worry about seeing one. Moms would think Mrs. Gold needed a psychiatrist for thinking I needed one.

"No I'm not afraid. I just don't think it's necessary. I can solve my own problems."

"Maybe so. Nevertheless I would like you to mention my suggestion to her. Will you promise to do that for me?"

"Sure. I'll mention it. I'll see what she says." I would mention it to my mother as a joke, and that's exactly how she would accept it.

In truth, Mrs. Gold's shrink talk did nag me for a while, caused me to ponder how much control I had over myself, over my own life, you know, whether I was the player or the played. But I finally shrugged off all that heavy reflection and became all the more disgusted with the counselor, another do-good worrier who wouldn't understand that none of my peers had any combination of powers greater than my own. Not even Harry Jenkins, whom she thought was the most unsuitable company for me.

Now Harry was our leader in a sense, a head taller than the rest of us, always clowning around but had a real solid punch. In fact, Harry sometimes punched too well. He cracked a White boy's jaw that spring outside the subway station on Queens Boulevard. Got himself arrested by detectives who hung around the school for two days before they nabbed him.

Although I didn't see it all, I understood it as a little shoving match that only became a criminal matter because of the racial climate of the times and the fact that Harry hit so hard. There was no real right or wrong I could determine, only that it was right that Harry, like Louis and Ali, should win his fights. But the loser saw it very differently, saw himself as the victim of an unprovoked attack. So the issue had to be decided in court, a formal place, not such a good venue for the home team. First there would be an Information and Evidence Hearing, then maybe a trial.

I decided to help Harry, much to his delight, by volunteering to serve as a witness. Although I was pretty sure he was going to lose the case, I thought I could at least shorten the odds. I just knew I could handle myself in the courtroom much better than most of the others who said they would support him. I figured they would panic or freeze or overtell the story or walk into some verbal trap and contradict themselves. Or perhaps they would stare down at the floor too much, or get too hostile or hysterical, or sound too "street." Just telling the truth would never be quite enough. Only this White guy in Harry's class was a person I felt good about as a witness. I thought he was even better than me.

I dressed a bit preppy for the court hearing. Put on my bright yellow button-collar shirt with the red paisley print around the inside of the collar. My tie, which I searched far and wide for, precisely matched that fashionable blaze of a pattern.

Harry's lawyer thought the tie was fine. Said so when he introduced himself, had caught me, in my somber radiance, eyeing the bus from the Youth House that was parked out on 89th Avenue and seemed to take up too much of the street. Cars could barely squeeze by in a single file. The lawyer mentioned my appearance again before the judge, emphasized my clean-cut nature while he led me through a retelling of my story.

The Corporation Counsel, the only other person in the room, which surprised me, had no compliments for me. Nor sympathy. He paced back and forth, clad properly in conservative tweed and standard cordovans. Lingered by the judge's bench, gave me plenty of time to get nervous, to stay in touch with the clamminess of my palms. His voice boomed as he began the cross examination.

"You say you saw Harry Jenkins push and then punch the plaintiff, Jonathan Craig. Is that correct?"

"No sir. That's not what I said. I said I saw the other boy push him first. Then I saw Harry push back; then the other boy pushed back harder, and then Harry punched him. *That* is what I said." I looked directly at him and kept my own voice loud, but well short of defiant.

"Oh I see," he countered. "I wasn't sure I understood. Then you did see Harry punch him in the face? Is that so?"

"Yes it is. I did see that. Just as I already said."

"I see. . . . Tell me, did you hear any nasty words exchanged between the two of them? Any racial insults?"

"You mean did I hear any derogatory stuff?" Boy did I stretch out that "derogatory." A one word poem.

"Uh, yes, uh, that's precisely what I mean. Did you hear anything of that nature?"

"No I did not."

"You didn't? Then you must be positive there was no such language used."

"No. I can't say that at all. As I said before, I was in the candy store when the whole thing started. I know some people are talking about hearing, uh, how do you say it? (I faked) Epithets? Yeah that's it. Epithets. I know some people are talking about that kind of stuff but I can't say anything about that at all. All I can be sure about is what I saw. I came out of the candy store and saw the other guy push Harry. Harry pushed him back, got pushed back hard, and then Harry punched him. That's what I saw." I tried to sound apologetic.

The Corporation Counsel suddenly waved toward the judge. "That's enough for me your Honor." And I was abruptly excused. Didn't get a chance to try to read the judge's face, get some feedback.

When I came back out into the waiting area I exchanged small talk with the other witnesses about "how it was." I then wandered again to the window overlooking the bus from Spofford and the deliberate cars easing down the road in the direction of King's Park.

In little more than an hour the case was resolved. The judge ruled that there wasn't enough evidence for the court to consider the matter further. Harry showed his joy by hugging or shaking hands or slapping five with all who had testified on his behalf. He was talking about throwing a party. His father was more restrained, but obviously as pleased, as though he too had been vindicated. I only caught a glimpse of Jonathan, his jaw still wired. But one couldn't tell from his expression if, on a legal level, he had won or lost. His dad, though, seemed distraught. I don't know; maybe the medical bills were too heavy.

VI

My last year of junior high was my worst one in terms of grades. I was warned several times that I might be dismissed from S.P., but that didn't happen. Besides, because of my test scores, I gained admission to

Stuyvesant High, one of the Board of Education's special academic high schools. Even though the prospects may not have been so great, I was a candidate for redemption. Ninth grade was actually the freshman year of high school, and the grades received would appear on the transcript to be sent to any college to which I eventually applied. A 70 average for the freshman year was no way to make Harvard or Yale or some other top think tank.

Stuyvesant proved to be an apt metaphor. It was named after Peter Stuyvesant, that peg-legged, last colonial governor of New York who lost a leg on a colonizing raid through St. Martin. I wasn't ripping folks off for land, but the good leg / bad leg part was certainly me.

I was tuned in more and more to the streets, the ones I walked and the ones on fire in the news. After a traffic accident involving a White motorist and a Black pedestrian, there was a riot right on Northern Boulevard in the spring of 1967. Angry residents vandalized White-owned businesses that were repaired subsequently with money from the higher prices the rioters themselves had to pay. Something absurd about it, of course, but that's the way those things went down. And in matters of ghetto sociology, Corona stayed up to date.

Maybe the high school could save me. Maybe old peg leg peering down from the portrait in the lobby could show me how you handled obstacles with one leg. And I did come out of the blocks fairly well. Got excellent marks in Biology and Geometry. A few of my S.P. classmates had entered the school with me, and Eddie Goldstein and Marty Rosenberger from P.S. 149 were also on hand although, having chosen two-year S.P. programs, they were now juniors. We didn't get too close this time around. I mean nobody said drop by. There were even a few brothers down there from the other side of the tracks (how some of us referred to East Elmhurst). But Danny Baylor had taken his struggle to the Bronx High School of Science.

The high school *was* saving me. I didn't mind the three-hour daily commute, looked forward to the four or five hours of homework. The old crew didn't much get in the way. Corona never had a high school, so we were sent to various schools all over the borough. Flushing (where Sherry was), Bryant, Bowne, Long Island City, Woodrow Wilson (where Wallace was), Bayside, Newtown. Everyone had plenty new things to get into. Some were sent out of the state altogether. Down south, a remedy for urban waywardness a number of parents would attempt. They hoped the old could cure the new.

Most times when I walked up First Avenue to the school—that is, when I happened to come in by way of the Canarsie line—I would see this redheaded guy on the corner, one of the seniors, dressed in an army jacket and boots. He would be passing out or selling pamphlets or newspapers expounding the position of the left. There was always something about oppression and the military-industrial complex. Boone spoke about student radicals in the barbershop. He said they were all socialists while their parents were still footing the bills. Nonetheless, I was still surprised to find a guy like that down at Stuyvesant. I was hip to the Panther thing in the air, the fight for rights thing, the antiwar Ali thing. But students generally fretted most about their averages, SAT scores, what colleges they could gain entry to, what scholarships they could obtain. Although I never viewed our corner propagandist as a serious player, there was something about his presence that nagged me.

Before the term ended Martin Luther King Jr. was dead. I was sixteen, hadn't yet decided to participate in any actual protest demonstrations, and they already seemed quite beside the point.

I pulled my overall average up to within a fraction of 80 in just one year, topping off the performance with a perfect 100 on the Regents Examination in Geometry. My mother was pleased and proud, and I was clearly back in the race for college. I needed three more semesters of 90 plus grades to increase my overall average to at least 85; I had to nail those SATs early in my senior year. Then I would be in line for a shot at a noteworthy institution. Would make it too. If I could protect Raymond from Keith.

That summer I landed a job with the Neighborhood Youth Corps. I was sent out to Brooklyn to work in Livonia Yard helping to maintain subway cars. I received forty-five dollars per week, thirty-eight and change after taxes, which was all right back then. I could offer Moms a few dollars although she would never accept as long as she saw visible signs, like needed clothes, that I was using the money in positive ways.

Most of the other youth workers were from Brooklyn and other parts of Queens. This one guy, Melvin, was drawn to me immediately. He was friendly enough, but more competitive than friendly. Would have dominated if I didn't hold him at bay. After he bragged about how well he played basketball in tournaments out at Lincoln Park, I beat him easily one day during our lunch break. He said his jump shot was off but he didn't exactly beg for a rematch. Then he used to say that Corona was nothing and I would invite him to come deliver that speech on Northern Boulevard. Then he would want to box and I would tell him I didn't play with my hands, but if he wanted to get serious. . . . As initiation tests go, it was pretty easy and we were cool.

The only thing Melvin had on me streetwise was that he was using heroin. Snorting. That shouldn't have bothered me so much, but it did. I had done my share of abusing drugs by then while I was getting ready for high school—reefer, snaps, wine, cough syrup. But I hadn't done anything since I started Stuyvesant but smoke an occasional joint. The heroin plague had certainly reached the neighborhood, touching or about to touch my own circle of friends. However, I hadn't thought much about it until Melvin talked about getting high, never suggesting I try it, but hooking me all the while.

I vomited at first. Used a fingernail file to shovel a bag of the shit up my nose over at Gary's. Gary was weird, a bright guy who was somewhat new in the neighborhood. I couldn't understand why someone with only a year left at a highly regarded school like Brooklyn Tech would want to be fooling around with this stuff. He didn't understand me either.

When I went to work I couldn't wait to tell Melvin what I had done.

"So you put the thing in your nose, hunh?"

"That's what I just told you, ain't it?"

"Yeah well dig this. It's done but don't get crazy with it. Sit back, think about it. Think about what you doing, you know, dip and dab. You don't wanna catch no habit, no chippie."

I was snorting again that same night. And by that weekend, I was ready to hit the main line. Weird Gary, old standby Wallace, and I went down to 127 playground, which, although on the right side of the tracks, was becoming a major trade center for drugs.

"So get the money right," Gary said. "We want an organized move here. How many things we gettin in all?"

"I want two bags," I replied. "What they got down here, fours?"

"All depends on who we catch. They mostly got fours down here, but we might catch treys. I even heard there were some deuces around like uptown. But it's a rumor thing. We better just count on the fours."

I fished a ten from my pocket, the only money I had, and handed it to Gary. He got eight dollars from Wallace, who had his money partially wrapped around the soda can from which he was sipping, and gave me two of those.

"So we gettin six things," he uttered mostly to himself. "We straight."

After a few more strides Wallace broke in, "You sniffin these Keith? Or you gonna skin pop?"

"I don't know. I'm thinkin about poppin one and holding one. Supposed to feel it more, right?"

"Yeah, and feel it a lot quicker too."

"I may as well pop then. What you think, Gary? You Tech guys are supposed to be so smart though downtown we know you ain't nothin."

"Skin pop it man," he chuckled. "You can handle it."

So that's how we decided I'd take the next step down the snort–intramuscular injection–intravenous injection ladder. After Gary copped over by the handball courts, we cut across onto the baseball field and headed for the first base dugout. It was a spot secluded enough for our planned activity, yet with enough light coming from the nearby streetlamp. As we approached the dugout we could see that someone had beaten us to the spot. Which actually didn't matter. They were neighborhood. We knew them. And there was room on the bench for all. In fact, I knew one of the guys too well. Another competitor, one with whom I shared a mutual dislike.

Everyone nodded ambiguous greetings and asked the muted rhetorical question: "What's happenin?" They were winding down their "operation get high" and we set about the task of firing up. Wallace went to rinse out the soda can at the water fountain. Gary pulled out his works. They were encased in aluminum foil and tucked inside an eyeglass case. I had seen them before. Glass dropper with the nipple from a baby's pacifier secured to the wide end with a rubber band. A small spike inside a plastic case. A bottle cap with a small wad of cotton inside and a bobby pin attached as a handle. Tough elastic string. Gary laid the works on the bench, gently unfolding the foil. He peeled the scotch tape off one of the glassine packets, unfolded the bag and dumped the dangerous dullish white powder into the bottle cap, the "cooker." He announced, "You're up first, Keith." This provoked the guy I disliked. He picked at me through Gary.

"What he doing? Maining? I know he ain't maining." Meaning I wasn't hip enough to shoot drugs intravenously like him. His speech was slurred. He slid a hand down inside his pants to scratch his groin, rubbing the side of his neck with the other hand. Gary ignored him but I reached over for the string and balled it up in my fist. By the time Wallace returned with the water, Gary had torn off a piece of the border on a dollar bill. He wet it in his mouth and wrapped it around the open end of the eyedropper. He jammed the spike, still in its cover, onto the dropper, shaking the instrument vigorously a few times to make sure the spike held. Then he drew about a half dropper of water from the can and squirted it into the cooker.

"This is Keith's shot," he announced in hushed tones to Wallace. "Gimme a light." Wallace already was pulling a book of matches from his pocket. He struck one and held the flame under the cooker. I had seen the procedure a couple of times by then, but I was fascinated anew by the chemistry involved. Wallace shielded the flame with one hand like a smoker trying to light a cigarette in the wind. Gary moved the cooker in a slow circular motion until he brought the contents to a simmer. He held the cooker with his left hand and had the homemade hypodermic in his right. He drew the mixture into the dropper by squeezing the nipple, inserting the tip of the needle into the cotton and releasing it, slanting the cooker a little so that all the fluid would run into the cotton.

I handed Wallace the string, which prompted both him and Gary to stare at me in wonderment. The three of us knew you didn't need to tie up if you were only skin popping. Usually just took the injection back in the triceps area.

"What you doin?" Wallace asked.

"What it look like? Tie me up." I offered my left arm and after hesitating Wallace wrapped the cord around it a few inches above the elbow. As my arm wasn't very vascular, he had to loosen the tie and then retie it more firmly. Moving swiftly, Gary picked the vein running along the outside portion of the crook. He grabbed my arm, pressed his thumb hard against the chosen vein with a pulling downward motion, and deftly pricked the skin. Blood spurted up into the dropper. Wallace released the tourniquet and Gary squeezed the nipple to inject the shot. But he didn't squeeze the nipple all the way, didn't want to shoot any air into the vein. He released the nipple and blood began flowing back into the dropper. This was called booting, was supposed to make you feel it quicker. I didn't need to boot much that night. The dropper was less than a quarter full when the shot hit me. A triple assault. Head spinning dizzily, mouth tasting the bitter quinine that was used as the cut, stomach hinting at turning over.

"Feel it?" Gary asked.

"Yeah," I whispered.

Gary squirted the fluid back into the vein, this time squeezing the nipple all the way. As he removed the spike from my arm, he grabbed my arm just above the injection spot and pressed down on the vein so it hurt. He stroked the vein back in the direction of the injection spot, doing this to make sure to squeeze out any air bubbles. When he finished he headed over to the water fountain to rinse out the works. I sat dazed, head bowed, slightly rocking back and forth, stroking my vein in the manner that Gary had done, though not nearly as hard. The other group were collecting their belongings to slink away in agitated bops. I didn't catch the eye of the disliked one. And appearing, coming across the baseball field, was more neighborhood.

Melvin was a mainliner by the time the summer ended. And I had fallen deeper. On as slow a day as you could get in the streets, on one of those Sundays when wasn't no money happening for nobody, my nose started running and I got a few cramps in my stomach. As definite as registered mail, the chippie had arrived. I told myself what most novice addicts did: I could stop whenever I wanted. I didn't though. I took the whole conundrum back to the portrait of the peg-legged governor.

VII

Back at Stuyvesant I became obsessed with college. I daydreamed about it constantly, wishing I could forgo the final two years of high school. I even made certain practical moves.

Having a study period in my schedule, I volunteered to work in the college office under Mr. Wechsler whose son, in fact, was in my home-room section. I read all the information that came in about colleges, application procedures, standardized tests, scholarships, and other forms of financial aid. I wrote away for numerous catalogs to be sent to my home. At one time I thought my sister would benefit from them also since she was in her senior year, but she joined the maternity club and didn't make it out that term. I shared them with Gary who was rather disinterested. I think he knew he wasn't graduating either.

Heroin was the first thing that I feared could make me late. No, not like for a class, appointment, or job, but late in life. Although I hadn't always fulfilled my best capacities, I had still managed to make it on time to the places I needed to be. But you don't cheat dope for long. It collects its dues.

Gym classes were expressly participatory. We had to be in uniform every day and I didn't feel like being bothered with responding to Mr. Davis's ever-insistent urging to "move with alacrity." I dressed for gym sporadically, finally failing it. However, it was a minor subject and the grade wasn't computed as part of my academic average, so I really wasn't too upset. After all, I was holding on in the classroom. I could still keep much of my act going. Get down with Trigonometry and Chemistry and Hawthorne's *Scarlet Letter*. A 90 average was a thing of the past but I ran high eighties for the fall semester, which wasn't too shabby among the eager beaver, one-dimensional, no social concern types. They had no interest in the Mark Rudd parts of Columbia or the Free Speech Movement aspect of Berkeley.

Failing the gym class was just a warning of course. The overall inevitable decline soon followed. So that spring, while Ronald Reagan was sending the National Guard into Berkeley and imposing a curfew on the town, and Black students with guns held control of a building at Cornell, my main pursuit was for money for drugs.

I became involved in a series of crimes that initially ranged from purse snatching to burglary. Ripping off some White woman down in Jackson Heights, descending through the skylight of a cleaners or grocery store, squeezing through air ducts to plunder concession stands inside the airport, lifting television sets from those airport area motels where they hadn't yet been bolted down. It was convenient and sometimes crucial to have ready transportation, so stealing cars became part of the curriculum. You looked mostly for GM models. Back then GM was still using the old "turn ignition," the kind that could be activated without use of a key—that is, if the owner were careless. If he or she only turned the knob to the "off" position and not the "lock" position, you could start the car simply by turning the knob back to "on." At other times, you would take car keys obtained through various means and roam the streets trying them on like models. It never took long to find a fit. Sophistication wasn't necessary, no hot wiring or anything like that.

As the heroin plague infested the neighborhood, a network of petty gangsters was formed, daily circumstances of need and greed often determining which members of this network would get together on a given occasion. By being in the network you came to know who was reliable, who had heart, who was likely to snitch, who could stand the weight.

I was a pretty good wheel man by the summer of 1969. That July I had a shiny blue 1968 Oldsmobile Cutlass with a black vinyl top. One Saturday, in fact, the day before Man first walked on the moon, I handled a wheel job for a couple of local union members. Afterward I got high, went to a couple of parties, and spread some favors around in case I needed to ask for some in the future. It was past four by the time I stashed the car and went home, only to find that I couldn't get in. Moms was enforcing her new regulation that if I didn't come home at a decent hour she would make sure I didn't get in. The rule was a good one. A seventeen year old had to have the wrong reasons for keeping the hours I wanted to keep, and some lessons had to be learned the hard way. That was an understanding and, I think, a strength my mother had. On the other hand, she hadn't grasped, and understandably so, the enormity of the problem with her son. First-generation northern urban youth were hard to figure.

I shrugged off my little housing problem and went back to fetch the Oldsmobile. Along the way I ran into Gary and a guy named Blue, so the three of us went to the diner on Junction Boulevard and then over to 127. The sun had risen and I was wide awake. I had barely settled down with the newspaper to read about the escapade to the moon when it started to rain. I thought of running for the car, but instead I went along with a suggestion to break into the school. We went through a front window in full view of a man out walking his dog. As you might suspect, the police arrived a few minutes later.

I was at a table in the cafeteria when I spotted the patrol car pulling up along 25th Avenue. Calling to Gary and Blue, who were using their newspapers as pillows, I dashed for the far exit. They scrambled for the door near the window through which we had entered. Theirs was a poor choice, I figured. Too close to the patrol car. However, the police apparently caught sight of me running toward the other exit and pulled the car up to that door just as I was emerging. I spotted Gary and Blue getting away. I ducked back inside and ran up a stairwell, finally settling into a hiding place in the dark fourth floor gymnasium. It was to no avail. An officer came in brandishing a flashlight and I was busted. He cuffed my hands tightly behind my back, his partner said I smelled like a goat, and they accused me of having stolen typewriters from the school for weeks. I didn't say anything in response.

At the 114th precinct I was interviewed by a detective who seemed primarily interested in my accomplices.

"OK pal, you want to tell me about the two guys who were with you?"

"What two guys?"

"Look buddy, I'm asking the questions. Understand?"

"I don't know them. I have seen them once or twice. But I don't know their real names and I don't know where they live."

"OK. It's your ass up the river by yourself." And that, surprisingly, was it. No real pressure to make me squeal.

For arraignment I was taken over to Atlantic Avenue in Brooklyn. Weekend court. I was placed in a cell by myself. As one of the legal aid people was coming down the line to do the customary interviews, the man in the next cell called me, though at first I didn't realize he was addressing me in particular.

"Yo homes, next door. Next door, homes. You."

"You talkin to me?" I asked apologetically. But as soon as I asked the question in that fashion I told myself to be more assertive, though not defiant.

"Yeah man. You. You hear that punk comin down here for the info. Fuck him. Don't tell him nothin. He ain't gonna do nothin for you. Askin all them bullshit questions. What you got this time?"

This time? I wondered. I thought the veterans asked "*first time in kid?*" or something like that. Well, I sure wasn't going to give away that it was my first. What if my mother didn't show and I had to remain in this joint for a while? It was a thought that just sneaked up and horrified me.

"Burglary," I responded, trying to make it sound like murder one.

"Yeah? Well don't tell this punk nothin cause he ain't doin nothin for you."

By this time the interviewer had reached this man's cell.

"I just want to ask you a few questions for the report."

"Man, get the fuck out of here. Who you kiddin? I got one bid in already. They droppin four armed robberies on me now. What kinda fuckin probation am I gettin? Or bail? Or any of that fuckin shit."

"But it's for your own good."

"Fuck you I said. Leave me the fuck alone." Then he called to me. "Don't tell em nothin youngblood."

"I have to," I told him, the words fluttering hesitantly from my mouth. "I can walk on this one. It's a meatball."

"Go ahead then," he advised after a pause. "But I'm tellin you homes, they ain't gon do nothin but fuck you up."

I was out early that afternoon. Paroled in the custody of my mother. Caught a legal aid attorney who happened to be a graduate of Stuyvesant High. He showed me his ring and said he couldn't understand what a fellow peg leg was doing in criminal court. So I sanitized the explanation as much as I could. Presented the whole matter as harmless mischief, that's all. Same way with Moms. Left the drug part out. Though in two more days she would know it all.

Wallace and I were on a fundraising mission. I still had the Cutlass and Wallace had a .22 revolver. I was no stickup kid but had confidence that we could handle something minor, you know, not get in over our heads.

Wallace had scouted a few sites down in Elmhurst and Woodside that he thought were worth another look. We picked up another local desperado named Tango, who was alleged to have enough nerve in matters like these, and were on the go, Wallace directing me to a Chinese laundry on 31st Avenue. We circled the block after passing the laundry, parking in the side block a car length or two shy of the avenue. There was a fire hydrant in front of us so the odds were we wouldn't get jammed in by another car. The getaway would be smooth. I left the keys in the ignition as Wallace and I exited the car. Then Tango got cold feet on us.

"I'll lay and get the seats ready."

"Seats ready?" Wallace exploded. "Man, what the fuck are you talking about? You suppose to be the lookout. Don't tell me you can see around corners."

"What's happening Wallace? I thought you double-checked his references."

"Jay and them boys said he was cool. Fuck it. You still down?"

"Yeah." Wallace was already several yards ahead of me. I told Tango to wait right there.

There were no customers when we entered the laundry, only the woman behind the counter who had a fit when Wallace pointed the pistol at her. She began backing away slowly, shaking her head "no no no" with her hands pressed up against the sides of her face. She formed words with her mouth but no sound issued forth. I had leaned across the counter to open the cash register when a man came from the rear of the establishment. Upon seeing us his first impulse was to charge, but the image of Wallace leveling the pistol at him made him change his mind. He retreated, not with a look of fright, but as though he had an equalizer. I grabbed a small stack of bills and scooted out the door just ahead of Wallace. We sprinted around to the car, I fired up the engine, and we were in the bleachers at 127 in a matter of minutes. Tango was still with us but we ignored him until, after watching me divide the money evenly between Wallace and myself, he inquired, "What about me?"

"Should I shoot him?" Wallace asked me.

"Naw man," I replied, my mind on the real business at hand. "We ain't got time for that."

"Only take a second."

"Naw man, stop jiving." However, I wasn't totally convinced he was. Tango was quietly pathetic, what you might call a hope fiend.

The take was mostly singles, less than $20 altogether. We could get high but not complacent, and later that evening we were back on the prowl. This time we picked up Smitty, a bit undersized but generally game, although the pistol thing was new for him too.

We cruised out to Woodside to case a bakery, but it was too busy. We looked at a few drugstores and liquor stores but at least one of us would have an objection, would sense that something wasn't quite right. Frustrated, I began to think that my opinions were the only valid ones, that Wallace and Smitty were losing their heart.

Working back to the east, back through Corona–East Elmhurst, on through Flushing, we eventually wound up on Bell Boulevard in Bayside. There was a drugstore we all agreed was ripe for the picking. No one inside but the proprietor, chubby, balding, White, our type. Wallace and I approached the counter as Smitty stationed himself by the entrance.

"This is a stickup," my partner declared as I made my move for the register.

"Oh yeah?" the intended victim responded. Without flinching he reached down and drew a gun. Fortunately, my instincts had me backing away. The barrel of that gun seemed so huge he wouldn't have had to shoot to capture me. He could have lassoed me. By the time I turned to take full flight, Wallace and Smitty were scooting out of the door. If not for the situation I would have laughed at how they seemed to go through the doorway simultaneously, the doorway actually seeming to expand as in a cartoon.

We were entering Corona an hour or so later still not having made any money. As we rolled down Roosevelt Avenue up under the El train, we saw a White pedestrian entering the parking lot of Shea Stadium.

"Let's get him," Smitty suggested.

"Fine with me," I responded, slowing the car down only to speed up again when it turned out that the headlights of an approaching vehicle belonged to a patrol car. I held the Oldsmobile steady, tried to stay relaxed. I picked up the patrol car in the rearview mirror and watched it recede into the distance.

"Everything's cool," I reassured. "They ain't notice nothin." But the moment to hit the new target had been lost. I proceeded along Roosevelt. At the corner of 111th Street I spotted another White man descending the stairs leading from the train station.

"I'm getting him," I said impulsively and sprang from the car.

"No Keith no," I heard Wallace calling behind me. He was following me but I was gone. I pushed the man hard against the wall of a building.

"Now gimme that money!"

"Take it. Take it." he shrieked. As I went to empty his pockets a patrol car was screeching to the curb right behind us. This is what Wallace had been trying to warn me about. The instant I turned I could see the car almost hit Wallace who then started running back across Roosevelt. The man tried to grab me but I elbowed him viciously in the solar plexus, spinning around and following that up with a right cross to the jaw. He staggered, a cop was closing in, lights were swirling, I couldn't comprehend the shouting.

I took off down Roosevelt. As luck would have it, I happened to be on the longest block in the area. I could hear the cop behind me. That wasn't my major problem. Unless he were Bob Hayes in disguise, he didn't figure to be able to run me down. No, the major problem was that if the officer in the car chose to pursue me rather than Wallace, he could easily cut me off on the long straightaway.

Cutting into an alley, I encountered a high fence topped with a short row of barbed wire and didn't hesitate to scale it. I ripped my shirt going over but managed to jump down to the other side and scurry behind a clump of bushes just as the cop entered the alley.

"Freeze," he bellowed, his gun drawn. Hell, I wasn't planning to move at all. Figured I would blend into the scenery and make him think I had escaped. There was another fence to climb and no way I could make it.

He shined a flashlight. "Come out of those bushes with your hands up." I thought about trying to escape but with the losing streak I was on, I knew better than to count on a fence to block bullets. So I surrendered. The patrol car turned into the alley with no prisoner inside. Just me and the law again.

I was arraigned the next morning in Kew Gardens. The judge did a double take at my yellow sheet, realizing that my prior arrest had been only three days before.

"Appears as though he needs a rest," he considered before setting a cash bail of one thousand dollars.

My mother turned to me, repressed hurt and anger twisted together in her face, and whispered tersely, "I guess you're satisfied."

I used my phone privilege to call Uncle Howard, my best, perhaps only shot at bail. He said he would see what he could do. In the meantime I was on my way to Rikers Island, cell block 5, cell 5A6. Like most folks who made it to the Island, I turned reflective. I would lie on the top bunk staring at the red lightbulb above the cell door mulling how I got to this part of the script, the trip, whatever. Got to the part with the stomach cramps. No sensationalized Hollywood gorilla jones stuff. Just a baby monkey thing I could handle. Every morning you could see at least one inmate with a strong habit, or maybe a weak constitution, fall out in the mess hall. Actually, you could have admitted to being a drug user on entering the facility, but that made you a registered addict in the new Rockefeller Program. There were early advantages for some in terms of medication and leniency, but the state kept more tabs and labels on you in the long run. Copping to the Rockefeller only made sense if you had a heavy beef, but if the beef were too heavy they wouldn't let you cop anyway.

Got to the part of worrying about time. After all, I was caught red-handed. Wasn't like I should waste the court's time and anger a district attorney by pleading innocent.

Got to the great reunion. Half the neighborhood was on the Rock. All the folks whose falls I had heard about and the ones whose disappearance I hadn't stopped running long enough to notice. Even old Lonnie Blair, who was all smiles when we ran into each other during a movement. He broke from his line to greet me with a hug. The officer in charge let him get away with it.

Got to the around-the-clock fear. Avoiding direct eye contact but not shying away from it all the time either. Didn't want to issue challenges or have to accept any. But if I had to, I was committed to rumbling, to holding my own.

Conversations filled with lies echoing up and down the tiers. Ass kickings promised on the lockout. Landing in the day room watching news broadcasts monopolized by the trip to the moon.

I was supposed to be only fourteen months away from college. I had to get back on track. The dope game was a sucker play, not just in terms of lost opportunities. That was the obvious part. But more interesting was to understand drugs in terms of being controlled by others. This Black cop really made me see that one night on Northern Boulevard. He pounded his beat, taking his payola here and there, but he left a gem for me. He asked me had I ever seen any ocean liners dock in Flushing Bay or any 747s land on the Boulevard. Since I hadn't and told him so, he wondered how I didn't know that the only way I could get any heroin was because there were some people who wanted me to have it. It was not so much self-destruction that I was engaging in, but designed destruction.

By the time Uncle Howard came to get me I was ready to tell him, my parents, and anyone else who cared to listen what the hustle was all about and how I resolved to beat it. It's just that resolve didn't yet hold the upper hand with me.

VIII

I felt old for someone still in high school. Like if I did manage the course load, get a favorable disposition from the court, beat the latest phase of my drug involvement, and gain admission to college, I might be too worn out to attend.

A few of the brothers also started to age too much, began experimenting with heroin. I tried to discourage them as Melvin had done for me, but of course they didn't listen, which, in one sense, was fine. They made my hustle safe and easy. You see, heroin usually cost more in their communities. So I would cop deuces in Corona, bring the supply to school, and give them a bargain. Give them two bags for seven, say, if they were used to fours. This would work until they traveled more and/or prices stabilized all over town. The few dollars generated were plentiful. I didn't have a habit. Knew I couldn't afford to ride that white pony hard with two cases already before the court. Besides, I really did talk to myself a lot about quitting.

Attempting to fit some productive activities in my schedule, I took a job uptown at the arcade next to the Apollo Theater. Needed to save for future educational expenses. At that point I didn't worry much about high school matters. I could do enough in class to get by and make sure my average didn't slip too far. No school official mentioned my legal problems so I assumed none of them knew how I had spent part of my summer vacation.

I scored a shade under 1200 on the SAT, which wasn't too poor given the circumstances. And I sifted through my catalogs at home, focusing in on the University of Connecticut and the University of Notre Dame. My average was four or five points off what I desired, but because of my test scores and the fact that both schools were making highly publicized efforts to recruit Blacks, I managed to receive scholarship offers from both. Against the advice of my English teacher from the previous year, who thought the atmosphere would prove too constricting, I chose Notre Dame. Had visions of dusting off my athletic skills and becoming a scholar-athlete of renown.

During the fall semester I handled my academic subjects as expected. But I failed gym once again, my attendance being so spotty. This forced me into the position of taking back-to-back gym classes during the spring semester. On many occasions those were the only two classes for which I showed up. English was on my schedule after gym. When I bothered to stick around, I didn't really participate. I might ask why we couldn't discuss books like *The Outsider* and *Manchild in the Promised Land* only to get a retort about curriculum and classics. Sometimes I would sit at my desk in the back row (my usual position in all classes by then) and model social consciousness rhetoric into the form of the Shakespearean sonnet.

When I was off in my own world in class one day, a student in the next aisle patted my arm to get my attention and motioned toward the rear door of the classroom. I saw the big blond dean, Mr. McGinn, and my shop teacher, cool black-haired Mr. Valenti, peering through the thick glass. McGinn beckoned me and I responded while trying to figure out what he wanted. McGinn didn't frighten me. I had hookied too much, cut too many classes, had too much raw, real world experience to be shaken up by a high school dean. But although he couldn't scare me, he could antagonize me endlessly, warning me that I didn't have it made yet, that the school in Indiana was but a phone call away.

"Are you tired Raymond? It doesn't seem as if you're especially interested in English." His tone was matter-of-fact, not accusatory.

"Well you know," I replied while remaining civil. "I have those two gym classes."

"Are you sure that's it? Take a little stroll with us. It'll energize you."

"Energize?" I laughed. "I told you I am *enner-vated*."

"Aw come on," Mr. Valenti intoned mildly. To myself I asked *what's the angle?* as I consented to walk.

When we came to an empty classroom, Mr. Valenti opened the door and McGinn asked me to step inside and take a seat. My mind was fully puzzled by then, but I didn't have to remain agitated for long. Clarity was cloaked in the dean's next request.

"Would you roll up your sleeves please?"

"What?"

"Would you roll up your sleeves?"

"For what? You think I'm a magician or something?"

However, the real question was how he finally put it together. *Observations? Probably where Valenti comes in. A court inquiry? A snitch?*

"Just roll them up," he snapped. Actually I didn't mind obeying his order. I wasn't carrying anything and was curious to see what they knew.

However, in complying with McGinn's request I felt compelled to remind him that he didn't strike me as being the least bit intimidating.

"No problem," I stated while staring defiantly into his eyes.

I unfastened the cuff buttons on my shirt and rolled the sleeves up past the elbow. I thrust my arms forward in a gesture that indicated I had nothing to hide.

McGinn took my arm, the left one first, the one hardly ever pricked. Then he examined the right arm and saw, along the thickest vein, the pattern of needle marks, one as fresh as that morning, as well as the skin made dark and callous by prolonged puncturing.

"So you're using dope."

"Used to, which is not exactly the scoop of the year." Then I looked up at Mr. Valenti, who seemed mesmerized by my arm, and decided to lighten up. "As I said, I used to. But I stopped."

"What about these needle marks?"

"They're old," I said evenly. "Very old."

I'm sure McGinn didn't believe me, but he seemed confused. He took Mr. Valenti over near the door where they consulted in whispers, eventually deciding that I should be taken across the street to be examined at Beth Israel Hospital. Parental permission was required for this, so my father was called. I wasn't unnerved by all the fuss; I mean it wasn't like I was being arrested. I could go to Beth Israel Hospital as long as it didn't turn into Rikers Island while I was there.

I repeated my claims to the attending physician, which he received with professional detachment. He was primarily interested in whether I was presently under the influence, which I was not. He shined a light into my eyes, checked my reflexes, and had me sit in the emergency room for an hour or so before he informed me I was free to leave. That night I tried to ease my mother's worries. I told her I hadn't done any new wrong. Everything was old stuff.

The next day the guidance counselor, Mrs. Brody, called me in for a long talk. She was a nice person, engaging. This was serious talk. No sermonizing. Just a realistic look at things. She suggested I enroll as an outpatient at Greenwich House, a rehabilitation center over on 14th Street off Sixth Avenue. I walked over for the intake interview but didn't enroll.

I was around school less and less after that. Well on my way to a grand total of 56 official absences for the spring semester alone. Not to mention the classes cut after being marked present in homeroom. I didn't get interested in everyday attendance again until four students at Kent State University in Ohio were killed by the National Guard. There were demonstrations at the school and rallies over in Union Square. A relatively radical faction of students issued a demand for certain changes within the school and organized a student strike, which, in terms of numbers, was successful. In 1970 the spirit of the '60s had reached the White folks at Stuyvesant High. An assembly was called at which several instructors urged students to work through the system. Students blew off steam verbally. And in a few days it was back to business as usual although I don't recall that any concessions were made by the administration. Well, I already knew not to take White student activists too seriously. Boone had made me skeptical enough about that. But if I needed a more vivid reminder, the wait would not have been long. Five Black students were killed at Jackson State University in Mississippi, time for sho nuff demonstrations in my view, and the members of the relatively radical faction were too preoccupied with thoughts about graduation to interrupt classes again.

But not all the brothers were too busy. Several windows were smashed. The piano in the auditorium was set afire. Before stepping in line for their diplomas, they offered testimony as a new crop of eighteen year olds that Black martyrs also count.

After that particular fervor faded, I realized something that was perhaps the most incredible fact of my senior year. I still had a chance to graduate myself. I cleared court on the third of June, given youthful offender treatment, which meant that in return for my pleas of guilty my record would remain sealed if I encountered no further trouble with the law. My lawyer, proud of my scholarship, told me a joint or two was the best thing for loosening up. He said the hard stuff was strictly bad news. The judge, after sentencing, instructed me to go to school, do well, and stay out of her courtroom. She sounded sincere.

I couldn't make any grades to speak of for the eighth semester, could sort of just squeak by the way I had left junior high school three years earlier. But classroom grades weren't the only concern at that point. Regents Examinations were required in several classes and there was a stipulation that students with more than 20 absences in a class would not be permitted to sit for an exam. However, Mrs. Brody pulled me over that hurdle, consulting all the parties involved in waiving the attendance requirement once I assured her I could pass the three exams I had to take.

I kept my end of the bargain. 82 in Physics. 79 in History. And English was the irony of ironies. There was an essay question on the overcrowded judicial system that I handled on the way to an 83. Despite passing the Regents, I was given a 40 in English, but it was decided at a special meeting that I would be given credit for the course and allowed to graduate. Time to bid old peg leg good-bye.

Advancing to college was another matter. I convinced myself that I would not show up on the campus of Notre Dame addicted to heroin. But the way I began to run the streets that summer, you would have thought I intended to kick on the bus ride to South Bend. I stole some more, did a little dealing, shot the highest dosages of dope I ever had. Jail was a more likely destination than a university.

Father Hepsburgh had his say on where I would be when he sent me a letter halfway through the summer canceling my admission. Said something about my not being ready for college at that time. No doubt he knew what he was talking about. But besides being angry, I wondered what the decision had been based on. Had my old adversary, the dean, tripped me with telephone wire? Did the folks out there know about the legal piece? Had it simply been the eighth semester grades or attendance?

My mother received the news stoically, probably thankful not to hear worse. I think my father had allowed himself to be more adventurous in his dreaming, so he appeared much more distraught. I tried to reassure him by telling him that although the past had caught up with me, I was in command of the present and would bounce back. Still make it. We called the University of Connecticut to see if the offer previously made could be reactivated. No chance. The scholarship had gone to someone else.

So there would be no college in September. After all those years putting in time with the White folks, they finally had the chance to leave me behind. That was bad enough, but I felt defeated among the brothers, especially in Corona, where I had been a bearer of collective hope. Sure we all ran together, but several of them depended on me not to be an authentic loser in the end. Like Wallace, for example, recent recipient of a three-year sentence for robbery. He kept writing to tell me to tighten up the school thing.

Fortunately, there was encouragement to be found in the streets also. I had a friend named Alan Jennings, tough survivor in his own right, who was on his way to Queensborough Community College. Whenever we would come across each other that summer, he would have a pep talk for me or some advice. He suggested I apply for February admission to Queensborough, put in a few good semesters, and reevaluate my academic position at that point. Naturally the drug use would have to cease and I twice tried to quit on my own. However, because I knew I had my biggest habit yet, as soon as I caught a cramp I became fearful and, fully cognizant of how weak I was, dove back into the cooker. It took a newspaper headline to yank me out for good.

On August 8th the paper blared in bold print the story of how Jonathan Jackson walked into a courtroom in California, announced that he was taking over and had come to free his brother, celebrated prison writer George Jackson, and got himself smoked during the subsequent shootout. Most people on the street were buzzing about the derring-do involved, the fireworks. Most poignant to me was that Jonathan was only seventeen years old. Here was a kid younger than I who put his very life on the line because he still believed in dreams. Had to believe in them, that is, if he really thought he could pull off such a stunt. I understood dreams, idealism. I understood living in the future. But the trick is to know when the future has arrived.

Almost as soon as I finished reading the story I knew I was out of the drug life. The truth of that proposition was as clear as the bright caps of angry ocean waves hurtling toward a shore in clear darkness. A rhythmically sparkling clarity to which one who is amid the turbulence of the sea would be blind. That afternoon I visited my father. After watching a baseball game on television I announced I was spending the night. Dad was at the post office by then working the night shift, and I was certain to have the solitude I needed when I invited that often feared jones to come on down.

Oh, the stomach cramps were there, the runny nose, the diarrhea, the chills alternating with outbursts of sweat. The first night was the worst of course, with no sleep to be had. But I rolled to and fro across the sheets, actually welcoming the struggle, the fluorescent peaks of those waves collapsing just before me. The images I hadn't gathered myself to decipher. Yo-yo heads bobbing up and down in nods of escapism decorating

Northern Boulevard, Lenox Avenue, Eighth Avenue, Avenue D. Gorgeous women transformed into apparitions of slurred speech and desperate thighs. Everyone scratching, lazily slapping their own faces. Yellow-eyed hepatitis sufferers. The man who needed no needle because he kept holes in his arm large enough to drip dope into them directly from the dropper. Spike marks in necks. Alongside vaginas. On penises. Drops of blood on my diploma because I got careless while showing it off to win a bet. Shoving ice down Gary's drawers after an overdose. Shooting a salt shot in his arms, walking him back to consciousness.

I welcomed it all, the sight, the roar. Keith was going to college.

9

Conclusion

With a rap or two of the magistrate's gavel punctuating my junior high school experience, I reached new sociolinguistic heights. I had successfully wielded language as an instrument of power in the often-intimidating world of the legal system. This tactical success gave me greater confidence than ever in my ability to manage impression in novel situations, using language as the primary device, and it also served as dramatic notice of a truth I was well aware of by then: inadequate language skills would not be my downfall. By the close of eighth grade, with my reading level at a solid 12.2 according to my performance on the Metropolitan Achievement Exam and with a healthy 86 percentile ranking on the Iowa Test of Educational Development (see Table 4 in Appendix), I had moved far beyond any barrier constructed solely with Standard English. A major purpose of this book has been to describe this movement, yet this book is not simply about positive accomplishments. Contrary to what some might have anticipated, mastery of the standard dialect did not in and of itself lead to outstanding formal academic progress and, as the narrative indicates, I foundered badly.

My average in academic subjects dropped from 84 at the end of seventh grade to 79 at the close of eighth grade to 70 at the close of ninth grade. As indicated, I made a comeback upon entering Stuyvesant High, finishing the tenth grade with a 90.2 average for the spring semester. In the process of doing so I scored the previously reported 100 on the Regents Examination in Geometry, received a grade of 94 in English, and earned a 91 in Spanish II (after failing Spanish I with a 55 just one year earlier).

Then the heroin usage began and the grades plummeted once again. I averaged 78 for the latter half of my junior year and 61.7 the last half of my senior year, this last feat highlighted by the 40 in English and 56 general absences. I was torn between institutions, between value systems. At times the tug of school was greater, therefore the 90.2 average. On other occasions the streets were a more powerful lure, thus the heroin and the

40 in English and a brief visit to the Adolescent Remand Shelter. (I couldn't talk my way out of that one.) I saw no middle ground or, more accurately, no total ground on which anomalies like me could gather. I tried to be a hip schoolboy, but it was impossible to achieve that persona. In the group I most loved, to be fully hip meant to repudiate a school system in which African-American consciousness was undervalued or ignored; in which, in spite of the many nightmares around us, I was urged to keep my mind on the Dream, to play the fortunate token, to keep my head straight down in my books and "make it." And I pumped more and more dope into my arms. It was a nearly fatal response, but an almost inevitable one.

Several recent and popular books can be used to shed further light on my predicament. In fact, *Hunger of Memory* by Richard Rodriguez (1983) helped motivate me to produce this present work. Rodriguez, a Mexican-American, reveals the storm of torment he has weathered in order to assimilate into the culture of mainstream America. He has chased the middle-class dream and caught it, but the psychic costs have been enormous, as he himself well knows. He has suffered alienation to the point of feeling apart from his own family, has virtually given up his native tongue, has zealously pursued the ideals of his upper-middle-class companions, has endured the caustic rebuttals of opponents who dislike his anti-affirmative action and anti-bilingual education views, and he has felt that all the pain has been worth it. Whether it has indeed been worth it is something only Rodriguez can decide, in fact, must decide, but he is mistaken to advocate an educational policy under which his type of pain is to be justified rather than prevented. Early on in his book he writes, "I remember what was so grievously lost to define what was necessarily gained" (p. 6); I immediately scribbled a question in the margin: But was it necessarily lost? The answer, however, is not easily arrived at. Of course it (his culture) was necessarily lost inasmuch as he chose to give it up. What one does is necessary in one's own eyes. But in a larger sense, we are asking if such cultural loss is a desirable aim of public education, and this question has only one answer: No! More specifically, getting back to the issue of language, the eradication of one tongue is not prerequisite to the learning of a second. Rodriguez participated in such self-annihilation *for as long as he did* because he thought it benefited him personally. It would be tragic, however, to translate his own appraisal of his pain into pedagogy.

Rodriguez asserts that "radical educationalists meanwhile complain that ghetto schools 'oppress' students by trying to mold them, stifling native characteristics. The truer critique would be just the reverse: not that schools change ghetto students too much, but while they may promote the occasional scholarship student, they change most students barely at all" (p. 68). If one has ever watched the gleam in the eyes of kindergarteners fade to smoldering anger before they even reach adolescence, if the children Kohl or Kozol or Levy or Fader or Collins has taught are at all real characters, then one knows all too much about some of the damaging changes that the public school system has wrought.

Rodriguez just ignores reality. His thinking is characterized by the failure to stretch his own arguments out to logical conclusions, by the passing off of his own transactional choices as outer-determined inevitabilities, again, by pushing his pain as policy instead of using it to question policy. One would expect him to fumble a discussion of Black English and, predictably, he delivers:

> I remember the black political activists who have argued in favor of using black English in schools. (Their argument varies only slightly from that made by foreign-language bilingualists.) I have heard "radical" linguists make the point that black English is a complex and intricate version of English. And I do not doubt it. But neither do I think that black English should be a language of public instruction. What makes black English inappropriate in classrooms is not something *in* the language. It is rather what lower-class speakers make of it. Just as Spanish would have been a dangerous language for me to have used at the start of my education, so black English would be a dangerous language to use in the schooling of teenagers for whom it reinforces feelings of public separateness. (pp. 33–34)

Rodriguez has surely hit upon a dilemma, one not to be taken lightly. But I think the most potentially dangerous thing concerning public education is to allow it to remain pretty much as it has been. Important works concerning language instruction, several of which I have cited thus far, contain quite clear warnings against suppressing students' language. Such action helps create failing students, provides an inadequate support system for scholarship students, and may promote within the latter group negative self-concepts. Rodriguez is aware of these dangers, particularly those involving scholarship students. After all, he was a victim himself. However, he doesn't see that part of the solution to the problem lies in using the children's own languages in school. He insists on cultural suicide, a conclusion totally unappealing to me, one I rejected as an adolescent.

John Edgar Wideman's book, *Brothers and Keepers* (1984), provides related insights. Wideman, whose career has been even more distinguished than that of Rodriguez, has lived through a similar process of cultural self-denial. Part of what makes his book more refreshing to me, though, is that he is still trying to come to grips with his personal history; he doesn't ask anyone to emulate him. Much of this critical self-examination is motivated by the guilt he feels over the fact that his brother is doing a life sentence for murder; nevertheless, his self-exploration is quite honest and revealing.

A question that keeps nagging Wideman is this: How could he and his brother, both from the same background, undergo such vastly different experiences? But actually the answer is not all that complicated. They had different visions. John, a child of the fifties, strongly identified with mainstream America, and like Rodriguez, he was willing to commit cultural suicide to gain membership. He writes:

> To get ahead, to make something of myself, college had seemed a logical, necessary step; my exile, my flight from home began with good grades, with good English, with setting myself apart long before I'd earned a scholarship and a train ticket over the mountains to Philadelphia. With that willed alienation behind me, between us, guilt was predictable. One measure of my success was the distance I'd put between us. Coming home was a kind of bragging, like the suntans people bring back from Hawaii in the middle of winter. It's sure fucked up around here, ain't it? But look at me, I got away. I got mine. I didn't want to be caught looking back. I needed home to reassure myself of how far I'd come. If I ever doubted how good I had it away at school in that world of books, exams, pretty, rich white girls, a roommate from Long Island who unpacked more pairs of brand-new jockey shorts and T-shirts than they had in Kaufmann's department store, if I ever had any hesitations or reconsiderations

> about the path I'd chosen, youall were back home in the ghetto to remind me how lucky I was. (p. 27)

I had no desire, as John did, to alienate myself from my community.

Robby Wideman, a child of the sixties, ten years John's junior, only fourteen months older than I, did not, as I did not, share his brother's aspirations. His adolescent perspective could be summed up as follows:

> In the real world, the world left for me, it was unacceptable to be "good," it was square to be smart in school, it was cool to be cold to your woman and the people that loved you. The things we liked we called "bad." "Man, that was a bad girl." The world of the angry black kid growing up in the sixties was a world in which to be in was to be out—out of touch with the square world and all of its rules on what's right and wrong. The thing was to make your own rules, do your own thing, but make sure it's contrary to what society says or is. (p. 58)

Robby's reasoning was the type of reasoning that often made sense to me. It was more than coincidence, therefore, that in the summer of 1968 we both took that hard fall down into the world of heroin addiction. Robby just didn't make it back in time to avoid prison.

No one paid more for the type of cultural conflict being discussed here than Edmund Perry. He lost his life. A teenager from Harlem, Perry finished four years at Phillips Exeter, one of the most prestigious prep schools in the country, only to be killed less than two weeks after graduation, allegedly during the act of mugging an undercover police officer. A cop's bullet canceled Edmund's full scholarship to Stanford University. Edmund's brother, Jonah, a student at Cornell University, was tried as an accomplice but was subsequently acquitted. During the furor surrounding the case, when the Perry boys were symbols of general Black rage directed at the police department or useful icons for self-serving types, one thing became increasingly clear. Not many people, especially Blacks, allowed for the complexity of Edmund or Jonah. Reporter Robert Sam Anson (1987) illustrates this point well in *Best Intentions*. The argument that scholarship students couldn't be involved in street crime is a shallow conception. I happen to think the Perrys were guilty. I was saddened by the event but not surprised at all. The very day Edmund Perry died, I took my oral examinations at New York University. As the last step in earning a doctorate in English Education, I was called upon to discuss much of the information contained in the book now before you.

It is significant to note that many of the students Anson interviewed at Exeter said that Edmund was too hung up on "Blackness," said that they had grown tired of hearing it. Easy enough for them to say, it wasn't their immediate problem. Many educators, however, must continue to listen. Edmund Perry wasn't the last person to suffer a kind of enforced educational schizophrenia, and the world is a more complex place than a Michael Jackson video in which the Harlem-boy-at-prep-school dilemma is resolved with a series of sublime dance steps capped by a sermon. As part of the present movement for educational reform, along with the call for increased salaries, professionalization, greater teacher input in shaping curriculum, mandatory preschool, less powerful bureaucracies, and so on, there must be an insistence that educators understand and indicate by their actions the importance of cultural and linguistic pluralism in educational settings. Why fight for better salaries for teachers so they can do a higher paid job of alienating and attempting to eradicate?

That teachers break the confines of monoculturalism is more crucial than ever before. It has been suggested in some circles, given the history of Black-White classroom confrontations, that the solution is an increase in the number of African-American teachers. If such candidates were not into cultural self-denial (a phenomenon too widespread), it seems a reasonable remedy and, indeed, there is no question that the recruitment of minority teachers should be a priority. Nonetheless, current data show that the percentage of African-American public school teachers is decreasing and probably will continue to do so. Whitaker (1989) reports that because of low pay, undesirable work conditions, and overall frustration with school systems, African-Americans are shunning careers in education. It is predicted, he reveals, that by the turn of the century 40 percent of the students in public schools will be Black while less than 5 percent of the teachers will be so.

Aside from this specific concern, demographics indicate that schools all over the nation are becoming more and more ethnically diverse. Raspberry (1988) reports that ethnic diversity is potentially upsetting to the "civic paradise" of Minneapolis–St. Paul: "For the first time, whites are on the way to becoming a minority in Twin Cities public schools. The new immigrants include Filipinos, Vietnamese, Hmong from Laos and an influx of blacks quite different from the upwardly mobile managers, technicians and educators the area is used to dealing with" (p. 3B).

As this whole educational enterprise proceeds inexorably but unsteadily toward the twenty-first century, language educators in particular must prepare themselves to function productively in multicultural classrooms. Terry Dean (1989) has suggested specific techniques that may be useful. Having worked with students from over thirty ethnic groups, he assigns writing topics about culture itself, about language itself, to ensure that student-centered discussions of difference, collision, and assimilation, are central to the course of study. Dean understands that "how students handle the cultural transitions that occur in the acquisition of academic discourse affects how successfully they acquire that discourse" (p. 23). Add a multicultural literature to the mix and you have a good start toward a model language arts classroom.

Over the years, roughly 85 percent of Dean's students have expressed the belief that they do not have to give up their home and cultural values to succeed in school. This has been the attitude of thousands of African-Americans all along. What has been commonly referred to by educators as "failure" to learn Standard English is more accurately termed an act of resistance: Black students affirming, through Black English, their sense of self in the face of a school system and society that deny the same. It is not at all shocking to me, as it was to many, that a more recent study by Labov (see Stevens 1985) demonstrates that the language of many Blacks is diverging more and more from Standard English. With continued lack of equal opportunity in many areas, with increased racial polarization, only those who underestimate the significance of language as a symbol of protest or group solidarity could expect otherwise.

It can be said that the cultural conflict that has confronted African-Americans in schools "got me later," as it did Robby Wideman and Edmund Perry. However, it finished off many students "sooner," caused them to shrink away from formal education before they could gain or, more importantly, even appreciate the enormous power to be had through encounters with a wide variety of books, of articles, of conversations, and by way of writing, through encounters with their innermost selves. These students were helped to fail before they could fully develop the sociolinguistic ability necessary to educate themselves.

. . . and mostly they lead marginal lives of regret and self-blame and eventually they preach to their children about, uh hunh, the virtues of the school system. . . .

I have tried to show in this book that language instruction and school education in general can only be a widespread success, in the humanitarian sense of the word, when teachers stop assuming that students are inferior and/or have nothing to contribute to the educative process other than to sit and absorb. I don't know all that must be done, however, to break the cycle of failure. But to successfully challenge current practices that justify eradicationist attempts aimed against African-American identity and the language variety in which that identity is most clearly realized is a worthwhile place to begin.

Appendix: Records

Tables 1–4 have been retyped because the print quality of the original documents is too poor for reproduction purposes.

TABLE 1 Guidance Data

Date	Outstanding Abilities
6–64	Raymond is an eloquent speaker and very much interested in social studies. He is also a fine athlete.
	Outstanding Disabilities
6–61	Father not living with family. Raymond needs supervision.
	Outstanding Interests
6–63	Poetry—Creative writing.

TABLE 2

PERSONALITY (Check one in each group with an X)		CLASS								
		K-1	1-1	1–4	1–3	2–1	3–1	4–1	5–1	6–1
RELATIONSHIP TO OTHER CHILDREN	A. Works and plays well with others.	X	X	X	X			X	X	X
	B. Does not get along well with others.					X	X			
ATTITUDE TOWARD GROUP CONTROL	A. Usually non-conforming.									
	B. Occasionally resents group control.	X				X	X	X	X	X
	C. Responds well to group control.		X	X	X					
LEADERSHIP	A. Good leader, accepted by others.	X	X						X	X
	B. Fair leader on occasion.			X	X	X	X	X		
	C. Does not possess leadership qualities.									
RESPONSIBILITY	A. Usually not dependable.									
	B. Occasionally evades responsibility.					X	X	X	X	X
	C. Usually dependable.	X	X	X	X					

PERSONALITY (Check one in each group with an X)		CLASS								
		K-1	1-1	1-4	1-3	2-1	3-1	4-1	5-1	6-1
NEED FOR ATTENTION	A. Requires inordinate amount of attention.									
	B. Satisfied with reasonable amount of attention.	X	X	X	X	X	X	X	X	X
STABILITY	A. Usually well controlled.	X	X	X	X	X	X	X	X	X
	B. Occasional temper outbursts.									
	C. Frequent temper outbursts.									
AGGRESSIVENESS	A. Does not assert himself.									
	B. Moderately aggressive.	X	X	X	X	X	X	X	X	X
	C. Over-aggressive, fights frequently.									
SOCIAL PARTICIPATION	A. Shy, withdrawn, does not participate.									
	B. Participates actively in group projects.	X	X	X	X	X	X	X	X	X
SELF CONFIDENCE	A. Usually works with confidence.	X	X	X	X	X	X	X	X	X
	B. Needs frequent encouragement.									
	C. Lacks confidence, needs constant encouragement.									
ACTIVITY	A. Usually lethargic.									
	B. Normally energetic.	X	X	X	X	X	X	X	X	X
	C. Usually restless, hyperactive.									
WORK HABITS	A. Rarely attends to work.									
	B. Generally works with sustained attention.									
	C. Works with sustained attention.	X	X	X	X	X	X	X	X	X
INITIATIVE	A. Frequently makes original contribution.	X	X	X	X	X	X	X	X	X
	B. Requires direction.									
NERVOUS HABITS	A. Has numerous nervous habits.									
	B. Is relatively free of nervous habits.	X	X	X	X	X	X	X	X	X

PERSONALITY (Check one in each group with an X)		CLASS K-1	1-1	1-4	1-3	2-1	3-1	4-1	5-1	6-1
RELATIONSHIP TO PARENTS	A. Seems free in relationship to parents.	X	X	X	X					
	B. Parent-child relationship seems disturbed.					X	X	X	?	

TABLE 3

YEAR BEGINNING		SEPT 1957	SEPT 1958	SEPT 1959	SEPT 1959	SEPT 1959	SEPT 1960	SEPT 1961	SEPT 1962	SEPT 1963
LANGUAGE ARTS	READING		S	S	S	S	S	E	E	E
	WRITTEN COMMUNICATION					S	S	G	E	E
	SPELLING					S	S	G	E	E
	HANDWRITING			S	S	S	S	G	E	E
	ORAL COMMUNICATION	S	S	S	S	S	S	G	G	E
	APPRECIATION (LITERATURE GRADE 7 & 8)					S				
	GENERAL RATING					S	S	G	E	E
SOCIAL LIVING			S	S	S	N	N	F	F	G

TABLE 4 Examinations

Date	Exam	Result
10–65	Iowa	86th percentile composite score
1–65	Met. Rdg.	11.0
10–65	Met. Rdg.	12.4
5–66	Met. Rdg.	12.2
4–67	Met. Rdg.	12.3

FIGURE 1

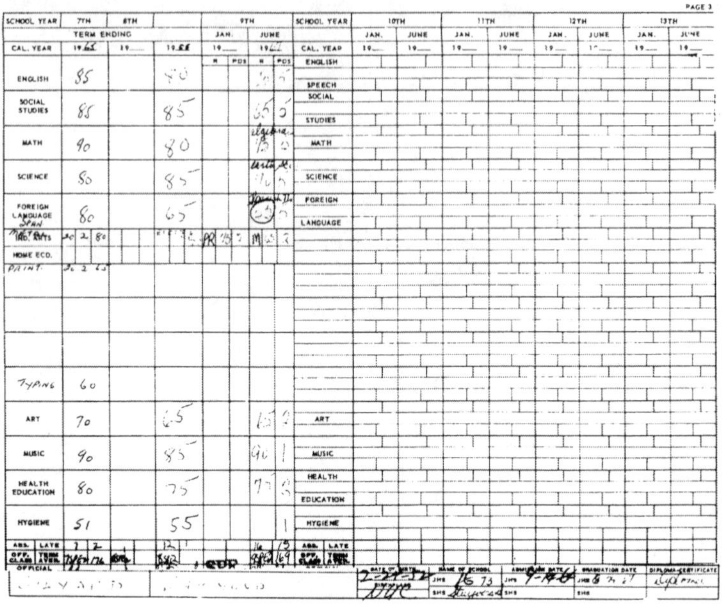
PAGE 3

SCHOOL YEAR	7TH	8TH		9TH JAN.	9TH JUNE
CAL. YEAR	19 65	19__	19 66	19__	19 67
ENGLISH	85		80		
SOCIAL STUDIES	85		85		65
MATH	90		80		Algebra
SCIENCE	80		85		Earth Sc.
FOREIGN LANGUAGE SPAN	80		65		Spanish
TYPING	60				
ART	70		65		
MUSIC	90		85		90
HEALTH EDUCATION	80		75		77
HYGIENE	51		55		

FIGURE 2

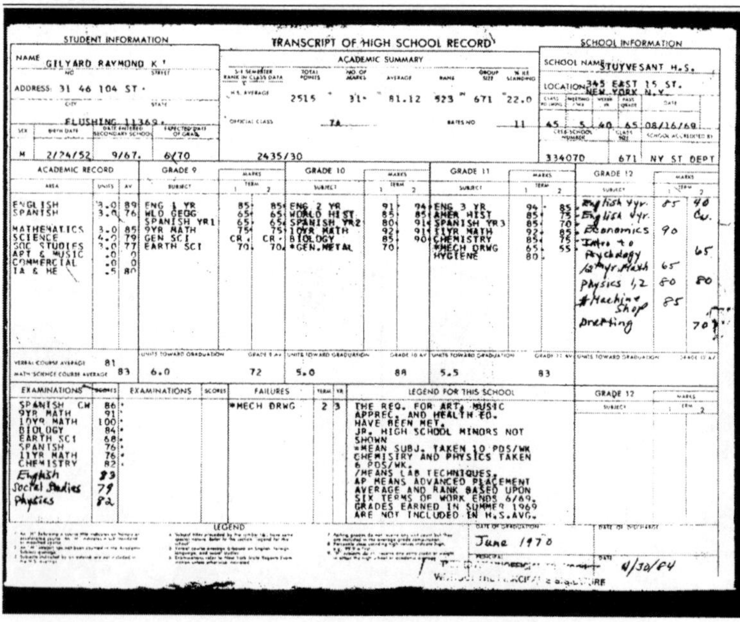
TRANSCRIPT OF HIGH SCHOOL RECORD

STUDENT INFORMATION

NAME GILYARD RAYMOND K

ADDRESS: 31 46 104 ST.

FLUSHING 11369.

SEX M | BIRTH DATE 2/24/52 | DATE ENTERED SECONDARY SCHOOL 9/67. | EXPECTED DATE OF GRAD. 6/70

ACADEMIC SUMMARY

H.S. AVERAGE | TOTAL POINTS 2515 | NO. OF MARKS 31 | AVERAGE 81.12 | RANK 523 | GROUP SIZE 671 | % RE STANDING 22.0

OFFICIAL CLASS 7A | RATES NO 11

2435/30

SCHOOL INFORMATION

SCHOOL NAME STUYVESANT H.S.

LOCATION 345 EAST 15 ST. NEW YORK N.Y.

45 | 5 | 40 | 65 | 08/16/69

CEEB SCHOOL NUMBER 334070 | CLASS SIZE 671 | SCHOOL ACCREDITED BY NY ST DEPT

ACADEMIC RECORD AREA	UNITS	AV
ENGLISH	3.0	89
SPANISH	3.0	76
MATHEMATICS	3.0	85
SCIENCE	4.0	79
SOC STUDIES	3.0	77
ART & MUSIC	.0	0
COMMERCIAL	.0	0
IA & HE	.5	80

VERBAL COURSE AVERAGE 81
MATH SCIENCE COURSE AVERAGE 83

GRADE 9 SUBJECT	TERM 1	TERM 2
ENG 1 YR	85	85
WLD GEOG	65	65
SPANISH YR1	65	65
9YR MATH	75	75
GEN SCI	CR	CR
EARTH SCI	70	70

UNITS TOWARD GRADUATION 6.0 | GRADE 9 AV 72

GRADE 10 SUBJECT	TERM 1	TERM 2
ENG 2 YR	91	94
WORLD HIST	85	85
SPANISH YR2	80	91
10YR MATH	92	91
BIOLOGY	85	90
*GEN.METAL	70	

UNITS TOWARD GRADUATION 5.0 | GRADE 10 AV 88

GRADE 11 SUBJECT	TERM 1	TERM 2
ENG 3 YR	94	85
AMER HIST	85	75
SPANISH YR3	85	70
11YR MATH	92	85
CHEMISTRY	85	75
*MECH DRWG	65	55
HYGIENE	80	

UNITS TOWARD GRADUATION 5.5 | GRADE 11 AV 83

GRADE 12 SUBJECT	TERM 1	TERM 2
English 4yr.	85	40
English 4yr.		Cu.
Economics	90	
Intro to Psychology		65
12th yr. Math	65	
Physics 1,2	80	80
#Machine Shop	85	
Drafting		70

EXAMINATIONS	SCORES
SPANISH CH	86
9YR MATH	91
10YR MATH	100
BIOLOGY	84
EARTH SCI	68
SPANISH	76
11YR MATH	76
CHEMISTRY	82
English	83
Social Studies	79
Physics	82

FAILURES	TERM	YR
*MECH DRWG	2	3

LEGEND FOR THIS SCHOOL

THE REQ. FOR ART, MUSIC APPREC. AND HEALTH ED. HAVE BEEN MET.
JR. HIGH SCHOOL MINORS NOT SHOWN
*MEAN SUBJ. TAKEN 10 PDS/WK
CHEMISTRY AND PHYSICS TAKEN 6 PDS/WK.
/MEANS LAB TECHNIQUES.
AP MEANS ADVANCED PLACEMENT
AVERAGE AND RANK BASED UPON SIX TERMS OF WORK ENDS 6/69.
GRADES EARNED IN SUMMER 1969 ARE NOT INCLUDED IN H.S.AVG.

DATE OF GRADUATION June 1970

DATE 4/30/84

References

Anson, R. S. 1987. *Best intentions: The education and killing of Edmund Perry*. New York: Random House.

Baratz, J. C. 1969. Who should do what to whom . . . and why? *Florida FL Reporter* 7 (Spring/Summer): 75–77, 158–59.

Beck, M. S. 1979. *Baby talk: How your child learns to speak*. New York: Plume.

Bereiter, C., & Engelmann, S. 1966. *Teaching disadvantaged children in the preschool*. Englewood Cliffs, NJ: Prentice Hall.

Bissex, G. L. 1980. *Gnys at wrk: A child learns to write and read*. Cambridge, MA: Harvard Univ. Press.

Britton, J. 1972. *Language and learning*. Harmondsworth: Penguin. Originally published 1970.

Britton, J. 1982. English teaching: Retrospect and prospect. In *Prospect and retrospect: Selected essays of James Britton*, ed. G. M. Pradl, 201–15. Montclair, NJ: Boynton/Cook. Reprinted from *English in the eighties*, papers presented at the Third International Conference on the Teaching of English, Sydney, 1980.

Burling, R. 1973. *English in black and white*. New York: Holt, Rinehart and Winston.

Byers, P., & Byers, H. 1972. Nonverbal communication and the education of children. In Cazden et al., 3–31.

Cazden, C. B., John, V. P., & Hymes, D., eds. 1972. *Functions of language in the classroom*. New York: Teachers College Press.

Chomsky, N. 1957. *Syntactic structures*. The Hague: Mouton.

Chomsky, N. 1972. *Language and mind*. Rev. ed. New York: Harcourt, Brace and Jovanovich.

Collins, M., & Tamarkin, C. 1982. *Marva Collins' way*. Los Angeles: Tarcher.

Corbett, E. P. J., ed. 1974. Students' right to their own language. *College Composition and Communication* 25 (Fall). Special issue.

Dean, T. 1989. Multicultural classrooms, monocultural teachers. *College Composition and Communication* 40 (1): 23–37.

Dillard, J. L. 1973. *Black English: Its history and usage in the United States*. New York: Vintage. Originally published 1972.

Eisner, E. 1981. On the differences between scientific and artistic approaches to qualitative research. *Educational Researcher* (April): 5–9.

Elgin, S. H. 1979. *What is linguistics?* 2d ed. Englewood Cliffs, NJ: Prentice Hall.

Fader, D. 1971. *The naked children*. New York: Macmillan.

Fishman, J. A., & Leuders-Salmon, E. 1972. What has the sociology of language to say to the teacher? On teaching the standard variety to speakers of dialectal or sociolectal varieties. In Cazden et al., 67–83.

Flesch, R. 1955. *Why Johnny can't read—And what you can do about it*. New York: Harper & Row.

Flesch, R. 1981. *Why Johnny still can't read: A new look at the scandal of our schools*. New York: Harper Colophon.

Geertz, C. 1973. *The interpretation of cultures*. New York: Basic Books.

Goffman, E. 1959. *The presentation of self in everyday life*. Garden City, NY: Doubleday Anchor.

Goodman, K. S. 1967. Reading: A psycholinguistic guessing game. *Journal of the Reading Specialist* 4: 126–35.

Greer, C. 1976. *The great school legend: A revisionist interpretation of American public education*. New York: Penguin. Originally published 1972.

Haskins, J., & Butts, H. F. 1973. *The psychology of Black language*. New York: Barnes & Noble.

Holdaway, D. 1979. *The foundations of literacy*. Sydney: Ashton Scholastic.

Hudson, R. A. 1980. *Sociolinguistics*. Cambridge: Cambridge Univ. Press.

Isakson, R. L. 1979. Cognitive processing in sentence comprehension. *Journal of Educational Research* 72: 160–65.

Jensen, A. R. 1969. How much can we boost IQ and scholastic achievement? *Harvard Educational Review* 39: 1–123.

Joiner, C. W. 1979. Memorandum opinion and order on civil action 7-71861, Martin Luther King Junior Elementary School children et al. vs. Ann Arbor School District Board. 473 F. Supp. 1371 (E. D. Mich. 1979).

Jones, R. 1982. What's wrong with Black English. *Newsweek*, December 27, p. 7.

Kelly, G. A. 1963. *A theory of personality: The psychology of personal constructs*. New York: Norton.

Kohl, H. 1968. *36 children*. New York: Signet. Originally published 1967.

Kozol, J. 1968. *Death at an early age*. New York: Bantam.

Labov, W. 1972. *Language in the inner city: Studies in the Black English Vernacular*. Philadelphia: Univ. of Pennsylvania Press.

Labov, W. 1981. *The study of nonstandard English*. Rev. ed. Urbana: NCTE.

Levy, G. E. 1970. *Ghetto school: Class warfare in an elementary school*. Indianapolis: Pegasus.

Martin, N., Williams, P., Wilding, J., Hemming, S., & Medway, P. 1976. *Understanding children talking*. Harmondsworth: Penguin.

Mayher, J. S., Lester, N., & Pradl, G. M. 1983. *Learning to write/writing to learn.* Upper Montclair, NJ: Boynton/Cook.

McCracken, G., & Walcutt, C. C. 1963. *Basic reading: Teacher's edition for the pre-primer and primer*. Philadelphia: Lippincott.

O'Neil, W. 1973. The politics of bidialectalism. In *Black language reader* ed. R. H. Bentley & S. D. Crawford, 184–91. Glenview, IL: Scott, Foresman. Reprinted from *The Politics of Literature*, ed. L. Kampf & P. Lauter. Random House, 1970.

Penalosa, F. 1981. *Introduction to the sociology of language*. Rowley, MA: Newbury.

Perkins, E. 1975. *Home is a dirty street: The social oppression of Black children.* Chicago: Third World Press.

Perkinson, H. J. 1977. *The imperfect panacea: American faith in education. 1865–1976*. 2nd ed. New York: Random House.

Philips, S. U. 1972. Participant structures and communicative competence: Warm springs children in community and classroom. In Cazden et al., 370–94.

Purkey, W. W. 1970. *Self concept and school achievement*. Englewood Cliffs, NJ: Prentice Hall.

Raspberry, W. 1988. 'Diversity' changing twin cities' schools. *St. Louis Post-Dispatch*, November 21, 3B.

Rodriguez, R. 1983. *Hunger of memory: The education of Richard Rodriguez*. New York: Bantam. Originally published 1982.

Rogers, C. 1982. *A social psychology of schooling*. London: Routledge & Kegan Paul.

Rosenthal, R., & Jacobson, L. 1968. *Pygmalion in the classroom*. New York: Holt, Rinehart and Winston.

Rouse, J. 1978. *The completed gesture: Myth, character and education*. NJ: Skyline Books.

Sledd, J. 1973. Doublespeak: Dialectology in the service of Big Brother. In *Black language reader*, ed. R. H. Bentley & S. D. Crawford, 191–214. Glenview, IL: Scott, Foresman. Reprinted from *College English*, January 1972.

Sledd, J. 1983. In defense of students' right. *College English* 45: 667–75.

Smith, F. 1971. *Understanding reading*. New York: Holt, Rinehart and Winston.

Smith, F. 1979. *Reading without nonsense*. New York: Teachers College Press.

Smith, F. 1980. Making sense of reading—And of reading instruction. In *Thought & language/language and reading*, ed. M. Wolf, M. McQuillan, & E. Radwin, 415–24. Cambridge, MA: Harvard Educational Review. Reprinted from *Harvard Educational Review*, 1977.

Smitherman, G. 1977. *Talkin and testifyin: The language of Black America*. Boston: Houghton Mifflin.

Spache, G. 1964. *Reading in the elementary school*. Boston: Allyn and Bacon.

Stevens, W. K. 1985. Study finds Blacks' English increasingly different. *New York Times*, March 15, A14.

Stewart, W. A. 1969. Urban negro speech: Sociolinguistic factors affecting English teaching. *Florida FL Reporter* 7 (Spring/Summer): 50–53, 166. Reprinted from *Social Dialects and Language Learning*, 1965.

Taylor, D. 1983. *Family literacy*. Exeter, NH: Heineman.

Troike, R. C. 1972. Receptive bidialectalism: Implications for second-dialect teaching. In *Language and cultural diversity in American education*, ed. R. D. Abrahams & R. C. Troike, 305–10. Englewood Cliffs, NJ: Prentice Hall.

Trudgill, P. 1974. *Sociolinguistics: An introduction*. Harmondsworth: Penguin.

Whitaker, C. 1989. The disappearing black teacher. *Ebony*, January, 122–26.

Wideman, J. E. 1984. *Brothers and keepers*. New York: Holt, Rinehart and Winston.

Williams, F. 1973. Some research notes on dialect attitudes and stereotypes. In *Language attitudes: Current trends and prospects*, ed. R. W. Shuy & W. Fasold, 113–28. Washington, DC: Georgetown Univ. Press.

Wright, R. 1966. *Black boy: A record of childhood and youth*. New York: Harper & Row. Originally published 1945.

Index

Let's Flip the Script

AN AFRICAN AMERICAN DISCOURSE ON LANGUAGE, LITERATURE, AND LEARNING

Contents

Introduction

Much to my benefit, I have friends and colleagues who encourage me to say things about language and education, particularly with respect to African Americans. They solicit writing, invite me to forums, and prop me up at podiums. They generally seek insight, decisiveness, and controversy, though I wonder sometimes which they most prefer. Notwithstanding, I am thankful for the opportunities to influence discussion and, possibly, to shape actual maneuvers. The eleven essays in this book, each written upon request, indicate the major themes with which I have been concerned during the past five years. They furthermore represent my overall attempt to shift discourses and activities, to turn the tide or flip the script.

The first two essays, "A Heightened Sense of Language" and "The Social Responsibility That Writing Is," deal pointedly with confluences of language and politics. Within the context of considering diversity issues, I demonstrate how language resonates politically and how value-laden writing pedagogy is. Although I admittedly digress a bit, my specific purpose is to spark resistance to counterproductive language arts instruction.

The next three essays comprise a sort of unit on literature and teaching. When my 1980s research in sociolinguistics made me conscious of the frequency with which musings about linguistic strength and weakness constituted motifs in African American literary works, I began to write a series of pieces reflecting this understanding. "Genopsycholinguisticide and the Language Theme in African American Fiction" is the most expansive. "Tucept HighJohn and the Limits of Language Programming" carries the argument and way of reading a step further, and "Julius and Jesse in 003" shows how the critical agenda I pursued can meaningfully inform writing classrooms.

The remaining essays can profitably stand alone. "One More Time for Professor Nuruddin" is a "knowledge loan" to Yusuf Nuruddin, the resident scholar of Bedford-Stuyvesant. I have tried to lay out in concise and accessible fashion the origin, development, and educational implications of Africanized forms of English. It is a pleasure to do so, but Yusuf still has to pay me back.

"Language Learning and Democratic Development" is in many ways a homage to the "NYU crew." In consulting and learning with people affiliated with New York University's Program in English Education, some of whom I'll name later, I was pressed to consider seriously, always with the intent of shaking things up, notions of democracy and their relationship to various educational practices.

"African American in Process" investigates the claim, to which Lisa Delpit's work is central, that writing-process methodology is inappropriate for African American students. I argue, conversely, that process instruction is indeed fitting instruction for such students and that teachers can more fruitfully challenge the abuse of process methods than the process paradigm itself.

"A Legacy of Healing" largely examines the generative power of African American folkloric, literary, and educational traditions with the idea of harnessing some of that power to revamp schooling. In addition, recounting my role in one contentious discussion of education, I aim to illustrate briefly how language theorists can contribute to practical debates.

"Getting Off the Hook" encodes my obligation to respond to *The Bell Curve*. There is hardly need for further prefatory comment on this score. On its own, the essay won't win an intellectual tug of war with the Herrnstein and Murray book, but I know there's plenty of help out there, with more coming.

Writing the closing essay, "Playing with the Patterns," was perhaps the most fun. I have tried to account for the early influences on my present teaching beliefs and style. Such an autobiographical attempt inevitably falls somewhat shy of the mark, but I think it reveals valuable perspectives on (dis)connections between curricular and extracurricular activity.

This book should especially please those who put me up to it. I was not always an eager participant, and I am even tempted to abandon protocol at this point and take sole credit for whatever good parts there may be and blame them for the faults. Most of them would appreciate that bit of mischief, but I'll refrain and give propers in the usual way. All kidding aside, they have my utmost gratitude:

Lillian Bridwell-Bowles, former president of the Conference on College Composition and Communication; Geneva Smitherman, solid sista force throughout; Claire Wood and the members of the City University of

New York Writing Centers Association; Kenneth Peeples, editor of *Community Review*; James Raymond, Nancy Johnson, and Reginald Martin, editors of the special African American literature issue of *College English*; Edison O. Jackson, president of Medgar Evers College, CUNY; Frances Degan Horowitz, president of the CUNY Graduate School; Ira Shor and the faculty of CUNY's Ph.D. program in English; Brenda Greene, who pulled me into her NCTE panel on cultural and critical literacy; the students of Medgar Evers College, especially the data producers who have consented to assist; John Garvey of the CUNY Office of Academic Affairs; Rita Brause, Nancy Lester, John Mayher, and Cynthia Onore, that NYU connection; Ruth Vins and Clifford Hill, Teachers College, Columbia University; Yusuf Nuruddin once again, who keeps me on my toes; Clinton Crawford, a positive force as well; Steve Cannon, who forced me into the *Curve*, not to mention many previous ventures; and Richard Larson and Tom McCracken, who sought narrative. I'll even add a tad more.

"Education, education," the youthful man would repeat as his health failed beneath the Georgia sun. "Make sure to educate the boys," he would scribble in the diary to be left for his wife. He in fact had been promised by a friend, a school official, that the friend would see the man's two sons through college. The man also had two daughters, but he had a different vision for them. Quite predictably. It was 1936. But we also know that the twist, the flip, is often the most important part of the tale. One of the man's daughters, nine years old at the time of his death, grew up remembering her father's words. "Education, education," she would stress repeatedly, decades later, to her son, who, most days, is looking for some educational action.

Mad thanks to Charles Otis Lewis and his daughter Mary.

I also want to thank Juanita Horan and George Rhinehart, my colleagues in the Syracuse University Writing Program, for keeping technological breakdowns from becoming nervous ones. And lastly, I wish to acknowledge the contributions of Dr. Teresa M. Redd of Howard University and Dr. Charles Coleman of York College, CUNY. Possessed of brilliant minds and helping spirits, they reviewed the manuscript thoroughly and provided much-needed guidance. "My bad" if it turns out that I have not taken full advantage of their wisdom.

K. G.

LANGUAGE AND POLITICS

A Heightened Sense of Language as Educational and Social Critique

I have long been sensitive to how certain terminology informs my perception, partly because of my role in a mass search for an adequate name. Having been Colored, Negro, Black (sometimes with a lowercase b), Afro-American, and African American (sometimes with a hyphen) all in only four decades, I have had to examine closely several linguistic constructs just to figure out my cultural identity. Also, on a more personal level, I possessed an early sense of language as a tool to be manipulated beyond the purposes of everyday communication. I can recall writing poems as far back as the third grade. A teacher even noted on my permanent record card, a usually dreadful document maintained by the New York City Board of Education, that poetry writing was a great interest of mine. Of course, we know by now that I found my way into the English profession and into print as a poet, two results that do not often enough follow from childhood language experiences such as I have described. My language interest, inventiveness, and playfulness were kept alive and developed, despite various obstacles, and my book *Voices of the Self: A Study of Language Competence* exists as the most noteworthy extension of those urges. Perhaps some brief retrospection about creating the manuscript is appropriate before I comment upon the *Students' Right*[*] resolution and how the doctrine of linguistic equality it champions still sparks arguments. I also

[*]Drafted in 1972, the *Students' Right* resolution was adopted by the Conference on College Composition and Communication in Anaheim in 1974. The resolution affirms "the students' right to their own patterns and varieties of language" and that "teachers must have the experiences and training that will enable them to respect diversity." Later that year, a background statement and a bibliography were included in *College Composition and Communication*.

Presented April 1, 1993, at the Conference on College Composition and Communication at a session linked to a revisiting of *Students' Right to Their Own Language*.

intend, in raising the general question of language awareness, to offer my own sociolinguistic takes on the war in the Persian Gulf and the uprising in Los Angeles, as well as to consider a few terms that are not understood well enough by many educators—namely, *whiteness*, *multiculturalism*, and *dialect interference*.

I arrived at the 1983 convention in Detroit in search of a dissertation topic. Gordon Pradl, the faculty member with whom I worked most closely during my days at New York University, had been encouraging me to conduct research related to Black English Vernacular, as we called it at the time. His suggestion was an outgrowth of discussions about language acquisition in a course he taught. Of particular interest to me was how bidialectal speakers, such as myself, grow to assign values and uses to each dialect, and I began a review of the literature. However, I was not confident about the contribution I could make until I attended a session in Detroit entitled "Black Student Writers and Linguistic Implications for Social Change" and heard Geneva Smitherman cite the need, as a complement to other theoretical work, for self-investigations by those who alternate or code-switch between BEV and Standard English.

I had my project. I dusted off an autobiographical narrative I had shelved several years earlier, decided to make the case academically that it represented a valuable record of bidialectal language development, and planned to pair the story in some way with analyses I would make of selected scholarship pertinent to BEV and education. I consulted works such as Albert E. Stone's *Autobiographical Occasions and Original Acts* and James Olney's *Metaphors of Self*, growing certain in the process that my narrative, though necessarily inaccurate as chronicle, was yet legitimate psychological history. From Elliot Eisner's work, I drew intellectual justification for artistic research, thus ridding myself once and for all of anxiety about validity and the lack of statistical data. In addition, I delved deeper into linguistic and educational literature, coming across assertions such as R. A. Hudson's, in *Sociolinguistics*, that "one of the most solid achievements of linguistics in the twentieth century has been to eliminate the idea (at least among professional linguists) that some languages or dialects are inherently better than others" (191), and J. L. Dillard's, in *Black English*, that "it's possible to characterize a peach as a deficient apple; in fact, it's the only conclusion you can come to if you judge the peach by the apple's standards" (33). I discovered the remark of Joshua Fishman and Erika Lueders-Salmon in "What Has the Sociology of Language to Say to the Teacher?" that "the home and regional speech can be used for many purposes in school" (78). And perhaps most important, I happened upon *Students' Right to Their Own Language*, a special issue of *College Composition and Communication*, a document that synthesizes progressive sociolinguistic thought and mightily informs *Voices of the Self*.

There has been a professional dimension, then, to my heightened language sensibility. In my work I have remained true to the spirit of *Students' Right* and stand ever ready to criticize attitudes and policies about linguistic difference that are harmful to students. Recently, for example, while I was mentoring a group of graduate students who were studying the teaching of basic writing, several principles of linguistic diversity became crucial to our discussion. The notion of linguistic competence—that is, the idea that every speaker has unconsciously mastered the language variety of his or her native community—was easy enough for them to accept. But some took exception to my contention that any such language variety mastered was equal to any other in terms of ability to express concepts. We had a spirited debate. Students made arguments that certain Asians would be unable to say "I want to be left alone" because individualism is not a desirable cultural trait for them, that some languages lack a highly technological or scientific vocabulary, even that Joseph Conrad's choice to write in English must have had something to do with the superiority of the language. My rebuttals, however, flowed easily. Assuming that a yearning for solitude is odd in an Asian culture (and none of my Asian friends and colleagues have assured me that this is categorically the case), it is still not an impossible idea to hold individually or to express linguistically. I could argue for African American political superiority in the United States, a rather remote possibility but not at all difficult to put into words. I can easily enough *say* that Black folk should control all the money, munitions, media, and legislatures. As for terminology, any language can add it, just as *AIDS* has shown up in recent dictionaries. And Conrad's choice had exclusively to do with his feelings toward English, not any particular merits of English itself. Similarly, his choice to be known as Joseph Conrad instead of Jozef Korzeniowski (first and last names) or Jozef Konrad (first and one of several middle names) had nothing to do with the superiority of English names or English spelling, not to mention that one of Conrad's contemporaries, Henryk Sienkiewicz—a Pole writing in Polish—won the Nobel Prize for Literature.

Although our debate centered on comparisons among languages, I stressed that the concept of linguistic equality holds true for dialects of any given language as well. Chauvinism about foreign languages and chauvinism about dialects, an idea more relevant for most writing teachers, are but two sides of the same coin.

An expressly sociolinguistic viewpoint continues to help shape my larger social outlook as well. In fact, it's impossible to distinguish at times between my macro-level social concerns and strictly educational ones because all my language insights eventually find expression in my classrooms and lead to increased awareness about both writing and language in general. A few more examples will underscore this point.

The Persian Gulf War brought us a baffling array of terms such as *aerial sorties* and *collateral damage*, words aimed to distance combat from carnage in the minds of the American public and make the conflict palatable. There have been voluminous remarks in this vein. But I submit, too, that certain justificative language was directed specifically at the African American community by Secretary of State James Baker, who, upon returning from a tense negotiating session with Iraqi representative Tariq Assiz, declared that Assiz had "dissed" him. I had never known Baker to be an aficionado of the African American vernacular—never *could* know from all the Standard English he spoke in public. Is it far-fetched, therefore, to suggest that his use of *dissed* was an effort to pitch the war to the African American community, one overrepresented in the military, in phrasing it could understand and support? Certainly many Black folk, for better or worse, accept the premise that harsh retaliation must follow being "dissed." We witnessed a major demonstration of such thinking after the verdict in the Rodney King case, another situation (w)rapped in language that should be scrutinized. The idea of revolt or organized violence was played down in media reportage, where the explosive aftermath of the verdict was generally characterized as a "riot," a relatively thoughtless outburst.

How you respond to these messages has to do with your political sense, of course. I have no particular interest in that at this point. But even to recognize the issues I am raising reflects the heightened language sensibility I am concerned with as a citizen and educator. Reportage of the war and the King case became subject matter in my courses, a practice in line with the sentiment expressed by participants at the 1987 English Coalition Conference, who wrote in the conference report that one of their goals was to have students "recognize and evaluate the ways in which others use language to affect them" (Lloyd-Jones and Lunsford 19).

Another interesting item for students and teachers to consider is one current proposal for countering social ills: the abolition of the white race—linguistically. This is the position taken by the editors of the journal *Race Traitor*, who view "whiteness" as a construct of privilege and not as a biological or racial descriptor (something it can only be inadequately). As they explain:

> Our primary intended audience consists of those people commonly called "whites" who sense whiteness to be a problem for themselves and others. For these people, "race treason," in our view, best sums up the meaning of consistent opposition to white supremacy. We hope that Afro-Americans [they're a few beats behind with that term] and other people of color will see this project as consistent with their own efforts, and we hope it will stimulate discussion among all opponents of white power. We appreciate the unique contributions that persons of color, who have a wealth of experience with white authority, can make to undermining it, and we invite all interested persons to write for *Race Traitor* and make whatever use of it they can. (Garvey et al. 126–27)

"Race treason" imbues public discourse with freshness, a quality also needed in educational debates. Theorists like John Mayher are keenly aware of this imperative. His trademark word, *uncommonsense*, moves discussion forward in ways that *progressive* and *conservative* do not—at least not any longer. Mayher knows that the theories we hold implicitly are the ones that generally guide us most powerfully. We will not change what we never bother to call into question. Uncommonsense, then, is a strong empirical questioning of common sense ideas and a commitment to examine our received wisdom at the conscious level. It insists upon change, not boisterously, but nonetheless. We can unearth, rather dispassionately, the authoritarian and behaviorist underpinnings of transmission-style instruction. Only through such activity can we meaningfully adopt the developmental and constructionist perspectives we are urged, sometimes in shrill tones, to embrace.

Not all new language, however, serves to clarify. *Multiculturalism* is a case in point. Flawed as an educational concept at the outset, it is now hopelessly clichéd and does what all clichés do: name complex phenomena vaguely. It is best used to describe a population, not an educational program, for any coherent program has to take up deeper questions. How, for example, do we avoid trivializing the struggles of certain groups whose confronting of racism and exclusion led, as was proper, to the rhetoric of multiculturalism in the first place? The more "multi" multiculturalism gets, the more it deflects attention from the cultural contributions of any one ethnic group. So a successful African American challenge, say, to exclusion may subsequently lead, in many current multicultural programs, to virtual re-exclusion. This is not to argue that wide representation is uncalled for; I am merely suggesting that the matter is quite complicated and not resolvable through hackneyed expressions. I have been offering the term *transculturalism* as a better description of certain educational initiatives that emphasize specific transactions among students from various cultural and ethnic backgrounds as opposed to being primarily concerned with "exposure."

I will call attention to one more coinage, *dialect interference*. Although not a new term, I hear it frequently and confusedly associated with writing instruction or, more precisely, writing problems. As such, it requires renewed inspection.

It is a simple matter to demonstrate how any variety of English *may* interfere with the production of an alternative variety. I jotted down the following conversation I had with a student from Jamaica as I was entering the building where I work. She owed me an assignment:

(1) You get my paper, professor?
(2) No, where did you leave it?
(3) I leave it in your mailbox.
(4) When?
(5) I leave it in your mailbox yesterday.

Sentences 3 and 5 represent a Jamaican language variety that features a largely uninflected verb system that marks time by context and helping words such as *yesterday*. *I leave* in each instance represents what we would commonly call first-person past tense. If this student's intention were to write in Standard English and she produced these types of sentences in her texts, dialect interference would be cited by many, somewhat correctly, as the reason. I would add, however, that a nonstandard dialect can only be a writing problem to the extent that the writer relies solely upon native oral resources to meet the demands of writing Standard English. If, to the contrary, strong reading ears and writing voices have been developed relative to Standard English, those tools, not the nonstandard dialect, would dominate writing situations where producing Standard English is the writer's goal. In other words, nonstandard dialect cannot function in isolation as a writing problem. The student who employed in her speech the verb system demonstrated above used no such constructions in any of her papers, most of which were written in class. No dialect correction program is necessary in her case or in the case of any other writer. Time is best spent fostering the differentiation that generally must occur between speech and writing personae.

A librarian in Brooklyn invited me to her institution to make a presentation about African American literature. During the session, I read from several of Charles Chesnutt's Uncle Julius stories, which are written partly in African American Vernacular English. During the ensuing exchange, an African American woman asked me bluntly, "What do you think about Black English?" Before I could answer, she declared, "I hate it." I could not persuade her to feel otherwise (or, at least, she wouldn't admit it), though our dialogue was very time-consuming. In fact, I didn't get to discuss with the audience Chesnutt's considerable literary skill.

In a university workshop, several writing instructors told me quite forcefully that part of their responsibility is to correct the speech of students, an activity that, even if they could do it, which is highly doubtful, contributes nothing, as I hope to have illustrated, to sensible writing instruction. Fortunately, not all their colleagues agreed with them.

These exchanges happened much closer to the millennium than to 1974, when *Students' Right* appeared. A major mission for us is to continue, the best we can, to disturb the intellectual comfort zones of those whose views of language variety would penalize rather than aid students. Our understanding of language and our language itself must be superior if we are to reflect our discipline at its most accomplished level and help move educational programs forward productively.

Works Cited

Corbett, Edward P. J., ed. *Students' Right to Their Own Language*. Special issue of *College Composition and Communication* 25 (Fall 1974).

Dillard, J. L. *Black English: Its History and Usage in the United States*. New York: Vintage, 1973.

Eisner, Elliot. "On the Difference between Scientific and Artistic Approaches to Qualitative Research." *Educational Researcher* (April 1981): 5–9.

Fishman, Joshua A., and Erika Lueders-Salmon. "What Has the Sociology of Language to Say to the Teacher? On Teaching the Standard Variety to Speakers of Dialectal or Sociolectal Varieties." In *Functions of Language in the Classroom*, ed. C. B. Cazden et al. New York: Teachers College Press, 1972. 67–83.

Garvey, John, et al. "Correspondence." *Race Traitor* (Winter 1993): 126–27.

Gilyard, Keith. *Voices of the Self: A Study of Language Competence*. Detroit: Wayne State UP, 1991.

Hudson, R. A. *Sociolinguistics*. Cambridge: Cambridge UP, 1980.

Lloyd-Jones, Richard, and Andrea A. Lunsford, eds. *The English Coalition Conference: Democracy through Language*. Urbana, IL: NCTE/MLA, 1989.

Mayher, John S. *Uncommon Sense: Theoretical Practice in Language Education*. Portsmouth, NH: Boynton/Cook, 1990.

Olney, James. *Metaphors of Self: The Meaning of Autobiography*. Princeton, NJ: Princeton UP, 1972.

Stone, Albert E. *Autobiographical Occasions and Original Acts: Versions of American Identity from Henry Adams to Nate Shaw*. Philadelphia: U of Pennsylvania P, 1982.

The Social Responsibility That Writing Is—and Writing Instruction Too

Writing is not an activity that features social responsibility as an option. Writing *is* social responsibility. When you write, you are being responsible to some social entity even if that entity is yourself. You can be irresponsible as a writer, but you cannot be nonresponsible.

This issue probably has been discussed most in literary circles, couched in the long-running debate between those who view art as propaganda and those who subscribe to the notion of art for art's sake. I am obviously in the former camp and feel, for example, that the late critic Addison Gayle spoke compellingly when he asserted at the National Black Writers Conference in 1986 that "if Black people are being shipped to die in Grenada and you choose to write poems and novels about sunsets and trees, you are being responsible. You are just being responsible to the status quo."

At the same gathering, the poet Jayne Cortez reasoned:

> If information is a resource for advancement and development and is the basis by which people make their decisions, then one of the responsibilities of the poet to the community is to provide information. I don't mean merely news reports, statistics, advertisements, or the kind of information some leaders use to assault and manipulate the public, but information detailing significant experiences that would allow a person to use her or his imagination, intelligence, and emotions to gain a greater awareness and understanding of self and the outside world.

Inauguration poetry is certainly intended to be socially responsible writing, whether it is Maya Angelou's official inaugural poem, "On the

---

Presented February 6, 1993, at the Conference of CUNY Writing Centers Association. The conference theme was "Writing and Social Responsibility." Later published in *Community Review* 13.

Pulse of Morning," which seems to fit the Cortez prescription, given Angelou's heartfelt vision of who we are and ought to become as a nation, or Allen Ginsberg's "New Democracy Wish List," the entry, published the same day, that Ginsberg would have read at the ceremony had he been invited. I offer a brief extract:

> Purge U.S. military death squad subsidies in Salvador, Guatemala, etc. We backed up dictators in Zaire, Somalia, Liberia, Sudan, Angola, Haiti, Iran, Iraq, Salvador, we're responsible: admit it then figure ways out. Encourage international trade in Eco-technology in place of enabling codependency on weapons trade. Open CIA & FBI & NSA archives on Cointelpro raids, Government drug dealing, Kennedy/King assassinations, Iranian Contragate, Panama Deception, Vatican, Hand & Lavoro Bank thuggery, etc. including Bush-Noriega relations and other CIA client-agent scandals. (78)

Ginsberg harbors no illusions about art for art's sake. While some readers surely will want to discuss the quality of form, Ginsberg as poet is clearly more interested in the quality of the presidency and other political matters.

Other viewpoints on writing and responsibility, ones more directly related to our work in composition, are revealed in the academic discourse on literacy. Several are touched upon by James Paul Gee in his review of Harvey Graff's *The Legacies of Literacy: Continuities and Contradictions in Western Culture and Society*. Gee first takes up Graff's idea of the literacy myth—that is, the popular notion that literacy is not only requisite for higher-order consciousness but ensures critical thinking, governmental complexity, economic development, and social equity. Concerning the strictly cognitive claims supporting the literacy myth, Gee points to the work of Sylvia Scribner and Michael Cole, *The Psychology of Literacy*, which demonstrates that literacy is not a key variable in the development of ability to reason abstractly. Context proves more salient than the mere fact of literacy.

Graff himself provides ample historical evidence to debunk the social constructs underpinning the literacy myth. For example, the fact that Sweden was the first Western nation to achieve near-universal literacy did not lead to tremendous economic development or social progress.

However, one need not scour historical texts very much on this point. Most of us would agree—we know Ginsberg would—that overall development hasn't been ideal in the latter-day United States, where, although the rate of illiteracy is alarming to many, a lot of our most important bad decisions are made by literate people. Even where major social gains have taken place, and the United States fits in here as well, the causes are quite complex. Literacy cannot be extracted from the social matrix and highlighted as the determining factor. In fact, it has been argued that because it privileges certain language interaction, school-based literacy is not a means of ameliorating social inequity but a tool for reproducing it, serving mainly the purposes of the elite. Their particular brands of speech and writing are celebrated; other types are undervalued, discouraged, and penalized. Students generating the latter patterns realize early on, sometimes quite clearly, that the linguistic playing field is tilted against them. Some relish the uphill climb. Many don't even bother, thus falling victim to school systems that purportedly serve their best interests.

The argument being traced here is not that formal literacy instruction has no merit. We should not cease writing and resign our jobs. It is one thing to recognize that some claims about literacy and cognition have been exaggerated, but one need never to have considered literacy and orality a hierarchal proposition, much less one of either/or. Americans of African descent, for example, spring from a tremendous oral tradition but know full well the power of literacy, know it to be strong medicine if for no other reason than the fact that it was in large measure legislated away from them. We're not ambivalent about needing to master both the spoken and the written word. We need to be empowered in as many ways as we can. I would not want to choose between dialogue and writing, between oral tradition and text, between the Negro spirituals that clearly form the basis for Angelou's poem and that poem itself, between this paper I am presenting and the oral exchange I hope will ensue. Literacy has no monopoly on profundity but unmistakably contributes to it—as I am sure any academic who feels he or she has written a brilliant and insightful critique of literacy would agree. Scholars and others are right to warn against abuses of literacy and to rage against language practices that are exclusionary and exploitative. This has been a focus of my own professional endeavors. But any written argument against literacy, including any academic argument against academic literacy, is ultimately, as a philosopher-colleague of mine would say, self-refuting. It reminds me of the paper I heard arguing against the further spread of the English language being delivered, in English, at a conference of English teachers.

This is not a criticism of Gee. He has not taken the position, either in the review essay or in his own book, *Social Linguistics and Literacies*, that literacy is irrelevant. Far from being "anti-literacy," his goals are to force a more careful examination of issues surrounding literacy instruction based on the understanding that such instruction per se guarantees no particular form of social activity or organization and to keep open the question of how literacy instruction can best contribute to the public good. Gee is as aware as anyone—argues explicitly, in fact—that there never is a neutral literacy agenda. Just as there is no nonresponsible writing, there is no nonresponsible writing instruction. In every act of teaching there is complicity. Or, as he phrases it:

> A text, whether written on paper, on the soul (Plato), or on the world (Freire), is a loaded weapon. The person, the educator, who hands over the gun, hands over the bullets (the perspective), and must own up to the consequences. There is no way out of having an opinion, an ideology, and a strong one. . . . Literacy education is not for the timid. ("The Legacies of Literacy" 208)

What Gee fails to point out, but conceivably could have, is that revolts do occur. Perspectives fall into disfavor. Rulers are toppled. Slaves do forge freedom papers. Personal radicalization can, like Richard Wright's, begin in libraries. In other words, the process of initially becoming literate does not overdetermine how we continue to proceed in our "literateness" since, potentially at least, we are always becoming. Reading, writing, and instruction do act powerfully upon us; at the same time, we can act powerfully on and through reading, writing, and instruction. This is the heart of the matter. The urgent query is not whether we can or cannot write or teach devoid of social responsibility, but whether we dare specify a role for ourselves in situating students in the strongest possible positions relative to our teaching (which means, of course, that in a sense they can overthrow us). Do we deliberately encourage students to be agents of social change? How often, in fact, is the idea that students should change things spelled out in curricula? And I don't mean anything really controversial at this point. (My thing is to restructure society so that material profit for the few is not more important than mass human need, but I know I can't sell this to everybody.) I am merely suggesting that social change is always necessary because, at the very least, what exists is not perfect. But even this mild form of agitation is not championed enough in schools.

In *Writing and Sense of Self* Robert Brooke distinguishes between the roles of writing students and the roles of writers. In the student role, one habitually follows the dictates of the instructor, learning the strategies and values—both stated and implied—that are issued forth. However, Brooke finds this arrangement unsuitable, possibly debilitating, because it is an attempt to teach writing that has little in common with what motivates practicing writers or how they produce work. He argues, instead:

> Learning to write meaningfully in our culture requires developing an understanding of the self as writer, as someone who uses writing to further personal thinking and to help solve public problems. The development of such a role, such a self-understanding, is more important than developing any set of procedural competencies. Developing such a role, however, depends crucially on connecting the role of self as writer with other roles in the culture outside the classroom, especially writers' roles in the culture at large—including roles for the self as reflective thinker and community influencer. (5)

To Brooke, writers' roles—along with writing itself—are best promoted in a workshop setting steeped in writing-process methodology (multiple drafts, collaboration, alternative purposes and audiences, deferred emphasis on correctness, etc.), and over the years he has shifted his courses in that direction and away from a sequential curriculum emphasizing rhetorical principles. However, because they function within a university, none of Brooke's workshop members fully escape the student role. But in Brooke's view they are able to minimize and/or benefit from the tension involved in negotiating identities relative to both student and writer roles. Joy Ritchie, a participant-observer in a class taught by Brooke, writes that "the workshop classroom values personal experience and self-reflection, tolerance and consideration for plural perspectives, dialogue, responsibility, and commitment to action" (Brooke 139).

Brooke's workshop is admirable, undoubtedly in line with a significant strand of thought in the profession, and is an approach I generally endorse. There is, though, a disturbing aspect. For all their talk about "influencers" and "commitment to action," Brooke and Ritchie avoid indicating what deeds they find commendable. They forward a vague notion of democratic participation as a desirable outcome for their student writers or writer students. Beyond that, they adopt a politically neutral posture, which by now we understand is not an apolitical stance at all, merely one that reflects an unwillingness to articulate political persuasion. To simply advocate social responsibility, once we understand all professional educational activity to be socially responsible, is to advocate nothing. I have asserted the same nothingness many times—quite recently, for that matter—so I am not ridiculing anyone else for doing the same. But I now feel that teachers, including myself, should embrace the honesty that comes with delineating their political views. The point is to truly model mature literacy, to show that literacy always means something in particular. Recalling Gayle, we may pose a question: to whom are you being responsible? Gee causes us to question which type of ammunition is being used. Or, as Richard Bullock, John Trimbur, and Charles Schuster, editors of *The Politics of Writing Instruction: Postsecondary*, explain, "we prefer a disciplinary perspective that makes its politics explicit so that all involved—from students and instructors to administrators and theorists—can make intelligent, knowledgeable, informed choices about their own actions" (xviii).

Trimbur closes his own essay in the volume, "Literacy and the Discourse of Crisis" (the literacy crisis is an intellectual kin of the literacy myth), by maintaining that "To counter the growing privatization of education, we need to revive the movement of the late 1960s and early 1970s to democratize higher education through open admissions to *all* colleges and universities, free tuition, and a liveable student stipend" (294).

I don't think this referendum will fly. I think public institutions should remain or become tuition-free, open-admissions entities. I will continue to argue this even though the fight possibly will be lost. I won't, on the other hand, invest much energy debating the stipend issue or the status of private colleges because, though Trimbur's ideas appeal to me, I don't think there is the remotest possibility that fundamental changes will be made in those areas, at least not preceding greater equity and access to quality education in public schools. Although, like Trimbur, I range so far left that I wouldn't register a blip on the radar of what passes for fashionable political conversation in our country these days, there are some struggles I am actually trying to win. But the most important point regarding Trimbur's writing and my pondering it is that his writing about education is expressly political, as must be any response. Writing and writing instruction are socially, not naturally, occurring phenomena. They are never heading nowhere.

Works Cited

Brooke, Robert E. *Writing and Sense of Self: Identity Negotiation in Writing Workshops*. Urbana, IL: NCTE, 1991.

Bullock, Richard, John Trimbur, and Charles Schuster, eds. Preface. *The Politics of Writing Instruction: Postsecondary*. Portsmouth, NH: Boynton/Cook, 1991. xvii–xx.

Cortez, Jayne. Speech at First National Black Writers Conference at Medgar Evers College, CUNY, March 22, 1986.

Gayle, Addison. Speech at First National Black Writers Conference at Medgar Evers College, CUNY, March 22, 1986.

Gee, James Paul. *Social Linguistics and Literacies: Ideology in Discourses*. New York: Falmer Press, 1990.

———. "The Legacies of Literacy: From Plato to Freire through Harvey Graff." *Harvard Educational Review* 58, No. 2 (1988): 195–212.

Ginsberg, Allen. "New Democracy Wish List." *Newsday*, January 20, 1993. 44, 78.

Graff, Harvey G. *The Legacies of Literacy: Continuities and Contradictions in Western Culture and Society*. Bloomington: Indiana UP, 1987.

Scribner, Sylvia, and Michael Cole. *The Psychology of Literacy*. Cambridge, MA.: Harvard UP, 1981.

Trimbur, John. "Literacy and the Discourse of Crisis." In Richard Bullock et al., eds., *The Politics of Writing Instruction: Postsecondary*. Portsmouth, NH: Boynton/Cook, 1991. 277–95.

LANGUAGE AND LITERATURE

Genopsycholinguisticide and the Language Theme in African American Fiction

> You are a victim of . . . of, let's see, we need a new word for it. . . . How about: genopsycholinguisticide. Sure, why not: "first there was the word . . . and the word was nigger," and you became—nigger. And that, dear nigger, dear lost, blown-up bleeding, stumbling, raggedy nigger, that is genopsycholinguisticide.
>
> Arnold Kemp, *Eat of Me: I Am the Savior*

These sharp words emanating from Yaqui Laster's subconscious create a key thematic link between *Savior* and numerous other fictions in the African American tradition. In conceiving of genocide from a psycholinguistic perspective, Kemp has reflected a characteristic language sensibility, an awareness of the linguistics of subjugation. Virtually endless examples abound to reveal the fascination of African American writers with the Word, with the idea of language as a force either to prevent or foster the development of authentic selves. As Henry Louis Gates Jr., has observed, "the concern to depict the quest of the black speaking subject to find his or her voice has been a repeated topos of the black tradition, and perhaps has been its most central trope" (*Signifying Monkey* 239).

Language as subject matter is not restricted to Black writing. Much of Herman Melville's and Mark Twain's work, for example, stands as evidence in "mainstream" American literature. Frederick Busch views the dead letter as a central metaphor of Melville's life and work. He explores this idea, in part, by alluding to *Pierre*, the story of a woman who waits seventeen years in vain for a letter from her husband, by noting the report that Bartleby had been a clerk in the Dead Letter Office in Washington, and by citing Billy Budd's stuttering and subsequent silence (analogous to mail not getting through). And in *The Adventures of Tom Sawyer* and *The*

Published in *College English* 52, No. 7.

Adventures of Huckleberry Finn, Tom's authority over his friends derives from his book knowledge. Pap Finn, on the other hand, forbids Huck to pursue literacy. But in the African American canon, commentary about language is much more common, almost required, and often of a different nature. Any casual critic of the work nods knowingly when Jesse Robinson, the central character in Chester Himes's *The Primitive*, frustrated with racism in general and the racialized politics of corporate publishing in particular, stabs his manuscript with a knife, a scene foreshadowing (quite predictably) the murder of Kriss Cummings.

Houston Baker has traced a language motif in Zora Neale Hurston's *Their Eyes Were Watching God*, as has Barbara Johnson. Mary Helen Washington has contributed a metalinguistic analysis of Gwendolyn Brooks's *Maud Martha*, and Kimberly Benston has advanced a theory, "the topos of (un)naming," that addresses the question of characters choosing or casting off labels as an affirmation of freedom. Language motifs are especially evident in the work of Toni Morrison. Much of *Song of Solomon*, for example, can be viewed in terms of two voyages: the protagonist's journey from Milkman to Macon Dead III to the great-grandson of Shalimar, the flying African, and the movement in the song from Sugarman to Solomon to Shalimar. So if authors have laid out this specific expressive pattern as one of the distinguishing features of African American literature and laid it out across boundaries of ideology and style, and if eminently qualified critics have responded to it, then what do I propose to add to the mix? The answer is twofold.

First, I am not satisfied with or clear about (which could mean the same thing) explanations offered for why this pattern has manifested itself or, for that matter, about what, outside the author's ethnicity, makes texts "Black." There are those who bristle at the suggestion of racially determined differences in, say, American literature and bristle justifiably (as mongrelized as America is) if a viable cultural-historical explanation of such phenomena is not provided and certain possibilities of texts are ignored. Andrew Delbanco is right, to a degree, when he indicates that a problem in current African American literary criticism is that Black critics tend to exalt what they wish to explain, relying overmuch on a vague concept of Blackness. However, though I think theorists do tend to overstate cases in their zeal to organize canons and/or achieve professional legitimacy, in this matter it is relatively easy to establish an underpinning that supports one distinctive Black quality of the African American literary corpus viewed as a whole.

Consider the oft-debated notion of African survivals, in this instance the conception that cultural practices in Africa can account for certain forms that literature by African Americans has taken. A concise treatment of this idea can be found in Geneva Smitherman's *Talkin and Testifyin*:

> The preslavery background was one in which the concept of Nommo, the magic power of the word, was believed necessary to actualize life and give man mastery over things. All activities of men, and all movements in nature, rest on the word, on the productive power of the word, which is water and heat and seed and Nommo, that is, life force itself. . . . In traditional African culture, a newborn is a mere thing until his father gives and speaks his name. No medicine, potion, or magic of any sort is considered effective without accompanying words. So strong is the African belief in the power and absolute necessity of Nommo that all craftsmanship must be accompanied by speech. (78)

This concept, the argument goes, forms part of a rather fixed African worldview, fuels the much-discussed African oral tradition, and eventually infuses African American written forms with such qualities as testifyin—"a ritualized form of black communication in which the speaker gives verbal witness to the efficacy, truth, and power of some experience in which all blacks have shared" (Smitherman 58)—and signifyin—"the act of talking negatively about somebody through stunning and clever put downs" (82).

The idea of continuity with a generalized African past is provocative but could hardly support a theory by itself, given the shattering transitions surrounding slavery along with a variety of cultural exchanges. But just as features of African languages themselves have survived in creolized forms of English, one would have to assume that African perceptions of language have also become part of the African American cultural matrix. There certainly is enough testifyin and signifyin going on in the literature. Add to this the reality of plantation linguistics—that is, the vocabulary of suppression, the denial of literacy, the devoicing and identity-eradicating imperatives of masters and overseers.

It is obvious, then, why textual comments about language are integral to the African American tradition and why numerous musings about voice imbue the writing of slaves, ex-slaves, and the descendants of slaves. As Gates writes in *Figures in Black: Words, Signs, and the Racial Self*:

> The command of a written language, then, could be no mean thing in the life of the slave. Learning to read, the slave narrative would repeat again and again, was a decisive political act: learning to write, as measured against an eighteenth-century scale of culture and society, was an irreversible step away from the cotton field toward a freedom larger even than physical manumission. (4)

All this is not to delimit explications. African American authors are not solely influenced by African American culture. And as I mentioned earlier, they aren't the only ones to use language as theme. But for historical reasons, they do it overwhelmingly, almost inescapably, which is the point.

Among Americans, African Americans know the most about genopsycholinguisticide. Why wouldn't these writers, some of whom are still only four or five generations removed from slavery and living in a society where African Americans to a large degree are still devoiced, take time out to testify? They know they are fortunate to be able to do so. And why not signify? In one sense, they are all taunting lions from trees.

My second purpose in this essay, because I feel theory and practice should remain consciously connected, is to illustrate briefly an interrelationship among African American texts along strict language-as-theme lines. Although, as I pointed out, there is no shortage of critics attentive to sociolinguistic aspects of Black prose, their comments have generally been offshoots of other critical endeavors.

The novels of Alice Walker and Ishmael Reed illustrate my specific concerns. These two writers often have been on opposite sides of the literary fence, so to speak, and, therefore, the choice is a good one to demonstrate that various ideologies often function in African American literature primarily as subsets of an overall preoccupation with the interplay of language and liberation.

II

In *Meridian*, Alice Walker relates the tale of the slave and master storyteller, Louvinie, who has her tongue cut out by her master because she tells a tale of horror so vividly it gives the master's son a fatal heart attack. Mutely, Louvinie begs Master Saxon for the tongue, believing she will be cursed if her tongue, having been removed, is not at least put in a resting place she can designate. If she fails to have this control over her tongue, then the singer in her soul will be doomed, according to the folklore of her native land, "to grunt and snort through eternity like a pig" (44). Louvinie retrieves her tongue from the dirt and buries it under a magnolia tree, a tree that outgrows all others. Other slaves deem the tree magical. They hold that, among other things, it can talk and obscure vision so that slaves in its branches remain undetected.

During a 1960s riot at Saxon College, built on the site of the old Saxon plantation, Louvinie's tree, known as The Sojourner, is destroyed by students. This is the only significant damage they inflict, even though Meridian, one of the students, urges them to wreck the president's house instead. Such disregard or disrespect for their own myth indicates an inability on the part of the so-called radicals to choose effective courses of action. In destroying the fruit of Louvinie's tongue, they forgo mastery of their own.

Walker indeed fingers a problem of the 1960s. One of the difficulties then was judging the sincerity of those who spouted the popular slogans. Without question, there were legions of the committed, but the various shallow ones weren't so easy to distinguish. If the singers in their souls hadn't been lost, those singers couldn't always be trusted. Meridian, who tries to save The Sojourner, is genuine. Metaphorically, she becomes that tree, dedicated to positive advocacy. During a voter registration drive, she tells a man, "You have to get used to using your voice, you know. You start on simple things and move on" (205).

Of course, Louvinie's tongue is not Walker's only tie to an African American fictive tradition. Like Morrison, she's always ready for a naming ritual. In *The Third Life of Grange Copeland*, the naming process defines both a character and society's direct effect upon him. After the Copelands have a child, the father, during his negative "first life," turns despairingly to his equally depressed wife and asks what the boy's name is going to be.

She, in turn, names him Brownfield after the brownish, autumnal Georgia cotton fields that blanket their entire world. "That'll do as well as King Albert," the new mother laments. "It won't make a bit of difference what we name him" (178).

The Copelands are the pessimistic or realistic counterparts to the mammy in Charles W. Chesnutt's "A Deep Sleeper," who wants to name her babies Caesar or George Washington. The Copelands don't even dare to hope. Brownfield, then, doesn't start out with much of a chance. It is an explanation of character we don't get concerning Brownfield's literary twin, Mr. _____ of Walker's *The Color Purple*.

Brownfield, like Mr. _____, abuses his wife. Quite naturally, he has to conquer her voice in the process:

> The tender woman he married he set out to destroy. And before he destroyed her he was determined to change her. He was her Pygmalion in reverse. The first thing he started on was her speech. They had begun their marriage with her correcting him, but after a short while this began to wear on him. He could not stand to be belittled at home after coming home from a job that required him to respond to all orders from a stooped position. When she kindly replaced an "is" for an "are" he threw her correction in her face.
>
> "Why don't you talk like the rest of us poor niggers?" he said to her. "Why do you have to be so damn proper? Whether I says 'is' or 'ain't' ain't no damn humping off your butt." (56)

We could side with Brownfield, recalling Celie's comment that "only a fool would want you to talk in a way that feel peculiar to your mind" (*The Color Purple* 194), except that we must recall that Brownfield was initially attracted to Mem because of her knowledge and her educated voice. She had taught him the alphabet and to write his name. He is the one reneging on the deal, relentless in his efforts to make her talk like what she was, "a hopeless nigger woman who got her ass beat every Saturday night" (56). Brownfield eventually murders his wife, an unfortunate woman trapped in the wrong novel. She could have used a Meridian, Shug Avery, that songstress as deliverer, or even Shug's prototype, Hurston's Tea Cake.

In Walker's *The Temple of My Familiar*, the machinations involving language are once more indispensable as the action unfolds. Early in the novel, Carlotta wonders how she and her mother, Zedé, had been able to escape from South America. She thinks that maybe one of the guards was her father and had been perhaps fascinated by the fact that Zedé was literate. Literacy directly associated with the literate subject's freedom is, as we know, common fare. However, Walker inserts a twist. Zedé's literacy frees, instead, Mary Ann Haverstock, a student-victim in La Escuela de Jungla, where Zedé had come to work as a maid-slave. Zedé's fondness for Mary Ann prompts her to write the letter notifying Mary Ann's parents of their daughter's plight, but she is also inspired to "rebel against the gringos and assert who I was. That I could read and write. That I knew reading and writing to have great power" (80). After being taken home by her parents, Mary Ann eventually returns to liberate Zedé and Carlotta and escort them to California, where Carlotta grows up to assume, among others, the role of "guerrilla literaturist."

Another set of characters in *The Temple of My Familiar* achieve knowledge through literacy. Suwelo begins to know his uncle Rafe and become curious about Lissie through the scribbling Rafe left behind on books, notepads, boxes, and napkins. Later, however, Suwelo's failure to read the books that excite Fanny results in their estrangement. Then there is the voice of Lissie Lyles:

> I have always been a black woman. I say that without, I hope, any arrogance or undue pride, for I know this was just luck. I speak of it as luck because of the struggle others have trying to discover who they are and what they should be doing and finding it difficult to know because of all the different and differing voices they are required to listen to. (53)

We find later that Lissie has been insincere: she has experienced incarnations as someone other than a Black woman and has indeed suffered the strain of competing voices. Coming to grips with all of them is her essential struggle. Rounding out the novel's obsession with language are Arveyda, a songster; M'Sukta, the African maiden who is held captive in the British Museum of Natural History for fifteen years and who asserts that the words of her native language, inscribed in a mud wall in the simulated village exhibit, were all that kept her going; and Ola, the revolutionary African playwright.

In this novel, which reads to a large degree like a series of seminars, interwoven with the tale are the anticipated linguistics lessons. Ola, for example, addresses the very necessity and origins of language:

> Talk . . . is the key to liberation, one's tongue the very machete of freedom. We are the only species, some say, who have created speech. But that is only because, being far less intelligent than the majority of other animals, and more prone to disastrous blunders, in our relationships with others speech is so necessary. (315)

And in a scene that harks back to the Louvinie episode in *Meridian*, Olivia examines an intersection of language and the psychology of oppression:

> If you tear out the tongue of another, you have a tongue in your hand the rest of your life. You are responsible, therefore, for all that person might have said. It is the torturers who come to understand this, who change. Some do, you know. (310–11)

Literary politics is also covered. Olivia contends that by using the Bible to perpetuate slavery, the white man has "spoiled even the most literary form of God experience for us" (147). Ola advances, on behalf of Walker, a thinly veiled addendum to *The Color Purple*. Explaining why he doesn't portray his people at their best, he exclaims, "When my people stop acting like the white man, I can write plays that show them at their best!" (182)

An additional topic for discussion is the shift from oral to written traditions, indeed the tyranny of written traditions. And of course, there is the not-so-startling series of names to underscore the struggles for dominance that break out all through the novel. Carlotta's father remains silent when he is beaten by his captors. He would never reveal his name to them, so they simply called him Jesús instead. Zedé was alternately dubbed Consuelo, Connie, or Chaquita by the people for whom she worked. She, too, refuses to reveal her true name. Mary Ann Haverstock changes her name to Mary Jane Briden as she is "eager to give up being who I was" (207). Arveyda, who was named after a bar of soap, discovers that the mother he had known as Katherine Degos started out in the world as Georgia Smith. Suwelo began as Louis Jr.; Ola was once Dahvid. Fanny's therapist,

Robin Ramirez, uses "Robin" because it doesn't sound Mexican. Fanny Nzingha received her name because "Fanny" represented sassiness and rebelliousness to her grandmother, Celie, and "Nzingha," the name of a woman who ruled Angola, was seen as a much better middle name than Lou or Jean by her mother, Olivia. And when Shug founds her own religion, it is decided that G-O-D should have no name at all.

The *Temple of My Familiar* is Walker's fullest rendering of the language theme. She hasn't fallen far from Louvinie's ill-fated magnolia.

III

One cannot get very far into an Ishmael Reed novel without encountering commentary or symbolism relative to the role of language in social, political, or cultural struggle. Such comments are essential to the overall development of his work. In fact, in *Mumbo Jumbo*, *Flight to Canada*, and *Reckless Eyeballing*, language assumes the force of main characters.

In *Mumbo Jumbo*, there is in the 1920s an outbreak of Jes Grew, a positive disease that makes folks feel good. Reed describes it as "an anti-plague, enlivening the host, as electric as life, the delight of the gods" (9). Not being among those "germs that avoided words," Jes Grew is drawn toward New York in search of its text, which it needs to attain permanence (36). Without its text, Jes Grew can achieve no more than periodic flare-ups. As the hoodoo detective, PaPa LaBas, expounds: "Jes Grew needed its words to tell its carriers what it was up to. Jes Grew was an influence which sought its text, and whenever it thought it knew the meaning of its words and labanotations it headed in that direction" (241).

Jes Grew's search, however, is fraught with peril. The Atonist's henchmen, the Wallflower Order, seek to suppress Jes Grew and abort the prospect of Jes Grew Carriers in possession of their text shattering artistic norms. The text is eventually destroyed, and Jes Grew does not catch on. The epidemic dissipates, and the Wallflower Order retains control. But the peace is temporary, for in writing *Mumbo Jumbo*, Reed has created another text for Jes Grew and thereby fulfilled a prophecy of LaBas. When asked by Earline if Jes Grew has come to an end, LaBas replies that Jes Grew will return and flourish and that "we will make our own future Text. A future generation of young artists will accomplish this" (233).

In *Flight to Canada*, a novel set against the background of the Civil War, Reed reverses the action. Instead of tracing a search for the text as he does in *Mumbo Jumbo*, Reed constructs a text that is on the move itself. The speaking protagonist is a runaway slave named Raven Quickskill. The skill at which he is quickest is, of course, words. He has written a poem called "Flight to Canada." Then the poem pursues him: "Little did I know when I wrote the poem 'Flight to Canada' that there were so many secrets locked inside its world. It was more of a reading than a writing. Everything it says seems to have caught up with me" (7).

Because the issue of language is germane to the plot, the novel is both vintage Reed and a classic example of African American fiction. Literacy is Raven's liberation: "Raven was the first one of Swille's slaves to read, the first to write and the first to run away" (14). Of course, Swille, the old Massa, has a negative view of Raven's actions, but he also realizes the power of the written word:

> And the worst betrayal of all was Raven Quickskill, my trusted bookkeeper. Fooled around with my books, so that everytime I'd buy a new slave he'd destroy the invoices and I'd have no record of purchase; he was also writing passes and forging freedom papers. We gave him Literacy, the most powerful thing in the pre-technological pre-post-rational age—and what does he do with it? Uses it like that old Voodoo—that old stuff the slaves mumble about. Fetishism and grisly rites, only he doesn't need anything but a pen he had shaped out of cock feathers and chicken claws. (35–36)

In addition to the deeds on the plantation, the freed Raven submits a bill for all of his previous labor, an action that repeats the rite performed by the former slave in Chesnutt's "Tobe's Tribulations." But Raven does far better than he expects. After Swille's death, he eventually returns to take control of the estate. His language skills have served him well.

In *Reckless Eyeballing*, the text has become a play. Raven the poet is replaced by Ian Ball, playwright. This time, the text will make Ian a successful playwright and get him off the sex list compiled by feminists who control the theater. Ian explains his strategy to his mother over the phone: "I've written a play that's guaranteed to please them. The women get all the good parts and the best speeches" (3). Ball does become a commercial success, but the victory is tainted because his compromise has been too great. He lacks the commitment to his own voice displayed by Chorus in *The Last Days of Louisiana Red.*

Chorus, an actor, shoots Minnie Yellings because she talks too much. Chorus has had his lines reduced and his career ruined by hysterical leads dating back to *Antigone*. Nevertheless, he is on the rebound:

> His agent wanted him to fly to New York to check out its dimensions, its acoustics. His voice had been stifled so much over the years through bad distribution, poor and often hostile salesmen, indifference from those at the top that he insisted that a clause be added to his contract giving him the right to satisfactory acoustics. (171)

With the description of the stifled voice seeking self-expression, we are on familiar ground. Chorus's flight out of San Francisco is skyjacked, which in itself is of no great concern to Chorus as he readily forks over his money to avoid a hassle. But the voice of Minnie, one of the skyjackers, irks him to no end. She drones on and on, all the while reminding Chorus of his life since *Antigone*, until he can endure no more:

> Minnie moved down the aisle as the men kept an eye on the passengers. She caught Chorus' eye. She paused in front of him. She said she had seen his last performance. She said that she didn't think it was "relevant." She started calling him obscene names, standing in the aisle with her hands on her hips. She went on and on, and every time he tried to get a word in edgewise, she would scream, "YOU LISTEN TO ME, NIGGER. YOU LISTEN TO ME. LET ME FINISH. LET ME FINISH!" Chorus knew what he had to do because he'd be damned if he were going through this scene again. (172–73)

Chorus is more concerned about his voice than about material property or possessions; he is a more serious actor than Ian Ball is a playwright.

Early in *The Free-Lance Pallbearers*, as Bukka Doopeyduk is about to drop out of school, he confers with the dean of Harry Sam College, a figure strongly reminiscent of (though less treacherous than) the Dr. Bledsoe of *Invisible Man* (one of several points at which this novel parodies Ellison's). The dean's name is U2 Polyglot. We can transform this strange moniker to You Are Too Polyglot—that is, one of too many tongues, thereby lacking a strong sense of self. Since his chief activity in the book is pushing around a ball of excrement with his nose as part of his research for a paper on literature, this characterization rings true. Doopeyduk apparently is fortunate not to be swayed by the dean's exhortations to stay enrolled.

Bukka gets married to hen-pecking, lesbian-on-the-sly Fannie Mae and settles down to a life in the Harry Sam Projects, a conscientious worker and disciple of a cult of quixotic do-gooders called the Nazarene Bishops. In the hall of a project building, the following verbal exchange takes place:

> "You must be the couple that moved in here a few weeks ago."
>
> "That's right. My name is Bukka Doopeyduk. What's yours?"
>
> "My mother lost my name in a lottery, Mr. Doopeyduk. Why don't you jess call me the neighbor, and so's you kin 'stinguish between me and my wife, refer to me as M/Neighbor and my wife as F/Neighbor."
>
> "Fine with me," I said. "I have a hard time remembering names anyway." (21)

The projects are compared to prison, the M/Neighbor and F/Neighbor tags being analogous to the numbers by which inmates are officially identified. M/Neighbor and F/Neighbor don't question their misfortune, and Bukka naively helps to perpetuate it. His vision is jaded. To maintain the metaphor, we might say that his tongue is not knowledgeable enough. Only when he finally asserts himself, speaks out, does he assume the role of hero. Unlike the enlightened voice possessed by the protagonist at the end of *Invisible Man*, Bukka's informed voice results in direct social action. His speaking out against Harry Sam brings an end to the Harry Sam regime.

Language also is a major theme in *Yellow Back Radio Broke-Down*. Young rebels—fed up with the same old story, a position their spokesman articulates succinctly—have seized control of the town called Yellow Back Radio, chased out the traditional authorities, and decided to create their own fiction. Drag Gibson spearheads the counterinsurgency, but the Loop Garoo Kid, the hoodoo cowboy who is the novel's hero, helps to secure a win for the new generation. It once emitted signals so faint "it seemed that the whole valley would soon be off the air"; now, however, Yellow Back Radio is again on its feet and communicating well (118).

The language theme is not pervasive in *The Terrible Twos* and *The Terrible Threes*, the first two books (Reed's sixth and eighth novels overall) of a proposed trilogy entitled *The Terribles*, but it remains significant. Although the overriding concerns are the presidency, big business, and international politics, the plot involves an impostor Black Peter who throws his voice through an impostor Santa Claus, having Santa criticize the commercialism surrounding Christmas and calling for a boycott. Black Peter, spotted in his earlier role as a sidewalk hustler, is described by an observer:

> The fellow was a ventriloquist. He could talk at the same time as his little dummy who was engaging the crowd in a game of three-card monte. He said that he was a descendant of a slave named Pompey, a master ventriloquist of the Old South who escaped from slavery by throwing his voice. I've never seen anything like it. He could talk and puff on a marijuana cigarette, imitating President Eisenhower, Winston Churchill, and other famous world leaders. He said that although he was an ordinary, insignificant, and barely literate speaker, he was fortunate that someone named Jah made it possible for the Emperor to speak through him. (*Terrible Twos* 25)

Reed also embellishes the tale with several choice tidbits about language such as the California Supreme Court's decision outlawing the naturalist novel and Satan's concern, because he doesn't understand them, about "microbiologists, deconstructionists, New Age Freaks." Satan contemplates opening a new area for these sinners called Jargon City (*Terrible Threes* 147).

With organisms searching for a life-sustaining sacred text; poems chasing poets; consciously manipulative playwrights; authorial comments on forms of fiction; characters named Chorus, Yellings, and Polyglot; a town called Yellow Back Radio; and a ventriloquist on the loose, Reed's stories strongly echo a dominant impulse in the African American literary tradition. They are, in fact, the tradition's most imaginative examples.

Works Cited

Baker, Houston. *Blues, Ideology, and Afro-American Literature: A Vernacular Theory*. Chicago: U of Chicago P, 1984.

Benston, Kimberly. "I Yam What I Am: The Topos of (Un)Naming in Afro-American Literature." In Henry Louis Gates Jr., ed., *Black Literature and Literary Theory*. New York: Methuen, 1984. 51–72.

Busch, Frederick. Introduction. *"Billy Budd, Sailor" and Other Stories*. By Herman Melville. New York: Penguin, 1986. vii–xxiv.

Chesnutt, Charles W. "A Deep Sleeper." In Sylvia L. Render, ed., *The Short Fiction of Charles W. Chesnutt*. Washington, D.C.: Howard UP, 1969. 115–22.

——. "Tobe's Tribulations." In Sylvia L. Render, ed., *The Short Fiction of Charles W. Chesnutt*. Washington, D.C.: Howard UP, 1969. 97–105.

Delbanco, Andrew. "Talking Texts." Review of *The Signifying Monkey: A Theory of Afro-American Literary Criticism* and *Figures in Black: Words, Signs, and the Racial Self*, by Henry Louis Gates Jr. *The New Republic* (January 1989): 28–34.

Ellison, Ralph. *Invisible Man* (1952). New York: Vintage, 1972.

Gates, Henry Louis, Jr., ed. *Black Literature and Literary Theory*. New York: Methuen, 1984.

——. *Figures in Black: Words, Signs, and the Racial Self* New York: Oxford UP, 1987.

——. *The Signifying Monkey: A Theory of Afro-American Literary Criticism*. New York: Oxford UP, 1988.

Himes, Chester. *The Primitive* (1955). New York: New American Library, 1956.

Hurston, Zora Neale. *Their Eyes Were Watching God* (1937). Urbana: U of Illinois P, 1978.

Johnson, Barbara. "Metaphor, Metonymy and Voice in *Their Eyes Were Watching God*." In Henry Louis Gates Jr., ed., *Black Literature and Literary Theory*. New York: Methuen, 1984. 205–19.

Kemp, Arnold. *Eat of Me: I Am the Savior*. New York: Morrow, 1972.

Melville, Herman. *"Billy Budd, Sailor" and Other Stories*. New York: Penguin, 1986.

——. *Pierre*. 1852.

Morrison, Toni. *Song of Solomon*. New York: Random House, 1977.

Reed, Ishmael. *Flight to Canada*. New York: Random House, 1976.

——. *The Free-Lance Pallbearers*. Garden City, NY: Doubleday, 1967.

——. *The Last Days of Louisiana Red* (1974). New York: Avon, 1976.

——. *Mumbo Jumbo* (1972). New York: Avon, 1976.

———. *Reckless Eyeballing*. New York: St. Martin's Press, 1986.
———. *The Terrible Threes*. New York: Atheneum, 1989.
———. *The Terrible Twos*. New York: St. Martin's Press / Marek, 1982.
———. *Yellow Back Radio Broke-Down*. Garden City, NY: Doubleday, 1969.
Render, Sylvia L., ed. *The Short Fiction of Charles W. Chesnutt*. Washington, D.C.: Howard UP, 1969.
Smitherman, Geneva. *Talkin and Testifyin: The Language of Black America*. Boston: Houghton, 1977.
Twain, Mark. *The Adventures of Huckleberry Finn*. 1885.
———. *The Adventures of Tom Sawyer*. 1876.
Walker, Alice. *The Color Purple* (1982). New York: Washington Square, 1983.
———. *Meridian* (1976). New York: Washington Square, 1977.
———. *The Temple of My Familiar*. San Diego: Harcourt, 1989.
———. *The Third Life of Grange Copeland*. San Diego: Harcourt, 1970.
Washington, Mary Helen. "Taming All That Anger Down: Rage and Silence in Gwendolyn Brooks's *Maud Martha*." In Henry Louis Gates Jr., ed., *Black Literature and Literary Theory*. New York: Methuen, 1984. 249–62.

Tucept HighJohn and the Limits of Language Programming: A Coda

Arthur Flowers taps out, in *De Mojo Blues*, a tale of post-1960s stagnation. His chief concern, socially, is the collectively weak soul of the African diaspora, and his attempt, artistically, is to paint a vision of ultimate triumph. He forges a modern myth out of African American culture, particularly relying upon the hoodoo aesthetic, which is personified most fully in the protagonist, Tucept HighJohn of Memphis, Tennessee.

The controlling dynamic in the novel is the transformation of Tucept from a disenchanted Vietnam veteran into a hoodoo master selected to deliver "THE CALL" to his people. This drive toward "THE CALL" and the linguistic preparation pertinent to it cleverly mark the novel as one in the African American literary tradition. Moreover, the novel resounds with the blues, the sharp verbal play, and the various allusions to the value of language skill one comes to expect in fiction by African Americans.

Early in the story, as Tucept, upon his return to Memphis, settles into his Riverside Park habitat, he contemplates his postwar existence. His preoccupation with the power of the Word is revealed:

> Tucept cooled out, lulled by the slow crawl of the river, the water lapping softly at the banks. Old man river. He pulled out Chancellor Williams' *Destruction of Black Civilization* and was soon deep into the ancient glories of Mene's Memphis. Old Memphis on the Nile. Ptah's city, the Egyptian god of scribes. He who thought the world, said it in a word and then it was so. (35)

Tucept has thus, perhaps inadvertently, outlined his own mission: to be a god of the Word himself. But at that point he is unable to respond

Presented March 5, 1993, at the Graduate School and University Center of the City University of New York at a forum sponsored by the Ph.D. program in English.

in full to his calling. Although he possesses some political resolve, he has women to chase, marijuana to smoke, and brooding to do. He finds a river-soaked chair in the Mississippi and spends two years restoring it, often accompanied by the recordings of Lou Rawls. Steadily, albeit slowly, Tucept does move beyond mundane pleasures. He considers more seriously his past and his purpose, an aspect of which is to honor the memory and carry on the work of his late army buddy, Jethro Tree, who first interested him in hoodoo. The Word, naturally, had been at the core of their relationship.

Jethro had inquired about Tucept's surname, which echoes the story of HighJohn the Conqueror, a tale Tucept characterizes as a "slavery myth about some tricking man" (61). This precipitates a rebuke from Jethro, who feels that Tucept lacks proper appreciation of his own heritage. Jethro insists that HighJohn the Conqueror is real and will, in fact, be reappearing soon because African Americans need him desperately. The prophecy is contained, according to Jethro, in the Lost Book of Hoodoo. "Dat's de black book of power," Jethro claims. "De mojo book number one" (61).

There are obviously strong overtones here of Ishmael Reed's *Mumbo Jumbo*, And as Jes Grew must find its text in order to sustain itself, Tucept must locate the Lost Book of Hoodoo to fulfill his potential. The wrinkle that Flowers provides is that the book is not an inanimate text but a hoodoo master named Spijoko who takes Tucept on as an apprentice and teaches him, among other things, that "the Will, the Word and the Way is the whole of sorcery" (87).

Immediately following this particular instruction, when Tucept's sister performs her own version of sorcery, we see a variation on the theme, emphasizing the importance of the Word in the trinity. After years of frustration and financial neglect suffered at the hands of her son's father, who does not acknowledge the child as his own, she torches her ex-lover's luxury car. Caldonia expresses the Will and the Way in the act of arson. But she does not feel completely avenged without sending a note:

> What kind of car was it? [Tucept]
>
> Deuce and a quarter. Fire engine red.
>
> Do it Cal.
>
> It did feel good, she said, sitting across from his whistling with the coffee pot, Caldonia, Caldonia, what makes your big head so hard?

> You think he'll figure out you did it?
>
> He will when he gets the letter.
>
> The letter? said a suddenly horrified Tucept, you wrote a letter telling him you did it?
>
> I couldn't help it. (91–92)

Perhaps Caldonia isn't too wise, but she is certainly in the tradition, providing the word to match the deed. And the episode serves to foreshadow, in broader strokes than Tucept's early invocation to Ptah and Jethro's cryptic prophecy, the course of action to be taken by the protagonist. For Apprentice HighJohn's forte is to be myth, the Word, and his task is to incorporate, through the most advanced type of neurolinguistic programming imaginable, a story of dominance into the souls of people of African descent.

De Mojo Blues is thus linked to what is often called the Whorfian hypothesis—that is, the belief that language shapes, almost exclusively, the way we perceive the world. Allen Walker Read is a prominent exponent of Whorf's position and cites, in turn, the work of Alfred Korzybski to advocate the reorganization of mass character along neurolinguistic and neurosemantic lines. Read warns that correct pronouncements by leaders mean little if not subsequently expressed in the everyday actions of those on the popular level. He argues that through neurolinguistic retraining—brainwashing actually—that end can be achieved.

There are, of course, two major problems with this line of thinking. First, Whorf's position is an overstatement in that, as Eleanor Burke Leacock indicates in "Abstract versus Concrete Speech: A False Dichotomy," Whorf "did not take sufficient account of nonlinguistic cognition" (114). Fortunately, especially since many of us are in reality already being subjected to negative "language programs" on a daily basis (such as the labels some of us have to survive), we are not as language-bound as is generally considered the case. Second, even if we were as dependent upon language as Whorf suggests and susceptible to the type of retraining that Read favors, there could be no consensus reached about who would be responsible for prescribing *the* correct message. Who decides for all whether pronouncements by leaders are, in fact, correct?

Tucept HighJohn, however, will not grapple with such questions. Although Whorfian thought lies at the heart of his own conception (which is also, by the way, a problem with the description of Yaqui in Arnold Kemp's *Eat of Me: I Am the Savior*), he commands power far greater than any social scientist could muster. Through the gift of conjuration, he aims for direct access to and total control over the central nervous system of the Black masses. He will determine all impulses, linguistic and otherwise, present and future. He seeks the limit.

Despite all this movement toward lofty ritualism, the story is kept lively because Tucept remains for most of the novel so recognizably human. He wavers in his commitment to become a hoodoo master, yet he never abandons his work completely. He takes time, as mentioned earlier, to fool around with ordinary things like one-on-one romance. The relationships never work out because, as one may anticipate, it isn't easy for the women he knows to comprehend why he spends so much time pursuing hoodoo. When one of his girlfriends, Lynn, presses him on why he bothers with "mumbo jumbo," he responds that "it's going to get me some sayso" (102). Lynn remains bewildered:

> Some what? She questioned, head cocked off to the side.
>
> Some sayso, he said, voice suddenly throbbing with restrained passion, Some people in this world have sayso, most don't. I want to be one of the people with sayso.
>
> He hated being a bit player in this world, a little man without sayso, helplessly watching his people go down because they lacked understanding of the way of things. (102)

Tucept values nothing above the exercise of his voice, experimenting with the Word. After the breakup with Lynn, and partly because of it, he pursues his studies with Spijoko more intently, closing in on his goal. Finally, as he strides through the park on a stormy day, he creates his masterwork of myth and is ready to program it into the soul of the Tribe. He will take care of genopsycholinguisticide (recall *Savior*) once and for all:

> The saga of the Blacks began to shape itself in his head according to what he wanted to program into the soul of the Tribe. What first, he pondered. Arrogance. He wanted a proud, arrogant people. He conjured up the first monkey tribes to stand and struggle to humanity

> and called them Firstborn. Firstborn! To rule is your birthright! He chronicled the founding of civilization, the isolation and sloth of an elder race, the decline of a once mighty people. He built a commitment to the destiny of the race in the Tribe's soul by carving in its conquest and enslavement in hard brutal strokes. He showed the conquest and dispersion of the Folk to the four corners of the earth and called these the Leanyears. We survived.
>
> And then the Longmarches. The Ascension of the Blacks. Tales of relentless struggle and ruthlessly strategic commitment to the destiny of the black generations. Tales of power. Because more than anything he wanted a people bred to the instinct of power. A race of rulers. And so he forged his myth accordingly. A saga of struggle and mastery. The Longmarches. Generations and generations of struggle. Working the Tribe's soul with swift and sure strokes he programmed in traits like discipline and dignity, selfresponsibility and selfdirection, the ability to grow from both victory and defeat. With all the patience of a master craftsman pleased with his work HighJohn carefully weaved an inexorable Will to Power into the soul of the Blacks and exulted in the length of his game. I am HighJohn he howled, and this I swear, the Blacks will never again be enslaved. By the gods and all that's holy I shall forge a race of rulers.
>
> And so into the heart of his myth he placed his survivor's vision. The Blacks still marching where others have long since fallen. Survival of the black generations unto eternity. The Promised Land. His myth came alive, its heart a burning sunheat thing, a beacon in times of both celebration and despair.
>
> The storm around him grew in intensity and he felt its fire in the small hairs of his arm. As he worked he constantly checked his myth for alignment with the Board of Destiny. A good fit. A good Work. He was proud of it. (192–93)

All that remains is for the myth to be planted into the Tribe by means of "THE CALL," the assembling of the masses. Tucept has joined ranks with Ptah himself, has delivered upon Jethro's prophecy, has harnessed and then unleashed, with a Jungian twist, the power of the Word. "I have named the thing and it is done. I am a mighty sorcerer and reality shall yield to me" (215).

Some detractors of *De Mojo Blues* claim that it is an instance in which ideology has hampered craft. They find the closing pages of nationalist rhetoric, as opposed to final dramatic action or concrete expression of the mojo, disturbing to their aesthetics. They wonder, too, why HighJohn is, as Aun Peggy was back in Chesnutt's Uncle Julius tales, leery about throwing the goopher on the oppressors. If the mojo is so powerful, why can't it be put to immediate political ends? But despite these criticisms, and they do have considerable merit, it is clear that Arthur Flowers has made a stunning contribution, extending, in one sense, the language theme in African American fiction to its logical conclusion. He has absorbed and magnified the sociolinguistic impulses of his predecessors. Think of Harriet Wilson's Frado, coming into her own only when she recognizes the power of her voice to determine, or at least influence, social arrangements; the runaway slaves in the work of Chesnutt and Reed submitting invoices to their ex-masters for services rendered; Janie's struggle, at the heart of Hurston's *Their Eyes Were Watching God*, to become more than a voiceless ornament; Fred Daniels, Richard Wright's underground man, lacking the language to survive; Ellison's Invisible One, described as possessing more big words than a pocket-sized dictionary, hoping to ascend a mountain of words to the top of the Brotherhood; Langston Hughes's Jesse B. Semple, constantly quarreling over semantics; the elaborate naming rituals that are hallmarks of the Morrison and Walker canons.

All these Flowers invokes. These writers and characters have played HighJohn to him.

Works Cited

Flowers, Arthur. *De Mojo Blues*. New York: Dutton, 1985.

Leacock, Eleanor Burke. "Abstract versus Concrete Speech: A False Dichotomy." In Courtney B. Cazden, et al., eds., *Functions of Language in the Classroom*. New York: Teachers College Press, 1972. 111–34.

Read, Allen Walker. "The Contribution of Sociolinguistics to the Peacekeeping Process." *Et cetera* 39 (1982): 16–21.

Julius and Jesse in 003

Feeling a need to shake things up, flip the script, depart from the skill and drill stuff that transpired in most basic writing courses dubbed ENGW 003, I decided to have students read several stories that deal extensively with the theme of language empowerment. I wanted them to understand that in some respect these stories address their struggles as language users, particularly ones of African descent who had been classified as remedial writers. However, the specific connections between the texts and their lives would be something the students mostly articulated themselves. I planned to provide commentary, but not before the students had given theirs. The main task I set for myself was to be relatively unobtrusive and allow students to do their work.

The first text was "Dave's Neckliss," a story from Charles Chesnutt's Uncle Julius series (I can never get away from Julius). The stories, or frame tales, contain anecdotes about plantation life related by the former slave, Uncle Julius, within the framework of a larger story narrated by John, the male member of the couple that employs him. Julius's purpose for telling a tale is ultimately to secure some advantage for himself. In this instance, he covets the remainder of a ham that John's wife, Annie, has shared with him. Julius begins to weep and spins the story of how the ham reminds him of a slave back on the plantation who was falsely accused of stealing a ham from the smokehouse, was forced to wear the ham around his neck on a chain as punishment, went insane, even imagined seeing ham trees, eventually thought he was turning into a ham himself, and finally hanged himself over a fire he set in the smokehouse. Touched by the story and for the moment, unlike Julius, turned off by the prospect of eating more ham, Annie gives him the rest. Blended into the story are portrayals of plantation life in which attacks on humanity and voice are foregrounded. For example, it is discovered that Dave has

---

Presented November 18, 1990, at the Annual Convention of the National Council of Teachers of English. The working title was "Using Literature about Literacy."

secretly learned to read and has been studying the Bible. Naturally, his master is distressed by the news and, in confronting Dave, asks him what he's learned from the Holy Book. Dave replies adroitly that he has learned not to steal, lie, or be disobedient. His master then decides that the Bible hasn't done Dave any harm and quickly invites him to preach to the rest of the slaves. However, after Dave is framed for the theft of the ham, his Bible is confiscated and burned.

In the ensuing discussion, students did focus, as I had hoped, upon the interplay of language, enslavement, and freedom, but not immediately. Initial reactions addressed how difficult the text was to read because it is written in dialect. In fact, as we read the story in class, several students stopped at various points to protest being given work featuring such poor English. They reasoned that, because one needs good English to make it, people like Julius would never get anywhere in life.

I think, for the most part, the students were telling me what they thought I wanted to hear. After all, this was a writing class, always in their view a place to chastise folks about poor grammar. Besides ignoring the author's use of alternate voices, what they hadn't understood in being intolerant of Uncle Julius is that I valued a clear and effective story above Standard English and believed that their efforts to produce acceptable academic writing depended upon the degree to which they could stress elaboration and clarity over the grammar they were so worried about. I pointed out that I didn't have as much trouble reading "Dave's Neckliss" as I had reading some of their papers, a comment they didn't appreciate at first, although they did affirm that walking off with the ham is a measure of how competent a language user Julius is. When asked, none of them thought they were better storytellers than Uncle Julius. A few, though, were bold enough to claim they were his equals.

As the students further explored the story, their responses grew more varied and unpredictable. One student said the story shows that one shouldn't steal and blame others. In other words, what happens to Dave is sad and shouldn't have happened. On the other hand, others suggested that the aspect of the tale involving the framing of Dave is only a minor issue. Some students doubled back to stress how well Julius gets his point across. I think this was partly another case, since I had argued that Julius's linguistic ability is to be praised, of students catering to what they perceived to be my expectations.

The discussion then shifted to how bad slavery had been. After a spell of communal lamenting, one student posed a rhetorical question: How much freedom do we really have? He promptly declared that we (meaning our enslaved ancestors) had no right to read or preach unless it benefited the master. Several of his classmates chimed in. And although I, myself, am ever prepared to speak at length on this theme, I felt there was nothing for me to add in that vein other than to inquire how that understanding may further inform present perceptions. The students, primarily on their own, had hit upon several features I deemed important.

Certain students, not used to this sort of classroom discourse, pressed for a definitive explanation. They were concerned to know who among them was most right, an impulse highlighted during discussion about what Julius had accomplished. A segment of the class perceived Julius as a trickster figure who "got slick" and "used psychology on the white folks." This group became extremely agitated when an opposing faction felt that Julius was not conniving at all. They figured he was genuinely moved by sad recollection to tell the story about Dave and that the truth and brilliance of the story just happened to strike a receptive and charitable chord in Annie. Despite knowing the trickster figure interpretation to be obvious in the wider literary community, I refused to resolve the dispute, pick a winner, because to tell the supporters of the "naïveté theory" that they were wrong would have constituted a setback for both them and me. I had told them that any reading of a story involves subjectivity, and I didn't see how they could maintain faith in this view if I were willing to call them wrong, even though in some way I felt I had to, about the first major subjective response they cared to air in class. Why would they bother again?

The solution to this dilemma was to distribute another Uncle Julius story, an unscheduled action, in order to expand the frame of reference. "The Goophered Grapevine," the first of the Julius stories chronologically, more clearly spells out how beautifully scheming Julius can be. Upon meeting his future employers, who are contemplating buying land that is of special interest to Julius because of the money he makes from the abundant supply of grapes, the cunning former slave tells them a story about how the property is haunted. The story doesn't work as well for him as the one that gets him the ham, but it left no doubt in any of my students' minds that Uncle Julius is an accomplished con artist. The story wasn't read in class, but comments about it were enthusiastically brought to my attention. Those whose prior notions were validated displayed obvious satisfaction. Just as important, the others seemed pleased to have discerned something without being explicitly directed. When I tried to interject new doubt by intimating that perhaps Julius was sincere after all, one could not distinguish between the replies of the two groups. Neither was going for it.

Unfortunately, the class wasn't as committed to its own ideas in essays. Regardless of my warnings against doing so, one-third of the students summarized "Dave's Neckliss" and/or "The Goophered Grapevine." Those in this group still assumed their objective to be strictly informational as opposed to being an attempt to link the texts to their own experiences and the world as they knew it. Others went to the opposite extreme, almost totally leaving the texts behind. So for one student, "Dave's Neckliss" received a two-line mention prefatory to a lengthy indictment cataloging hardships visited upon African Americans by white America. Some, however, did manage to plant one foot in Julius's world and one foot in their own. One writer, for example, reflected upon why a particular rhetorical strategy had been employed:

> I also notice that Julius must have been a extra ordinary man to be able to use something about slavery to accomplish something so simple and a bit funny. I think that most people find slavery something very serious and do not like speaking about it. But for Julius to have actually experience it and used it like that is different. Then may be that is why he used a story about slavery because he knew people felt serious about it.

Another became involved in a comparison of legal systems:

> The story makes me think about justice. Aren't you glad that your innocent until your proven guilty? I know I'm glad about it. Thank God for the justice system. You know I also think about being in the hot cotton field. Picking cotton. Imagine me saying yes sir, no sir. My master would have lynched me.

Yet another chose to pursue the language angle mentioned earlier by another student in the class:

> The plantation owner had punishment on his mind. The owners of plantations knew that learning how to read would give slaves knowledge and with knowledge comes power. Slaves are suppose to be powerless.

As we shared the papers in class, the strongest negative reactions were reserved for summaries (my influence again), and even those responses were by no means malicious. Discussion of the remaining papers was characterized by receptiveness, and students mainly wanted assertions supported by the text. I was badgered somewhat to finally deliver my own, as if an absolutely correct answer were yet in the offing. But I insisted instead that the stories were the sum total of what had been forwarded by the students and still more. And I left the matter at that, moving on to other crucial questions I wanted them to mull over: How much Uncle Julius can you be? How much Uncle Julius do you need to be?

One writer had anticipated me. She began:

> Often in our lives, there are changes that occur. We can either use these changes to benefit us or let it go to waste. In "Dave's Neckliss," both Julius and Dave are affected by circumstances around them.

The student briefly recapitulated the story and proceeded to write:

> These two characters, Dave and Julius, have similar personalities. They are both free from the shackles that entangled them physically and psychologically; however, they wish to remain in their past situation. This maybe due to the fact that they are afraid of the unknown, since their minds are not yet freed. I can relate to this aspect of the story, since I, sometimes, unconsciously hold myself back from doing something that I can do. I think the key message in this story is to show us how to make use of the opportunities given to us. . . . I consider my college years the primary years of me expressing myself.

I elected to follow up considerations of language power and self-expression by introducing the class to Jesse B. Semple, Langston Hughes's memorable character, who is one of the most astute language users to be found in any literature. Possessing a strong ego, Semple—or Simple, as he is also known—uses his highly polished wit and oral skill to impress his ideas upon others, usually his barroom buddy, Boyd, narrator of most of the tales. Although Boyd is a man of education—"colleged," as Simple puts it—he holds no advantage over the verbally combative Simple and is never able to change Simple's mind. Acquired in rural Virginia, Baltimore, and Harlem, Simple's experiences form a fortress of meaning more than equal to the assault of the academy. Consider his reaction to Boyd's complaint in "Two Sides Not Enough":

> "I thought you'd get around to race before you got through. You can't discuss any subject at all without bringing in color. God help you! And in reducing everything to two sides, as usual, you oversimplify."
>
> "What does I do?"
>
> "I say your semantics make things to simple."
>
> "My which?"
>
> "Your verbiage."
>
> "My what?"
>
> "Your words, man, your words." (214)

Simple is actually putting Boyd on, for he really understands him all along, as one who had witnessed their conversation in "Concernment" would know. After the narrator has paraphrased a line from *Hamlet*, Simple initiates the following exchange:

> "Boyd, your diploma is worth every penny you paid for it," said Simple. "Only a man who is colleged could talk like that. Me, I speaks simpler, myself."
>
> "Simplicity can sometimes be more devious than erudition," I said, "especially when it centers in an argumentative ego like yours."
>
> "Of course," said Simple. (152)

Of the Simple stories we read, "Puerto Ricans" generated the most controversy, as Simple asks why the language a Black person speaks, in this case Spanish as opposed to English, leads to more privileges for the speaker. After widespread, almost obligatory observations that race and discrimination are matters central to the story, several students delivered harsh opinions of Simple, accusing him of putting down foreigners and having a defeatist attitude, so hung up on what the system would not allow him to do. These students, who happened to be from the Caribbean and who identified with the Puerto Rican being, in their view, mistreated by Simple, asserted that the story reminded them of how Blacks in the United States discriminate against immigrants from the Caribbean. Some of their U.S. counterparts conceded that this type of discrimination exists but that they themselves were above such thinking and practice. They did venture to add, however, that Blacks from the Caribbean arrive with the conception that they are better than the Blacks already here. After a few heated exchanges (in easily the liveliest, almost too lively, session of the semester), the presence of those who emerged as peacemakers eventually began to dominate. The talk shifted to how all Black people should stick together.

All this was interesting but had little to do with the story. It is fairly easy to demonstrate among the wider literary community that Simple's beef is not with immigrants but with white Americans. I had to postpone illustrating the point in class, however, because I had announced that my only role during class discussions that preceded the next batch of papers would be to answer questions about information—for example, to define the term *Jim Crow*. As I sought to boost student confidence and encourage interpretive risk taking, I would neither introduce comments nor field questions that had to do with confirming or disconfirming student readings. This placed me in a frustrating posture, but part of what reassures me that it was the correct move is the fact that of eighteen papers I subsequently received, none were strictly summaries, and only in one was summarizing still the dominant tendency.

Of course there was a price to be paid for the activities chosen. As noted, there was a misconstruing of texts and (or because of) too much reliance upon personal experience. There was trouble again with appreciating mood, many failing to imagine the pieces as humorous, probably their most outstanding quality. Authorial viewpoint was largely ignored, several students mentioning, in fact, that Simple *wrote* the stories. This recalls a problem encountered while dealing with the Uncle Julius stories. In general, whatever comments John made about Julius were judged by students to be unquestionably true. That Chesnutt may have provided John's appraisals to show the extent to which people like John misunderstand the Juliuses of the world was not envisioned.

So there was more work in reading to do, more stories, some essays, additional response assignments. While comprehending, to be sure, the subjective nature of textual interpretation, I simultaneously maintain that some subjectivities hold richer explanations than others. I want my students as a whole to be able to perform some fuller "reads," which I believe can help them produce better "writes."

Specific writing problems were indeed addressed. For example, I taught the student who wrote about judicial processes that her audience could think some bridging statements are needed between "Imagine me saying yes sir, no sir" and "My master would have lynched me." Perhaps something like "I wouldn't have done it and, therefore, as punishment..." I also indicated that because a slave was valuable property, it was unlikely that a slaveholder would have lynched one based solely upon the type of insubordination she described. I almost threw in some remarks about God and the justice system—but I kept those to myself. The key point is that this student did flesh out her paper through continued drafting.

I showed the student who wrote about self-expression (who was in a basic writing class, not ironically, only because she didn't write enough on the writing assessment test) that to write "their minds are not yet freed" is to contradict her previous claim in the same paragraph that "they are both free from the shackles that entangled them physically and psychologically." This student became a stickler for logic, habitually asking me if her sentences "go together."

In conjunction with a push for greater clarity, time was, yes, spent dealing with matters such as inflections, pronoun usage, and punctuation, as related to their essays, with various rates of improvement among the students over the course of the semester. Some will have an ongoing struggle with mechanics; it's part of the process.

The central point I wish to state here is my belief that the writing activities described above were meaningful and successful—both for the students and for me—mostly because students had been given enough incentive and authority through the stories we read and the discourse surrounding them to develop keenly vested interests in their own writing voices within the confines of a writing classroom. A student noted in reference to Hughes's "Promulgations," "The author write about the way he feels about it. He writing about the situation is a lot and a very good way of dealing with it."

Realizing that simply to exercise the voice, to exercise *author*ity, can be significant action is a good understanding of what Julius and Jesse, and Chesnutt and Hughes, are up to. The student may have been responding, and in a manner very much as I have, to Simple's comment that "right now I cannot do much, but I can say all." And to begin to say all, for students who have been labeled remedial, is, as my student hints, a crucial achievement.

Works Cited

Chesnutt, Charles W. "Dave's Neckliss" (1889). In Sylvia L. Render, *The Short Fiction of Charles W. Chesnutt*. Washington, D.C.: Howard UP, 1981. 132–41.

———. "The Goophered Grapevine." In *The Conjure Woman*. Ann Arbor, MI: U of Michigan P, 1969. 1–35.

Hughes, Langston. "Concernment." In *Simple's Uncle Sam*. New York: Hill and Wang, 1965. 146–52.

———. "Promulgations." In *Simple's Uncle Sam*. New York: Hill and Wang, 1965. 160–64.

———. "Puerto Ricans." In *The Best of Simple*. New York: Hill and Wang, 1961. 216–18.

———. "Two Sides Not Enough." In *The Best of Simple*. New York: Hill and Wang, 1961. 213–16.

LANGUAGE AND LEARNING

One More Time for Professor Nuruddin

Yusuf Nuruddin, my brother. Surely the best arrangement is for me to be there at Medgar Evers College to visit your Black Studies courses. But now that I live two hundred fifty miles from Brooklyn, that option is no longer convenient. So as per your request, I have sent what you need to do justice to the language unit in your classes. I hope you'll appreciate that I treat African American and Caribbean varieties of English together. You may catch some flak for this. As you know, you teach at the college with the largest concentration in the country of Caribbean students with African bloodlines, many of whom insist upon a cultural distinction in every detail between themselves and African Americans. On the other hand, as you are also well aware, African American students on campus haven't always welcomed their Caribbean schoolmates warmly. So expect some tension. But hold your ground, for this is the way to go. And perhaps this current crop is much hipper anyway, past all that jingoism.

My examples of linguistic features are purposely restricted to the sentence level. I feel you can talk well enough about discourse features such as call-response, talking sweet, toastin', and so on. If not, we can consult some more sources. That analysis is never as complicated as the syntactic stuff, and I imagine it would be more interesting for you to read.

You may get to repay this favor, as I may need a good sociological and historical analysis for an English class soon, you know, with new historicism and all. I'll call.

Overview

Certain language varieties spoken by African Americans and Afro-Caribbeans have often been termed "Broken English" by teachers, students, and the general public. The underlying assumptions are that the language varieties in question are unsystematic, inferior, and the direct cause of poor reading and writing. Nothing could be more inaccurate. These language varieties are rule-governed systems that have developed as a result of conflict, conquest, and cultural mixing. They are equal in a linguistic sense to any other varieties of English and are not a major obstacle to literacy.

Origin and Development

Just as English grew and changed because of the Anglo-Saxon invasions, the Danish raids, the Norman conquest, and class divisions within Great Britain, the language changed again when it was exported overseas. Because of British colonizing activity in the New World accompanied by the mass importation of African slaves, the dialects, to use the most familiar label, spoken by most African Americans and Anglophone Caribbeans represent a merging of some aspects and practices of English and several languages of Africa. Although it was standard procedure to mix slaves from different groups together in an attempt to stifle their verbal interaction, some degree of verbal communication among them was necessary for plantations to operate effectively. In addition, masters and overseers needed to be able to address and receive reports from their workers. To accomplish these ends, new language varieties were created by combining what appeared to be the simplest (which usually meant least redundant) elements of two or more existing languages. Such newly created language systems are called *pidgins*.

In time, children are born who acquire a pidgin as their first language. The language combination is then said to have *creolized* and is referred to as a *creole*. People from the Caribbean sometimes say they speak Creole, which is true, but they are really talking about a particular creole, as *creole* also functions as a generic term. Jamaican Creole, for instance, also known as *patois*, is indeed a creole. But so are the range of dialects we generally call Black English.

The language varieties being considered can all be classified, following the lead of John Holm, under the heading *Atlantic Creole*, *AC* for short.* Creoles basically contain the syntax of the language of less or least prestige and the lexicon of the privileged tongue. AC, then, is an amalgam of English and structures from several African languages. But proportions

*Atlantic Creoles also include those based on other dominant languages like Dutch, French, and Spanish. For convenience, I limit the term's use to English-based creoles.

are not absolute. Some brands of AC are closer to Standard English syntax than others, and African lexical items have been incorporated into Standard English. Words borrowed from Africa include *yam*, *tote*, *gumbo*, *gorilla*, *elephant*, *okra*, *jazz*, *oasis*, *sorcery*, *cola*, *banana*, and *banjo*.

The above view of language formation is known as the *creole hypothesis* and is the explanation for AC given the most credence by contemporary linguists. Competing claims that AC symbolizes cognitive deficiency, or attests to physiological differences, or derives from white regional speech, or mostly signifies an evolution of Portuguese trade pidgin lack compulsion.

Creoles change over time, as all varieties do, usually moving closer to the dominant language. This is *decreolization*. Language varieties can also *recreolize*—that is, move in the opposite direction. It all depends upon social activities at large. That African Americans have been a numerical minority in the United States accounts for the great degree of decreolization in this country. Differences between AC in Jamaica and Barbados result largely from different histories of colonization and economic organization. Jamaica, for example, was ruled by Spain, then Britain, and housed large sugar plantations with relatively high slave-to-master ratios, while Barbados, "Little England," was never colonized by anyone but Big England and featured mainly small farms and low slave-to-master ratios.

Geography also accounts for differences. Jamaica, after all, is one thousand miles from Barbados, roughly the distance from New York to St. Louis. Usage is also influenced by gender, class, education, attitude, age, degrees of assimilation, contact with languages other than English, and so on. AC will vary slightly, therefore, from nation to nation and within nations, similar to how Standard English varies from Australia to New Zealand and from New England to Texas. What must be stressed, however, is AC's essential character. Despite differences among varieties, their similarities are far greater. They don't vary as much from one another as they do from Standard English. As J. L. Dillard points out, "The English of most American Blacks retains some features which are common to both Caribbean and West African varieties of English" (6).

Language Features

The following examples come from speech samples or student essays. The country where each subject spent his or her formative years is noted in parentheses. Although I approach them from the angle of inflections and spelling, there are other classification schemes for discussing syntax and phonology issues. I am not attempting an exhaustive or theoretically sophisticated review. I wish to keep this both condensed and useful.

INFLECTIONS

Inflections are changes in word form that indicate how a particular word is being used. For example, in the statement "We are interested in Malcolm's ideas," the *'s* is a suffix that completes the possessive construction. Generally, inflections proliferate when word order is relatively unimportant. That is why English, centuries ago, deriving mainly from German, had many noun and verb inflections. Word order wasn't an overriding feature of the language then. It since has become so. Subject, object, and possession can all be demonstrated by word order, and inflections are not needed to convey meaning—the reason, in fact, many have become obsolete. Even the distinction between *who* and *whom* is weakening and perhaps disappearing.

Inflections were not a feature of West African languages, and in the merger of those languages with English, inflections, being unnecessary to making meaning, did not become a significant feature of the creoles. Speakers of AC systematically eliminate certain redundancies relative to nouns, pronouns, and verbs. Instances commonly described as subject-verb (dis)agreement, tense, pronoun, or possessive errors are directly tied, as illustrated below, to this practice.

1. *She have* a Benz that she and Carl call the Status Symbol. (Guyana)
2. When *a young child have* a baby she is not ready for, problems come. (Guyana)
3. *A student do* have some say in the matter. (Jamaica)
4. *He need* to get with the program. (U.S.A.)
5. *Blacks* in South Africa *is refused* decent health care. (Barbados)
6. *He play* four instruments. (Trinidad).

No doubt, these types of constructions irk more than a few speech and English teachers, many of whom would be quick to assert that the speakers or writers don't know grammar or, even worse, that the sentences make no sense. But these configurations result from the application of a specifiable rule, in this case that only one form of a verb be used with all subjects. In an absolute sense, these constructions are no less meaningful or more ambiguous than their Standard English translations:

7. *She has* a Benz that she and Carl call the Status Symbol.
8. When *a young child has* a baby she is not ready for, problems come.
9. *A student does* have some say in the matter.
10. *He needs* to get with the program.
11. Blacks in South Africa *are refused* decent health care.
12. *He plays* four instruments.

The substitutions of *has* for *have*, *does* for *do*, *needs* for *need*, and *plays* for *play* don't clarify the statements. That the latter forms indicate singularity is true, but they don't create it. A *student* and *a young child* would not be confused with plural forms by any native speaker of English. To inflect a verb to show singularity, plurality, or person is redundant because the subject alone denotes these attributes.

AC speakers will sometimes produce forms like *they does* because they are struggling with conflicting rule systems. This is called *hypercorrection*. Hypercorrect forms are actually incorrect in all varieties of English. It is the same type of overgeneralization committed when a speaker learns how to indicate past tense but says *he goed* instead of *he went*. An additional example:

13. Sometimes in life we experience certain *things that tells* us we have to make a decision. (Guyana)

As stated previously, speakers of AC often do not mark for tense:

14. I was on my own. 15. It was very hard because I *have* to work day and night. (Jamaica)
16. Back when I was fourteen, I *drop* out of school. (Antigua)

17. Most of the factors *mention* about teenagers in my paragraphs are trends followed by most teenagers today. (Grenada)
18. I finally got away from my family. 19. Then I *start* having children right after I got married. (U.S.A.)

One would be justified in saying, to the horror of many language guardians, that AC represents an advanced variety of English, historically speaking, particularly with respect to verb usage. As Frederic Cassidy explains:

> Those of us who were brought up on Latin Grammar sometimes do not realise that the Standard English verb today has only three living inflectional suffixes: *(e)s* of the third person singular (*goes, sings*), *(e)d* (or *t*) of the weak past (tas*ted*, swep*t*) and *ing* of the present participle (*coming*). One cannot even include the *(e)n* of such verbs as bro*ken*, since it is never added to new verbs, and survives in a decreasing number of old ones. In the course of its history the English verb has been discarding inflection more and more. (57–58)

AC varieties of English assign a fixed form to nouns, usually the Standard English singular. Thus, we obtain the following:

20. Teenagers especially in America have the attitude of separating most *adult* from them. (Grenada)
21. Especially in those high technology *continent* such as America and Europe. (Grenada)
22. The hard facts hit us about a few *week* later when we had to start finding jobs to support ourselves. (Jamaica)

Hypercorrect utterances include:

23. I did not think *an adults* could say much.

One form of a pronoun is generally chosen or repeated. The subject pronoun may serve as the possessive pronoun also:

24. They still don't think that we are *they* equal. (Barbados)

25. They better bring *they* best! (U.S.A.)

Sometimes the Standard English subject pronoun becomes the object pronoun. Instead of *her* and *they*, we get:

26. Look at *she*! (Trinidad)
27. There are too many young people having babies and *them* themselves are still babies. (Guyana)

Along with possessive pronouns and "apostrophe *s*" (*town's people*), possession is indicated in Standard English by preposition (*people of the town*) or by juxtaposition (*townspeople*) Speakers of AC rely almost exclusively on juxtaposition:

28. *My parents business* was about to collapse. (Jamaica)

The convergence of AC pronunciation and the redundant aspect of all inflections determine the nature of auxiliary constructions:

29. This *has strengthen* me to be an example for my peers. (Trinidad)
30. But where his kids *were concern*, nothing was too strenuous for my dad. (Trinidad)

Hypercorrect forms produced include:

31. But he *did not succeeded* in doing so. (Jamaica)
32. This *could indicated* that this area was new to her. (Guyana)

SPELLING

Anyone can have trouble with words that sound alike. Speakers of various English varieties confuse your/you're, no/know, to/ too (and even two), and there/their. One can, of course, add other examples. Speakers of AC share the potential for these problems, and, because of pronunciation rules of AC, they have additional sets of homophones. Influenced heavily by the phonology of West African languages, speakers of AC soften consonant clusters at the beginning and end of many words. The initial *th* sound, for example, becomes *d* or *t*. So where *taught* and *thought* are not homophones to speakers of Standard English (in this case, not for speakers of the U.S. creole either), they are to many speakers of AC. Sentences like these are written frequently:

33. Fred wrote an essay he *taught* was excellent. (Grenada)
34. One must be *thought* responsibility. (Trinidad)
35. The kids who were being *thought* by Miss Moore didn't have much pride because of their environment. (Trinidad)

Although the softening of the initial *th* is only one of many AC phonological rules, it receives a lot of attention because initial *th* is a feature of many of the most commonly used words in English.

The softening of final consonant clusters also creates homophones specific to AC. For example: *mine/mind, fine/find*:

36. I really wouldn't *mine* having an Acura Legend. (U.S.A.)
37. In the 1980s you will *fine* more people having sex than in the 1960s. (Guyana)

Among AC speakers, Jamaicans possess a distinct feature:

> *h* behaves in a non-Standard way. It is, as often as not, prefixed to stressed vowels or diphthongs, as in *heggs* and *hice*, and dropped irregularly from other words—*'ow, 'igh, 'ouse*. This is very much like Cockney usage—indeed, some historical connection is not at all impossible; yet the Jamaican and Cockney confusions with *h* may merely result from the same conditions: loss of the sound, followed by an attempt to replace it that goes awry and puts it in the un-Standard places. (Cassidy 36–37)

Educational Implications

I promise not to take you too far afield here, but I think it's important to indicate the major camps in terms of dialect and education issues. I term them *eradicationists*, *bidialectalists*, and *pluralists*.

The eradicationists would argue that schools should attempt to eradicate AC because it represents deficient speech and interferes with the acquisition of Standard English. But while linguistic variation can contribute to minor problems of reading and writing, it is not the major cause of reading and writing problems. (Remember, dialects of English are far more alike than they are unalike.) Grapholects (writing systems) bridge dialects, which is why people from various English-speaking regions can read common texts in Standard English, or even in dialects such as AC. People don't read solely the way they speak. Nor do they write the way they speak unless they draw only upon native oral resources. To develop a Standard English "writing voice" is the key, and that comes through continual and plentiful practice by motivated students, not through drills aimed at eliminating the vernacular. To spend time on eradicationist attempts, given the badge of identity that language is, invites cultural resistance that hampers, perhaps even dooms, instructional efforts. This is not to argue that teaching Standard English, the language of wider communication, is never a legitimate school goal, only that it is not likely to happen through a policy of eradicationism.

Pluralists would maintain that most of the educational problems encountered by speakers of AC stem from who they are, not which language variety they utter. They understand that AC and Standard English are linguistically equal and know that the fact that they are not equal in society is a matter of society, not linguistics. The crucial work for pluralists is expressly political: shake up school and society so language variation doesn't play out so negatively in classrooms. Get AC some real respect, some acceptance. Pluralists wouldn't ignore Standard English, but they do feel that in a more equitable societal arrangement and school situation, students generally would want to expand their use of Standard English and, in fact, do so very well.

Bidialectalists know what pluralists know—namely, that AC is not inferior to Standard English in a linguistic sense. However, they would make the seemingly pragmatic argument that AC speakers will need Standard English to succeed in the mainstream. Theirs is an accommodationist strategy: they don't want to make much of a fuss.

I'm down with the pluralists. Educational initiatives that fail explicitly to consider or address social relations and student perceptions are impoverished in my view and are geared to fail students, like many of those of African descent, who feel reasons not to melt on into the program.

I'll stop for now. You easily have one whole class period covered. Maybe two. And you can assign fieldwork.

Works Cited

Cassidy, Frederic G. *Jamaica Talk: Three Hundred Years of the English Language in Jamaica* (1961). London: McMillan Education, 1982.

Dillard, J. L. *Black English: Its History and Usage in the United States* (1972). New York: Vintage, 1973.

Holm, John A. *Pidgins and Creoles: Reference Survey*. Cambridge: Cambridge UP, 1989.

———. *Pidgins and Creoles: Theory and Structure*. Cambridge: Cambridge UP, 1988.

Smitherman, Geneva. *Talkin and Testifyin: The Language of Black America* (1977). Detroit: Wayne State UP, 1986.

Language Learning and Democratic Development

I have sought to avoid hopping from one bandwagon to another, a behavior characteristic of American educators. My decisions to embrace or reject phonics or teaching grammar or back-to-basics or writing-process instruction or critical thinking courses have not been based on the shrillness or popularity of rhetoric but upon cautious consideration of practice and theory. As I have argued, often in a winding and inductive way, in favor of pluralistic educational initiatives, against monocultural ideals, in favor of emphasizing literature in basic writing courses, I have been approaching, sometimes unwittingly, a deductive vantage point from which I can efficiently analyze educational proposals. This viewpoint mainly entails a concern with democratic schooling and affords an extremely useful typology: either educational proposals promote democracy and thus are to be favored, or they do not. This is how I am viewing language arts learning proposals for all levels, including adult education programs.

Let me confess at this point, while I'm being purposely political, that a small part of me leans toward benevolent dictatorship as the superior form of government. I believe it was Sartre who asserted that when one chooses, one chooses for all, and I take those words too literally at times, as I'm sure Sartre would discourage. At any rate, since I would never trust any dictator to be totally beneficent other than myself, the greater part of me sees true democracy as our nation's best hope. If we're not struggling toward that as educators, we're not struggling toward anything worthwhile.

Our work as teachers is political—whether we construe it that way or not—and our obligation, which we sometimes shun, is to provide clarity of political vision regarding our teaching endeavors. My vision yields the following mission statement: literacy educators further the development of authentic democracy—enlightened citizenry and all that—by helping to

---

Presented December 9, 1992, at the Graduate School and University Center of the City University of New York, as part of the Distinguished Speakers Series in Adult Learning sponsored by the CUNY Office of Academic Affairs.

create informed, critical, powerful, independent, and culturally sensitive student voices.

Of course I'm not pretending to be original. Thomas Jefferson knew the value of heightened dialogue and asserted more than two hundred years ago that given a preference, he would choose newspapers without government rather than government without newspapers, although Jefferson may have softened that stance somewhat had he been around to watch newspapers beat up Gary Hart and Bill Clinton or to discover how susceptible to propaganda, especially in the television age, many Americans have become. There can be no democracy in the full sense he envisioned without universal, critical literacy. This condition does not exist in our society and is why I have been qualifying the term *democracy* with descriptors like *true* and *authentic*. Because Jefferson was a slaveholder, he was more than a little bit hypocritical, but his better notions, like his understanding that governance by internal authority requires widespread informed debate, are yet worthwhile.

John Dewey took this conception a step further. In *Democracy and Education*, which appeared more than eighty years ago, he wrote:

> A democracy is more than a form of government; it is primarily a mode of associated living, of conjoint communicated experience. The extension in space of the number of individuals who participate in an interest so that each has to refer his own action to that of others, and to consider the action of others to give point and direction to his own, is equivalent to the breaking down of those barriers of class, race, and national territory which kept men from perceiving the full import of their activity. These more numerous and more varied points of contact denote a greater diversity of stimuli to which an individual has to respond; they consequently put a premium on variation in his action. They secure a liberation of powers which remain suppressed as long as the incitations to action are partial, as they must be in a group which in its exclusiveness shuts out many interests. (87)

Paulo Freire also develops this idea of culturally diverse stimulation, while examining more directly the relative positions of students and teachers. In *Pedagogy of the Oppressed*, which appeared more than twenty-five years ago, he asserts:

> A careful analysis of the teacher-student relationship at any level, inside or outside the school, reveals its fundamentally narrative character. This relationship involves a narrating subject (the teacher) and patient, listening objects (the students). The contents, whether values or empirical dimensions of reality, tend in the process of being narrated to become lifeless and petrified. Education is suffering from narration sickness. (57)

There was enough of a Jeffersonian-Deweyan-Freirean strain kept alive among language arts professionals to bring about the English Coalition Conference of 1987, convened in a nation probably more diverse and booming with more narration than could have been predicted by these intellectual antecedents of the conference participants. At the gathering, the theme of which was "Democracy through Language," old ideas were reworked and invigorated. An excerpt from the conference report reads:

> The increased heterogeneity of our society also gives new urgency to enhancing students' ability to appreciate cultural diversity and multiple ways of reading and writing. The information explosion makes learning how to read and write absolutely vital for living, because without these abilities students will not be able to assimilate, evaluate, and control the immense amount of knowledge and the great number of messages which are produced every day. The development of new media similarly requires of citizens an enhanced ability to use different ways of reading and writing, and language arts instruction has an important role to play here. (86)

Perhaps no students have been more shut out, objectified, and bewildered than those who eventually enroll in adult education programs or those who enter so-called remedial programs in open-admissions colleges. These two groups can reasonably be viewed as one in some respects. I have, in fact, seen students proceed from adult education programs into colleges as discretionary admits, meaning without high school diplomas, and subsequently be referred back to adult education programs. The important matter is that most of these students have not prospered in our system of public education.

Many adult education students are members of ethnic minority or immigrant groups, of a people whose numbers on these shores are tied directly either to bloodshed or to dreams. When we meet them, they have not given up hope of securing credentials that will, they feel, enable them to succeed. Unfortunately, however, a large percentage of these students (like too many students overall) will be subjected to instructional practices that will not help them toward their goal. They are eager yet passive, maybe the worst disposition, in the long run, any group of students can possess. They search for saviors, instead of guides, in teachers, many of whom all too willingly accept the role. These students search for magic in methods; they settle for getting taught at while they fail to see themselves as largely responsible for their own learning. And what is especially ironic and painful to realize, as a spectator to some of this educational parade, is that these students' lives in many instances are the very case studies that indicate the ineffectiveness, from the standpoint of their own benefit, of dictatorial teaching. They indeed suffer—they, not education; personally, not abstractly—from narration sickness. And we lose them again.

I always hope to get in my class students who have been rather rebellious in previous schools and who prove to be somewhat contentious in general. I want to work with these spunky souls, who often not only know where they want to go (which most students know at least vaguely) but may have some strong and sensible ideas about how they want to get there. But alas, I don't start out with these nervy types very frequently. I see instead remedial students doing the good old remedial thing, waiting on the remedy. They are expecting isolated, prepackaged grammar lessons. They are waiting on presentation of written format divorced from ongoing reading. I have had basic writing students ask me why I put so many reading assignments on the syllabus. After all, they reason, ever mindful of their convoluted prose, they have taken the course to learn how to write. And they are almost hopelessly intimidated by literary texts. I'll stretch this last point out a bit further, for I think that attempting to resolve the problem indicated here is perhaps the most important work I have done in class.

Several years ago, when reading essays students had submitted after reading a William Faulkner short story, "Dry September," I encountered a startling beginning: "This story was written in 1931 on a hot dry day in the month of September."

I was taken aback because a hot dry September day is simply the backdrop *in* the tale, and 1931 is the publication date indicated on the opening page of the story as it appeared in the anthology. The student demonstrated no understanding of a writer's ability to use language to create a world. In her mind Faulkner was doing the work of a stringer, and she was content to summarize what she perceived to be his impartial recording of events.

When I shared my own reading of "Dry September," a story on one level about a rumor of rape, I started explaining how it spoke to me about a certain psychosexual sickness that lies just below the surface of Southern life easily exposed by even the slightest suggestion of black-on-white rape and how the description of aridity illustrates that sickness. This same student interrupted me. Peevishly she inquired, "Where did you get that from?" She wasn't challenging my originality; she didn't understand my symbol making. Prepared to scour the text for literal evidence, for some words she had missed, she failed to see that an examination of my belief system was more appropriate if she wished to know the total sources from which I derived meaning. Despite my subsequent request for interpretive papers, she penned one of the most detached efforts ever given to me in an English class. Indeed, she was far more concerned with her usage—which, no surprise to me, was poor—than with interpretation. This was a Freshman English class, not a basic writing course, mind you. She had passed one of those already.

Although the most memorable case of what I call low literary self-esteem, this student's plight is not uncommon. A number of students have, like her, staggered through watered-down basic skills or adult education courses only to be left with little or no conception about how to proceed successfully in, say, College English I. This episode helped to convince me that work in literary response should be a mainstay of all reading and writing courses I teach, basic and developmental classes as well as those designated Freshman English. But I still didn't have a broad view, not anything like a theory of democratic schooling. I saw myself as simply making a reasonable response to an immediate problem. As a practical matter, I figured, if students could write critical papers on literature, they could fulfill their English course requirements. The sooner they started working toward that goal, the better. Addressing the question of teaching literature, Peter Roberts writes:

> One answer to this argument is that in the teaching of Appropriate and Effective English, because people have always drawn on the techniques of persuasion inherent in the language of written literature, the study of written literature is the most fertile ground for understanding language use. In other words, the traditional categories of literature study—theme, structure/plot, style, content, purpose—are the very same factors that govern Effective English. Therefore, where once literature was an objective in itself, whose appreciation was aided by knowledge of its constituent factors, it can now also be treated as general exemplification of factors which are used in specialized forms of persuasion (i.e., in advertising, labels, newspaper articles, etc.). (*West Indians and Their Language* 201)

Influenced by the work of James Britton, through his book *Language and Learning* and such essays as "The Role of Fantasy" and "English Teaching: Retrospect and Prospect," I became acutely aware of the possibilities of using literature as a way to expand students' conceptual powers and to foster expressive ability. Naturally, I held a vague notion that it had worked that way for me. Literature has always been a powerful way of reminding me that I am not just in the world but of it. Writing about literature or attempting to compose some myself makes up the bulk of the scribing I have managed. Through the realm of literature, it can be argued, runs the clearest path to proficiency in both reading and writing. In the wider world, stories engage people much more deeply than drills or restricted assignments, a relationship that should also hold in educational circles provided students are given a proper forum.

I came to recognize that the problem with students like the one who summarized the Faulkner story is not that they are totally devoid of critical ability. However, because they have learned to be intimidated, they usually don't bring what are at times substantial evaluative talents into the arena of formal education. They don't cope well with the surprising experience of being asked to pass judgment on texts already certified as great works, or so it appears, signified by their presence in an anthology or on a teacher's syllabus. Teachers themselves, sometimes merely by the sureness and forcefulness with which they speak about a piece of literature, frequently dominate class discussion and give the impression that their opinion is really the only important one, even as they push transactional or reader-response theory. I know I have quoted Louise Rosenblatt on the one hand, trying to persuade students that the primary subject matter of their papers had to be "the web of sensations and ideas that they spun between themselves and the text" (*The Reader, the Text, the Poem* 137), while on the other hand becoming too directive of their spinning. Such intrusion short-circuits the interpretive endeavor and fails to lend strength to student voices. Rather than look to deficit and skills models to explain student withdrawal from classroom literary encounters, teachers would do well to examine their own roles during such activities. There certainly are specific strategies that readers at every level can learn to employ to make better sense of texts, but these strategies are not the discrete "skills" about which many reading teachers are concerned. We could introduce teachers themselves to deconstruction, for example, as a critical tool without assuming a skills or decoding deficiency on their part. If we did assume deficiency of this sort, they would be right to feel insulted.

As my outlook broadened, with graduate study and the like, as well as finally and consciously linking political ideas I had held more explicitly to my work, I was able to articulate more substantial reasons for using literature in all language arts classes. I understood that along with passing courses and becoming more literate, it is fundamental that students gain practice in developing beliefs that are to be defended, amended, or discarded as they participate in the discourse of academic and wider formal settings, since informed and powerful voices existing in dialogic and critical relationships is the form of discourse this society supposedly privileges. Other voices, less informed, less powerful, generally are excluded from the dominant societal conversation. I wrote a few years back that surrounding a text in class, being united by it, being at odds with others because of it, approving and/or disapproving it, discussing it confidently, feeling passionate enough to write about it and want to share that writing (which then means attention to conventional usage), seeking new texts, and searching out new talk are some of the most important activities students can undertake—not because they are good ideas in and of themselves, I see now, but because they support democratic development and are on that basis to be favored.

By 1987, I was ready for the English Coalition Conference—if only I had been called. I'm not sure I would have gone anyway. It was held on an old plantation in Maryland, and that's a spooky kind of thing to me. Nonetheless, in my painstaking manner, I had moved very close in spirit to those who participated. To cite another section of their report:

> Teaching students how and why different ways of reading can find different meanings in the same text can provide important experience in understanding and appreciating opposing perspectives. Learning about the many different kinds of writing and ways of thinking which are the subject matter of the language arts curriculum can expand the capacity of students to imagine and value worlds other than their own. The ability to communicate their views in oral and written form and to listen with comprehension to the views of others is also indispensable to citizens in a democracy, and enhancing this ability is a major aim of language arts education. (86)

So neither I nor the folks at the conference would support narrowly defined skills curriculums in adult literacy programs or in any other programs. Interpretive work should characterize the academic lives of students. Reader-response theory, though a step in the right direction, is no miracle cure for all that has gone wrong. And there were no miracles in the class I alluded to earlier. Some students showed marked improvement as critics, while others, including the woman who struggled with the Faulkner story, did not. And even the students who did progress significantly were not as ready for College English II as I would have liked. They were still too afraid of "literature" and not trusting enough of themselves. They didn't display enough of the arrogance that is part of the temperament of all good readers and writers—and viewers, too, I might add, having observed the critical activity surrounding the movie *Malcolm X*.

Some moviegoers pointed out the historical inaccuracies of the film, legitimately so, given that many less informed viewers were ready to accept the film as historically accurate in every detail. Director Spike Lee, equally correct, insisted the film was a dramatic representation of Malcolm's life, not a documentary. As a result, Lee felt justified in taking artistic license. I had no quarrel with any party on this score. In fact, I found this particular debate relatively boring. A more interesting activity for language arts classes is for students and instructors to question how valid the division is that Lee made between dramatic and documentary.

Could any film, even a documentary, be completely objective? Or consider *The Autobiography of Malcolm X*, a text regarded as a virtually indisputable source of authority by Lee and many others. Does autobiography have an absolute claim on truth or just a particular one—a subject requesting that we believe the one story of his or her life that only he or she can narrate in first person? I'm not anywhere near commending Bruce Perry's misguided psycho-babble about Malcolm, and I'm certainly not disparaging autobiography as a genre. I wrote one myself. I raise these questions to suggest more ways of talking and getting students to talk about textual authority, maybe to change relations of power between students and texts, to get students to see that they can act powerfully on stories, that stories don't just act on them.

Oprah Winfrey, at least three times on her television talk show discussing Lee's film, implored people not to worry about *Malcolm X*'s length, 201 minutes, but to go see it anyway. I would have liked to hear students talk about why Winfrey felt such exhortation was necessary. To whom did they think Oprah was specifically addressing her remarks? Did they think that a comment was being made about their interests and abilities? If so, what was their response? And what I'd be most interested in regarding any venture involving Malcolm X is what do students, especially adult education students (of whom Malcolm was one), think is the crucial lesson to be learned from his life? Do they accept the weak, tepid line that the central import of his life is that he overcame obstacles and had a tremendous capacity for reinventing himself? I know I don't accept it. You can run to your nearest politician to find a master of hurdling and reinvention. Malcolm stood straight up and aimed a fiery verbal assault directly against white supremacy and economic exploitation. That is what thrilled me on the verge of adolescence. I didn't care that he liked jazz and danced the Jitterbug. I liked Motown and did the Brooklyn Hustle. I didn't care what hard times he had gone through to get to that stance. I had my own hard times to go through. No, what was essential was that he was on the scene by whatever circumstances, tall, majestic, being defiant, and mostly being right. While I am witness to the commodification of X, I'm looking for some X-ification, if you will, some basic decency and far less greed in our structures of commodity. I'm seeking some X-ification, some gentle equalities and student empowerment, in our establishments of education. This is how I am reading X as text.

I may seem far afield from my basic argument, but actually I have merely stepped inside it for a moment, personifying critical reading ability conceived broadly, though, of course, I don't imagine that everyone shares my views or endorses my explication.

Before I begin to wind down, and point out some specific contrasts between authoritarian and democratic practices, I want to be as clear as possible about some of my previous remarks concerning students. I don't mean to imply that all adult education students are so easily victimized or that all programs are set up in such a way as to achieve victimization. Neither do I mean to underplay psychological strategies that account for student behavior, a passive rejection of certain kinds of formal instruction, for example. Nor do I ignore external social factors that undermine success. I simply wish to emphasize what I feel most familiar with, a seemingly enabling eagerness and availability to learn rendered nearly useless in school by a learned passivity about how schooling should proceed.

A view of knowledge as lore, then, as accumulated information, is an authoritarian view. A teacher holding this view would consequently conduct classes in an authoritarian manner, assuming his or her rightful function to be that of distributing knowledge to his or her charges. This promotes the student passivity I have been describing. On the other hand, from a democratic view, knowledge is a process that is only successful in schools with active student participation, which is proper preparation for the active, participatory lifestyles envisioned by some of the scholars mentioned earlier.

The construct that admirable progress is being made as teachers "cover the material" is an authoritarian construct. That more meaningful activity occurs when students "uncover material" is a democratic construct.

To focus exclusively on teachers' purposes is authoritarian. Cointentional education, as Freire puts it, is preferable—not because it has a nice ring to it, but because it is democratic.

A deficit model of language differences is also authoritarian. Deviations from standard or target usage are treated as deficiencies. Black English is "Broken English" and has to be repaired. Jamaican Creole is "Broken English" and has to be operated upon. There is a line on the back of the City University of New York Writing Assessment Test booklet on which students are to indicate their native language. Many students from the Caribbean indeed write "Broken English" on this line. The first few times I saw this, I thought the students were being facetious. But I soon changed my mind. The rate at which they were failing the exam was no joke. Students, not dialects, have been broken, and negative responses to language differences have been much of their problem. An equality model of language variation, the only one supported by modern sociolinguistic scholarship, does not support repair-model instruction. Understanding, as George Bernard Shaw did, that "a language is a dialect with an army behind it," democratic educators focus upon repertoire expansion. They accept the legitimacy of various types of English and study them so as to contribute to an enlightened discussion of learning and teaching with respect to the various speaking populations to be served.

I think the history of English, if only in a rudimentary way, is an important topic for language arts classrooms. We could all stand to know how closely the earlier evolution of English was tied to politics and warfare. We could start with the collapse of the Roman Empire in the fifth century, talk some about clashes among Jutes, Celts, Angles, and Saxons, and how this activity led to the development of certain Englishes, as did conflict with the Norse, from whom were borrowed such essential items as the pronouns *they*, *them*, and *their*. We could talk about Duke William and his posse of Normans, their (remember a word from the Norse) conquest causing a considerable "Frenchifying" of English. *Government*, a word central to this presentation, is a French word. Then we have to notice the Anglo-Saxons, back in charge and growing strong enough to export English around the world to become the tongue upon which the sun never set. During this period dictionaries and prescriptive grammar books were produced. Standards of usage were established.

Writing instruction in schools has much to do with standards set by powerful groups. Being able to produce texts that meet that standard may be a valuable ability. However, a focus on the standard to be reached, accompanied by disregard for different ways students may try to get there, is authoritarian and disabling. An approach in which the prevailing spirit is to take advantage of varying talents, strengths, and interests of students is more enabling, more democratic.

The final area I want to talk about is *multiculturalism*. I find it a term that obscures more than it illumines when forwarded as an educational concept; at least, that's what my conversations with people have led me to conclude. It is easy enough to argue against a monocultural ideal. To privilege one culture amid the wealth of diversity in this nation is certainly to be authoritarian. To celebrate cultural diversity is sensible. But of what is the celebration to consist? I often hear discourse on multiculturalism reduced to the level of cuisine, a chicken chow mein, chicken fettuccine, Southern fried chicken, arroz con pollo kind of multiculturalism. I hear leaders say our nation's strength lies in its diversity, though I don't often hear them articulate why, that the real virtue of multiculturalism or ethnic diversity is that it supremely tests the nation's resolve to live up to the rhetoric contained in its most cherished documents. Will we comprehend the teasing oxymoron near the end of Ellison's *Invisible Man*? To quote:

> It's "winner take nothing" that is the great truth of our country or any country. Life is to be lived, not controlled; and humanity is won by continuing to play in the face of certain defeat. Our fate is to become one, and yet many—This is not prophecy, but description. (564)

Ira Shor, who is on the faculty at CUNY's Graduate Center, posed to me a question: what would college language arts classes look like if we took multiculturalism seriously? The obvious answer is that the content of curriculums would change. It would become more diversified. More and more literature by authors from so-called minority groups would be incorporated, and so on. Again, that's the easy answer. I contend, however, that three other results, usually overlooked, of taking multiculturalism seriously are ultimately more important than mere diversification of the canon.

The first result I'm thinking about is that whole departments would be more serious about multiculturalism. This may seem an odd point to make, since I have already mentioned a diversified canon. But such progressive activity is often confined to only a few members in a department. It becomes someone's specialty. We create a cadre of experts on multiculturalism when, in fact, we should all be striving for expertise. Some usually well-intentioned colleagues are still asking me to, quote, "give them something on multiculturalism," like my name is Mr. Multicultural or something like that, like I'm not just one African American man. I see the term on numerous job announcements these days: "Candidate must have demonstrated commitment to multicultural education." I surmise that the insistence on this quality in applicants is because the employers possess so little of it themselves.

The second result I foresee is that the ethnic composition of classrooms would change, especially in upper-level literature courses. A higher concentration of students from so-called minorities might even become language arts professionals. I'm not sure what the exact effect would be on adult education programs, but it would ultimately be positive.

The third result, most important, of taking multiculturalism seriously is that it would disappear—that is, as a distinct educational concept, at least in the sense it now exists. At present, it is an *ism* that circumscribes the failure to take full advantage of the diversity that has always surrounded us. The United States has been a polylingual, multicultural nation since its inception, and if the educational system had reflected this reality all along, there would never have been a need to propose this particular *ism* as a panacea for educational ills. If a multicultural ideal were ever present, it would not have become a special movement. In fact, it may be time for another movement, one that stresses not just recognition of diversity but diverse interaction. This new movement, really an eve-of-the-twenty-first-century update of an intellectual tradition I sketched earlier, would emphasize not just multicultural existence but transcultural dialogue.

One evening in a restaurant, I remarked to my friend and colleague Nancy Lester that with all the new experts on multiculturalism running around, it was a clear signal to stop using the term to explain anything. It was time to light out, as Huck Finn might put it, for other rhetorical territory. I was amazed by the numbers. As I reexamined the program for the Annual Convention of the National Council of Teachers of English in 1981, the first year I attended, I hardly noticed any reference to multiculturalism, though by then I had heard the term used among literary artists for at least a decade. Of approximately two hundred panels and workshops at the six-day conference, only three were billed as multicultural or multiethnic in perspective, and one of those panels was composed entirely of presenters from Canada. The conference theme was "Sustaining the Essentials." For the 1989 NCTE annual convention, the theme was "Celebrating Diversity." Did I hear someone say bandwagon, that it won't last? We'll see.

Insofar as *multi* means diverse fluidity, it sounds good to me. But where *multi* means distinct, as the fixed tile in a mosaic, I think we have problems. This is one reason I enjoyed Toni Morrison's book *Playing in the Dark*. Her ideas about American Africanism—Morrison's phrase to describe how the African presence in the United States profoundly affected the work of writers such as Willa Cather, Ernest Hemingway, and Mark Twain—make for good cross-cultural conversation.

It is all before us now. There is a past to draw on but not to duplicate. What about the golden age of American education when all was fine? Forget it. It never happened. Numerous scholars have argued convincingly that American education has generally focused on producing a highly literate elite and a minimally literate general populace. Never was it the most widely held view among administrators to provide high-level literacy for everyone, what business leaders are calling for urgently. It is indeed a new literacy challenge we and our students face, a task we must be equal to if we are to have the most favorable participation in civic and business affairs, if our society is genuinely to become more inclusive and approach its full potential for humanism.

Works Cited

Britton, James. "English Teaching: Retrospect and Prospect." In Gordon M. Pradl, ed., *Prospect and Retrospect: Selected Essays of James Britton*. Montclair, NJ: Boynton/Cook, 1982. 210–15.

———. *Language and Learning* (1970). Harmondsworth: Penguin, 1972.

———. "The Role of Fantasy." In Gordon M. Pradl, ed., *Prospect and Retrospect: Selected Essays of James Britton*. Montclair, NJ: Boynton/Cook, 1982. 38–45.

Dewey, John. *Democracy and Education* (1916). New York: Free Press, 1966.

Ellison, Ralph. *Invisible Man* (1952). New York: Vintage, 1972.

Freire, Paulo. *Pedagogy of the Oppressed*. New York: Continuum, 1970.

Lloyd-Jones, Richard, and Andrea Lunsford, eds. *The English Coalition Conference: Democracy through Language*. Urbana, IL: NCTE, 1989.

Morrison, Toni. *Playing in the Dark: Whiteness and the Literary Imagination*. Cambridge, MA: Harvard UP, 1992.

Perry, Bruce. *Malcolm X: The Life of a Man Who Changed Black America*. Barrytown, NY: Station Hill Press, 1991.

Roberts, Peter. *West Indians and Their Language*. Cambridge: Cambridge UP, 1988.

Rosenblatt, Louise. *The Reader, the Text, the Poem: The Transactional Theory of the Literary Work*. Carbondale, IL: Southern Illinois UP, 1978.

African American in Process

In 1988, Lisa Delpit achieved a masterstroke of irony. Writing in the *Harvard Educational Review*, she broached the subject of silence and subsequently hushed much of the audience she was imploring to speak. Her goal in "The Silenced Dialogue: Power and Pedagogy in Educating Other People's Children" was to initiate or redirect conversations about writing pedagogy and to amplify remarks made in a 1986 article entitled "Skills and Other Dilemmas of a Progressive Black Educator." Although praiseworthy in several respects, especially for an analysis of what Delpit calls "the culture of power," the two-part entry also represented somewhat muddled thinking about writing instruction, which undermined her own aims. She argued, even as she offered disclaimers, that writing-process pedagogy is inappropriate for African American children. Such pedagogy, she vaguely contended, emphasizes fluency at the expense of teaching specific skills, a belief supported by several of her African American colleagues.

Delpit recalled how she had learned writing-process pedagogy as a graduate student at a prestigious university. She declined to name the institution. She also offered that she "never wrote any text longer than two sentences" until tenth grade and suggested that the key to her Standard English literacy development was having her speech constantly corrected and spending hours on writing drills ("Skills" 380). She added that when she employed an open classroom model, her white students from "Society Hill" thrived while her African American students from "South Philly" faltered. And her indictment against process strategy was completed when she revealed that Black teachers who confided in her held the opinion that the method is not for Black children and may even be part of a white conspiracy to keep them uneducated. Her friend Cathy (no last name was given) declared: "This is just another one of those

---

Excerpts presented November 17, 1994, at the Annual Convention of the National Council of Teachers of English.

racist ploys to keep our kids out. White kids learn how to write a decent sentence. Even if they don't teach them in school, their parents make sure they get what they need. But what about our kids? They don't get it at home and they spend all their time in school learning to be *fluent*. I'm sick of this liberal nonsense" ("Skills" 382).

Delpit quoted other Black teachers but didn't give even their first names. She did not identify sites, provide detailed scenarios, or dispute the ideas of particular educational theorists. There were several reasons, then, she should have received plentiful feedback. She was clearly open to the charge that she had misrepresented process pedagogy; the issue of substantiation seemed germane as well. There were no formal citations, for example, in the 1986 essay. Perhaps most important, her stereotypical images of African American students and of teachers, both African American and European American, were certainly assailable.

Although she received calls in reaction to her work, Delpit's challenge to process pedagogy did not provoke great public response among language arts professionals. Her ideas weren't featured prominently, say, at conferences of the National Council of Teachers of English, a group with enough deconstructionists, problematizers, "site contesters," other assorted contestants, and multiculturalists to boot, to get a good argument going about almost anything. On the other hand, I believe her articles were passed around frequently. In fact, that's how I got them, delivered with some agitation. So the interest was there, but not the noise.

I was approached by colleagues at convention sites several times, most often during the 1992 NCTE Spring Conference in Washington, D.C., where Delpit appeared on a panel I helped to organize. In rather cautious tones, they would ask me about her writings. Much to their relief, I would express a general disagreement with the articles while acknowledging the valuable insights contained therein. My colleagues would respond softly, carefully.

Of course, what accounted for our muted dialogues were the complexions of the people who had approached me. They were the Euro type. They had been stumped, not intellectually but rhetorically. Delpit had played the so-called race card, positing a variation of the basic argument "I'm Black, so I know what's best for Black kids." Not many European Americans seemed willing to call her on that—not out loud. They thereby avoided a possible nationalistic rebuttal. They didn't want to be called racists for expressing legitimate intellectual concerns. At the 1992 conference, only one person, African American educator Dorothy Strickland of Rutgers University, subjected Delpit's analysis to a degree of oppositional scrutiny. At least, this is what I was told. I was primed to speak out also, but in our session other issues came to the fore, and I decided to postpone airing my criticism.

Delpit had also employed a verbal stratagem of "I didn't do it that way, so it's not necessary." But this tactic lacked the impact of the racialized one, and if it had been the major contention in her essays, they wouldn't have drawn much attention, perhaps wouldn't even have been published. Surely they would have quieted no one.

It has also been pointed out to me that gender was a factor in the silence. Women, the explanation goes, are hesitant to criticize publicly other women because it's so hard for women to gain professional acceptance in the first place. Maybe there is something there, although I never heard any women whispering about Camille Paglia. The more cynical read is that white people weren't going to invest much energy debating methodology for African American children. They would argue the product-versus-process issue among themselves, do their best for white children, and leave it at that. However, I couldn't subscribe to that notion because, as indicated, too much European American traffic had come my way. No, the race card was trump.

What I am angling for, then, is fulfillment of Delpit's original goal, which was to spur as many exchanges as possible about the relevance of writing-process instruction for African American children. I think this is best done by specifying the tenets of such instruction, diminishing suppositions, whether they be racialized or otherwise, that don't address the model presented, and then sending invitations for further discussion that people can feel comfortable accepting. I am not concerned primarily with disputing Delpit. I don't presume she holds those exact views today. In fact, the reason I have dispensed with the academic convention of writing about her texts in the present tense, as you may have already noticed, is to stress my use of them as historical reference points that merely tip an iceberg of contemporary dialectics about writing-process instruction. I have heard many of the same things she has. I, too, talk with Cathys. I am trying to treat their ideas, those of my wary colleagues in convention halls, and Delpit's also, more seriously than has been the case.

Steven Zemelman and Harvey Daniels, in "Defining the Process Paradigm," provide fifteen concepts that, as they say, "should provide a sufficient definition of the process model of writing instruction" (345). As I talk further about Delpit's work, then, I do so with this list in mind:

> 1. Teachers who understand and appreciate the basic linguistic competence that students bring with them to school, and who therefore have positive expectations for students' achievements in writing.
> 2. Regular and substantial practice at writing.
> 3. Instruction in the process of writing—learning how to work at a given writing task in appropriate phases, including prewriting, drafting, and revising.
> 4. The opportunity to write for real, personally significant purposes.
> 5. Experience in writing for a wide range of audiences, both inside and outside of school.
> 6. Rich and continuous reading experience, including both published writing and the work of peers and teachers.
> 7. Exposure to models of writing in process and writers at work, including both classmates and skilled adult writers.
> 8. Collaborative activities that provide ideas for writing and guidance in revising drafts in progress.
> 9. One-to-one writing conferences with the teacher.
> 10. Inquiry-oriented classroom activities that involve students with rich sets of data and social interaction, and that focus on specific modes or elements of writing.
> 11. Increased use of sentence-combining exercises, which replaces instruction in grammatical terminology.
> 12. Mechanics of writing taught in the context of students' own compositions, rather than in separate exercises and drills.
> 13. Moderate marking of the surface structure errors in student papers, focusing on sets or patterns of related errors.
> 14. Flexible and cumulative evaluation of writing that stresses revision. The teacher's written comments include a mixture of praise and criticism, with praise dominating.
> 15. Writing as a tool of learning in all subjects across the curriculum. (345–53)

No teacher is expected to give attention to every dictum, and the authors resist pushing any particular combination. As they explain: "The danger we face in our field today, and it's now a serious threat, is the idea that there is only one right way to handle a given kid, a given grade level, a given chunk of curriculum, a given element of writing. This is not just wrong; it is profoundly, dangerously, insidiously wrong" (355).

Zemelman and Daniels don't seem to be the ones with whom Cathy was upset. They all identify the same problem, a sort of mindless orthodoxy. But where Zemelman and Daniels blame practitioners for the misapplication of writing-process theory, Cathy blamed the paradigm itself. I have some sympathy for her complaint and for Delpit's representation of it. A little hearsay (I've used some already) and the prospects of a good conspiracy theory always pique my interest. However, both Cathy and Delpit failed to develop the story line. To make all students spend all their time on one aspect of writing—say, the fluency that Cathy commented on—is at odds with serious attempts to instantiate writing-process instruction, clashing, at the very least, with features 1, 3, 8, and 14 presented above. So while I am definitely willing to accept the word of Cathy and other informants that they had encountered inflexible, insensitive, and racist teachers as well as poorly managed writing projects, I don't, on the other hand, see a need to privilege their vague interpretation of educational ideology. The reasoning most useful for the dialogue Delpit urged would expose the stark contradictions between clearly articulated theory and poor practice.

Also useful would be avoidance of unnecessary binarism and reductionism. In Delpit's 1986 article, Blacks were said to fail in the open classroom and fare better in a more rigid, skills-based curriculum. The same was not true of whites. Although the class difference between "Society Hill" students and "South Philly" students was mentioned, it was not acknowledged as a possible explanation for the performance and attitude of each group. One is led to conclude, for example, that *no* African American child prospers in an open classroom and that *all* white students do. Further essentializing occurred when it was claimed that all African American students were already fluent and that work on fluency functioned in opposition to needed work on skills. That African American children wrote elaborate rap songs is cited as proof of the fluency they possessed. Ignored is the reality that fluency is relative to tasks and modes of discourse. People may exhibit different degrees of fluency in different genres. Operationalizing fluency is, in fact, a skill. I am a far less fluent essayist than rapper. I have to push myself much harder to get the essay work done. I free-write, dismiss conventional structures, really force the issue of fluency at times. I push through the relative discomfort. If I didn't, we wouldn't have this text to discuss.

One more word about raps. Students can write them *in* school, a notion not forwarded by Delpit's informants but one that is consistent with item 5. And they can be helped to become more fluent in that activity. I don't buy the stereotype that they are all fluent rappers any more than I believe that they are all natural experts at singing, dancing, and dribbling basketballs.

The most curious dichotomy Delpit used was to pit Black teachers against writing-process teachers. As she wrote in "Skills and Other Dilemmas":

> Writing-process advocates often give the impression that they view the direct teaching of skills to be restrictive to the writing process at best, and at worst, politically repressive to students already oppressed by a racist educational system. Black teachers, *on the other hand* [emphasis mine], see the teaching of skills to be essential to their students' survival. (383)

In this setup, one cannot be Black *and* a writing-process advocate—quite ironic because that is exactly what Delpit herself was and perhaps yet is. And there are others.

African Americans Janis Epps and Jacqueline Royster endorse writing-process instruction in *Tapping Potential: English and Language Arts for the Black Learner*. Epps, in "Killing Them Softly: Why Willie Can't Write," provides a scathing polemic against the restrictive, she would even say genocidal, skills instruction foisted upon African American youth. More important than skills instruction, in her view, are critical thinking and "respect for their own personal experiences and those of their people" (156).

Royster, less strident but equally committed to the education of African Americans, writes in "A New Lease on Writing" that the current trend toward process-oriented teaching seems to be a key asset (163). However, she does note the inconsistencies that may accompany attempts to enact a process model; nevertheless, she reasons that "there is still the potential for great rewards, especially in the areas of inquiry, problem solving, and revision" (163). Royster concludes, quite significantly:

> The fundamental point to be made is that a process-oriented approach to the development of the writing skills of black students has the same potential that it has for the skill development of other students. If we do move in this direction, what we will have to acknowledge first is that even though black students may be different from other students in a variety of ways, the process of educating them may be essentially the same as the process for students in general. We, then, might be in a position to stop identifying black students as forever atypical and to start concentrating our attention on the pressing battle to determine how children with all of their individual differences learn—and how and when we as educators can intervene positively in the learning process. (166)

African American Carol Lee, addressing Delpit's work, writes in her 1993 publication, *Signifying as a Scaffold for Literary Interpretation*:

> I have some reservations about Delpit's specific comments about composition instruction within the process approach or what Hillocks . . . identifies as the natural process mode of instruction. However, I do agree with the basic thrust of her argument about the need to empower students from disenfranchised communities by teaching strategies that will lead to mastery of particular skills and the need for the research community to listen to perspectives articulated by minority researchers. (151)

So one cannot intelligently deny African American scholars their complexity and their ability to engage theory. They will use what they can and discard the rest, not merely because of ethnicity but because of sophisticated intellects at work. African American educators do want African American students to acquire language skills, but they don't all rule out writing process as a means to that end.

Indeed, Delpit's own sophistication belied her report of her own literacy development and that of those she represented. Anyone who reads the 1988 article knows she understood that any form of language use is a manifestation of personal motivation and social dynamics. Nonetheless, the literacy success she cited is attributed solely to skills instruction. To gain a fuller, more accurate sense of that development, we need a more elaborate account of motivation. Her eyes and her classmates' were on the prize, the sparrow, or something similar. One also wonders what to make of her disclosure that she didn't write texts longer than two sentences until the tenth grade. That can't be a recommendation to defer essay writing by African American students until the sophomore year of high school, can it? One wouldn't think so. What would Cathy say?

Actually, in the 1988 article, Delpit lent a powerful voice to the writing-process movement. In conjunction with the aforementioned analysis of the culture of power, a brilliant treatment in which she cogently argued the need to explicitly teach African American students the linguistic and cultural codes that may enable more effective participation by them in the wider realms of language and power (I recommend it highly), she made several strong statements about writing instruction. She warned, for instance, that "merely adopting direct instruction is not the answer. Actual writing for real audiences and real purposes is a vital element in helping students to understand they have an important voice in their own learning processes" ("The Silenced Dialogue" 288).

This sounds like a combination of features 4 and 5. Delpit added that what she meant by skills was "helping students gain a useful knowledge of the conventions of print while engaging in real and useful communicative activities" (295). I take this to be strong affirmation of feature 12.

Perhaps her most clearly rendered suggestion is as follows:

> I suggest that students must be *taught* the codes needed to participate fully in the mainstream of American life, not by being forced to attend to hollow, inane, decontextualized subskills, but rather within the context of meaningful communicative endeavors; that they must be allowed the resource of the teacher's expert knowledge, while being helped to acknowledge their own "expertness" as well; and that even while students are assisted in learning the culture of power, they must also be helped to learn about the arbitrariness of those codes and about the power relationships they represent. (296)

Having argued both sides of the skills/process debate, Delpit called for an end to it. She blamed the whole thing on academics, presumably white ones, and asserted that successful teachers have not confined themselves to either approach. The call is somewhat on target, but I don't think resolution is so simple. There are people who believe that teaching "decontextualized subskills" is the proper path. I have African American colleagues who teach about parts of speech and parts of sentences because, the way they view pedagogy, those are the building blocks students will subsequently employ to write paragraphs and then, if they make it far enough, essays.

I recently observed a basic writing class being taught by an African American instructor in which the students were doing workbook exercises, taking turns supplying answers aloud. One student, a young African American, had arrived late and had barely turned to the proper page by the time his turn came. Trying to orient himself, he asked the instructor, "What are we doing this for?" He didn't know how wise his question was. There was an uneasy and telling silence until a fellow student explained that the class was preparing for the upcoming writing examination and that the exercises were for that purpose. The questioner, seemingly satisfied with the explanation, replied, "Oh, OK," and joined in. To the extent that teachers pursue skills activity *at the expense of* writing, they function in opposition to the process paradigm. The pedagogical space thus created excludes a skills/process intersection. There is a real reason to debate. Textbook companies, like the one that produced the book used by the students mentioned above, know this perfectly well and are scurrying to get bets down on both sides, a fact I became aware of when a salesman visiting my office, undeterred that I lacked interest in a skills-based book, assured me that his company's process textbooks would soon be available.

Enough of hearsay. As we converse, we should pull all the players out into the open. We need to identify fully all the Cathys and push them to make their critique more rigorous, to point fingers explicitly and compel specific responses. We must honor their experiences but not fetishize them. The value of self-report as argument is directly related to how well the experience is theorized. We must remain hesitant to assign causality to correlation. Skills instruction may have been the breakfast of some champion writers, but we hardly need conclude, as I hope the analogy I have chosen makes obvious, that skills instruction alone *created* their success. We must also hear more, loudly, from the colleagues who collar me in the halls. European American teachers are, after all, going to teach the majority of African American children in the foreseeable future. If they can bear the load of that awesome responsibility, they can carry the weight of helping the skills/process dialogue be as productive as possible, specifying, along with the other participants, their particular perspectives and the grounds upon which they are willing to be persuaded about issues.

The skills/process issue is never going to be decided by strict empiricism. Tightly controlled experiments, for obvious ethical and methodological reasons, cannot be applied to most educational processes. The talk that settles the matter, insofar as talk can, will have to contain marvelously insightful descriptions and high-quality rationales. This is the talk I am trying to promote. African American children deserve it.

Works Cited

Delpit, Lisa. "The Silenced Dialogue: Power and Pedagogy in Educating Other People's Children." *Harvard Educational Review* 58, no. 3 (August 1988): 280–98.

———. "Skills and Other Dilemmas of a Progressive Black Educator." *Harvard Educational Review* 56, no. 4 (November 1986): 379–85.

Epps, Janis. "Killing Them Softly: Why Willie Can't Write." In Charlotte K. Brooks, ed., *Tapping Potential: English and Language Arts for the Black Learner*. Urbana, IL: NCTE, 1985. 154–58.

Lee, Carol D. *Signifying as a Scaffold for Literary Interpretation: The Pedagogical Implications of an African American Discourse Genre*. Urbana, IL: NCTE, 1993.

Royster, Jacqueline. "A New Lease on Writing." In Charlotte K. Brooks, ed., *Tapping Potential: English and Language Arts for the Black Learner*. Urbana, IL: NCTE, 1985. 159–67.

Zemelman, Steven, and Harvey Daniels. "Defining the Process Paradigm." In Linda Miller Cleary and Michael D. Linn, eds., *Linguistics for Teachers*. New York: McGraw-Hill, 1993. 339–56.

LANGUAGE, RACISM, AND RESISTANCE

A Legacy of Healing: Words, African Americans, and Power

To claim that "words will never hurt me" is the all-time number one act of denial. Only a person profoundly hurt by words would attempt this psychological maneuver. I have, in fact, been rather adept at the sticks-and-stones competition but have been nicked quite a bit, along with others of my ethnic group, by the master narrative in which inferiority is ascribed to those of darker hues. I plead no special case here. African Americans aren't the only ones who don't fare well in the American script of exploitation—just a prominent example. My aim, therefore, is not merely to highlight the victimization of African Americans but to explore adaptive responses to that victimization along the axis of language. In other words, I am considering the healing qualities contained in the counterstory about language that has been central to the African American intellectual and expressive traditions. I don't argue that language alone oppresses or that a magic combination of syllables could alone secure full empowerment. I simply choose to pay particular attention to the Word, even as I acknowledge that Word and Deed inevitably interact to shape destiny.

Imagine the first African slaves ever captured by Europeans. As soon as they were called *totally out they names*, they had to know they were up against a different game. They weren't losers in a mundane intracontinental conflict; they were to be subjected to the largest program of dehumanization ever seen in the western hemisphere, complete with tales and labels, sanctioned by respected intellects, that rationalized enslavement. *Nigger*, because of the variety of powerful reactions it can spur and because of the particular history and present it inscribes, remains to this day the most potent word in the American vocabulary.

Presented November 4, 1994, at the Third Annual Conference on African American Language and Communication at Teachers College, Columbia University.

Although captured Africans were suffering huge losses in the skirmish about self-definition (we did call ourselves Negroes well into the twentieth century), they managed some impressive gains along other verbal fronts. Patricia Turner points out in *I Heard It through the Grapevine*, her fascinating study of rumor in African American culture, that the 1839 mutiny aboard the *Amistad* probably began because Cinque and other Africans believed the rumor that they were about to be literally eaten by their captors. That slavers were cannibals, in more than the obvious metaphoric sense, was an idea widely held by Africans. When Cinque and company made their move, therefore, they were propelled toward their eventual freedom by a specific linguistic form. So while rumor generally connotes negativity, it has functioned systematically in the African American community, as Turner carefully and brilliantly documents, as a method of protection and resistance. Recent and popular rumors suggesting that there is an ingredient in certain fast-food chicken to sterilize Black males, or alleging Ku Klux Klan ownership of clothing companies like Troop, or asserting that Reebok sneakers were manufactured and/or distributed in South Africa circulate as sites of teaching and survival.

The Reebok rumor even convinced supposed empiricists like my wife and me. The Boston-based manufacturer was, in fact, the first major U.S. shoe company to pull its products *out* of South Africa. But when some folks told us about the South Africa angle, and when we pondered how South African the word *Reebok* sounded, we soon vowed never to buy a pair of Reebok sneakers as long as South African apartheid existed. This really bothered our children. It was:

"Mommy, Daddy, but the sneakers is phat!"
"Yeah, but you not gittin em."

Through dialogue about sneakers, a very powerful channel, we taught our children much about colonialism, the Mandelas, and boycott. And to communicate this most effectively, all we had to do was not purchase a few pairs of sneakers, which cost too much anyway. In fact, when one considers that every other major sneaker company has been hit by a rumor connecting it to the predemocracy South African government or the Ku Klux Klan, one understands that some folk are doing fine cultural work in trying to discourage African American youth, an audience specifically targeted by these manufacturers, from so intently, and sometimes perilously, accumulating so many pieces of overpriced leather and rubber. Health is one of the issues here, and not all the rhetoric can be pretty. As Turner concludes, "Like a scab that forms over a sore, the rumors are an unattractive but vital mechanism by which the cultural body attempts to protect itself from subsequent infection" (220).

I'm not trying to start any trouble, but Crooked I, a company that produces malt liquor and fruit drinks, may easily be hit by a rumor. Some brother or sister may notice that the company's juices, whatever the flavor, are packaged in black cans and are available almost exclusively in the African American community. Someone else may notice that the product is produced in North Carolina and then associate it with the Ku Klux Klan. Another may discover the ultimately damning scoop—that is, if you dissect the company logo, the Crooked I, vertically, which you can do, say, by covering half of it with your finger, you will clearly see three K's. Opinion then spreads that in KKK-owned Crooked I products there is a chemical (beyond, but clearly connected to, the alcohol in the malt liquor our youth drink too much of) designed to destroy African Americans.

The grapevine also extends to literature. In his 1967 novel, *The Man Who Cried I Am*, John A. Williams has a character discover a document describing the King Alfred Plan, a "final solution" for African Americans in case of continued racial unrest. Agencies such as the FBI, CIA, National Security Council, Department of Defense, and local police forces are to coordinate their efforts in order to neutralize Black leadership and then "terminate, once and for all, the Minority threat to the whole of the American society, and, indeed, the Free World" (372). This conspiracy theory grabbed hold of the mass Black imagination. Black folk skipped past the first twenty-seven chapters to get to this King Alfred Plan they had heard about. They didn't care anything about Harry Ames or Max Reddick or Marion Dawes. The Black Topo-graphical Society based a three-hour political awareness session, one I sat through in the early 1970s, on a version of the proposal. Speakers would explain, for example, that superhighways like the Dan Ryan Expressway in Chicago were always routed through Black ghettos to facilitate eventual military operations against those communities. I told one of the presenters that the King Alfred Plan came out of a novel. He replied that the novel was just telling the truth. And it is certainly easy to comprehend why it could ring true for anyone who had witnessed the suspicious assassinations of Martin Luther King Jr., Malcolm X, and a long list of others, and who had seen or been a part of the post-Watts wave of inner-city uprisings.

Although it provided ample grist for the rumor mill, Williams's novel is, in addition, firmly linked to texts in the African American literary tradition. The Wright-like figure Harry Ames asserts, "I'm the way I am, the kind of writer I am, and you may be too, because I'm a black man; therefore, we're in rebellion; we've got to be. We have no other function as valid as that one" (49). The story is—as most stories in the tradition are—largely about the tension between expression and repression of the Black voice. This dynamic is manifest, for example, in the very first novel by an African American published in the United States, Harriet Wilson's *Our Nig; or, Sketches from the Life of a Free Black* (1859).

After being abandoned by her mother at the age of six, Frado begins a period of indenture in the New England home of the Bellmonts. She quickly becomes a favorite of men working around the farm, who "were always glad to hear her prattle" (37). However, Frado is soon silenced. When young Mary Bellmont accuses Frado of pushing her into a stream, Frado's true account of events is ignored. Mrs. Bellmont, with the aid of her daughter, beats Frado, props her mouth open with a piece of wood, and locks her in a dark room. Frado cannot even talk things over with herself, as many of us are wont to do in times of extreme distress.

As Frado grows older, the Bellmonts' son James, Aunt Abby, and Mr. Bellmont himself all try to shield her somewhat from Mrs. Bellmont's cruelty. But her mistress only becomes more selective and clandestine about the beatings, never failing to warn Frado that she wouldn't hesitate to "cut her tongue out" if she exposed her (72), threatening to do physically to Frado what she has been accomplishing symbolically all along. Frado tells anyway as her voice, encouraged by her advocates, is gaining in strength, which prompts a desperate Mrs. Bellmont to resort to one of her favorite techniques. She forces a wooden block into Frado's mouth and whips her with a rawhide strap.

Frado is undeterred. She reads and continues to converse with those willing to entertain her. And in the novel's climactic scene, when Mrs. Bellmont raises a stick to strike Frado because she feels Frado is taking too long with her chores, Frado loudly declares that if she is struck, she will never work again. Mrs. Bellmont, amazed at the direct verbal challenge, declines to test Frado's resolve. Frado, her period of indenture nearing its conclusion, becomes intensely interested in a wide range of reading material and pursues literacy with vigor. She keeps a book nearby even as she toils.

Charles W. Chesnutt explores nineteenth-century expression/repression conflict against a Southern backdrop, particularly in his Uncle Julius tales. He illustrates how tightly the voices and literate behaviors of slaves were monitored by slave owners. Dave, the central character in "Dave's Neckliss," hardworking and obedient, encounters no special problem with his master until he is found reading the Bible. Dave uses his wit, however, to escape trouble. Mars Dugal, in contrast, cunningly attempts to reinforce control. As Julius narrates:

> "'Dis yer is a se'ious matter,' sezee; 'it's 'g'in de law ter l'arn niggers how ter read, er 'low 'em ter hab books. But w'at yer l'arn out'n dat Bible, Dave?"
>
> "Dave w'an't no fool, ef he wuz a nigger, en sezee: 'Marster, I l'arns dat it's a sin fer ter steal, er ter lie, er fer ter want w'at doan b'long ter yer; en I l'arns fer ter love de Lawd en ter 'bey my marster.'"
>
> "Mars Dugal' sorter smile' en laf' ter hisse'f, like he 'uz might'ly tickle' 'bout sump'n, en sezee: 'Doan 'pear ter me lack readin' de Bible done yer much harm, Dave. Dat's w'at I wants all my niggers fer ter know. Yer keep right on readin', en tell de yuther han's w'at yer be'n tellin' me. How would yer lack fer ter preach ter de niggers on Sunday?'" (134)

When Dave later is framed for a theft, his Bible is taken away and burned by the overseer.

African American writers have never lost sight of the language problematics posed by Wilson and Chesnutt. Toni Morrison, for one, always foregrounds, perhaps most notably in *Beloved*, the dialectic of expression/repression. Sixo, one of the Garner slaves, a bit more fiery than Dave, decides to stop speaking English because he sees no future in doing so. One can sympathize with Sixo's position after witnessing the conversation, a thoroughly postmodern one, between him and schoolteacher when Sixo is accused of stealing a pig:

> "You stole that shoat didn't you?"
>
> "No, sir. I didn't steal it."
>
> Schoolteacher smiled. "Did you kill it?"
>
> "Yes, sir. I killed it."
>
> "Did you butcher it?"
>
> "Yes, sir."
>
> "Did you cook it?"
>
> "Yes, sir."
>
> "Well, then. Did you eat it?"
>
> "Yes, sir. I sure did."
>
> "And you telling me that's not stealing?"
>
> "No, sir. It ain't."
>
> "What is it then?"
>
> "Improving your property, sir."
>
> "What?"
>
> "Sixo plant rye to give the high piece a better chance. Sixo take and feed the soil, give you more crop. Sixo take and feed Sixo give you more work." (190)

Schoolteacher beats Sixo anyway to show him that, as the authorial voice puts it, "definitions belonged to the definers—not the defined" (190). Of course, Sixo knows this by then, and he seeks to become a definer. So he leaves the masters their language, only resorting to English again while formulating plans to escape. His plan is defeated, but he goes to his death singing his own song, laughing, and calling out, because his Thirty-Mile Woman (not her master's label) is pregnant, "Seven-O! Seven-O!" (226).

Baby Suggs also practices self-definition. After her freedom is purchased by her son and she is escorted out of bondage by Mr. Garner, she asks why she was always referred to as Jenny. Garner informs her, naturally, that the name on her invoice is Jenny Whitlow. She bitterly rejects it. Another of the story's free elders has cast aside his given name of Joshua and renamed himself Stamp Paid because he feels he has settled any debt he might have owed in this world.

If Zora Neale Hurston and Ralph Ellison have written the most artistic "discovery of voice" books in the African American literary tradition, then *Beloved* will probably go down as the most accomplished "claim your name" book. It is *The Bluest Eye*, though, that conveys most powerfully

Morrison's concern with both the debilitating and therapeutic aspects of overall language practices.

The story opens with a paragraph that could have been excerpted from a typical primer: "Here is the house. It is green and white. It has a red door. It is very pretty. Here is the family. Mother, Father, Dick, and Jane live in the green-and-white house. They are very happy" (7).

The major trouble with primers is that characteristically they have depicted the happy, white, suburban, nuclear family, which discounts the reality of most of the nation including, of course, African American children like Pecola Breedlove, who wishes for, above all things, a set of blue eyes.

In the second paragraph of the novel, Morrison repeats the wording of the first, only she removes standard punctuation marks. The spaces between the lines of type are smaller. In the third paragraph, she removes the spaces between the words and even ignores conventional syllabification.

The reader soon realizes, even more so as similar phrases are repeated at the outset of later chapters, that a narrative of domination contributes directly to Pecola's plight and eventual insanity. Undeniably, there are other crucial factors: neglect, abuse, incest, rape. But the fact that no voice is stronger to Pecola than the one that encourages self-loathing is an essential element. So is the fact that her father, Cholly Breedlove, who eventually passes the sickness of his life to her, hasn't grabbed hold of an enabling tale. In describing Cholly's relationship with his wife, Morrison pens a line reminiscent of the description of *Native Son*'s Bigger Thomas: "He poured out on her the sum of all his *inarticulate fury and aborted desires*" (emphasis mine; 37).

Contradistinct to the inadequate language system most available to Pecola are the rich verbal experiences shared by Claudia and Frieda MacTeer, who habitually tune in to the vibrant verbal interplay of their mother and her friends. As Claudia narrates:

> Their conversation is like a gently wicked dance: sound meets sound, curtsies, shimmies, and retires. Another sound enters but is upstaged by still another: the two circle each other and stop. Sometimes their words move in lofty spirals; other times they take strident leaps, and all of it is punctuated with warm-pulsed laughter—like the throb of a

> heart made of jelly. The edge, the curl, the thrust of their emotions is always clear to Frieda and me. We do not, cannot, know the meaning of all her words, for we are nine and ten years old. So we watch their faces, their hands, their feet, and listen for truth in timbre. (16)

With ready access to a collaborative, self-affirming language community, the MacTeer girls have a shield against the dominant narrative.

Morrison's work advances significantly the African American literary project. Although not all characters in the tradition successfully counteract repression, many do achieve autonomy, expressive and otherwise. African American literature as a whole, much like protective African American rumor mechanisms, has been a grand gesture toward healing.

Rap, at its best, is on the same mission. A blend of urgent beats and reinvigorating Black orality, rap is recent testimony that the contesting Black voice in every generation will somehow force itself upon a broad audience. Ready or not, brand-new flava will be kicked in your ear. Referring to the Stop the Violence Movement and HEAL (Human Education Against Lies), and to stars like KRS-One and Chuck D, Houston Baker argues that "these positive sites of rap are as energetically productive as those manned by our most celebrated black critics and award winning writers" (59–60). Baker, one of those celebrated critics, sees the connection between "this DJ be Warren G" and "this PHD be Houston B." He adds that "rap is the form of audition in our present era that utterly refuses to sing anthems of, say, STATE homogeneity" (96–97).

Tricia Rose, one of the most informed people on the planet about rap, amplifies Baker's comments:

> Rap music is, in many ways, a hidden transcript. Among other things, it uses cloaked speech and disguised cultural codes to comment on and challenge aspects of current power inequalities. Not all rap transcripts directly critique all forms of domination; nonetheless, a large and significant element in rap's discursive territory is engaged in symbolic and ideological warfare with institutions and groups that symbolically, ideologically, and materially oppress African Americans. (100–101)

Obscenity trials, widespread media attention, and the multibillion scramble over rap revenues indicate the power and importance of this verbal form. Also interesting is the elbowing over who gets to tell the most persuasive academic story about rap. The participation of Skip Gates in the 2 Live Crew trial is called careerism by Baker, who sees Gates as an uninformed outsider pimping the music for publicity. Baker, in turn, is criticized by Rose for marginalizing the female voice in his version of rap's origin and development. And Tricia, just beware. I don't know who is right on these questions, but it's amusing and gratifying to see rap on the agendas of professors at Harvard, Penn, and NYU.

General African American literacy initiatives have run parallel to folkloric and artistic concerns with language power. Immediately after the Civil War, Black folk took the lead on the issue of literacy and schooling for the newly freed population. Black illiteracy had been state-sanctioned, so it is little wonder that a widespread Black literacy project was conceived primarily as a self-help endeavor. These educational pioneers understood that to be literate was to be able to construct textual knowledge for oneself. They didn't want former slaves to be tricked by the textual interpretations of others, as was often the case during slavery when a literate ruling class would lie to slaves about the contents of abolitionist writing. It is common nowadays to hear the slogan "knowledge is power" associated with African American educational campaigns, but Thomas Holt reveals that the phrase has been in use at least since 1865, when the South Carolina Black Men's Convention used it in the preamble to a resolution to establish schools.

Holt also demonstrates quite clearly that there has been no greater dedication to the ideal of popular education in this nation's history than that made by the African American community in the South. The secret schools that operated during slavery, the free schools that were founded shortly after the war, contributions of money that were an amazingly high percentage of contributors' incomes, abundant in-kind resources made available, even the institution of voluntary tax collection systems to support schools when federal and state monies were withheld all constitute remarkable commitment.

The African American literacy project even survived, though barely, both the postreconstruction white backlash and the subsequent attempts of philanthropists like Rosenwald and Rockefeller to gain control of the agenda and ensure that Blacks received only the type of education that kept them "in place," so to speak, in Southern society—a sort of Booker T.

Washington deal. W. E. B. Du Bois, as one probably would suppose, was prominent among the African American leadership who countered this idea. But as Holt writes, opposition came also, and perhaps more importantly in terms of history, from another formidable source:

> Resistance also came from students at Tuskegee, Fisk, Howard, and Hampton who, during the 1920s, went on strike against their school administrations and in many cases succeeded in getting new leadership. In the long run, all those struggles laid the basis for the student warriors during the civil rights movement in the late 1950s and early 1960s, because, next to the church, southern colleges were the most critical to the success of that movement. (99)

One thing that now has to happen is that we tap into the fundamental valuation of education that exists to this day in the African American community. Although African Americans have become highly skeptical about certain educational practices and remain dismayed because even institutional certification ensures equal opportunity for them only sporadically, they still view effective schooling to be a key aspect of communal healing. It still represents great possibility.

Language professionals can help to improve educational practice by bringing clarity to discussions of language-related matters. They can share state-of-the-art knowledge about language acquisition and verbal processing and assess how instructional designs are consonant or inconsistent with this information. In addition, they can indicate some of the social variables that affect language instruction and stress, above all, the importance of honoring the language varieties that students bring to school. The teacherly impulse to eradicate specific dialects, for example, is wrong, as Peter Trudgill cogently argues, on grounds of psychology, sociology, and practicality (80–81). Such corrective attempts usually send the message that students are inherently deficient and fail to facilitate expansion of students' verbal repertoires. Students may, in turn, understanding the message clearly, make language a site of resistance and thus reject Standard English so as to solidify their rebellious identities. Some think that these concerns, particularly as they relate to African American students, were laid to rest back in the 1970s. However, that is not the case.

On November 28, 1992, the *New York Times* ran a front-page story entitled "Caribbean Pupils' English Seems Barrier, Not Bridge." The article dealt with the poor performance of students from the English-speaking Caribbean, who were enrolling by the thousands in New York City public schools. To some extent, dialect was cited as the cause of failure, and I was reminded of the Black English debates of previous decades (which continue today, though more quietly). Wary about the impact this article could have, I was eager to author a response and shake things up a bit.

Fortuitously, a reporter from the *Carib News* visited me to solicit my opinion. I told him that if folks are committed to discrimination, they can almost always use language as a pretext. I further expressed that the problem was one of method, not language. It has been demonstrated repeatedly, especially during the celebrated King case (or Black English trial) in 1979, that inappropriate *responses* to language diversity, not language diversity per se, are a major educational problem. I definitely favored committing as much support as possible to helping the students in question; linking dialect with deficiency is what I was mainly arguing against.

I am fully aware of, and do not want to minimize, differences among Black English and a variety of Caribbean dialects. On the other hand, I feel a diasporic view with regard to African-derived language forms yields the most compelling analysis. Only diaspora aesthetics can properly explain rap, for instance, which could not have started as it did without Kool DJ Here and other Jamaicans. And both Black English and Black Caribbean dialects are examples of what linguist John Holm terms *Atlantic Creoles*. The *Times* article, in fact, describing the language patterns of Caribbean students, reported that "many forgo the past tense, drop the verb to be (he tall; she a princess) and switch subject and object pronouns (I tell she; him say). They express plurals and possessives differently (two house, or de house-dem; this is mines). Their words often carry different meanings, pronunciation varies greatly and sentence stresses fall in different places" (22). Every item mentioned here, with the possible exception of "de house-dem," is familiar to anyone who knows Black English.

Unfortunately, the reporter lumped my response with those of several other interviewees, not all of whom shared my views or academic background, in a piece entitled "American English Experts Respond!" As a group, we sounded as if there were no real problem at all. I wasn't surprised, then, when "Caribbean English Specialists Respond" appeared in a subsequent issue of the paper. A Caribbean scholar took us to task for being unqualified to address the matter, buying into West-Indians-as-cream-of-the-crop mythology, failing to properly understand the realities of bilingualism and bidialectalism, and ignoring the fact that the children were doing abysmally in school, scoring very low on standardized tests, and sitting in special education classes in disproportionate numbers.

I responded with a letter to the editor, which was graciously printed. I highlighted again that I objected to any belief that dialect differences alone can account for the rate of so-called failure in our schools. I conceded the fact of bilingualism, as there is the issue of mutual unintelligibility between English and certain varieties of Caribbean creoles. But I warned that we must not conflate bilingualism with bidialectalism.

I remain supportive of serious attempts to enhance academic performances of Caribbean students both in class and on standardized tests. Programs that recognize the uniqueness of the Caribbean immigrant experience and build upon strengths in that experience make sense to me. But a reassessment of standardized tests is also required, as is the deconstruction of special education. It's easy to wind up there if you're Black, no matter which sounds come out of your mouth.

I don't pretend that my analysis has drastically effected change. It's merely illustrative of the insight that language professionals can offer. To fully implement correct, not simply corrective, language pedagogy, a varied action agenda is needed along with participation from many types of individuals and groups. Schools ultimately are sensitive to occurrences in the larger society. Anyone working toward positive social change is to some extent helping to strengthen language instruction.

One more flashback as we move forward. Arna Bontemps explains that during the eighteenth century, when even greater than usual pressure was being applied to repress the literacy of slaves, the beautiful, gorgeously double-voiced spirituals were born. As noted earlier, the contesting Black voice will find a way. Marveling at that achievement, James Weldon Johnson paid homage to those artists in "O Black and Unknown Bards," some of which goes:

> There is a wide, wide wonder in it all,
> That from degraded rest and servile toil

The fiery spirit of the seer should call
These simple children of the sun and soil.

It's a beautiful poem, but it's also a script we want to flip. We want to bring all the righteousness of African American expressive and intellectual output to bear full force upon the creation of more Black *known* bards whose production will be wide and wonderful as well.

Works Cited

Baker, Houston A. *Black Studies, Rap, and the Academy*. Chicago: The U of Chicago P, 1993.

Chesnutt, Charles W. "Dave's Neckliss" (1889). In Sylvia L. Render, ed., *The Short Fiction of Charles W. Chesnutt*. Washington, D.C.: Howard UP, 1981. 132–41.

Gilyard, Keith. "Disappointed with Dr. Irish." *Carib News*, June 9, 1993, p. 19.

Gutman, Herbert G. "Schools for Freedom: The Post-Emancipation Origins of Afro-American Education." In Ira Berlin, ed., *Power and Culture: Essays on the American Working Class*. New York: Pantheon, 1987. 260–97.

Holm, John A. *Pidgins and Creoles: Reference Survey*. Cambridge: Cambridge UP, 1989.

———. *Pidgins and Creoles: Theory and Structure*. Cambridge: Cambridge UP, 1988.

Holt, Thomas. "'Knowledge Is Power': The Black Struggle for Literacy." In Andrea A. Lunsford, Helene Moglen, and James Slevin, eds., *The Right to Literacy*. New York: Modern Language Association, 1990. 91–102.

Ien, Seymour. "American English Experts Respond!" *Carib News*, Feb. 2, 1993, p. 6.

Irish, George. "Caribbean English Specialists Respond." *Carib News*, Feb. 16, 1993, p. 38.

Johnson, James Weldon. "O Black and Unknown Bards." In James Weldon Johnson, ed., *The Book of American Negro Poetry* (1931). New York: Harcourt Brace: 1969. 123–24.

Morrison, Toni. *Beloved*. New York: Knopf, 1987.

———. *The Bluest Eye* (1970). New York: Washington Square Press, 1972.

Rose, Tricia. *Black Noise: Rap Music and Black Culture in Contemporary America*. Hanover, NH: Wesleyan UP, 1994.

Sontag, Deborah. "Caribbean Pupils' English Seems Barrier, Not Bridge." *New York Times*, Nov. 28, 1992, pp. 1, 22.

Trudgill, Peter. *Sociolinguistics: An Introduction*. Harmondsworth: Penguin, 1974.

Turner, Patricia A. *I Heard It through the Grapevine: Rumor in African-American Culture*. Berkeley: U of California P, 1993.

Williams, John A. *The Man Who Cried I Am* (1967). New York: Thunder's Mouth Press, 1985.

Wilson, Harriet E. *Our Nig; or, Sketches from the Life of a Free Black* (1859). New York: Random House, 1983.

Wright, Richard. *Native Son*. New York: Harper, 1940.

Getting Off the Hook—I Mean Curve

Shortly after the publication of Richard Herrnstein and Charles Murray's tome on intelligence and social policy, I began to have a recurring and disturbing dream. I would be trapped between the covers of the *New York Times Book Review* impaled on a bell curve. I was an African American hanged one of the new ways—that is, by genteel and intellectual klansmen wearing robes of academe. "They just never stop," I would repeat in resignation until I lost consciousness.

In my waking hours I cannot afford to be resigned, precisely because, in fact, they never do cease and desist. Herrnstein and Murray's unleashing of *The Bell Curve: Intelligence and Class Structure in American Life* is a massive and dangerous reinsertion of social Darwinism and biological determinism into public discourse, particularly debates about how best to address issues of so-called racial inequality.

The advice to government officials from the authors, two Harvard graduates, is grim: you need not do a great deal because social problems are determined by low IQs, which are generally unresponsive to programs of social improvement. Affirmative action, it follows, will not yield much benefit; one can hardly hope to influence the biological design that accords less intelligence to Blacks than to whites. Attempting to hide behind a shield of scientific neutrality, though in reality their scientifically racist backsides are exposed, Herrnstein and Murray provide powerful, if polluted, ideological fuel for the Gingrich Gang.

Fortunately, many voices, including several from Harvard, have risen in opposition, a chorus I must join. I owe it to ancestors, elders, brethren, and progeny. I take no solace in, and as no compliment, the fact that Herrnstein and Murray would have found me remarkable, an African American who scored well on IQ tests. Herrnstein, recently deceased, who made his first public splash as an apologist for Arthur Jensen in the

Presented May 20, 1995, at a conference entitled "Educating People of African Descent for the Twenty-First Century," sponsored by the Medgar Evers College Psychology Club and the New York Association of Black Psychologists.

early 1970s, helped to oppress my ethnic group. As does Murray.* This is why I am in on the action.

The Bell Curve was released just as I was about to submerge myself in some good old Afro-rhetoric by reading the first volume of *Speech and Power*, a collection of African American essays edited by Gerald Early. I had meant to appropriate some rhetorical moves in general. The mission quickly changed to a frenzied one of *inventio*, the discovery of specific arguments to counter those of Herrnstein and Murray. Not surprisingly, W. E. B. Du Bois, a Harvard man as well, provides the first.

In a 1920 essay entitled "On Being Black," Du Bois sarcastically notes a range of discriminatory practices by whites then ponders the intriguing, as he calls them, Souls of White Folk. Anticipating Herrnstein and Murray, or already aware of early twentieth-century Herrnstein-Murray antecedents (they never do stop), Du Bois writes: "And yet as they preach and strut and shout and threaten, crouching as they clutch at rags of facts and fancies to hide their nakedness, they go twisting, flying by my tired eyes and I see them ever stripped—ugly, human" (6).

No doubt, Du Bois would have much to say about the facts and fancies in *The Bell Curve*. But even seventy-five years ago, in a comment following the one cited above, he indicates perhaps the best line of argument against works in which much of the analysis revolves around so-called racial differences as he, in essence, rejects the notion of races. Du Bois remarks:

> The discovery of personal whiteness among the world's peoples is a very modern thing—a nineteenth and twentieth century matter, indeed. The ancient world would have laughed at such a distinction. The Middle Ages regarded skin color with mild curiosity; and even up into the eighteenth century we were hammering our national manikins into one, great, Universal Man, with fine frenzy which ignored color

*Psychologist Arthur Jensen has argued that there are differences of IQ between whites and Blacks that are attributable to genetics and largely immutable. In 1971, Herrnstein echoed this sentiment in an essay entitled "I.Q." that appeared in *Atlantic Monthly*, and he expanded his claims in a 1973 book, *I.Q. in the Meritocracy*. Twenty-four articles written or coauthored by Jensen are included in the bibliography of *The Bell Curve*. Before now, Murray was best known for his conservative 1984 treatise, *Losing Ground: American Social Policy, 1950–1980*.

> and race even more than birth. Today we have changed all that, and the world in a sudden, emotional conversion has discovered that it is white and by that token, wonderful! (6)

Du Bois understands *whiteness* as a linguistic tag that validates the experience and privilege of the *one* at the expense of the *other*. It is a label of political dominance. To be sure, he has not in his essay thought through the deconstruction of whiteness thoroughly. Not able to escape totally the prevailing racialized constructs of his time (nor have enough current scholars escaped the dominant thinking of his time), Du Bois occasionally refers to race as an objective category. Nonetheless, his commentary points to contemporary considerations about race that bear directly upon the worth of *The Bell Curve* as science. Inasmuch as some of the book's central arguments rely heavily on a distinction between a white race and a black one, the arguments necessarily suffer to the same degree that such distinction is shown to be invalid. Yank the pillar of race from beneath Herrnstein and Murray's logical edifice, and the edifice begins to crumble.

Some of the pull comes from Steven Holmes, who in "Defining Race" asserts that "racial categories, especially in the United States, are often more poetry than science. American blacks almost invariably have some white ancestry, so their classification has more to do with politics and culture than with genes" (273).

Holmes reports that in a 1985 survey of anthropologists, only half the respondents agreed that race is a legitimate biological category. I am slightly amazed that the percentage was still so high, given that no one has ever adequately defined how human beings, Homo sapiens, break down into races. The most commonly talked about physical characteristic, skin color, is only one trait among thousands, hardly enough, at least one wouldn't think, to sustain a theory of races. I am not aware that anyone strictly bases racial groupings on human blood types, though it seems to me that blood type is at least as important as skin color, as anyone who has needed a transfusion should attest. Even if one tries to use skin color to conform to some American classification ideal of black and white, what does one label the East Indians or Arabs, many of whom are darker than I?

Blackness and *whiteness* as human labels are social constructions and signify specific conveniences. When Billy Paul sang "Am I Black enough for you?" he was talking not about genes but ideas. *Whiteness*, as Du Bois well knew, is a term that lends rhetorical sanction to societal inequity. And when white folk call us *blacks*, they are generally not calling us anything more complex or flattering than not white, the other. All this semantic juggling or race talk is to be expected in the expressly racialized social arena America is, but it cannot make for good physical science or even good conversation about physical science.

Herrnstein and Murray are acutely aware of the problem and try hard to tiptoe their way around it. As they explain:

> We frequently use the word *ethnic* rather than *race*, because race is such a difficult concept to employ in the American context. What does it mean to be black in America, in racial terms, when the word black (or African-American) can be used for people whose ancestry is more European than African? How are we to classify a person whose parents hail from Panama but whose ancestry is predominantly African? Is he a Latino? A black? The rule we follow here is to classify people according to the way they classify themselves. The studies of "blacks" or "Latinos" or "Asians" who live in America generally denote people who say they are black, Latino, or Asian—no more, no less. (271)

Cognizant of the impossibility of making real and physically scientific divisions concerning race, the authors resort to a curiously unscientific procedure. They accept what people say. We don't accept the simple declarations of motorists that they are sober when, in fact, they are drunk, yet Herrnstein and Murray would have us trust self-report on an issue that, by their own admission, is quite complicated. They try to turn a laudatory cultural stance, the acceptance of self-naming, into plausible biology. And it just isn't. Nor is their rhetoric of acceptance genuine, for on the very same page they write that "opting for common usage and simplicity, we usually use *black* instead of *African American* and *white* (which always refers to non-Latino whites) instead of *European-American* or *Anglo*" (271).

So what is all their fuss about? Despite protestations to the contrary, Herrnstein and Murray insist on keeping much of their discourse locked in black and white, as it were. Common use and simplicity mean more to them than good science. They care nothing at all about the cultures of African Americans, Latinos, or Asians. They care about objective categories of race, which are actually more of a concern for talk-show producers or hosts—Oprah, Ricki, Geraldo, and the like—than for serious scientists.

Manning Marable, in his almost mandatory "On Being Black" essay, published sixty-one years after the one by Du Bois, contributes a materialist slant to an understanding of *The Bell Curve*, a quality absent from most of the public debate about the book. To Marable, racism is a systemic feature of Western capitalism and functions to "withdraw the dominant group's sympathy from an 'inferior' race, to facilitate its exploitation" (23). Along with such factors as the disproportionate appropriation of African American labor and widespread segregation, racist societies like the United States are also characterized by ideologies that justify these practices. As Marable explains: "Whites as a group have historically approached blacks not in the light of their 'blackness'—perhaps a better term would be 'Africanness'—but in light of what whites believed that blacks must become from the vantage point of their own 'whiteness.' Racist societies must invent 'the Negro'" (26).

The Negro, or Black, is a mechanism that Herrnstein and Murray, who provide intellectual blessing to the existing social order, cannot bring themselves to discard, precisely because they are confirmed, privileged, and content—not to mention white—members of that order. For all their talk about deterministic encounters of the biological kind, they fail to account sufficiently for the social forces driving their own work, and it's no coincidence that the social outlook they articulate at the end of their book supports further segregation and economic disparity. They dismiss the idea that government intervention is a useful way to address social inequality; they're still pushing "trickle-down" economic theory; they entertain visions of a "high-tech and more lavish version of the Indian reservation for some substantial minority of the nation's population" (526). In insisting that the prevailing reality of the twenty-first century will be the reality of the cognitive line, a proposition neither Du Bois nor Marable would accept, and then factoring so-called race into how that line will be drawn (sorry, most folks of color, but you happen to be on the wrong side of it), the authors of *The Bell Curve* predictably, so predictably, serve as academic representatives of American racism.

I will not, however, make too strong a case for institutional determinism, as there are members of the academy—of Harvard, in fact—who are highly critical, based upon their own readings of their disciplines, of the type of thinking represented in *The Bell Curve*. Howard Gardner, for example, argues in his celebrated volume *Frames of Mind: The Theory of Multiple Intelligences* that IQ is a simplistic and counterproductive way of assessing intellectual capacities:

> If we are to encompass adequately the realm of human cognition, it is necessary to include a far wider and more universal set of competencies than has ordinarily been considered. And it is necessary to remain open to the possibility that many—if not most—of these competences do not lend themselves to measurement by standard verbal methods, which rely heavily on a blend of logical and linguistic abilities. (x)

In addition to linguistic and logical-mathematical capacities, Gardner considers musical, spatial, and bodily kinesthetic intelligences, as well as a set of abilities he terms *personal intelligences*. In his view, not only is intelligence irreducible to a single number on an IQ test; it is not even restricted to the range of abilities measured by such a test. Furthermore, Gardner believes a cultural approach to understanding intelligences yields richer explanations than purely genetic approaches, arguing, after noting the high heritability of physical and temperamental traits, that "when one comes to aspects of cognitive style or personality, the case for high heritability is far less convincing" (35).

Herrnstein and Murray reject Gardner's theory on grounds of both terminology and methodology. They insist that proficiency in, say, music represents talent, not intelligence. Gardner, for his part, would accept this designation but only on the condition that skill in linguistic and logical-mathematical operations be conversely regarded as talent, not intelligence. Obviously, this subdebate won't be resolved anytime soon, nor will the one about methodology, as Herrnstein and Murray suggest that Gardner's work, which is narrative, is an inappropriate approach to issues they construe to be quantitative. They steadfastly maintain that the weight of statistical evidence supports the claim that intelligence is a general ability, signified by what is known in psychology as the g factor, and that IQ tests measure it accurately.

Gardner, however, does not go quietly. In a review of *The Bell Curve*, he writes:

> Science goes far beyond the number-crunching stereotype; scientific inquiry involves the conceptualization of problems, decisions about the kinds of data to secure and analyze, the consideration of alternative explanations, and, above all, the chain of reasoning from assumptions to findings to inferences. In this sense, the science in *The Bell Curve* is more like special pleading, based on a biased reading of the data, than a carefully balanced assessment of current knowledge. (62–63)

Then shifting gears, reminding us bluntly of the so-called racial ideas entwined with psychometric considerations in *The Bell Curve*, Gardner, after mentioning his debate with Murray on National Public Radio, states:

> Herrnstein and Murray, of course, have a right to their conclusions. But if they truly believe that blacks will not be hurt by the hints that they are genetically inferior, they are even more benighted—dare I say, even more stupid—than I have suggested. (72)

Stephen Jay Gould, commenting on *The Bell Curve* in a piece entitled "Mismeasure by Any Measure," contends that the authors fail to employ sophisticated enough mathematical procedures and that, in reality, they don't make much of a case either for the existence of g or the worth of an IQ score. Gould adds that a proper understanding of statistical procedures reveals that "their own data indicate that IQ is not a major factor in determining variation in nearly all the social behaviors they study—and so their conclusions collapse, or at least become so greatly attenuated that their pessimism and conservative social agenda gain no significant support" (11).

By debunking race theory, seriously challenging restrictive concepts of intelligence, and casting considerable doubt on procedure, one significantly dispels the logical power of *The Bell Curve*. Even so, the book has plenty of spunk left. It's a slick text, relying heavily upon equivocation as a defense strategy. Also, on offense, its authors extend their rhetorical left hand for a shake while trying to clobber you with their right. For example, they agree that intelligence is ranked too highly among human virtues but spend more than eight hundred pages ranking it as highly as they can.

At the outset of the section entitled "Cognitive Classes and Social Behavior," they admit that "you cannot predict what a given person will do from his IQ score," but then they declare immediately that "large differences in social behavior separate groups of people when the groups differ intellectually on average" and further maintain that "intelligence itself, not just its correlation with socioeconomic status, is responsible for these group differences" (117). While admitting the silliness of trying to establish causality between IQ and behaviors such as crime and welfare dependency at the level of individuals, they offer some group correlations and then argue, without properly factoring in social explanations, that lower IQ causes such behaviors. They feature statistics but omit adequate explanations of what the statistics may mean.

Were I to commit crimes, Herrnstein and Murray obviously would not submit that the acts are driven by IQ or, by extension, genes. Were I to organize—by tapping into senses of rage, frustration, and powerlessness caused by life in the racist, economically exploitative U.S.A.—a large crew of "blacks" to commit crimes along with me, then in Herrnstein and Murray's view, our actions become explainable by IQ and genetics.

What IQ predicts at best, and I think this point is fairly noncontroversial, is educability or performance within given participant structures, usually those, like school, that emphasize linguistic operations and linear logic within certain cultural contexts and contain embedded in those contexts messages about power and the relative worth of cultures. I would expect groups that don't fare well in, say, school, whose members have often decoded, even if subconsciously, negative "power" signals as inscribed in society at large, often long before they take intelligence exams, to have lower IQs. The scores, more than anything else, reflect that school as generally structured is not designed for them to do as well as they can. They, in fact, would be the group most susceptible to "failing." Similarly, once the disappointments and social penalties for not succeeding in school are factored in, I would anticipate significant correlations among IQ, crime, poverty, welfare dependency, and so on. This does not mean those correlations are the most important correlations. The correlation between crime and a specific organizing of school, for example, may be more important than the correlation between crime and IQ. Now, I am not arguing that a given school organization actually causes crime, and neither should Herrnstein and Murray argue that crime is caused by given IQs.

The Bell Curve's authors are really conceding that they can tell us virtually nothing about complex people, particularly not complex African

Americans, which is a severe flaw. Theirs is a thick book with a thin vision. The tone, however, is not overly threatening. They anesthetize African Americans with disclaimers before they hang them up on the curve, but the important thing to remember is that they hang them nonetheless.

Of the policy recommendations in *The Bell Curve*, I am most concerned in this space, as you would suspect, with those that affect public school education. Herrnstein and Murray argue that the most crucial problem in American education is the underfunding of programs for the cognitively gifted, we really should say IQ gifted, who are being denied sufficient opportunities, in the authors' view, to develop their considerable potential. Not that these students need to be made any more intelligent, mind you. Herrnstein and Murray insist that they will in any event fulfill their genetic destiny to attend elite universities, embark upon distinguished careers, and run the country. But they won't necessarily possess, in Herrnstein and Murray's eyes, the ability to maximize their effectiveness as leaders unless they receive educations in wisdom and are instructed in "their responsibilities as citizens of a broader society" (443). Toward this end, Herrnstein and Murray support voucher systems, tuition tax credits, greater choice for parents about which public schools their children attend, and the rechanneling of funds targeted for disadvantaged students, who, after all, don't have much to gain, to programs for the IQ gifted.

The authors of *The Bell Curve* never explain why everyone shouldn't be instructed more with respect to civic responsibility. It is an informed citizenry, not merely an informed elite, that makes democracy work. Instead, they remain content to submit a characteristic barrage of data about test scores and surveys, with no accompanying social insight, that speaks to the "dumbing down" of education in general, a quality they claim harms the cognitively elite more than anyone else. They never speak of political and cultural tensions in relation to schools. They never address the poor funding of school systems attended by most African Americans and other so-called minorities or the fact that most of the students they identify as cognitively gifted—coming as they do from, in the authors' own admission, economically privileged homes—are already the beneficiaries, despite what the authors say about underfunding for the cognitively gifted, of preferential treatment.

Of course, public schools need to be improved. No one has to labor hard to convince African Americans, who have received some of the worst that public education has to offer. It is fairly easy to understand as well that the gifted, however we define them, ought to be educated more broadly. The ethical sense of the whiz kids who would swarm Wall Street—or D.C., for that matter—could certainly stand some attention. However, the policies advocated by Herrnstein and Murray, rather than representing genuine cures for public problems, invite the undermining and ultimate dismissal of educational efforts to help the majority of our children. Too narrowly focused, and enslaved to a notion of the elite versus the "at risk," the authors of *The Bell Curve* write off millions of nonelite students who are, nevertheless, genetically "at promise," to borrow a phrase from Gardner, and in need of vital nurturing for their potential to be realized.

They never do stop. Nor can we. Sweet dreams.

Works Cited

Du Bois, W. E. B. "On Being Black" (1920). In Gerald Early, ed., *Speech and Power: The African American Essay and Its Cultural Content, from Polemics to Pulpit*, vol. 1. Hopewell, NJ: Ecco Press, 1992. 3–7.

Early, Gerald, ed. *Speech and Power: The African American Essay and Its Cultural Content, from Polemics to Pulpit*, vol. 1. Hopewell, NJ: Ecco Press, 1992.

Gardner, Howard. *Frames of Mind: The Theory of Multiple Intelligences* (1983). New York: Basic Books, 1985.

Gould, Stephen Jay. "Mismeasure by Any Measure." In Russell Jacoby and Naomi Glauberman, eds., *The Bell Curve Debate: History, Documents, Opinions*. New York: Times Books, 1995. 3–13.

Herrnstein, Richard J. "I.Q." *Atlantic Monthly*. September, 1971. 43–64.

——. *I.Q. in the Meritocracy*. Boston: Atlantic-Little Brown, 1973.

Herrnstein, Richard J., and Charles Murray. *The Bell Curve: Intelligence and Class Structure in American Life*. New York: Free Press, 1994.

Jacoby, Russell, and Naomi Glauberman, eds. *The Bell Curve Debate: History, Documents, Opinions*. New York: Times Books, 1995.

Holmes, Steven A. "Defining Race." In Russell Jacoby and Naomi Glauberman, eds., *The Bell Curve Debate: History, Documents, Opinions*. New York: Times Books, 1995. 273–75.

Marable, Manning. "On Being Black: The Burden of Race and Class" (1981). In Gerald Early, ed., *Speech and Power: The African American Essay and Its Cultural Content, from Polemics to Pulpit*, vol. 1. Hopewell, NJ: Ecco Press, 1992. 20–28.

Murray, Charles. *Losing Ground: American Social Policy, 1950–1980*. New York: Basic Books, 1984.

A FINAL WORD

Playing with the Patterns

There are two main reasons I have resisted, despite considerable urging, following up on the memoir sections of my book *Voices of the Self*. One, I don't kiss and tell. So I would have to leave a large hole in a narrative about adult life compared to the small one (barely noticed by some) that I left in the tale of my adolescence. I can work with cracks in my story but not craters. Two, I haven't considered my adulthood to be all that remarkable. Interesting, yes, exciting at times, but nothing I would read a whole lot about—the pressure not so intense, the days not so desperate. However, as two colleagues have set the task for me of reflecting upon some of the values and experiences that account for my teacherly orientation, I find that I can pick up a strand of the story line (lifeline) with which I don't mind playing.*

January 1971. Queensborough Community College. Laid out among the hills and valleys of the former Oakland Country Club in relatively privileged Bayside, Queens. From there you could peep across the city line into even more privileged Nassau County, into Jay Gatsby territory, a fact I would soon learn in an English class.

I made a bit of a splash on the African American social scene, primarily because I was a new face, starting as I did in the middle of the academic year. The first day of the semester I was walking down a corridor in the Humanities Building when I began to hear all this hoopla. A group of sistas were holding cheerleading practice. But there were no short skirts, oxfords, bobby socks, and pom-poms. These sistas were decked out African style, bright-colored bubas, matching géles. Bright greens. Browns and yellows. Verdant, summer, and autumnal beauties bouncing around a classroom in the middle of winter. Fine young women preparing to root for the Queensborough entry in the Black Brothers Basketball League, an alternative to traditional varsity leagues that weren't, one way or another,

*Dick Larson and Tom McCracken prompted me to write this piece. I intended to submit it for a collection they planned to edit. However, when it grew to be a longer manuscript than they requested, I decided to include it here.

doing justice to the brothas. The league was supposed to have a political platform, though I never quite figured out what it was. What I do know is that the QCC cheerleaders brought the most flava. And I had a lot of good times with some of those sistas. But remember, we won't go *there*.

I had two courses dealing with the study of communication: English Composition I and Voice and Diction. Comp was fine. I had a whole lot to say and didn't have too much trouble saying it. Whatever the assignment was, I bent it to my purposes. That's how I figured you did it. Show teachers enough of their own style, then bend the rest yo' way. Know what I'm sayin? Even if they give you some passé protocols to work with, you cover them, sign them the way Aretha Franklin or Luther Vandross push against commonplace delivery to place their inimitable vocal signatures on ballads. Of course there's always a tension about just how hard to push, but I was managing quite well. I didn't feel oppressed by the institution's language or that I couldn't write my way into academic conversations. I am now aware of the current voice-versus-social construction argument, you know, whether we should teach students that they write the culture or that the culture writes them. When kept so narrow or dichotomous, the debate is frivolous. I knew I was socially constructed, and I knew I had something peculiar to say about it as well. I saw no contradiction, or at least not one I couldn't live with. Besides, there was an overriding question that held my attention: What's any of this got to do with Black liberation? After a mental hibernation of sorts, I was a bear on the prowl for energetic, even radical, ideas.

The political, then, was important to me along with the affective. As a writing instructor, I try to create spaces for negotiation, innovation, and the exploration of political views. Writing had to mean something to me if I were going to write with meaning. And I now feel that students who are vested in writing the way I was, in the sense of purposefulness, not necessarily particular persuasion, have the best chance to achieve the writing standards set by academic institutions. The interaction of formal essay writing and vernacular discourse generates specific and valuable verbal structures, thus understandings, not producible in any other way. It can strengthen one's entire intellectual package. Therefore, though I know full well and respect the critique that the implementation of language standards may oppress practitioners of nonstandard varieties, I also think it worthwhile to support the goal of students becoming at least "two ways strong," as Eve Fesl, first Koori (Aboriginal Australian) to receive a Ph.D. in Australia, put the matter, with her fists thrust in the air, at the 1990 conference of the International Federation of Teachers of English. She wasn't kickin no lame or tame bidialectalism for the marketplace rap; she was talking about mastering the language of wider communication as a way of tightenin up, as I said, one's whole intellectual thang, for struggle, for leadership, for whatever. My present articulation of these ideas is post grad school, post a lot of years of teaching, and post encounters with minds like Fesl's. Clearly, though, I already possessed some, we might even say the core, of this sensibility that first semester at QCC.

Voice and Diction was crazy. Unlike the writing placement exam, which I breezed through, I failed the speech test. A professor taped me, listened to me soften the initial consonant cluster for words like *these*, *there*, *their*, and *those*; noted how I dragged the vowel sound in *rice* and *ice*; then decided that I had a Southern accent. In my nineteen years I hadn't spent thirty days south of Brooklyn. But according to the professor I somehow had acquired this Southern accent. Me and most of the African Americans, mainly Northerners, too, at QCC. Now we knew a Southern accent, what we called "sounding country," when we heard one. That wasn't what we sounded like. Regardless: Remedial Speech. They had me spinning around for a moment, got me to thinking I was substandard. Had me in the mirror overarticulating and sounding stupid like I was in charm school or something. *These* may have begun to sound a little less like *dese*, but I know that *rice* and *ice* stuff didn't change one iota. Working on that just sounded too dumb, and I wasn't even tryin ta git wit it. At the postsemester taping, I glared at the examiner and then spoke pretty much as I had before. He said I passed.

Back then I hadn't heard about Beryl Bailey, Lorenzo Turner, or William Stewart. J. L. Dillard's *Black English* was still a year away. No one told me I was speaking a systematic, rule-governed variation of English. Even if construed as a problem, my "Southern accent" would not have been sensitive to isolated speech drills I saw as primarily pointless. But things worked out, I suppose. I handled my business. I couldn't help noticing, however, that several of my African American classmates never finished the course.

Perhaps the most significant thing about my experience in Voice and Diction is that it was simultaneous with my earning a grade of A– in

Composition. I would always recall this as I was working through the literature or listening to presentations about Black English and education. To this day, I'm very suspicious when folks try to lay writing problems at the doorstep of dialect. The analysis has to be deeper. Again, purpose, prior experiences, motivation, perceptions of institutional texts and subtexts all have to be factored into the mix. I was committed to Comp, not voice lessons.

About fifteen years after Voice and Diction, I was invited back to QCC to speak at a language symposium. My old instructor happened to be in the audience, and I told the story of how I had been required to take remedial speech, including the fact that he had done the requiring. He denied that such a thing could have occurred. I suggested we could scoot on over to the registrar's office for a little archival research. He declined.

Back in 1971, there was some serious outside schooling to be continued, a vibrant and vital extracurriculum. Someone had the good sense to build the Langston Hughes Library & Community Cultural Center two blocks from my home. It became my office. When my homies couldn't find me at the crib or out on Northern Boulevard, they began to check the library. Then they started checking the library first. "He probably in his new crib wit dem books," they would say.

That Black liberation question was largely guiding my actions. What could I snatch from books to help Black folk? I read history, political science, psychology. You could obtain a healthy dose of each just by reading Frantz Fanon. *Black Skin, White Masks* and *Wretched of the Earth*. But I read poetry most of all. Black arts, baby. And poetry was king of all that. Creative writing as instrumentality. As Amiri Baraka wrote in "Black Art":

> Put it on him, poem. Strip him naked
> to the world! Another bad poem cracking
> steel knuckles in a jewlady's mouth
> Poem scream poison gas on beasts in green berets
> Clean out the world for virtue and love,
> Let there be no love poems written
> until love can exist freely and
> cleanly. Let Black People understand
> that they are the lovers and the sons
> of lovers and warriors and sons

of warriors Are poems & poets &
all the loveliness here in the world

I wasn't really a cultural nationalist deep down inside. Cultural nationalism was more of a church I liked to visit. Made me feel good, but I wasn't looking for it to carry me too far. I knew serious struggle didn't revolve around cracking "jewladies" in the mouth or leaving references to Black daughters out of your verses. I had more Panther-like leanings (their male chauvinism notwithstanding), employing a social critique that incorporated both ethnicity and class. But even at that, I couldn't cut loose my nationalist bards. I consumed the entire library collection of recent Black poetry. Works by the likes of Baraka, Larry Neal, Don L. Lee (Haki Madhubuti), Sonia Sanchez, Johari Amini, and Carolyn Rodgers. Nikki Giovanni actually visited the library to read. Then I would go on a relentless hunt for even more poems. Uptown to Michaux's on 125th Street. Around to the Liberation Book Store on Lenox Avenue. Running down the material coming out of The East in Brooklyn. Checking the record stores for albums by The Last Poets, The Original Last Poets, Gil Scott-Heron, and Wanda Robinson. Far into most nights, often after I had put my school-work to bed, I would work on writing my own poems, mostly inferior agitprop stuff, but some good. I might ease into my sister's room and whisper them in the ear of my sleeping niece, Nicole (Nikki, of course), who was born the same week I enrolled at QCC.

We started a poetry group that operated out of the library. Myself, Ahmasi (Ronnie Lloyd), Randy Latimer, Eric Rawlins, Lorraine Taylor, and a few others. We put on poetry shows to read our work, and we also organized readings for other poets from the community. The latter events were probably more fun, as people would sometimes dash in off the street, grab the mic, and make up poems, some of them wine-induced, right on the spot. Hip-hoppers would call it free-stylin. And it was cool, not a whole lot different from the stuff most of the neighborhood poets were laboring to write down. You know the trip. Black King, Black Queen, let's stay tight and rule the universe after we dispense with the racist crackers and honkies. Raw and necessary stuff, but, as I said, I was trying to move beyond it. Make some other kinds of artistic mistakes. Which I surely did.

One night in the Village Vanguard, while listening to McCoy Tyner, I scribbled a poem on a napkin and gave it to him. My action was partly arrogance, partly sloe gin fizz, and partly the suggestion of my main QCC running buddy, Maurice Ford. I later knew that if you wanted to give props to someone as bad as McCoy, you had to come much stronger than a hasty napkin poem. So I disciplined myself to write a longer, stronger poem, "The Piano Man Pulled Some Along," though I doubt he's seen it.

I thought I would eventually place a book with Dudley Randall's Broadside Press or Lee's Third World Press. I think a couple of others in our group felt the same way. In the meantime, since everybody with two sheets of paper and a stapler was publishing poetry, Lorraine, Eric, Randy, and I produced our own anthology near the end of 1971, which we called *White Paper, Black Poem*. Didn't sell much, but I felt it was the perfect way to cap the year.

We also had a newspaper going on. The *Transition Press*. Eric was the editor, and the *New York Times* kicked in some loot in addition to sending newspapermen out to the neighborhood on Saturdays to show us the journalistic ropes. We certainly had enough local data to draw upon, as the Corona–East Elmhurst area was a microcosm of the Black urban situation in America. For example, in just a five-block stretch of Northern Boulevard, say from 100th Street to 105th Street, you had winos lining up outside the liquor store at eight in the morning (let's get our drink on), rampant drug activity around the clock (let's escape reality), storefront Christian churches (let's pray), the liberal integrationist Walter White Manpower Center (let's overcome, or at least sing about it), the Nation of Islam's Mosque 7A (let's separate from the white devils), the headquarters of the largest branch of the Black Panther Party in New York State (let's off the pig), and the writers in the library (let's figure all this out). Expand the frame of reference just a bit and you could see tensions between homeowners and the permanent underclass, between petit bourgeois and "illegitimate capitalist," and peep in on the movement of students going to and from various colleges, from public community colleges (like me) to the Ivy League.

Widen the scope some more. In the spring of 1971, the Panthers split into Newton and Cleaver factions. It's sometimes referred to as the East Coast–West Coast split, but in New York you had both Newton and Cleaver loyalists, which ultimately resulted in the assassination of Cleaver devotee Robert Webb in Harlem and the murder of Newton disciple Sam Napier in Corona, the branch office I mentioned above being set ablaze in the process. I remarked to a numbers runner on my block that the white folks got Webb and Napier. He replied that white folks certainly do their share, but they don't do it all. He warned against turning white folks into God.

The Louis Armstrong funeral was held on 103rd Street. Folks wanted to speak out on George Jackson and Angela Davis. The Attica uprising occurred upstate, and we knew brothas in the middle of it. So as I said, there was plenty to write about to see if we could get everybody's "right on" on right, as Eric (I think it was) would say.

I remember writing an article about Davis, but not what I actually reported or argued. Whatever it was I had penned failed to meet the approval of a sista, who had spent time in California and was willing to school a young reporter, make him wiser. This took me into Marcuse and Conforth, material like that. And a lot of personal tutoring. Now I can't say much more than that. You know my creed.

Around the same time, I cut into Ramón Jiménez and Hubert Hammond. To this day, I think they are two of the most stellar people I've ever met. They were trying to establish an alternative school, simply called The Community School, and were working out of a storefront a block from the library. Ramón had graduated from St. John's University and had plans to attend Harvard Law School. Hubert had been to Bowdoin College up in Maine. They pushed the Marxist tip but avoided, and this is the main point I want to make about them, being dogmatic. Ramón had already read Freire's *Pedagogy of the Oppressed*. Problem posing was a big part of his manner. Both he and Hubert could teach you a great deal with questions. I like to load up political questions the way they did. If it's just about ethnicity, then why did 15 percent of the African American electorate vote for Reagan? If it's just about class, then why do working-class white Democrats cross party lines to keep nonelitist African American Democratic candidates out of office? We talked 1971 versions of this stuff.

Hubert said there was an important role for Black literature, especially if the political consciousness therein was as sophisticated as possible. Needless to say, he wasn't impressed with any of the poets I talked about. And he never criticized my own work directly (still too nationalist for his taste), though I got his point. Study Richard Wright, he advised.

Ramón had more use for my work. Ordinarily the most ethical person I knew, he would take my poems, change all the African American references to Latino ones, and read his versions before audiences. Then he would laugh and tell everyone (still does) that he was my poetry instructor and that I liked to rip off his poems. Little matter. I owed him.

Ramón worked in an educational program in Harlem with Karen Troupe, who was married to the poet Quincy Troupe, who taught at Richmond College. I knew about him from Woodie King's anthology, *BlackSpirits*, and thought he worked the language better than most poets I read. His "Ode to John Coltrane" set a standard for Coltrane poems that has never been matched. Ramón arranged for me to meet him and even drove me to Quincy's home. I went on ultracool, you know, like I was invited to the home of notables all the time. Quincy mostly talked about the need to practice, to pursue the craft. He said political work was necessary but warned that you have to be careful about your running partners. You could be getting whipped up by the police while your crew was hiding around the corner. I knew about that one already, wasn't that naive. We talked about poets we liked. He said Amus Mor out of Chicago was bad. Then he asked the critical question: have you read Pablo Neruda? I had never even heard of Neruda, arguably the greatest poet of the twentieth century, much less read him. So that was the key info that night. I had to go on a Neruda mission.

Latin American surrealism exploded inside my head. Neruda's lines were like verbal depth charges. "A river that the feathers of the burning eagles are covering." I didn't see how you beat that imagery. The first book I bought (done by Robert Bly) also contained translations of Vallejo, who was masterful as well. I rapidly collected more titles, *Residence in Earth*, *The Captain's Verses*, *The Heights of Macchu Picchu*, *Twenty Love Poems and a Song of Despair*, *Selected Poems*, *Five Decades*, *Fully Empowered*, *The Captain's Verses*, *Spain*, *Take This Cup from Me*. Politics or personal passion, the brothas got down.

It seemed that because I was a serious student, I became everybody's favorite one. I had to duck people so they wouldn't add more titles to my list before I could catch up. I had to hole up with Nkrumah's *Consciencism*, *Neo-Colonialism: Last Stage of Imperialism*, and *Handbook of Revolutionary Warfare*. Aimé Césaire's *Discourse on Colonialism* and *Return to My Native Land*. Oh Césaire:

> My mouth shall be the mouth of misfortunes which
> have no mouth, my voice the freedoms of those freedoms
> which break down in the prison-cell of despair.

The Community School never became fully operational. It housed a couple of service programs for a while, then folded altogether. Ramón was off to Harvard, where I visited him several times. Once while I was there, he was invited to give a speech at an antiwar rally on Boston Common. The speakers had to climb up onto a high platform, and Ramón asked a friend of ours, Sonny Bargeron, and me to go up with him. That was the style back then. You spoke while your boys stood in back of you looking militant. I actually was more interested in my conversation with Dr. Daniel Ellsberg, he of the Pentagon Papers case, who was scheduled to speak after Ramón. I was like, "Yo Doc, you gon beat this case or what?" But we didn't get too far because Ramón was ready to begin, and I had to climb on up to the platform.

Ramón affirmed the antiwar efforts before launching into an attack on white leftists for copping out on other issues involving people of color. Somebody threw a whiskey bottle, and I told Ramón it was time to jet. I knew we could handle only so many drunken liberals. But he persevered and kept telling the truth, which is his way.

On those trips to Massachusetts, I picked up yet another mentor, Andrew Vachss. A once and future New Yorker, he was at that time living in Somerville and directing a juvenile facility. Andrew was a stone-cold action man. He could theorize with the best of them, but the bottom line for him was commitment, getting things done. Still is, as you can tell from both his law and writing careers. He's my top advice man to this day.

Extracurricular activity, then, especially the mentors I picked up along the way, figured prominently in my thoughts about learning and teaching. So-called multiculturalism was a given, silly to ignore. And I leaned toward an interactionist, critical mode of inquiry. I was miles ahead of all the talk about critical thinking that came into vogue years later. To me, critical thinking comes with the territory. If you read, write, and discuss texts critically, how could you not be experiencing critical thought? If you ran with the people I ran with, there was no other kind of thinking to do. Similarly, "teaching the conflicts" would be no new wrinkle in classes I was involved in either as student or teacher. It's the only way to be true to the game. Some of my teachers back at QCC thought I was too serious-minded; some were amused. I remember one saying she'd like to see me in twenty-five years. Well, twenty-five years later, 1 percent of the nation is pocketing 40 percent of the national wealth, and I'm still willing to beef about it.

My school reading list wasn't nearly so provocative as my outside one. However, there was plenty to debate. I didn't have to wait for reader-response theorists to know it's OK to stretch out on a text. I may have stretched too much at times, but I was never timid. After reading "The Rockpile," for example, a short story by James Baldwin that ends sort of up in the air, I wrote a paper contending that the boy (John) dies at the end, or at least gets hurt badly. My instructor countered that we couldn't assume that. But I felt that the symbolism and internal logic of the story compelled such a conclusion, and that I had made the case. We had to agree to disagree and call it a day. Years later, when I was a graduate student at Columbia, I put the question to Baldwin himself after he visited a class I was in. He didn't seem to recall the story, at least not readily. And I don't know why I thought he should. He was past fifty and had written a couple of million words by then. When I refreshed his memory and pushed the question again, he said the story does not suggest that John is to be assaulted. So I went back and read "The Rockpile" closely. Blood and death, or musings about blood and death, on all the opening pages. "Rockpile" suggesting prison. Seemed like some heavy foreshadowing to me. I won't say Baldwin was wrong, but D. H. Lawrence said that critics have the job of saving stories from the people who write them.

At times, my extracurricular sensibility caused me to take even more decisive action in school. I was enrolled in a poetry workshop and had an instructor whose sense of development, not to mention aesthetics, differed drastically from my own. He liked to call all of us beginning poets. To me, that meant, like, someone in the third grade. I thought of myself as a poet. Period. But in his view, we might, if we were good enough, become promising poets in our twenties, and mature poets after that. He would sound pretty reasonable to me today, but back then, because he had no idea of the circles I moved in, where there seemed to be all kinds of outstanding and mature poets in their twenties, including most of the ones I mentioned earlier, he turned me off. When you also consider that he only seemed familiar with European-style work and championed imitations of Euro-style masters—nary a word about a Neruda or a Troupe in that class—you understand why I dropped the course, the only English course I ever withdrew from in college except for one in which James

Fenimore Cooper was threatening to bore me to death. I left the poetry class because the instructor didn't bother to find out what I knew about poetry. Only his tastes, experiences, and the canon he paid homage to mattered. That squeezed me out, which has been instructive to recall.

I also thought about dropping Black American History, oddly enough, and probably would have if my homegirl Gerianne Scott and this brotha from Freeport named Phil hadn't been on the scene to absorb some of the tension. If we challenged, and challenge we did, some of the ideas being taught, the conversation always swung around to how disrespectful young Blacks were compared to older Blacks like the professor, and on the way to that point we had to hear that Black people in the ghetto deface and destroy the very places where they live and thus should stop bellyaching about what society won't do for them, something like that. Freeport Phil, sporting a big Afro and always on the case, stayed the most agitated, even got put out of the class a few times under threat of having security guards summoned. He did more intellectual scuffling than prescribed coursework. You can't effectively help those you don't respect, a fact to bear in mind.

I became an English tutor at QCC, worked for Linda Stanley, whom I still run into at CCCC. I tried to help students correct their errors, and I always had some sort of pep talk for them. They thought writing came easy to me or was a gift. I knew it had more to do with reading and work and practice and a sense of high stakes. Years later, when I was a basic writing adjunct at LaGuardia Community College, my first teaching appointment, I received an evaluation from the director of composition in which she noted that, in preparing the class for the departmental writing exam, I was exhorting the class like a coach preparing a team for the Super Bowl. The coaching metaphor has become popular since then and has a positive connotation, but the director was not complimenting me at the time. And I realized that. I was just disappointed that I couldn't make the test sound more important, to a group of largely African American and Latino basic writers, than a mere football extravaganza.

By the time I left QCC, I had completed eighteen courses, six in English. I had mainly sampled, unconcerned with the specific requirements of the A.A. degree. I transferred into a university-wide baccalaureate program and, praise to the extracurriculum, received life experience credits for various writing projects.

Andrew was back in New York. So was Ramón. I agreed to help them with legal work they were doing in the New Jersey prison system. We'd be regularly off to Rahway, Trenton, way down to Leesburg. Andrew had the idea of shooting a video inside Trenton State Penitentiary. Part of it would show me teaching a writing class we would convene for the occasion. After we rolled the tape, and this was still years prior to LaGuardia CC, I was thinking that I could actually do it. I could teach for real.

Index

Liberation Memories

THE RHETORIC AND POETICS OF JOHN OLIVER KILLENS

to Grace

Contents

Acknowledgments

For their general support and encouragement, I thank a host of people too numerous to name here. I trust that they know my gratitude. For their specific assistance with the manuscript, I am greatly indebted to Alvin Aubert, Adam Banks, Bernard Bell, Melba Joyce Boyd, Deborah Breen, Clinton Crawford, Lita Cunningham, William Daly, Arthur Flowers, Kaamilah Gilyard, Beth Howse, Grace Killens, Kelly Malarky, Vorris Nunley, Yusuf Nuruddin, Howard Rambsy, Elaine Richardson, Evelyn Richardson, Lorenzo Thomas, and Vershawn Young.

In addition, I wish to thank the entire staffs of the National Baha'i Archives, the Medgar Evers College Library, and the Schomburg Center for Research in Black Culture.

Introduction

On the night of March 22, 1986, septuagenarian John Oliver Killens made the last major public appearance of his career. He was received warmly by an admiring audience of hundreds who attended a dinner at Harvest Manor in Brooklyn, an affair held as part of the National Black Writers Conference. They showered appreciation upon a writer and activist who was the author of eight books, founding chairman of the legendary Harlem Writers Guild, a two-time nominee for the Pulitzer Prize, and a man regarded by some as the spiritual father of a generation of African-American novelists.[1] However, as the years pass and that buoyant occasion recedes further into the past, one is left to realize that despite the fact that Killens should be regarded as important, his literary reputation is far from secure. Much of his work is out of print. He has not been a popular subject for researchers. And although entries about him appear in several reference and critical works, he is not represented among the one hundred forty-nine selections discussed in *Masterpieces of African-American Literature* (1992). Nor is he among the more than one hundred writers included in the heralded *Norton Anthology of African American Literature* (1997) or among the dozens included in the *Prentice Hall Anthology of African American Literature* (2000).

His most notable African-American fiction-writing contemporaries, Ralph Ellison and James Baldwin, receive great attention and generate an abundance of ink. His fiction, viewed often as overly political or journalistic by detractors, fails to appeal to art-for-art's-sake advocates. Even those sympathetic to his message do not always embrace his technique. As Harish Chander observes relative to the fairly scant critical reception that does exist, "Appraisals of John Oliver Killens' fictional works that focus on his ideology and substance of his message have generally been positive, whereas those that focus on form and structure have generally been negative" (256).

Because no serious history of the development of the African-American novel from the 1950s onward can be constructed, as Addison Gayle and Bernard Bell have suggested, without considerable attention to Killens's contribution, we need a more informed and balanced critique that advances beyond the neglect of anthologists and the binarism indicated by Chander.[2] This book aims to support such a reckoning. The primary focus is an assessment of his novels from a rhetorical perspective. Rather than legitimizing the contention that so-called depoliticized writing is the cherished criterion that Killens's fiction fails to meet or the idea that technical blemishes in his work prevail, the governing premise here is that Killens's novels are best construed as tremendously artful renderings of African-American rhetorical forms and that the richest readings of his novels involve a knowledge of Black verbal traditions.

Killens was a novelist mainly concerned with articulating Black heroism, particularly within a family or community context, and offering a set of values he deemed liberatory. He often eschewed realism—assuming that by realism one means complex environmental and psychological portraiture—in favor of an insistence on noble and polemical characters. In his mission and view of art, he deliberately followed W. E. B. Du Bois, who, in a famous 1926 article titled "Criteria of Negro Art," wrote:

> All Art is propaganda and ever must be, despite the wailing of the purists. I stand in utter shamelessness and say that whatever art I have for writing has been used always for propaganda for gaining the right of black folk to love and enjoy. I do not care a damn for any art that is not used for propaganda. But I do care when propaganda is confined to one side while the other is stripped and silent. (296)

It must be noted that Du Bois was using *propaganda* in the more neutral sense the term conveyed, as Edward Corbett and Robert Connors remind us, before it took on "unfavorable connotations" (24–25). In addition, it must be stressed that the term *propaganda* for Du Bois did not imply any diminished artistry. He was merely affirming the persuasive aspect of art.

Killens was also a forerunner to Black Arts theorists like Larry Neal, who argued for the production of Black rhetorical art and the rejection of a Western critique.[3] For sure, only Black folks could put the "Black" in such art. On the other hand, to the extent that those critics meant "Western" to signify a uniform privileging by white critics of a restrictive formalism, they overstated their case. Wayne Booth, for example, had already effectively demonstrated the weakness and arbitrariness of the "pure art" position in his landmark book *The Rhetoric of Fiction*. Booth argued that any literary language that shows anything also serves to tell. He asserted that "the author cannot choose to avoid rhetoric; he can choose only the kind of rhetoric he will utilize. He cannot choose whether or not to affect his readers' evaluations by his choice of narrative manner; he can only choose whether to do it well or poorly" (149). Although certainly not flawless, the Killens fiction corpus represents a distinguished fusion of sociopolitical persuasion, or rhetoric, and literary artifact, or poetics.[4]

As I consider Killens's novels, individually or as a group, my investigation is organized sequentially, for the most part, in terms of three categories: vision, vehicle, and vernacular. This is similar to the taxonomy—theme, structure, saturation—that Stephen Henderson employed in the 1970s to examine the "new Black poetry," a poetry often viewed as parallel to Killens's fiction in the context of the Black Arts Movement. But while Henderson used *theme* to denote subject matter, I opt for *vision* because I want to emphasize that the writer is making an argument about a view of the world, not merely or neutrally trotting out provocative material for display. Thus my use of *vision* stretches Henderson's conceptualization of *theme*. On the other hand, by *vehicle* I mean something closely akin to what Henderson meant by *structure*, though I am more concerned with how the argument is articulated in rhetorical terms than I am with the genre elements typically associated with the novel. In other words, by *vehicle* I mean the most salient rhetorical devices used to carry the message. For the purposes of this inquiry, the primary topoi are the Black sermon; the elaborated folktale or epigraph; Du Bois's metaphors of the Talented Tenth, double consciousness, and the veil; literacy as emancipation; signifying, or humorous put-downs; the recurring image of Malcolm X; and the reinterpretation of community texts both sacred and secular. By *vernacular*, I mean the textual embellishments that derive from the linguistic, musical, folkloric, and religious practices of common African Americans. This is consonant with Henderson's notion of *saturation*, the detailed ways in which texts evince "Blackness." Or as Lumumba, narrator of *The Cotillion*, phrases the matter in the novel's foreword, "I decided to write my book in Afro-Americanese. Black rhythm, baby. Yeah, we got rhythm, brothers, sisters. Black idiom, Black nuances, Black style. Black truths. Black exaggerations" (6). Killens's use of the vernacular in *The Cotillion* and his other major novels will be detailed.

Incorporated into this book is examination of Killens's output as an essayist and cultural organizer. It helps to illumine his fiction; therefore, significant space is devoted to discussing those activities and the part they play in his overall message. More specifically, I am interested in the extent to which Killens's essays make up an African-American jeremiad, a major rhetorical form in the African-American intellectual tradition that expresses faith, unlike the tenets of the Black Arts Movement, that America's destiny is to become an authentic, pluralistic democracy. In addition, I demonstrate how the numerous conferences Killens organized serve as an elaborately constructed set of testimonials that endorse his views on cultural politics.

Chapter 1, then, deals with the major fictional statement that Killens made about the South, especially as related to heroic resistance, unity, and African-American folk wisdom. The relevant novels are *Youngblood* (1954) and *'Sippi* (1967). Chapter 2 revolves around *And Then We Heard the Thunder* (1962) and examines Killens's overall ideology and technique in more detail. The appeals at the heart of *Black Man's Burden* (1965), his collection of essays, form the third chapter's core topic, although significant references are made to several other Killens essays, to his relationship with Malcolm X as evidenced by the charter of the Organization of Afro-American Unity, and to the well-known criticism of Killens contained in Harold Cruse's *Crisis of the Negro Intellectual*. Chapter 4 considers *The Cotillion* (1971), perhaps the most popular Killens novel, and how it reflects the Black cultural revolution the author championed. Chapter 5 demonstrates how Killens's call for a literature of Black heroes, myths, and legends shapes *Slaves* (1969), *Great Gittin' Up Morning* (1972), *A Man Ain't Nothin' but a Man: The Adventures of John Henry* (1975), and the posthumously published *Great Black Russian: A Novel on the Life and Times of Alexander Pushkin* (1989). Chapter 6 illustrates how the various writers' conferences convened by Killens between 1965 and 1986 represent calculated amplifications of his voice.

Apparently Killens will always be associated with the Black Arts Movement, and he should be. His challenging the "pure art" position, his valorizing of African-American orality, and his creating idealized, heroic, and nationalist characters are hallmarks of the Black Aesthetic. As such, his work remains relevant as we continue to ponder the strengths and weaknesses of that aesthetic. Much of Killens's writing exists in dialogue with latter-day critics like Deborah McDowell and Madhu Dubey. McDowell, in "Boundaries: Or Distant Relations and Close Kin," claims that the artistic formulas of the Black Arts Movement make race the superordinate construct and thus engage in essentialism, subordinating, for example, gender differences. Dubey is sympathetic to McDowell's argument but also acknowledges, in *Black Women Novelists and the Nationalist Aesthetic*, that the critical project of the Black Aestheticians—particularly the debunking of art-for-art's-sake rhetoric and the privileging of vernacular forms, both ideas that were pushed strongly by Killens—made possible some of the subsequent literary achievements of Black female writers. This is undoubtedly a significant accomplishment of those theorists and practitioners. But although Killens's work should remain connected to deliberations about the Black Arts Movement, I argue for an even richer, more complex read. His ideas, as I hope to make clear, were more expansive and pluralistic than one might assume. I would even posit that Black nationalist writing by Killens is an example of what Gary Hatch describes as "community-based reasoning" (208–10). Using this technique, a rhetor does not forward the arguments most compelling to him or her if such arguments are not valued very highly by the community being addressed. Instead, reasoning is offered that aligns with the community's prevailing sentiments. This rhetorical move could be hypocritical—would be if the rhetor actually holds no belief in the propositions set forth—but it is not necessarily so. It is often like a witness telling the truth, indeed, maybe even nothing but the truth, but not the whole truth. As Hatch explains, "The trick is to find reasons that the community will find persuasive and that you can accept and believe in" (209).

Before Killens, Langston Hughes engaged in a celebrated example of community-based reasoning. About to begin a reading tour in 1931 before mostly religious and somewhat conservative Black Southerners, Hughes realized that his recent poems reflecting a radical socialist aesthetic would not be received well. So he wrote poems for the tour like "The Negro Mother" to glorify Black culture and Black pride in a way that would appeal to his envisioned audience. Hughes, of course, was genuine in his celebration—but he also celebrated more.[5] In a similar fashion, Black nationalist writing does not represent the sum of Killens's ideology, even post-1960s. Such writing aims, rather, to persuade African-American readers to unite and perform the hard and difficult task of building adequate mechanisms of power. This is a mission in which Killens truly believed. As such, he understood that one cannot ignore appeals to Black nationalism and reasonably hope to capture the attention of the Black masses. However, the window of his provincialism always opened onto broader prospects of liberation.

Wanda Macon writes, in *The Oxford Companion to African American Literature*, that "Killens's name will forever ring simultaneously with the bells of freedom" (420). But for how many? I hope that whatever the current count, this book helps increase the numbers of readers and listeners.

1

Southern Exposure

A major aim of John Oliver Killens as a fiction writer was to present his understanding of Southern experience and to counsel African-American readers and others. This brand of deliberative discourse involved departures on two fronts. First, he had to dispel the rather significant myth that happy, contented "darkies" got along on the whole with their white counterparts in a perceived pastoral Southland. His fiction would refute that notion explicitly and repeatedly. Second, he chose to challenge the American tradition of fiction, even that of African Americans, and develop stories around positive and generative Black families, which he viewed as essential elements of the most important social gains that had been and could be achieved by the general African-American populace. In addition, Killens interpreted politics for his readers by activating his characters quite polemically. Thus his novels have been criticized for being too rhetorical—that is, overly concerned with persuasion. Of course, the point is moot for these purposes because the present goal is precisely to examine a fair sampling of his persuasive gestures, attempt to account for its construction, and contend that his rhetoric, rather than being perceived as a literary defect, is best construed as crucial to an impressive artistry. The texts highlighted in this chapter are the novels *Youngblood* and *'Sippi*, his most extensive representations of life and political activism in the South.

Published in 1954, *Youngblood* signaled a new direction for the African-American novel. Its title alone, a surname, besides suggesting new energy and insights, announces its difference from Black existential works like *Native Son* and *Invisible Man*. Killens rejects the overriding singular (son) presence in Wright's novel and the isolated (man) absence in Ellison's. Particularly critical of *Invisible Man*, he wrote a harsh review in Paul Robeson's *Freedom* newspaper claiming that Ellison offered a commercial mix of sex, violence, red-baiting, and decadent African-American characters. He charged that Ellison portrays the incestuous

Trueblood as representative of Black sharecroppers, that the veterans in the asylum are meant to symbolize the average Black soldier, that Rinehart typifies the Black pastor, and that the novel's protagonist is an Uncle Tom who kowtows to rich white people. Killens argued further that "this book would give the impression that the Negro people as a whole are a hopeless bunch of dehumanized beings. This is exactly the Big Lie that the enemies of Negro freedom have been telling the world since slavery time—that the Negro is subhuman" (7).

As indicated previously, Killens considered novels to be propaganda as well as art and was preoccupied with the idea that most African-American characters be cast in a positive light. Unfortunately, this view, admirable in many respects, seriously compromised his evaluation of *Invisible Man*. For one, Trueblood is not offered as the norm among Black farmers. He is an anomaly, a veritable outcast. A casual observer like Mr. Norton has to be guided to him. Likewise, the veterans are not presented as paradigmatic, nor is Rinehart intended to be illustrative of the African-American ministry in general. Furthermore, it is contradictory to assert that the protagonist is consumed by the desire to ascend the social ladder, which requires intelligence and talent in his case, while maintaining that Blacks are categorized as hopeless and subhuman, in other words, lacking intelligence. Despite these flaws in his reasoning, or indeed because of them, Killens pressed onward to the conclusion that *Invisible Man* constitutes a "vicious distortion of Negro life" and asserted further that the "Negro people need Ralph Ellison's *Invisible Man* like we need a hole in the head or a stab in the back" (7). Although the artistic differences between Killens and Ellison during the 1950s should not be understated, it must be noted that Ellison was a favorite target of the left, both Black and white, in New York, who considered unflattering his depiction of leftist organizers.

The Killens viewpoint apparently prevailed inside the Harlem Writers Guild, of which Killens was the founding chairman. When *Youngblood* appeared, guild member John Henrik Clarke wrote in the August 1954 issue of *Freedom* that it was a story of "healthy Negroes" and called it "the best novel on Negro life that has appeared to date" (7). Killens would eventually soften his stance toward *Invisible Man*, and he even produced a Rinehart of his own nearly twenty years later in the satirical story "Rough Diamond." Nonetheless, the creation of positive Black characters remained his dominant concern.

Rather than portraying an individual's anguished quest for identity or self-fulfillment, Killens accepted an enabling Black identity as the rule, rather than the exception, and was driven to represent in *Youngblood* the heroic struggle of a family and community to persevere and thrive during the first third of the twentieth century. That Killens would perceive the family unit as the cornerstone of a successful mass confrontation with Jim Crow was predictable given the relative stability of his own upbringing. He shared a close bond, for instance, with his great-grandmother, Georgia Killens, whom he called Granny. She habitually regaled him with masterfully spun stories, which contained astute cultural criticism, often told as they walked the streets of Macon together. Although she died when Killens was five or six years old, she left behind plenty of material, much of it about her childhood years in slavery, that would show up in his work. She was, in fact, the model for Big Mama, the dominant figure in the early portion of *Youngblood*, whose forceful, deconstructive commentary infuses every scene. Echoing the wisdom dispensed by Granny, Big Mama refutes the idea that slaves felt there were benevolent masters worth serving. She remarks, "Crackers always talking about the slaves cried when Marster Lincoln sot us free. We cried all right, honey. Aah Lord—we cried. Won' a Negro's eyes dry that time. We cried for joy and shouted hallelujah" (6). This sentiment derives from that expressed by Granny, who informed young Killens, while criticizing a popular song about so-called mourning slaves, "Humph! Talking about 'All the darkies am aweeping.' We wept all right, honey bunch. We wept for joy and shouted halleluyah when Ol' Masser got the cold cold ground that was coming to him" ("The Half Ain't Never Been Told" 281).

Laurie Lee Barksdale, the central female character in the novel, benefits enormously from her grandmother's intellect and spirit. She is schooled by Big Mama always to resist oppression. Joe Youngblood, Laurie Lee's husband, is no less heroic. A dark and muscular six-foot-four, he goes to church on Sundays, sings bass in the glee club, and plays baseball on Saturday afternoons. Imagine Joe Louis, Josh Gibson, Paul Robeson, John Henry, and the most handsome and decent Baptist deacon ever all rolled into one. Having risked his life in Tennessee in an attempt to avoid being forced to perform involuntary labor on Mr. Buck's plantation, Joe has cut his teeth on struggle, though he somewhat regrets the solitary nature of his eventual escape, musing, "Shoulda brought some of them with me. . . . Shoulda talked them into it" (22).

After Laurie Lee and Joe marry, they settle in highly racialized Crossroads, Georgia, a metaphor for the Macon of Killens's youth and for a particular intersection. Pleasant Grove, the "colored section" of the town in which they live, is much like the Pleasant Hill community of real-life Macon. The Pleasant Grove School is the fictional counterpart to the Pleasant Hill School that Killens attended. The Youngblood children, Jenny Lee and Robby, were "born" around the same time as the author himself, Robby no doubt being a principal alter ego. With the idealized Youngblood family in place—mother, father, sister, brother—hardworking and virtuous, Killens has created his first major fictional vehicle to explore Black communal possibility within a social realm indelibly familiar to him.

The battle is pitched in both *Youngblood* and *'Sippi*; hardly a page goes by without Blackfolk having to resolve some crisis created by whites. Days upon days are wrapped in threat and death. Barely a conversation transpires without "boy," "sir," "nigrah," "cracker," "nigger," or "peckerwood." In the midst of these polarities, the author drives home the message that Black redemption can only come through Black unity. Building on solid foundations like the Youngblood family unit, the African-American community must construct an organized rebellion. Joe's favorite song, which functions as his (and the book's) mantra, is "Walk Together Children." Robby literally dreams of Black liberators:

> On one side was massed a great White army with ugly ghostlike faces, evil and leering. And on the other side the great Black army, proud and handsome and fierce and brave and everything else. And Mama was there and Daddy was there and Jenny Lee and Ben Raglin and Ida Mae Raglin and Fat Gus Mackey and everybody else. But most of all, Robby Youngblood was there, strong and mighty, leading the Black army to victory. (75–76)

Robby's dreams are commendable, but without manifest strength, Blacks remain vulnerable in a hostile white environment, a lesson spelled out painfully for Robby in an episode drawn from an incident Killens experienced while a student at the segregated Pleasant Hill School, a dilapidated structure without running water and sufficient heat. On the way to and from classes, Killens and several of his schoolmates passed the colonial mansions of wealthy whites, often crossing paths with white children going to and from their own segregated school. One day at the crossroads (hence Crossroads, Georgia), a white student asked a friend of Killens, "Hey nigger, what you learn in school today?" The quick-witted boy replied, "I learned your mother was a whore." As the Black boys laughed in approval, the white boy became enraged and slapped the Black boy in the face, touching off a melee during which punches were thrown, rocks hurled, and sticks wielded. No one, however, was seriously injured, and the battle ended indecisively. Killens and his friends continued home, proud of their scrapes, bruises, and hard-won dignity. The next morning a squadron of police officers came to Pleasant Hill School and dragged several frightened Black children from the building. Not all of them had participated in the fight, and some who had been involved had been fortunate, like Killens, to be overlooked. No white children were apprehended. After the children were taken to the courthouse, their mothers were summoned and afforded a choice. Either they could beat their sons in front of the authorities as a lesson not to fight white kids, or they could watch their sons, none of whom was yet a teenager, be carted off to reform school. As much as the mothers hated to do it, every one of them whipped her son to save him from the reformatory (*Black Man's Burden* 102–5).

Nearly thirty years later, Killens retells the story in his first novel, with slight modifications, upping the dramatic ante. Robby, for instance, is not fighting merely because he won a quick game of insult; he had come to the rescue of Jenny Lee, who was being assaulted by a group of white boys while on her way home from school. Like the early Wright, Killens provides little moral wiggle room. Robby had been taught by his mother, following the lead of Big Mama, that his resistance was appropriate. Laurie Lee did not subscribe, as Wright's mother did, to the part of the "ethics of living Jim Crow" that banned fighting against white boys.[1] In her eyes, you fought whomever you had to fight to protect yourself and your loved ones. Regardless of the omnipresent danger for an assertive Black male, and remembering that her own brother Tim had been ruined by reform school after fighting white boys, she nonetheless refuses, as the saying goes, to shove Robby back into her womb. She concentrates instead on consciously grooming him to become a man unbowed and unwilling to be treated as socially inferior. That she inevitably acquiesces to authorities and beats Robby is a crushing defeat for her family, as it was for the real-life and nameless mothers. Laurie Lee made the right call, but the decision offers her no immediate solace.

Despite setbacks like the courthouse debacle, which almost tears apart the family because of the children's resentment and the parents' combination of anger and guilt, the Youngbloods, Robby especially, recapture the momentum toward Black community. As Robby thinks wistfully one day after a trip to the swimming hole with his friends, "If they kept being buddies even after they had become grown men and never stopped being buddies ever, then white folks wouldn't be able to touch them with a ten-foot pole" (110). Robby also is the catalyst for resolving tensions between African Americans in the South and those from the North. Such divisiveness, ridiculous to Killens, who basically viewed the whole nation as Southern, stifles a valuable exchange of perspectives and impedes the development of the strongest possible African-American community in Crossroads and beyond.[2] So when Robby's friends disparage the idea of having a teacher from up North, even before they have met him, it is Robby who exhorts them to lay aside their prejudices and give the new teacher a chance. The children are rewarded immeasurably when the teacher, Richard Wendell Myles, brings to town a much-needed and ultimately appreciated radicalism. As Frederick Douglass wrote, as Mr. Myles remembers from college, and as Killens himself quoted countless times during his own public career: "If there is no struggle there is no progress. Those who profess to favor freedom, and yet depreciate agitation, are men who want crops without plowing the ground. They want rain without thunder and lightning. They want the ocean without the awful roar of its many waters" (*Youngblood* 136).[3]

Killens's father was Charles Myles Killens; thus he is the source of the fictional teacher's surname as well as one of the sources of his spirit. The author recalls with awe and fondness an incident that occurred in Macon in 1932 when his father managed a restaurant in the Black business district and sixteen-year-old Killens worked behind the counter. Two white men entered and one, who was apparently inebriated, demanded to be served. The elder Killens informed the man that it was against the law to serve him and declined. The man would not go easily or quietly; in fact, he became quite aggressive, creating a tense situation that was finally resolved when the elder Killens brandished a pistol. Young John was proud yet fearful, understanding that "Black manhood and Black womanhood were hazardous pursuits, inflationarily expensive" ("The Half Ain't Never Been Told" 283–84).

The Mr. Myles of *Youngblood* also derives, as Stephen Carey suggests, from the concept of the Talented Tenth. As he comments on Killens's characters generally: "In the social arenas of education, religion and politics, Killens develops heroic leadership as highly educated, as directly interested in the 'uplift' of the common masses, and as intensely active in directly resisting racial oppression. His protagonists must meet Du Boisian standards. Killens is particularly interested in developing heroes who serve as the Talented Tenth for the Black southern underclass" (2–3). Of course, Du Bois popularized the notion of the Talented Tenth in the early twentieth century, the idea being that the best among African Americans—the most capable, gifted, promising, and highly educated sector or "tenth"—would save the ethnic group as a whole from the worst social ravages. Not only did Du Bois posit that such aristocratic leadership eventually would be successful; he argued that it was the quickest way to effect the social uplift of the African-American masses. However, he later expanded and revised his thinking largely because, in his own view, he had failed to emphasize the importance of self-sacrifice in his initial conception. The Talented Tenth often operated more in its own interests than on behalf of the group. Du Bois also developed an appreciation for mass organization, activity he felt should be guided by socialist principles.[4] In any event, Killens, for whom Du Bois was a personal and invaluable mentor, was enormously influenced by Du Bois's more mature version of the Talented Tenth.[5] Thus the "Du Boisian standards" Carey references emanate, for Killens, from Du Bois's latter convictions as expressed in the 1948 "Talented Tenth Memorial Address."

The Du Boisian Mr. Myles has an immediate impact on Robby Youngblood. After learning in school about Harriet Tubman and the Underground Railroad, Robby has another dream: "Laurie Lee Youngblood was the conductor and Robert Youngblood was the engineer, and the train was long and black and beautiful, like the Mary Jane Special, but longer and blacker and even more beautiful. And black folks got on at every stop—Everybody headed for that thing called Freedom" (158).

Mr. Myles also presents his brand of activism to Laurie Lee and Joe, who have been rebels, at least in spirit, all along. Joe Youngblood is intrigued by how Mr. Myles's "book learning" essentially restates Joe's own heartfelt impulses. Joe understands that "We got to fight . . . *We?—We?* Yes . . .—*We*—We—You mighty right—*We*—We—We got to band together and fight— . . . We got to get together and fight these peckerwoods down to the ground" (203). Immediately thereafter, this idea is tested as Joe's paymaster at the mill continues his practice of shorting Joe on his pay. When Joe takes umbrage and successfully demands a proper accounting, he is supported by three of his African-American coworkers. As the four of them leave the mill, Joe feels that the combined strength of the others actually enters his body (211). While he strolls amid the African-American crowd on Harlem Avenue on his way to the barbershop, he is keenly aware—having been made hyperperceptive by the incident at the mill and his accompanying nervousness—of the Black throng's productive capability if they would only, as his most cherished song advises, walk together.

Laurie Lee, actually quicker to action than her husband is and who may be the stronger character, exclaims after hearing of the mill incident and the response of the three coworkers, "When a Negro's in trouble with the white man it's every Negro's business" (223). One recalls the fervent, community-spirited rhetoric—"injustice anywhere is a threat to justice everywhere"—later expressed by Martin Luther King Jr. in his "Letter from Birmingham Jail."[6]

As necessary as an activist Black solidarity is, it is not sufficient to revamp relations in the South in line with Killens's vision. His outlook required a coalition of revolutionary African Americans and progressive European Americans to fully address economic exploitation, a matter that was at least as important to Killens as civil rights. This inclination on his part is traceable, Du Bois aside, to his involvement in the labor movement. He was the first African American on the staff of the National Labor Relations Board, where he worked from 1936 to 1942 and again briefly after World War II. He was also an organizer for the Congress of Industrial Organizations, founded in 1938 under the direction of John L. Lewis, president of the United Mine Workers of America. His multiethnic vision may also have stemmed from his experiences at the Ballard Normal School, which he attended from the eighth grade until his graduation from high school. Established by the Congregational Church and the American Missionary Association, Ballard had an ethnically diverse faculty, which was very unusual in the Deep South. Most of the white teachers hailed from New England or out West and were considered pariahs by most white Maconites. One teacher, an Iowan named Lewis H. Mounts, impressed on Killens the need to be available for social service ("The Half Ain't Never Been Told" 284). Killens already felt this way, at least to some degree, because of his upbringing, but Mounts felt the idea could never be emphasized enough. Mounts was respected and genuinely liked by the African-American community in Macon and survives, in part, in Oscar Jefferson, the white character in *Youngblood* who most symbolizes the role that whites should play in the struggle according to Killens. Oscar, suspected by his own kind of being a "nigger lover," is the answer to the wry question Joe Youngblood had posed while listening to Mr. Myles: "Where the white friends at?" (204).

Having formed, or at least hinted at, his core coalition in the first half of the novel—rock-solid African-American Southern family, Northern Black intellectual, the heretofore underachieving Black masses, the white working class—Killens puts the group through its paces during the second half by exposing them to progressively more difficult challenges, prepping them for a final test of empowerment. One major battle concerns the rhetoric of Jubilee, an annual concert of Negro spirituals presented, grudgingly, by the students of Pleasant Grove School. The students resent singing for the amusement of a largely white audience and feel betrayed when Mr. Myles, whom they thought might resist, agrees to coordinate the show. However, Mr. Myles, inspired by Reverend Ledbetter, develops a twist, incorporating into Jubilee a narrative explaining the messages of rebellion encoded in the spirituals. The narrator, Robby Youngblood, would explain, therefore, that "Swing Low Sweet Chariot" and "Steal Away to Jesus" allude to escape via the Underground Railroad and that "Go Down, Moses" celebrates Harriet Tubman. For Myles and Ledbetter it is a question of unity and responsibility. As the reverend declares, "They will be singing for our fathers and our fathers' fathers back through the ages and for generations to come" (272).

Another comparison with King is instructive. As Keith Miller indicates in "Martin Luther King, Jr. Borrows a Revolution," "One of King's foremost rhetorical strategies was to locate his appeal within the context of cherished religious, cultural, and patriotic traditions" (249). This is exactly the stratagem Killens employs, using the highly valued spirituals, especially when explicated his way, as a mechanism of empathy, accessing a cosmology shared by the Black community of Crossroads and by much of his envisioned audience. Although Killens was not particularly religious, he knew his people were, so he prodded them to be simultaneously religious and revolutionary. He saw the "Sorrow Songs" as a ready medium.[7] As he recalls:

> I believe that those spirituals, like I said in one of those sections dealing with the spirituals, that the spirituals was a means for black people to organize themselves against slavery. I know that a lot of people I—I had a debate with a black woman singer, who said that I was reading some things into Negro spirituals that [only] do just what they seem to be, a childlike manifestation of black people, and their childlike belief in God, etc.—, I always thought the spirituals to be much more than that. All of the insurrections were planned in the church. (interview with Paul Lehman, included in Lehman 148–50)[8]

The reconstituted Jubilee is a huge hit with the African-American audience and Oscar Jefferson. In disgust, many of the whites leave midway through the program. This disgruntled group could have obtained the dismissal of Mr. Myles if his support from the Black community had not been so strong.

A second formidable task facing the coalition is to organize a hotel workers union at the Oglethorpe Hotel, where Rob Youngblood, now a young man, holds a job as a bellhop, work that Killens himself performed in Macon while in high school. As the Great Depression sets in, Black workers are afraid to make waves and risk what meager jobs they have. White workers prefer to accept unfit work conditions rather than cast their lot with Blacks. They are willing to endure exploitation and work against their own economic interests as long as they can retain white privilege. Of course, the ethnic split among the labor force only serves the owners.

Killens had observed firsthand that white working-class racists were the major impediment to the labor movement in the South, a region whose workers were among the most victimized in the nation. Having been both a nonunion worker and, subsequently, a labor organizer engaged in CIO endeavors in the South in the 1940s, a movement known as Operation Dixie, he bore witness that racialized identities were more important than class affiliation to many whites. They preferred segregated misery to integrated unions. As he later wrote in *Black Man's Burden*:

> When "Operation Dixie" invaded the South, Negroes hailed it as the Freedom Train, and they leaped aboard with great enthusiasm and profound dedication. But the train got bogged down very quickly and finally was derailed in the muck and mire of white supremacy. . . . The CIO's "Operation Dixie," like reconstruction, indeed like the American Revolution and every other movement that should have spelled freedom and equality for Americans of all colors and religions, died stillborn. To give the C.I.O. its due, it did not keep the Negroes *out*. The trouble was that it could not keep the white workers *in*. (62)

The task of galvanizing the support of white hotel workers falls to Oscar Jefferson, who manages to convince a few that an integrated union beats none at all. Rob Youngblood emerges as the central figure of Black unionizing activity. African-American workers are skeptical of eventually joining forces with whites, as Rob urges, but eventually realize they have no better choice. As Willabelle Braxton reasons, "If we don't use the crackers against Mr. Ogle, Mr. Ogle'll use them against us" (404).

During the labor movement section of *Youngblood*, Killens mischievously "enters" his own text—sort of like a Hitchcock cameo—a maneuver he would later repeat in *The Cotillion*.[9] As organizer Jim Collins, formerly known as Jim Kilgrow, returns to Crossroads after a long absence to promote union activity, Oscar Jefferson, who had been a childhood friend, recognizes him during a meeting:

> "Excuse me folks," Oscar said, "It's been such a long time since I seen this boy."
>
> "Boy?" Jim Collins said.
>
> "Mr. Kil—I mean Mr. Collins."
>
> "That's more like it," Jim said. He turned to the others. "Well let's get down to the case on the docket." (402–3)

The ultimate question for the Killens coalition is whether it will hang together and defend itself in the face of violent onslaught. After Joe Youngblood is gunned down during a second pay dispute at the mill, the Black community proves more than willing, chasing the Ku Klux Klan from Rockingham Quarters with volleys of bullets. Although Joe will no longer walk among them, they will still walk together. Robby's foreshadowing dreams reach fruition in some form. Laurie Lee and Jenny Lee stand majestic. Mr. Myles performs heroically in an attempt to save Joe's life, and Oscar Jefferson's son, whose blood type, unlike most of the African Americans tested, matches Joe's, contributes to a transfusion as Killens symbolizes the shortcomings of a purely racialized vision and further expresses his optimism about youth.

Joe Youngblood wonders how he is supposed to live in the white man's world. The answer from Killens is that Black people can only begin to live meaningfully when they live in harmony with one another and adopt a posture of self-defense. Killens had always been reminded that such action was needed. When he was participating in a discussion group as a college student in Atlanta during the 1935–36 academic year, a white student announced that he had the answer to the racial problem in the United States. As his audience tensely awaited his pronouncement, he declared that the "'nigrah' problem could be solved by drowning all the 'nigrahs' in the river" (*Black Man's Burden* 79–81).

'Sippi, published in 1967, begins in fictional time, June 1954, the same month *Youngblood* was actually released. The novel is virtually a sequel; in fact, some of the material in the latter story is drawn from the nearly two hundred pages that Killens trimmed from the original manuscript of *Youngblood* at the request of his publishers, who thought the one-thousand-page draft unwieldy.[10] Black solidarity and resistance are once again central themes. The characters lack the near-perfect nobility of those in the earlier book, which makes them somewhat more realistic. Notwithstanding, Charles (Chuck) Othello Chaney, the most important figure, is yet a close approximation of Rob Youngblood. His parents share most traits with the elder Youngbloods. Cora Mae, Bessie Mae, Little Jake Carson, Reverend Purdy, Phil Jacobson, and David Woodson correspond rather neatly to Willabelle, Ida Mae, Fat Gus Mackey, Reverend Ledbetter, Richard Myles, and Jim Collins. Carrie Louise Wakefield serves as the token, albeit embattled, white sympathizer. The working-class African-American community in Minksville is analogous to the one in Pleasant Grove, and a poorer community in the Bottom is similar to the one in Rockingham Quarters. As for setting, Wakefield County,

Mississippi, of the 1950s and 1960s is every bit as racially segregated and harsh as Cross County, Georgia, of the 1920s and 1930s—if not more so—which is why this rendition of the Killens coalition, a sort of Dream Team II, is assembled.

Additionally, Killens unveils variations of several set pieces used previously. The image of the "Big Black Burly Negro that ran amuck," part of a radio account of the Joe Youngblood shooting (443), becomes, in *'Sippi*, a newspaper boy's shout of "Extra! Extra! big burly negroes run amok!" as two of the Chaney sons are on the lam after a confrontation with a white department store salesman (34). Chuck Othello consumes too much ice cream and becomes sick just as Jenny Lee Youngblood gorges herself with birthday cake and falls ill. Both actions are responses to chronic deprivation. Young Chuck Othello shares Robby Youngblood's habit of dreaming about social progress for African Americans, writing out his fantasies on occasion:

> My home is my house and my land is my land and my country is my country, even though it is not really my home, or my land, or my country. Yet it must be. And I must make it be. All by myself and single-handed, if it's got to be that way. I will be a black knight on a black horse in a black and shining armor. I will be John Henry, Robin Hood, and Joe Louis and Paul Robeson and Abraham Lincoln and Matt Dillon and Jackie Robinson and Jesse Chaney Junior all rolled into one. And I will make the land my land. Our land. (82–83)

Killens even invokes the title of the earlier work when Bessie Mae writes to Chuck Othello, who is by then away at college, and conveys her wish that he were back home being active in local political affairs. "They needed *young blood*, especially with an education, to lead the struggle" (209, emphasis mine).

The primary difference in the "teams'" missions in the two novels lies in the specific nature of Black political engagement. Whereas in *Youngblood* the focus is on the founding of an NAACP branch and the development of a labor union, the major objective in *'Sippi* is to seize political power through the ballot and even up the body count between the African-American community and white supremacists. Writer David Woodson and Reverend Purdy provide the most compelling oratory for voter registration and aggressive political action. Purdy preaches *the* classic sermon in African-American literature, a moving message of freedom and unity delivered in the Black vernacular. For example:

> Douglass and Tubman and Turner was they brother's keeper. Yes they was. When they theyselfs got free, they didn't stop fighting like you woulda done. They dedicated they lives to the freedom of they black brothers and sisters! . . . Running around here talking about it's a free country and talking about you a citizen, and yet you scared to go down to the courthouse and register to vote. Well, you a lie and the truth ain't in you. . . . Talking about you tryna make a better life for your childrens yet you scared to do a little old thing like register to vote. You a lie and the truth ain't in you! . . . And when you don't vote . . . you cheating your children and your children's childrens. And cheating is ugly and God A'mighty sure don't love ugly. . . . Are you ready for the little black train? . . . Are you ready for the freedom train? That's the train I'm talking about this evening. (150–51)

During the course of the novel, Reverend Purdy assumes a heroic stance reminiscent of the role models he mentions.

Of course, a similar burden must be shouldered by anyone bearing the name Othello, a tribute to Paul Robeson and his legendary portrayal of the Shakespearean character. By Killens's own account, Robeson was the most significant male influence in his life next to his father. A large poster of Robeson hung in the Killens home.[11]

The Chaney surname invokes civil rights martyr James Chaney, and the first half of *'Sippi* is testimony to the worth of the civil rights movement. The latter half is a call for Black Power. And Killens keeps the action hot indeed; the temperature is symbolically kept above one hundred degrees for virtually all of the final two hundred pages. White supremacists have made it clear, particularly by the bombing murder of registration activist Luke Gibson and his family, that violence is the language they best speak. This is standard fare in Black protest writing. However, Killens provides a vision of the South in the 1960s that includes many white casualties as well when a veritable war erupts in Wakefield County after the assassination of Woodson. Killens articulates vividly that sufficient social redress cannot be accomplished by passive means. As Chuck

Othello explains to Mr. Wakefield, in phrasing the author himself would later employ in numerous speeches, "Rocking the boat—why should we black folk be worried about rocking the goddamn boat, when we're not even in the boat, but drowning in the open sea? Our job is to capsize the boat—and build another one with accommodations for everybody" (399).[12]

At the close of *'Sippi*, which, like *Youngblood*, concludes with the death of an African-American male hero and the promise of heightened political involvement by the African-American community, Killens elaborately reorchestrates the optimism that inflects the final passages of *Youngblood*, this time listing organizations that will effect political change instead of mentioning individuals:

> Came from SNCC, from SCLC, NAACP, the Urban League, CORE, NNLC, came from the Council of Negro Women, from the Federation of Colored Women's Clubs. The Muslims and Christians came. Jews came. Even infidels. The Deacons and the Elders came with their arms and ammunition. Men came from the labor movement. Came from the Willing Workers Club of Harlem, the Busy Bees, the Shining Lights, the Yorubas, the Climbers, the Ebonites, the Elks, the Masons. (433)

Although generally considered more nationalist by the late 1960s, Killens offers a view at the conclusion of *'Sippi* that, given the political postures of some of the groups mentioned, suggests multiple possibilities for struggle. While it is true that Carrie Louise Wakefield, the last prominent European-American character in Killens's fiction, is in effect banished from the African-American side of the civil rights movement by Charles Othello Chaney, a sharp contrast to the fact that Oscar Jefferson sits on the executive committee of the hotel workers union chaired by Rob Youngblood, it is also the case that Killens remained true to the idea of progressive pluralism or radical democracy. He was simply not interested much in, say, lunch-counter integration and felt that the most important function for white activists was to educate and organize members of the white community.

Youngblood and *'Sippi* make up a one-man Southern reconstruction. Killens consciously intended, as he points out in the introduction to the anthology *Black Southern Voices*, which appeared posthumously, to help build a Black Southern literary tradition distinct from, and in large measure oppositional to, that produced by the likes of Eudora Welty and William Faulkner, a body of work Killens terms "an apologia for the status quo" (2). Indeed, an examination of Welty's *One Writer's Beginnings* reveals no concern on her part with racist oppression in Jackson, Mississippi, where she grew up on the right (white) side of the tracks. From the other side hailed an African-American boy only seven months her senior who would also become known in literary circles, one Richard Nathaniel Wright. Concerning Faulkner, Killens satirizes him in *'Sippi*, using Mr. Wakefield as a mouthpiece: "Willie Faulkner was a friend of mine. He used to visit at the other house. All I'm saying is what he advocated. Take it easy right along in here, or else even if you win there'll be bitterness for centuries" (396). When such logic fails to persuade Charles Othello Chaney to abandon his belief in the ideology of Black Power, not to mention its exigence, Wakefield issues a blunt warning: "Don't fool yourself, boy. Willie Faulkner was right. My own Negroes will join up with me and kill other Negroes. All I got to say is, 'Come on boys, pick up your guns and follow me'" (399).[13]

Although Killens's fiction is obviously didactic, it is also immensely artful. With magnificent skill he melds key elements of the African-American rhetorical tradition into tales of dramatic force. This is not to say one should not criticize Killens's prose on the grounds that his work is sometimes too repetitious, overly journalistic, or less subtle than it could be. These are the familiar complaints. But to render the most informed judgment on style and structure, one needs to be familiar with, to invoke Geneva Smitherman, the "Black modes of discourse" on which Killens drew.[14] *Youngblood*, for example, is an African-American sermon in the form of a novel. *'Sippi* is a complex, recursive rewriting of an African-American folktale. All other textual aspects of the novels—inclusion of spirituals, biographical material, the Talented Tenth trope—connect within the context of these two basic structures.

Paul Lehman recognizes the secular Black sermon that is part and parcel of *Youngblood*. Each of the novel's four sections begins with a title and an excerpt from a Negro spiritual. Part 1, titled "In the Beginning," begins with "Didn't my Lord deliver Daniel / And why not every man?" Part 2, "No Hiding Place," starts with "I went to the rock to hide my face / The rock cried out—No hiding place." Part 3, "Jubilee," opens with "One of these mornings about five o'clock / This old world's gonna reel and rock / Pharaoh's Army got drowned." The last part, "The Beginning," commences with "And before I'd be a slave / I'd be buried in my grave / And go home to my Lord / And be free." Each pair of title and excerpt marks discursive boundaries relative to an overarching story of Black awareness, Black commitment, Black organization, and Black rebellion. Inside the identified subject, African-American history and culture are the preacher's texts. The aforementioned spirituals, for example, are used as opposed to the Bible. In this context, the activist Reverend Ledbetter is a deliverer of condensed sermons inside the master sermon delivered by Killens. At one point, Lehman extracts *Youngblood* from its literary genre by claiming that "*Youngblood* is not a novel; it is a black sermon" (52). There is no need to concede that much territory to formalists, and Lehman does later reclaim some turf. *Youngblood* is indeed a novel, but a Black sermonic one replete with an elaborate "call" to which it is hoped that readers "respond." Part of the call involves numerous examples of narrative sequencing, or the forwarding of stories, as Smitherman explains, to make a case. As she writes:

> The relating of events (real or hypothetical) becomes a black rhetorical strategy to explain a point, to persuade holders of opposing views to one's own point of view, and in general to "win friends and influence people." This meandering away from the "point" takes the listener on episodic journeys and over tributary routes, but like the flow of nature's rivers and streams, it all eventually leads back to the source. Though highly applauded by blacks, this narrative linguistic style is exasperating to whites who wish you'd be direct and hurry up and get to the point. (*Talkin and Testifyin* 147–48)

In the case of *Youngblood*, the "call" consists of numerous episodes, literally spanning hundreds of pages, about pride, self-determination, and self-defense designed to inspire readers to action.

Although *'Sippi*, like *Youngblood*, contains sermonic elements, the outstanding formal characteristic of *'Sippi* is that it essentially and intricately revolves around a single folktale. Lehman does not know the tale, "'Sippi," which is why, trying to account for the book's structural departure from *Youngblood*, he reasons that "this sermon follows one basic text" (61). But the sermon model does not yield the best description of *'Sippi*'s design. On the other hand, William Wiggins Jr., who has written the most extensive and insightful analysis of *'Sippi*, notes:

> Killens has made the customary literary use of this folklore genre; he uses them, that is, to invoke some response from his readers, such as humor or social protest. In many of his folktales humor and social protest are combined. In *'Sippi* he not only uses the message of the traditional folklore genre, but more importantly, he uses the structure of the folktale as a formal outline for his novel. Hence, it is not possible to remove the "'Sippi" folktale from Killens novel and have the same book: the novel *'Sippi* is a bigger and much more sophisticated offspring of her folktale father. (100)

The story Wiggins refers to was popular in the 1960s. He heard the version below from Reverend J. L. Parks of Louisville, Kentucky:

> Negroes getting mean now. They ain't taking no more stuff off the white man. Like this mad Negro who went up to these white folks that he's worked for all his life and said, "Ain't gon be no more Mister Charlie. It's just Charlie from now on." Then he looked at his wife and said, "Ain't no more Miss Ann. It's just plain Ann from now on." After saying this the Negro turned in a huff to leave. But when he got to the door he turned again and said, "And another thing! Ain't no more Mississippi! It's just plain 'Sippi from now on!" (101)

The mood of African-American rebellion that was in the air is symbolized by a man who will reject Southern custom, challenge the privilege and status of the white man, then the white woman, and fearlessly express total rejection of the overall structure of white supremacy.

Killens amplifies this folktale in *'Sippi*'s prologue. Jesse Chaney, who hears the news regarding *Brown v. Board of Education*, dashes from the cotton field to the home of Charles James Richard Wakefield, the biggest Mr. Charlie in the county. The following quote indicates in detail how Killens uses his gift for satire to expand on the common tale:

> As Jesse came within about a hundred yards of the Big House, Wakefield broke into a great big smile of friendly welcome. Jesse's mere

presence always gave him a genuine warm feeling of one human being to another, the kind of feeling that did not come easily these days. It also gave him a feeling of the rightness of his approach to *his* Negroes. But now the smile left his face, unknowingly, as he watched Jesse continue toward the front porch where he stood beneath the electric fan. Instead of his flanking movement to go around to the back door, old Jesse came straight across the yard. In the entire relationship between these lifelong friends, Jesse had never before come straight across the front yard. Never ever. Wakefield did not want to believe what his eyes beheld. But by the time Jesse was ten or fifteen feet away from the porch, it became obvious, even to a friend like Wakefield, that this particular day was different from all the other days in the world. And Jesse was not going to stand on tradition or formality. Wakefield was afflicted with lockjaw, momentarily. As Jesse kept coming toward the porch, he ultimately found his voice again.

He was more flabbergasted than angry with his boyhood friend. "What's the matter with you, Jesse boy? The heat got the best of you?"

"The Supreme Court done spoke!" Jesse shouted, like he had just got that old time religion and his soul had been converted. "Ain't going around to the back door no more. Coming right up to the front door from now on!"

"What'd you say?" Wakefield asked him, thinking maybe he had not heard properly. It was too hot to get angry with the best friend he had in all the world. Jesse was humility personified. Yet and still—

"And another thing—ain't no more calling you Mister Charlie. You just Charles from here on in. Or Jimmy Dick."

Wakefield's face lost color. The fan blew heat onto his forehead now. "Jesse, you going too damn—"

Jesse turned to saintly Anne Barkley Wakefield who wouldn't harm a mosquito if it were biting the tip of her turned-up nose. "And another thing—no more calling you Missy Anne. You just plain old common Annie from now on."

The sweet angelic woman gasped and put her handkerchief to her mouth. She stopped rocking momentarily. Her world was moving swiftly out from under her. This was too much for Charles Wakefield. Friendship or no friendship. Wakefield was completely out of control, a thing that seldom happened to him. Sweet and painful years of racial

> understanding and race philosophizing went by the everlasting boards. Even as he told himself, "Keep calm, C. J. R. Wakefield," almost against his will he heard himself shout:
>
> "Nigger, don't you know you're in Mississippi?"
>
> Wakefield immediately wished he could call the words back but they were gone from him forever. He had not meant to call his close friend, "nigger." Yet he felt a kind of cleansing of his heart and soul. He felt whiter, purer, inside. The atmosphere was clearer now. And he was somehow glad he had brought things out in the open, things that had been hidden between them all these many years. Sometimes the "word" had to be used to put things in perspective. Even between the best of friends. It had a therapeutic value for everyone concerned. Jesse would bow his humble head now, ever so slightly, and hide the hurt in his eyes with the noble savage's smile of profound humility. He would put his tail between his legs and go around to the back door, and God would be up in His Heaven again and all would be right with the world. Wakefield would forgive and forget. He was the biggest man in Mississippi. He could afford to be forgiving.
>
> Obviously, Jesse had not read the script. "That's another thing," the noble savage shouted, like he was preaching from a colored Hardshell Baptist pulpit. "Ain' no more Mississippi. Ain' no more Mississippi. It's jes' 'Sippi from now on!" (xviii–xix)

As one can see, Killens is totally faithful to the basic import of the folktale while at the same time embellishing the story to account for character, extended dialogue, and reaction as well as to establish the specific social and historical context.

Wiggins identifies eleven cycles in *'Sippi*, ascending from lesser to greater significance, that reflect the four-part motif of the "'Sippi" folktale. For example, Jesse Chaney's early insistence on manhood for himself and Chuck Othello eventually evolves into Othello's militant confrontation with Wakefield and Woodson's uncompromising call for Black empowerment. Single acts of Black defiance lead to mass Black defiance. Young Chuck Othello's innocent game of house with Carrie Wakefield is enlarged, when he later sleeps with her, into the adult flouting of a sexual taboo. Unpublicized repercussions for bucking the political order give way to ramifications that are tragic and epic in scope. The novel thus builds to its conclusion through a series of repetitive anecdotes within the thematic constraints of the "'Sippi" folktale. This gives the book an African-American oral quality because, as commonly noted, a hallmark of African-American storytelling, indeed of African art forms in general, is a series of "rising" repetitions often accompanied by insertions of self-reflective summarizing, or what is termed parallel phrasing. In addition, there is another rhetorical feature, known as parataxis (the creation of a string of statements that exist as interchangeable wholes within a fluid matrix), that Wiggins has cited as operative in *'Sippi*.[15] For example, there is an episode in which Jesse Chaney's cow is missing. He suspects that it has been taken by someone on the Wakefield plantation, but he is hesitant to reclaim it, only doing so after his manhood is challenged by his wife. The cow, Missy Anne, is alluded to several times later in the tale. The "Missy Anne" references are not, however, tightly bound to the story line, nor do they contribute to dramatic action; they seem, instead, sort of floating signifiers that emphasize the reduction of the status of "Miss Anne" to unremarkable—no more noteworthy than a cow—in the mind of the Black man. This particular, free-floating aspect of parataxis, associated with groups in West Africa, has been manifest in African-American ballads and the blues, and now hip-hop ("throw your hands up in the air"), where certain cherished stanzas or classic lines are repeated in a wide variety of songs.[16]

The lengthy, cyclical quality of *Youngblood* and *'Sippi* directly stems from Killens's adherence to the requirements of the African-American oral forms with which he experiments. His desire to reflect Black experience in this manner and his aim to capture the rhythms and nuances of the Southern folk characters who make up the bulk of his cast would not lead to the lean, sparse, densely symbolic novels that some critics prefer but to chanty, preachy, folkloric, elaborately oral ones.

Bound up with political vision and major tropes is a series of stylistic flourishes drawn from African-American culture. Killens writes much of his dialogue, as epitomized by Purdy's sermon, in Black Vernacular English, even commenting on his use of this language variety along the way. As Charles Chaney muses in *'Sippi* during a voter registration drive:

> He wondered why so many black folk preferred to call it "reddishing" instead of registration. He'd heard so many Negroes in the county say,

> and proudly, "I'm gon reddish if it's the last damn thing I do before I die." He'd heard others say, "I ain't studying about that reddishing mess." Did he say "reddish" before he entered the University? Maybe it was a sarcastic joke his folk played deliberately on the English language. They sure didn't owe the English language anything. It had been used against them ever since they were brought here to this place. (372)

Similarly, in *Youngblood*, Laurie Lee initially tends to "correct" Joe's English, causing him to withdraw from conversation. But she soon comes to appreciate his "unaffected dignity" and "mother-wit that no amount of education could take the place of" (26).

Robby receives early and important exposure to the game of insult known as the dozens when he witnesses an exchange between Fat Gus Mackey and Sonny Boy. Fat Gus initiates the verbal sparring by dismissing the "No Trespassing" sign on Mr. Rayburn's property:

> "To hell with Cracker Rayburn. I had Mizzes Cracker last night. She didn't say *No Trespassing.*"
>
> . . . Sonny Boy looked at Gus and said, "Now aintchoo something? Boy I bet you wouldn't know what to do with it if Old Lady Cracker offered it to you. Be so sked you wouldn't know what to do."
>
> "Your dear-rold mother didn't say that last night. She didn't say I didn't know what to do."
>
> Sonny Boy eyed Gus, made his face look serious. "Look out boy," he said good-naturedly. "You better watch that stuff. You know goddamn well I don't play no dozens." He picked up a rock.
>
> "Pat your damn feet then," Fat Gus told him. "Louis Armstrong plays it." All the boys laughed. (105)

Robby's immersion into this speech circle and, by extension, the broader African-American community enables the camaraderie that comes to inform his activism.

Killens also reworks standard phrasings to create Black semantics, which he uses to promote images of African-American beauty and dignity. For example, when Charles Chaney asks his mother to describe his older brother to him, she responds, "I done told you a hundred times—you his spitting image. He was tall and lanky just like you is. He had such a soft face and the sweetest disposition. Just like the Holy Bible say, Junior was black but he was comely" (139). At this point, Jesse Chaney, pushing an alternate aesthetic, intervenes, "He was black *and* comely," he corrected, proudly. "Ain't no *buts* about it" (139–40).[17]

Like Hurston and Wright before him, Killens makes ample use of folk political humor. In *'Sippi*, he gets mileage out of an old joke about the Civil War. Two young fellows engage Deacon Jimson in a ritualistic joke:

> One of them asked him, "Grampa, will you settle a argument for us? Who won the Silver War? The North or the South?"
>
> Rafe Jimson didn't have to study a second about it. "White folks won it," he told them without blinking, as if surely they must have known the answer to such an obvious question. His tobacco-chewing cronies sitting on his porch with him laughed and chuckled their agreement. And spat tobacco into the yard, stream after stream.
>
> The young men roared with laughter. "Grampa, you something else!" And they walked off up the road. They had asked him the same question (must've been a hundred times) and always got the same response. "White folks won the Civil War."
>
> "That's how come you ain't free yet," he shouted after them. "Cause you didn't win it. Git your hindparts down to that courthouse next Wednesday morning and registrate!" (262–63)

Killens, of course, does not settle for simply replaying the joke. In this brief scene, he illustrates a sense of community, positive interaction among different generations, and political advocacy. In *Youngblood*, Fat Gus relates a version of a common witticism about a Black man attempting to subvert segregation: "He went into this uppidy restaurant in Washington, D. C. and the cracker waiter walked over to him and asked him was he looking for somebody—see. The Negro said I ain't looking for nobody, I want something to eat. Cracker waiter told him we don't serve no niggers in here. Colored man looked at the waiter and told him—Man, I don't want no niggers for breakfast. Just give me some stew beef" (109).[18] As with the "'Sippi" folktale, the author includes this story as an argument to contest a racist social order.

There are literally hundreds of vernacular examples in *Youngblood* and *'Sippi*, and they contribute greatly to why Killens's fiction was valued highly by proponents, especially the critics, of the Black Arts Movement. The valorizing of Black folk culture, the view that art was instrumental or expressly rhetorical, and the focus on collective political struggle with emphasis on the realization of Black manhood all match the prescriptions those critics would formalize. Killens himself, however, shied away from the "Spiritual Father" tag hung on him by Addison Gayle.[19] As Gayle was aware, lines of literary influence can be difficult to draw in terms of rigid validity; he nevertheless saw Killens as the "leading edge" of a configuration of novelists that includes John A. Williams, Ernest Gaines, and William Melvin Kelley.[20] Killens thought more credit should be given to writers from whom he had himself drawn inspiration. The two most readily apparent were Du Bois and Wright (despite the latter's markedly different projections of Black families). He also felt indebted to Langston Hughes and Margaret Walker, both of whom exhibit in their work tremendous love for Black people along with visionary, at times politically radical, outlooks.[21]

2

Solomon, Highly Literate

The reintegration of Solomon "Solly" Saunders Jr. into the African-American grassroots community is the central movement in John Oliver Killens's 1962 novel *And Then We Heard the Thunder*. Solly grew up in Harlem and as a boy was once chased by the police for aiding fellow African Americans during a riot. However, after proceeding to become college educated and making it two-thirds of the way through law school, he is pursuing bourgeois individualism as opposed to community-oriented activism. He is one of the "exceptional men," a potential savior, even more educated than fellow Du Boisians Richard Myles, Charles Othello Chaney, and David Woodson.[1] He is the most elaborately and vividly drawn, as well as most cerebral, of the host of Du Boisian characters in the Killens canon. As much as any figure in African-American literature, he has felt his "twoness," the competing strivings warring inside one dark body.[2] Ideally, he would like to, as he personifies Du Bois's notion of double consciousness, "do my dancing in the Empire Room at the Waldorf but at the same time keep in touch with my folks who will still be stomping at the Savoy" (5).

After the United States enters World War II, Solly is inducted into the army. At the urging of his new bride, Millie, and propelled partly by his own beliefs, he enters the military determined to strive for personal success within its existing parameters; his plans include being admitted to Officer Candidate School. He is not looking to challenge the segregated system. His view is that in times of war American ethnic groups should unite against a common external enemy and settle their "in-house" differences at a later date. He is reluctant to adopt the motto "Double V," a call for both victory over fascism abroad and victory over white supremacy in the United States, an ethos embraced by many of the more than one million African-American soldiers who served during the war. Although the war was being waged, according to U.S. propaganda, to make the world safe *for* democracy, many African Americans had ample reason to fear for their well-being *in* the so-called democracy in which they lived. Black soldiers were serving both against and with the enemy, and uncompromised Black men like Joseph "Bookworm" Taylor, Jerry Abraham Lincoln "Scotty" Scott, and Jimmy "Quiet Man" Larker choose to resist continually, whatever the cost or personal loss, the adversary with which they are most familiar: the American white man. Solly himself cannot perpetually endure the emasculating abuse and indignities he suffers solely because of the color of his skin, and he eventually adopts an attitude like that of Scotty and the others.

After entrenching Solly in his ethnic peer group, Killens unfolds the remainder of the novel along lines similar to those in *Youngblood*. The major characters are confronted with increasingly harder obstacles that test their unity and resolve. Solly, also known as Sandy, grows stronger in his role as company spokesman. As Scotty announces to white officers during a successful protest against the segregated Post Exchange in California, "I'm not much of a talker, sir. I'm just naturally bashful, me, but we got Corporal Sandy here to speak for me and all the rest of the poor mistreated colored soldiers" (220).

At the beginning of the novel, Solly possesses the talent but not the strength of character to provide committed leadership. Thus the trials and tribulations he experiences serve as preparation. He sheds the illusion that he can be satisfied with individual success that is devoid of dignity and social responsibility or, more specifically, antiracist combat. By the novel's conclusion, such fighting is perilously real, and Solly proves equal to the challenge as he expertly commands African-American troops during the race riot in Bainbridge. He is not involved in the outbreak of the skirmish; his personal safety is assured. But if he, being the most skilled, intelligent, and articulate tactician among the African-American soldiers, refuses to participate in the battle, he condemns all the warring Black soldiers to death. Most perish anyway, but many whites die also. As he does in *Youngblood* and *'Sippi*, Killens offsets African-American loss with white casualties. White survivors, faced with the distinct possibility of their own demise, perceive, either rationally or through fear, the absurdity of the battle and cease their participation. Killens thus asserts, once again, the centrality of Black self-defense—along with dedicated high-level Black intellects—to fundamental social transformation.

Gatsinzi Basaninyenzi argues in "Ideology and Four Post-1960 Afro-American Novelists" that *And Then We Heard the Thunder* along with *Youngblood* typify "the integrationist tradition in Black American literature" (7). He contends that after *And Then We Heard the Thunder* Killens rejects such integrationist writing in favor of Black nationalism and its accompanying artistic ideology, the Black Aesthetic. However, Basaninyenzi's critical assessment is questionable, for Killens's early novels reflect several ideologies. There are Marxist leanings and civil integrationist gestures, as well as heavy overtones of Black nationalism. In addition, Killens's aesthetic was overwhelmingly Black from the outset. The linear reading by Basaninyenzi of Killens's novels is therefore too simplistic, largely because he distorts and overemphasizes the author's own analysis in "Reflections from a Black Notebook" that his novels became increasingly Blacker: "From *Youngblood* (1954), my first novel, to *The Cotillion* [1971], it has been a long sometimes tortuous but eventful journey. . . . Each book got Blacker than the one before, I hope. Which means, to me, that each book became more humanistic and universal. It has not been an easy struggle. The journey to Blackness is a rocky road" (12). What the ellipsis conceals is that the author clearly saw himself as operating within a Black Aesthetic paradigm before the term was even in vogue. The missing words: "The people and material of *Youngblood* taught me to tell their story in their words, in their own style, in Afro-Americanese, with Black nuances and Black rhythms and Afro-American idiom. It is what I was consciously into in *Youngblood* and developed it from book to book until finally, *The Cotillion*" (12). The deleted sentences and the qualifier, "I hope," which ends the sentence that follows the recovered statement, are thus significant.

It is true that Killens's public posture appeared more Black nationalist by the 1970s. By then he was aware of the Black Arts Movement—Larry Neal is mentioned in *'Sippi*—and enjoyed an expanded, nationalist audience, which he cultivated with vigor. It is also true that he had witnessed the failure of organizing efforts like that of the CIO and had become disillusioned about cross-ethnic strategies. But these developments are not *textual* evidence that his later work is "Blacker" than *Youngblood* and *And Then We Heard the Thunder*. That issue is still debatable. Surely Robby's dreams in *Youngblood* are as nationalist as any other statements made by Killens. Black and white armies fight and the Black army wins.

Armageddon tales in a Black, idiom-filled, folkloric novel. What could be more "Black Aesthetic"?

Integration in a strictly civil sense has little to do with Killens's vision in *Youngblood* and *And Then We Heard the Thunder*. Cross-ethnic alliances have to do with gaining and sharing economic and institutional power. They are about justice, not civility and socializing. So rather than viewing, as does Basaninyenzi, the donation of blood by Junior Jefferson (it is not Oscar as he states erroneously) as a crucial symbol of integration, the act can alternately be read as Killens's radically pluralistic deconstruction of purely racialized motivation. The point for him is not that the Junior Jeffersons and Joe Youngbloods of the world should unite just for the sake of interethnic harmony but, rather, that phenotype should not ultimately impede collaboration on serious, even life-and-death, issues. In the same vein, Bob Samuels, at the end of *And Then We Heard the Thunder*, is not the white liberal Basaninyenzi labels him (though he mistakenly calls him Samuel Rutherford). Samuels sides with Solly and the African-American soldiers during the race riot, actually killing white soldiers to save Solly's life. Solly then terms Samuels a colored man, a label Samuels rejects, preferring to affirm that he is a white man capable of siding with African Americans—when justice is the issue—in deed as well as word. This is not liberalism but action far more radical. White liberals do not pull the trigger against other whites to save African-American lives.

There is no doubt that Solly's primary identification at the end of *And Then We Heard the Thunder* is with the African-American community. Viewing the bodies of Billy "Baby-Face" Banks, Taylor, and Larker, he muses:

> And he knew what he hoped he would never forget again. All his escape hatches from being Negro were more illusion than reality and did not give him dignity. All of his individual solutions and his personal assets. Looks, Personality, Education, Success, Acceptance, Security, the whole damn shooting match, was one great grand illusion, without dignity. . . . He was a Negro and only with Worm and Jimmy and Baby-Face Banks could he achieve anything of lasting value. And Scotty and General Grant and Lanky. And Fannie Mae and Mama. And Junior. (482–83)

Solly's ultimate act of Black solidarity is to reaffirm his decision to become a writer in order to tell the story of his Black comrades. However, it is also the case, and equally important, that even as he speculates about "a new and different dialogue that was people-oriented" that might come out of Africa and Asia, he describes the small gathering of Black and white soldiers he is now a part of as "the place where the New World is" (485). Solly's expanded and final notion of community envisions African Americans as charter members, with others who can pass some semblance of a "John Brown test" invited into the club. This is neither integrationism nor nationalism but, as Paul Lehman indicates, utopianism, Killens's strongest and most consistent disposition over the course of his career despite otherwise shifting and subordinate positions (which did not shift as much as various detractors have maintained) on culture, politics, and economics.

Because of the complicated multisubjectivities his characters occupy, and given the authorial multisubjectivity that informs those characters, works like *And Then We Heard the Thunder* do not wear simple tags like "integrationist" well. It is interesting and perhaps ironic in this context to recall that in 1971, Killens, even after the commentary in "Reflections from a Black Notebook," rated his first two novels over *'Sippi*, the novel that signals to some his conversion to Black nationalism:

> Well, you know, like I think two of the great American novels are *Youngblood* and *And Then We Heard the Thunder*, but then again I may be prejudiced. I thought they were militant, ahead of their time, advocated self-defense and struggle, gave the literature Black heroes and heroines and were written in the Black idiom and rhythms of the people. I mean that's what I was trying to do. Consciously. I have a feeling that while *'Sippi* was a fairdemiddling novel, relatively speaking, it didn't come up to the level of the first two. ("Rappin' with Myself" 123)

Paul Lehman, although drawing very worthwhile conclusions overall as suggested previously, also employs too linear a model. A Black psyche in his view represents progression from ignorance, confusion, and self-hatred caused by racism to a stage of enlightenment or, if you will, endarkenment. As he elaborates:

> A black psyche is a process whereby a black individual gains a new perspective of himself and his world, based on a positive and conscious

> awareness and knowledge of his racial history and culture, and comes to view himself, not as a black individual, but as a black individual in common with blacks in his community, local and national, and the world—a black brother or sister to all blacks the world over. (27)

And Then We Heard the Thunder, Lehman further argues, most reflects this Black psychological development as Solly Saunders matures from lacking a Black psyche to attaining one. The problem here, though not the major one, is that the analysis proceeds from the belief that it is merely a knowledge deficit on Solly's part that stands in the way of group identification. In contrast, however, it is readily apparent that Solly is torn, his Du Boisian dilemma, his Empire Room / Savoy split, his accommodationist/activist schism, precisely because he has an abundance of knowledge, not because he lacks awareness of his heritage. He has always felt a community impulse, thus his actions as a child in the Harlem riot; it just has been layered over with bourgeois aspirations. His subsequent affiliative spirit results not simply from information gained in a detached manner but from insight forged, in cyclical fashion, within the experiential crucible. The end product of this process with respect to fellow Blacks is not merely recognition of commonality but commitment. In other words, Solly eventually hops off the psychic fence and starts making choices that reflect a Black psyche, one that he possessed in some measure all along.

Implied in the linear textual approaches of Basaninyenzi and Lehman is a characterization of Killens's theoretical development as a straightforward unfolding in response to societal developments between, say, 1950 and 1970. Neither seems aware that much of *Youngblood*, *And Then We Heard the Thunder*, and *'Sippi* was composed simultaneously—that is, many sections of all three novels were written *before* the 1954 appearance of *Youngblood*. *And Then We Heard the Thunder*, in fact, is the novel Killens was bursting to write when he reentered civilian life in 1945. Theodore Vincent, author of *Black Power and the Garvey Movement*, whose family knew the Killens family in the early 1950s, claims that Killens was subjected to censorship. Vincent asserts: "His left-wing friends promised to help him find a publisher and to promote his book when published, but they were not enthusiastic about his plan to write about the race riot; the subject seemed to smack of black nationalism. Killens conceded and turned out a polite novel about the civil rights struggle in the South" (256). One can quarrel with the description of *Youngblood* as a polite concession, but the Vincent anecdote, seemingly accurate in the main, confirms that *And Then We Heard the Thunder* was not strictly a post-*Youngblood* endeavor.[3]

Certain textual evidence compels the same conclusion. The first fiction published by Killens is a military story titled "God Bless America," which appeared in *California Quarterly* in 1952, two years before *Youngblood* was published. It is a story embedded, largely intact, in *And Then We Heard the Thunder*. Set during the Korean War, "God Bless America" opens as an African-American soldier, who is about to board a ship in California headed overseas, anxiously looks for his wife in the crowd. After he locates her, he begins to board the ship with his segregated unit. As the African-American soldiers approach the ship, the band switches from playing "God Bless America" to "The Darktown Strutters' Ball." An excerpt from the story reads:

> They were the leading Negro outfit, immediately following the last of the white troops. Even at route step there was a certain uniform cadence in the sound of their feet striking the asphalt road as they moved forward under the midday sun, through a long funnel of people and palm trees and shrubbery. But Joe hadn't spotted Cleo yet, and he was getting sick from worry. Had anything happened? (207)

In the novel, published ten years later, as Solly's company leaves California for the South Pacific during World War II, virtually the same scenario is depicted:

> They were the lead company in the regiment immediately following the last of the white troops. Even at route step there was a certain uniform cadence in the sound of their feet striking the asphalt road as they moved forward under the midday sun, through a long funnel of noisy people and quiet palm trees and gorgeous shrubbery. But Solly hadn't spotted Millie yet and he was getting sick from worry. Something must have happened to her! (247)

The 1952 version concludes:

> Luke grinned at him. "What's the matter, good kid? Mad about something? Damn—that's what I hate about you colored folks. Take that goddamn chip off your shoulder. They just trying to make you people feel at home. Don't you recognize the Negro National Anthem when you hear it?"
>
> Joe didn't answer. He felt his anger mounting and he wished he could walk right out of the line and to hell with everything. But with "The Darktown Strutters' Ball" ringing in his ears, he put his head up, threw his shoulders back, and kept on marching toward the big white boat. (209)

The episode in *And Then We Heard the Thunder* winds up:

> Worm grinned at him. "What's the matter, good kid? Mad about something? Damn—that's what I hate about you colored folks. Take the goddamn chip off your shoulder. They just trying to make you people feel at home. Don't you recognize the Negro National Anthem when you hear it?"
>
> Solly didn't answer. He just felt his anger mounting and he wished he could walk right out of the line and to hell with everything. Nothing had changed though. He would still do what he had to do. He would take care of himself, he would get ahead in the Army, he would come home safe and sound to Millie. He would hate it and at the same time take advantage of it. There was nothing else that he could do. His face filled up, his eyes were warm and misty too. With "The Darktown Strutters' Ball" ringing in his ears he put up his head and threw his shoulders back, and he kept on marching toward the big white boat. (250)

There are, to be sure, differences between the two versions. For example, Solly is by then an adulterer thinking as much about his girlfriend Fannie Mae as he is about his wife. Cleo is actually pregnant; Millie is only pretending to be. But the texts remain basically the same. *And Then We Heard the Thunder*, then, was being written as early as the 1940s, being composed at the same time that Killens was working on *Youngblood*, a manuscript that itself yielded parts of *'Sippi*. While it is possible that Killens's perspective could have shifted radically by the time the novels were published in 1954, 1962, and 1967, respectively, the point, of course, is that the textual and biographical evidence does not suggest that major ideological ruptures occur among his first three novels.

Additional insight about Killens's mindset before the publication of *And Then We Heard the Thunder* is contained in Maya Angelou's *Heart of a Woman*. Killens was the person most responsible for encouraging Angelou to pursue a writing career and convinced her to relocate from California to New York in 1959 to participate in the Harlem Writers Guild. Angelou, who briefly lived in the Killens residence, comments, regarding the Killens family, "Everyone except Jon, whose nickname was Chuck, talked incessantly, and although I enjoyed the exchange, I found the theme inexplicably irritating. They excoriated white men, white women, white children and white history, particularly as it applied to black people" (32). Even if one does not totally accept Angelou's depiction, it seems rather obvious that there was no profound "break" with integration to be achieved with either *And Then We Heard the Thunder* or *'Sippi*.

Angelou's account also captures the political passion and characteristic humor that saturate Killens's prose. Killens employed a popular joke to urge somewhat reluctant members of the guild to exhibit support for Fidel Castro:

> "There's no time like right now. You know about the slave who decided to buy his freedom?" Small smiles began to grow on the black, brown, and yellow faces. Grace chuckled and bit into her cigarette holder.
>
> "Well, this negero was a slave, but his owner allowed him to take jobs off the plantation at night, on weekends and holidays. He worked. Now, mind you, I mean, he would work on the plantation and then walk fifteen miles to town and work there, then walk back, get two hours' sleep and get up at daybreak and work again. He saved every penny. Wouldn't marry, wouldn't even take advantage of the ladies around him. Afraid he'd have to spend some of his hard-earned money. Finally, he saved up a thousand dollars. Lot of money. He went to his master and asked how much he was worth. The white man asked why the question. The negero said he just wanted to know how much slaves cost. The white man said he usually paid eight hundred to twelve hundred dollars for a good slave, but in the case of Tom, because he was getting

> old and couldn't father any children, if he wanted to buy himself, the master would let him go for six hundred dollars.
>
> "Tom thanked the slave owner and went back to his cabin. He dug up his money and counted it. He fondled and caressed the coins and put them back in their hiding place. He returned to the white man and said, 'Boss, freedom is a little too high right now. I'm going to wait till the price come down.'" (41–42)

Angelou recalls the impact the joke had on the immediate audience: "We all laughed, but the laughter was acrid with embarrassment. Most of us had been Toms at different times in our lives. There had been occasions when the price of freedom was more than I wanted to pay. Around the room faces showed others were also remembering" (42).

Although the accommodationist-revolutionary transformation is worked out in *And Then We Heard the Thunder* involving a host of reliable narrators, it is unconvincing to argue that the author was negotiating the exact same psychic movement in real time. A critical mapping from simple integrationism to simple nationalism ignores too much. Concerning his major novels, Killens is more profitably understood as a practitioner of what Bernard Bell, in *The Afro-American Novel and Its Tradition*, calls "critical realism," a method oppositional to capitalism and generative of figurative models for an envisioned society. This is a point Lehman hints at. Using one strand of critical method, the "outside" technique that Killens uses, the writer, as Bell explains, "derives exemplary character types from the individual and his personal conflicts; and from this base he works toward wider social significance" (247).[4] Like the noble Rob Youngblood before him, Solly Saunders reconciles personal angst and overcomes obstacles posed by racism to posit or symbolize broad solutions to the oppression of African Americans, which is conceived in terms of both race and class. A certain Black nationalism is always a part of Killens's work; the Black folkloric, vernacular-laced tales and the community-oriented activism and armed self-defense portrayed in his prose make that clear. But there is ever present, mingled with nationalist gestures, the undeniable strand of critical realism that speaks to wider transformation.

The ideologies conveyed in *And Then We Heard the Thunder*, therefore, are transmitted largely through Killens's manipulation of "double consciousness" as a description of mental condition and his use of critical realism as an articulation of vision. In addition, as is the case with *Youngblood* and *'Sippi*, the author bases the formal outline of the novel on a brief text and then employs a major African-American commonplace as the primary structural component. In this instance, the brief text is supplied by Harriet Tubman, and the dominant trope is "literacy for freedom."

The function of the song excerpts in *Youngblood* and the essential folktale in *'Sippi* is fulfilled by Tubman's partial account of a Civil War battle she witnessed, an account that serves as epigraph and is the source of the book's title: "And then we saw the lightning, and that was the guns. And then we heard the thunder and that was the big guns. And then we heard the rain falling and that was the drops of blood falling. And when we came to get in the crops, it was dead men that we reaped."[5] Part 1, "The Planting Season," chronicles the events that Solly and his comrades endure in a segregated unit in the Jim Crow South. The comparison of the section to Civil War strife suggests the views that many African Americans occupy neo-slave status and that the South itself is where you find it. In this instance, it is in the U.S. military. The seeds sown in the soil of a racist army will be grown and harvested over the course of the story. Part 2, "Cultivation," details the California stint of Solly and his unit as they are being primed, even as they are confined to the Booker T. Washington Post Exchange, for slaughter in the South Pacific. As penalty for their activism in Georgia, they are given four weeks, one-third the normal time, to get ready for deployment as a special amphibian force. Part 3, "Lightning—Thunder—Rainfall," portrays the action in the South Pacific, where Black U.S. soldiers die at the hands of foreign so-called enemies. Part 4, "The Crop," in which Black U.S. soldiers die at the hands of white U.S. counterparts—another Civil War—reminds us that the scene Tubman witnessed led to only a partial victory over racialized persecution. Thus the Tubmanesque outline of the book, which houses and serves as complement to the voluminous narration, urges readers to be, like Tubman—and Du Bois as well—socially responsible and heroic.

Solly's gradual conversion is facilitated by the practice of literacy, a development that represents one of the strongest structural ties between Killens's fiction and the African-American literary tradition. Black writers invariably explore connections between literacy events and liberation, an understandable and perhaps predictable preoccupation given that these writers, consciously or subconsciously, have largely considered themselves to be fortunate, in light of the odds against them, to be able to testify and bear witness. No Black writer has ever felt more blessed in this regard, or more responsible, than Killens. He had experienced much of the ambivalence that Solly Saunders does with respect to military involvement and middle-class ambitions, having himself been a law student whose studies were interrupted by World War II and having himself served in a segregated military unit. Like his character, he decided to become a writer during the war. Explaining his choice, he writes:

> After seeing all that blood and shit and suffering in the South Pacific, I had been turned by the experiences into some kind of half-assed revolutionary. With the stench of blood and shit still in my nostrils, I reasoned that a lawyer was not a revolutionary by the very nature of his position in society. His job, no matter how radical his inclination, was to fight for the rights of people under this system, not change the system, but to seek justice and equality under a system where no real justice or equality were possible. Right or wrong, this was my rationalization for not going back and completing my last year in law school. ("Rappin' with Myself" 98–99)

Solly first thinks of becoming a writer during his hectic early days at Fort Johnson Henry in Ebbensville, Georgia: "One of these days he would write it all down, he promised himself" (28). His barracks buddies vie for his attention and loyalty. Bookworm Taylor pulls him toward a community of rebels while William (Buck) Rogers, who exists as a caricature of Solly's bourgeois side and reads him best at the outset, affirms Solly's selfish ambitions. During a round of verbal jousting, Bookworm claims that Solly is a Race man, thus committed to collective Black advancement. Buck responds, directly to Solly, "You're a Race man from way back, all right. And you been racing ahead of the field a long time. And you aim to keep your distance" (48).

Solly next reflects on writing as he composes wistful poems about Fannie Mae Branton, a young woman he met in the PX: "Ever since he could remember he'd had this fierce obsession to write, to put something down on paper, and he had started many novels many poems ever since he was ten or eleven or twelve years old" (56). This description is true of Killens as well. But unlike the mature Killens, Solly isn't yet consumed with writing's social instrumentality. So although he feels "man, whole, complete, fulfilled" when writing, the satisfaction is temporary and only real to the extent that Solly can exist in isolation (56). The more he is socialized into segregated army life and gets in touch with his common, "Savoy" side, the closer he moves toward wielding writing as a political weapon. On a ten-mile hike, where he interacts with his fellow soldiers apart from his position as company clerk, he experiences "a warm and honest feeling of belonging" (66). When Captain Rutherford invites the men to speak about their troubles, Solly is the only one in the company to address racism in the military, drawing parallels between the Nazis and the American version of Herrenvolk. To be sure, he is still ambivalent about championing wholeheartedly the ideal of Double V, but on several occasions, to his credit, he does stomp with his company when they need him. This occurs much to the consternation of Rutherford, who, needing the continued services and cooperation of his superb clerk, keeps dangling the old trinkets in front of him to dissuade him from activism: promotions, Officer Candidate School, individual success.

Under the influence of alcohol one evening, Solly feels "good and big and comradery" (94) and suggests to the other men that they write a letter to the Black newspapers explaining the racism and hypocrisy at Fort Johnson Henry. However, exposing his hand to that degree would certainly jeopardize his advancement in the army, so he retreats from his own words and resists Bookworm's urging that they follow through on the idea to publish written protest, causing Bookworm to remark about the educated, "Anything they talk themselves into they can talk themselves out of without doing nothing" (96). Solly defers unconditional commitment as long as he can while still enjoying the comradeship of others who are paying heavier dues. Not until he is savagely beaten by the police in Ebbensville is he ready to agitate with the pen, even making a firm decision to abandon law studies to become a professional writer. When Bookworm once again, in response to Solly's complaining, issues the challenge to write up or shut up, they spend hours collaborating on letters to newspapers and prominent officials. Where previously he wavered, Solly now writes his way into the center of the African-American military community:

> We are Negro enlisted men but all of our officers are white and mostly Southern and mostly rabid Negro-haters. Our company commander is Southern to the core, and also of a Nazi mentality. The one thing he *has* to give Hitler credit for is his handling of the Jews. When we Negro soldiers go into town, we suffer all manner of indignities. We are looked upon with obvious contempt by the white people in the picturesque town of Ebbensville, beaten up with impunity by Ebbensville's finest and the Military Police. Our company commander intercedes on our behalf by sending us on a ten-mile hike. . . . We are voices crying out in a wilderness of hostility and UN-democracy, victims of a cruel, sadistic, perverted, and hypocritical hoax. Some of us feel that we do not need to go four or five thousand miles away to do battle with the enemies of Democracy. They are present with us here and now and spitting in our faces . . . riding on our backs and breathing down our necks. God only knows why we haven't taken matters in our own hands, or when we might—(173–74)

Solly's words not only highlight the contradictions of a Jim Crow military and represent an eloquent expression of the Double V rallying cry; they foreshadow the novel's apocalyptic ending—that is, the race war between Black and white troops in Bainbridge, Australia, a spin on an event that actually occurred in Brisbane.[6] More immediately, his words solidify the bond between the company clerk and his men despite the fact that as punishment for the letters they are rushed into combat without proper preparation.

On the ship to the South Pacific, the increasingly bitter Saunders begins to write a novel about the army and continues to ponder his politics. After subsequently being wounded in the Philippines, he is sent to recuperate in Australia. While hospitalized he receives a copy of Richard Wright's *12 Million Black Voices* from Fannie Mae, who still serves, along with Worm, Scotty, and the Quiet Man, as his conscience and functions in opposition to Millie, Rutherford, and Solly's "great white brother," Captain Samuels. After reading the book, Solly reasons, "If I'm proud of me, I don't need to hate Mr. Charlie's people. I don't want to. I don't need to. If I love me, I can also love the whole damn human race" (362).

Considering the impact of Wright's career on his own, Killens reveals profound respect:

> Richard Wright [is an influence] because of the awesome unadulterated power of his writing, his word power, his righteous anger, his indignation, his great success, his impact on the western world. He made me believe that a Black writer could make the literate world stand up and take notice. He taught me through his writing that you don't have to be a timid writer. You can be bold, you can say what you have to say without holding anything back. ("Rappin' with Myself" 100–101)

Killens goes on to acknowledge that his favorite books by Wright are not the more popular *Native Son* and *Black Boy* but *Uncle Tom's Children* and *12 Million Black Voices*. He thought there was an emphasis on Black beauty, collectivity, and possibility in the latter two books.

What specific phrasing made Killens rhapsodic about Wright's folk history of African Americans? One can easily understand the admiration of Killens for Wright's lyrical beauty, what the narrator in *And Then We Heard the Thunder* termed Wright's "awesome overpowering word images" (362). For example:

> Our southern springs are filled with quiet noises and scenes of growth. Apple buds laugh into blossom. Honeysuckles creep up the sides of houses. Sunflowers nod in the hot fields. From mossy tree to mossy tree—oak, elm, willow, aspen, sycamore, dogwood, cedar, walnut, ash, and hickory—bright, green leaves jut from a million branches to form an awning that tries to shield and shade the earth. Blue and pink kites of small boys sail in the windy air. (*12 Million Black Voices* 162–63)

Killens would have been drawn as well to words that speak of the restorative power of certain Black religious practices. He may, in fact, have plucked Saunders's first name from a section where Wright describes a Black preacher speaking "of Daniel, of Moses, of Solomon, and of Christ" (189–90). Because his protagonist's name is Solomon Saunders Jr. the character is both literally and figuratively the "son of Solomon" and evokes the wise and literary king.[7] In addition, because *12 Million Black Voices* contains more than eighty engrossing photographs, mostly of workers, families, and other groups, Killens had a powerful visual reminder of Black strivings. Finally, Killens would have embraced the call for collective resistance to oppression at the end of Wright's book, an ending akin to several of his own, including that of *And Then We Heard the Thunder*. In Wright's words, "We are the new tide. We stand at the crossroads. We watch each new procession. The hot wires carry urgent appeals. Print compels us. Voices are speaking. Men are moving! And we shall be with them" (241).

The identification Solly achieves with the "12 million" and his fellow Blacks in the military is facilitated by the vernacular. As in *Youngblood* and *'Sippi*, African-American folk practices are integral to psychological development. For example, *And Then We Heard the Thunder* literally begins with a blues:

> UNCLE SAM AIN'T NO WOMAN
> BUT HE SURE CAN TAKE YOUR MAN—(3)

The narrative then commences: "That was the very very funny song some guitar-playing joker sang like Ledbelly at Solly's wedding reception just a few days ago when he was a newly wed civilian" (3). This blues opening signals that Solly, like all blues sojourners, is going to be severely tested. As the tribulations unfold, Solly recalls lyrics from additional blues songs and other African-American popular music at particularly stressful junctures. Feeling pressure from his wife and mother to advance in the military and at the same time move cautiously enough to survive to resume legal studies, he recalls words sung by Bessie Smith and Billie Holiday (137). Later on, under the strain of battle, he remembers songs like James Weldon Johnson and Rosamond Johnson's "Lift Every Voice and Sing" (298–99). Folk lyrics are central to Solly's first real bonding with his fellow Black soldiers. On a company march, he joins in as Black soldiers change the lyrics of "Parlez-vous":

> They say this is a white man's war,
> *Parlez-vous;*
> *They say this is a white man's war,*
> *Parlez-vous;*
> *They say this is a white man's war,*
> *Well what the hell are we fighting for?*
> *Hinky, dinky, parlez-vous*—(67)

African-American song traditions and their improvisational quality are thus essential elements of the book. The story may even be said to have a blues ending as ten soldiers sit on the sidewalk in the aftermath of the race riot. They are at the crossroads, so to speak, looking for direction in a place that Solly asserts "the New World is" (485).[8]

Folktales also serve as models of behavior. One example occurs as the new Black recruits, being introduced to military life, are continually referred to as "boys." In response, Bookworm Taylor asks a captain whether the Blacks were in fact in the army, a question that initiates the following exchange:

> "Of course you're in the Army, boy. . . . Where in the hell did you think you were? The goddamn Boy Scouts?"
>
> Bookworm answered softly and sweetly as if he were licking an ice cream cone, "I *thought* we were in the Army, Captain, sir, with all these soldier suits and everything, all this 'Hunt, Hu, He, Ho,' and all that foolishness, marching up and down all day long, but you keep calling us *boys*, so I thought maybe we were somewhere else, cause I read in the *Daily News* where Mr. Roosevelt, the commander-in-chief his-self, said he wasn't going to bring nothing but men in the Army. Gonna leave the boys alone right long in here. So if I'm a boy, I just wondered if you could arrange it so I could go right back home to Mama and Papa, please, sir. I sure do miss em and I'm a heap too young to die on foreign soil. Khaki don't become me nohow. You understand—" (19–20)

For his oration, Bookworm is removed to the guardhouse. His desire to be released from duty is sincere, but he is also announcing that if he is to serve, he will do so while insisting on his dignity and manhood. Bookworm's words represent a spin on a series of tales and sayings that convey the central message of "call me Mister."[9] A one-line example, which appears in the *Encyclopedia of Black Folklore and Humor* under the title "To Whom It May Concern," simply states, "Don't call a Black man 'boy' unless he's under ten years of age" (454). The advice and Bookworm's rendition of it highlight Solly's dilemma at the outset of the novel. In other words, he has to decide which compromises of identity are worth making to achieve mainstream success.

Call-and-response, one of the Black modes of discourse, is another vernacular feature included in the novel, most notably the interplay among Solly, Scotty, and Bookworm. Scotty habitually gets into trouble with the establishment, difficulty in which he typically embroils Solly. Finally, Solly asks, "Why do you fuck with me so much, man? There are millions of other people in this Army" (221). Scotty replies that he likes Solly the best and will be supervising his activity. He states his intentions toward Solly emphatically: "Make a man out you or break you" (222). Killens symbolizes the relationship between Solly and Bookworm, and by extension with the other Black soldiers, by using call-and-response formally. During a discussion of written material supplied by the War Department, we witness the ensuing actions and words:

> But even Worm agreed and shook his big face up and down when Solly argued that there was nothing wrong with the War Department propaganda. The thing was, it was never put into practice.
>
> "This is good stuff. This is how our country has never been, but this is how we want it to be. If we can use their propaganda to make things better for us—now—and after the war is over, what's wrong with that."
>
> Worm shouted from the Amen Corner: "Ain't nothing wrong with that."
>
> Solly said, "We can say, 'Here it is in black and white—in your own words. Now let us practice what we preach!'"
>
> Worm said, "Ain't nothing wrong with that." (270)[10]

Through call-and-response, as with the blues and folktales, Killens further illumines Solly's tie to Black struggle. Solly proceeds haltingly at first, but he ultimately gains confidence in his commitment. He emerges as Killens's most fully developed and expertly drawn protagonist.

3

Patriots and Radicals

As the career of John Oliver Killens as a fiction writer unfolded, he also wrote nonfiction cultural and political commentary. The 1965 collection of essays titled *Black Man's Burden* stands as his major statement in the genre. But another popular treatise, one not generally associated with his name but to which he contributed, is "Statement of Basic Aims and Objectives of the Organization of Afro-American Unity," a document made public by Malcolm X on June 28, 1964.

The OAAU was the organization that Malcolm founded, or was attempting to establish, upon his return from Africa, a trip that followed his break from the Nation of Islam in early 1964.[1] The creation of the OAAU, according to George Breitman, signaled the beginning of Malcolm's final or most revolutionary ideological phase. As a spokesman for the Nation of Islam, Malcolm championed racial pride and uplift, but such exhortation remained wedded to a political philosophy of separatism and an organizational policy of abstentionism regarding Black political initiatives by others. After a transition period of several months during which Malcolm began to imagine a better political role for himself, he began the OAAU with the intention of leading a broad-based secular entity that would push an agenda of Black political empowerment.[2] Although an emphasis on Black self-determination would continue to be the core belief expressed by Malcolm, his emergent views, in Breitman's analysis, were also pointedly anticapitalist and more global as he conceptualized the Black struggle in the United States in the context of a worldwide rebellion against oppression. Breitman also notes that Malcolm, although he certainly did not stress the idea, admitted the possibility of solidarity with white allies. This "final phase," then, is allegedly marked by Malcolm's more elaborate and mature statement of his Black nationalism, what Breitman describes as a movement from "pure-and-simple black nationalism" to "black nationalism plus" (68). The "plus," in Breitman's mind, involved an impending embrace of socialism.

Breitman's view is hardly definitive. Michael Eric Dyson argues in *Making Malcolm* that "the nature of Malcolm's thought during his last year was ambiguous and that making definite judgments about his direction is impossible" (70). There is truth in both assessments. The point here, however, is that the Malcolm described by Breitman would have great appeal to Killens.

Malcolm and Killens met on several occasions at various venues, including the Killens residence, to work on the OAAU charter.[3] The author considered Malcolm to be his brother, both emotionally and ideologically, and *Black Man's Burden* and the OAAU charter are certainly "brother" texts.[4] Several essential passages appear in both. For example, it is stated in section 6 of the OAAU document that "we must launch a cultural revolution to unbrainwash an entire people. . . . Culture is an indispensable weapon in the freedom struggle" (563). In "The Black Writer Vis-à-Vis His Country," Killens writes that "a cultural revolution is desperately needed, here and now, to un-brainwash the entire American people, black and white" (*Black Man's Burden* 26). In the OAAU document, "entire people" refers specifically to African Americans. In *Black Man's Burden*, aimed at an expanded audience, European Americans are included in the equation.

The need for a cultural revolution is expressed further in the OAAU charter. Given that "our history and our culture were completely destroyed when we were forcibly brought to America in chains," it is concluded that "now it is important for us to know that our history did not begin with slavery's scars" (563). In "The Black Writer Vis-à-Vis His Country," Killens asks, "Who will write the songs for us to sing of our black heroes? . . . Who will recreate the ancient glory that was Timbuktu and Kush and Ghana and Songhay? It is important for us to know that our history on this earth did not begin with slavery's scars" (45).

Black Man's Burden and the OAAU charter also advance the same policy with respect to the social organization of the Black community. Section 5 of the charter calls for the creation of community-controlled drug rehabilitation centers, facilities for unwed mothers, health clinics, senior citizen homes, and orphanages. Also articulated is the need for a concentrated community effort against organized crime and for the establishment of a guardian system to direct Black youth. "We must take pride in the Afro-American community," it is declared, "for it is home and it is power" (563). In the essay "Downsouth-Upsouth," Killens notes that "we must make the Harlems of the U.S.A. sources of black strength, political and otherwise. For as my son, Chuck, wrote me after exposure to the Negro community of Washington: 'I suddenly realized that the Negro ghetto is not a ghetto. It is home'" (*Black Man's Burden* 94).

Obviously, the OAAU charter was composed while Killens was at work on the six essays to be included in *Black Man's Burden*. Perhaps an interesting question is which influence was greater, that of Malcolm on Killens or that of Killens on Malcolm. According to John Henrik Clarke, who also assisted with the charter, he and Killens made no exceptional contribution, mostly helping Malcolm commit to paper ideas he articulated orally.[5] This may, however, be an understatement. Malcolm indeed had a great impact on Killens, but it stands to reason that the author of *Youngblood* and *And Then We Heard the Thunder* was more than a recorder and that Malcolm profited significantly from their exchange. Textual evidence suggests Killens had a fairly active role in the charter's construction. In addition to the letter written by Killens's son, in the one other instance where the line of influence can be positively determined, Malcolm is quoting Killens. As the conclusion of the OAAU charter reads: "When the battle is won, let history be able to say to each one of us: 'He was a dedicated patriot: *Dignity* was his country, *Manhood* was his government, and *Freedom* was his land' [from *And Then We Heard the Thunder*, by John Oliver Killens]" (564).

Inseparably linked, though not identical in import, the OAAU charter and *Black Man's Burden* also share rhetorical strategies for the most part. Both are largely ethical, *ad populum* appeals, nestled in the disparity between the American ideal—expressed in documents like the Declaration of Independence and the Constitution—and the American reality of racialized oppression. As stated in the preamble to the OAAU charter, "The Charter of the United Nations, the Universal Declaration of Human Rights, the Constitution of the U.S.A. and the Bill of Rights are the principles in which we believe and these documents if put into practice represent the essence of mankind's hopes and good intentions" (559). Similarly, "The Black Writer Vis-à-Vis His Country" opens with the following paragraph:

> I believe it was George Bernard Shaw who once said that America was the first country in history to go from barbarism to decadence

> without going through civilization. I construe the statement of this estimable British gentleman of letters to mean that our country has been in such a hurry becoming the wealthiest and the most powerful nation in the world, it has hardly had time or stomach for the niceties of culture and civilization. Indeed, it has been in such unseemly haste, it has not even taken the time to bring into reality some of the most magnificent literature ever written about the rights of men. I refer, of course, to the Bill of Rights, the Declaration of Independence, and the Constitution of the United States. (25–26)

To the extent that faith is expressed in America's civil covenant, both Malcolm and Killens have evoked the African-American jeremiadic tradition, which itself is a variant of the dominant American one.

According to David Howard-Pitney, the rhetorical structure of the American jeremiad includes a citing of America's special and divine promise, chastisement because of present moral slippage or declension, and prophecy that the nation will transcend its decline and achieve its full potential (8). This construct, traceable to the identity formation of seventeenth-century New England Puritans, who saw themselves as "chosen," was a staple of condemnatory sermons by Puritan ministers and still forms the core of America's civil religion. African-American appropriation of the American jeremiad posits Blacks as a chosen people—among a chosen people—and thus, as Howard-Pitney points out, "characteristically addresses *two* American chosen peoples—black and white—whose millennial destinies, while distinct, are also inextricably entwined" (15).

The public figures who most consistently epitomized this African-American jeremiad were Frederick Douglass, W. E. B. Du Bois, and Martin Luther King Jr.—all leaders who influenced or interacted with Killens substantially.[6] Although all three by the end of their lives, and probably Killens as well, were rather doubtful that America, as a nation, was capable of renouncing its practice of racial inequity and oppression, the general optimism evinced by the three great leaders at the height of their respective careers still appealed to Killens in 1965. Their spirit informs much of *Black Man's Burden*, including the hopeful conclusion, where Killens poses the question of the correct development to pursue following the defeat of racism. Concerning white people, he wonders, "How are we going to integrate them into our New World of Humanity where racial prejudice will be obsolete and the whiteness of their skin will not be held against them, though neither will it afford them any special privileges?" (149–50). Strictly speaking, the question is moot at this point; it is only germane when the liberation referred to actually occurs, although it must be acknowledged that *how* racism is defeated impacts the *how* of the New World of Humanity, a point King would later stress. However, as Killens wishes to hasten the process, he delivers his appeal from the brink, in a sense, arguing that the long-standing gap between the national myth and everyday practice—in particular the disadvantaged position of African Americans in a land whose wealth was in large measure created from slave labor and the overall emphasis on profits at the expense of people—could soon cast the nation beyond any redemption that can be claimed peacefully. Never strictly the prophet of doom, however, he provides his characteristic finale, an ideological collage reminiscent of his novels:

> Come all you who labor for your bread, you radicals and liberals and intellectuals, you artists who would change the world, you educators, who would *really* educate, you preachers, priests, and rabbis, you Democrats and Republicans, you humanists, you winter patriots who love your country. Come and go with us. Man has just begun to live. Hurry! We black folk cannot wait another moment. The tide is with us. The black commander beckons. We must put our boats to sea. Git on board, little chillun. Git on board. (176)

Although *Black Man's Burden* is an amplification of OAAU tenets, it does differ from the shorter work in several important respects. As mentioned above, the essay collection speaks to a larger, therefore different, audience. Considerable space is devoted to Killens's utopianism in the multiethnic sense expressed in *Youngblood* and *And Then We Heard the Thunder*. This broader outlook and the possibility of multiethnic coalitions are not explicit in the nationalist call of the OAAU charter. Malcolm X, even at his most ethnically inclusive ideological stage, focused his energies on getting African Americans to achieve their full potential in the context of a Pan-African vision. He never embraced the "city on a hill" mythology, the notion that white Americans had a divine mission or were the chosen. Malcolm viewed white Americans as the oppressors of the chosen. So although for argumentation purposes he would exploit the variance between, say, the Constitution and contemporary reality, his rhetoric, unlike that of Killens, was never one that presumed enlightened whites—the true or winter patriots, to evoke Thomas Paine—could be a major force in the true liberation of African Americans.[7]

Despite this long-term visionary difference, there was ample immediate common ground, as already indicated, upon which to stand. The right of Black self-defense, an idea synonymous with Malcolm X in the minds of many, is also a central premise of Killens's novels. To be expected at this point, the stances on self-defense reflected by the OAAU declaration and *Black Man's Burden*, even some of the wording, are nearly the same. For example, the OAAU charter suggests that "since self-preservation is the first law of nature, we assert the Afro-American's right of self-defense. . . . Tactics based solely on morality can only succeed when you are dealing with basically moral people or a moral system" (559–60). In "The Myth of Non-violence versus the Right of Self-Defense," Killens first acknowledges the worth of nonviolence as an organizing strategy. He credits practitioners like Martin Luther King Jr., whom he greatly admired and considered a friend, with using it skillfully to attract worldwide attention to the plight of African Americans and garner the support of white liberals. However, Killens distinguishes between tactic and philosophy and ultimately insists, parting ways with King intellectually, on the right of self-defense, which, he says, "is the essence of the law of self-preservation, which is the first law of nature" (*Black Man's Burden* 109). He then explains that the major shortcoming of embracing nonviolence wholeheartedly is that "when non-violence evolves, as it has in this case, from a tactic into an ideology, and indeed into a way of life, it presupposes that one's opponent is a moral human being. But there is no evidence to support such a presumption" (112).

This is not the first time Killens criticizes King's brand of nonviolence. In 1963, at the funeral service of three of the girls murdered in the infamous church bombing in Birmingham, Killens, according to Coretta Scott King, made a statement to the audience, before Martin Luther King Jr. delivered the eulogy, that the tragedy signaled the end of nonviolence as a strategy in the Black Freedom Movement and that African Americans must protect themselves with guns (226). Naturally King disagreed, but neither King nor Killens could ever budge one another on this issue.[8]

Throughout *Black Man's Burden*, Killens rejects the popular notion of integration as well, arguing that "integration with dignity for the integrated can only come after the fact of freedom" (79). This is a line of reasoning, when it was repeated in a 1966 *Negro Digest* article, that drew a negative response from King, who engages Killens at length in *Where Do We Go from Here: Chaos or Community?*:

> At first glance this [Killens's argument] sounds very good. But after reflection one has to face some inescapable facts about the Negro and American life. This is a multiracial nation where all groups are dependent on each other, whether they want to recognize it or not. In this vast interdependent nation no group can retreat to an island entire of itself. The phenomena of integration and liberation cannot be as neatly divided as Killens would have it.
>
> There is no theoretical or sociological divorce between liberation and integration. In our kind of society liberation cannot come without integration and integration cannot come without liberation. I speak here of integration in both the ethical and political senses. On the one hand, integration is true intergroup, interpersonal living. On the other hand, it is the mutual sharing of power. I cannot see how the Negro will be totally liberated from the crushing weight of poor education, squalid housing and economic strangulation until he is integrated, with power, into every level of American life. (61–62)

King acknowledges that Killens's perspective might be valid if the Black struggle for freedom were against colonialists who would be expelled from the country. Given, however, the fact that the United States was home to both the oppressed and the oppressor in the matter under discussion, King ultimately reiterates his belief that "liberation must come through integration" (62). Like the impasse about nonviolence, Killens and King would not resolve this disagreement. More often than not, Killens remained fairly close to OAAU doctrine and more in line with the thinking of Malcolm X. He could, however, have lived comfortably in King's ideal world, and King in his.

Black Man's Burden, besides positioning Killens somewhere between Malcolm X and King, also addresses several of his long-standing concerns, each touched on in his novels: positive Black images, the need to tell an accurate history of enslavement, the importance of teaching African-American history and culture in schools. He rails, for example, in "The Black Psyche," against media proliferation of Uncle Tom or Gunga Din stereotypes, which, in his view, impede any real understanding of African Americans by others. The Gunga Din metaphor, spawned by Rudyard Kipling's "dirty 'ide—white inside" creation, becomes, in fact, central to the psyche of Mr. Wakefield in *'Sippi* and governs his relationship with Charles Othello Chaney, whom he counts on to become a Gunga Din and side with the exploiters against his own people.[9] As part of his criticism of the media, and of movies like *Gone with the Wind, Virginia*, and *Kentucky*, Killens insists that images of African Americans be more richly rendered. He says that contrary to the idyllic depiction of slavery in these movies, his own research showed that slaves had been ever subversive and insurrectionist, often burning the very cotton patches they labored in. This insight would directly inform the climactic scene of his 1969 novel, *Slaves*, in which the enslaved workers burn the cotton patch as Jericho and Cassy escape.

In "The Black Writer Vis-à-Vis His Country," Killens deplores the fact that an African-American child rarely saw a reflection of himself or herself either in the popular media or in schoolbooks, a potentially debilitating blow to a Black child's self-esteem. In prose that would fit unobtrusively into current tracts about inclusive curricula, Killens argues that children need to develop positive cultural identities by being taught that their ancestors made valuable contributions to world civilization. He recalls the positive impact made on his son, Chuck, by Langston Hughes, who, on a visit to the Killens home, gave him a copy of *Famous American Negroes*, which Hughes himself had written. Like the French needed a legendary figure like Joan of Arc, Killens subsequently reasons, African Americans need to be taught about Saint Harriet of the Eastern Shore, referring to Harriet Tubman, one of his sources of inspiration.

Subsequent to *Black Man's Burden*, which ultimately has to be viewed as no less than a sparkling African-American jeremiad, Killens continued to publish regularly about culture and politics. In a 1966 essay titled "Broadway in Black and White," he points to the impressive accomplishments on stage, screen, and television by the likes of Lorraine Hansberry, Harry Belafonte, Sidney Poitier, Bill Cosby, and Cicely Tyson. However, he believed that African-American cultural contributions would have been much greater if not for the racism of the entertainment industry. Accordingly, in his view, African Americans must, simultaneously with pushing for further achievement inside the establishment, create their own cultural institutions. This type of thinking led to the formation, in 1969, of the Black Academy of Arts and Letters, presided over by C. Eric Lincoln, with Killens serving as vice president. A companion article, "Hollywood in Black and White," disparages Hollywood's constant production of negative stereotypes, particularly those of Native Americans and, of course, African Americans. Killens claims that "the Negro is the nation's midcentury protagonist" and must be central to any fresh and dynamic tale about America, a positioning that, to him, can only be rendered authentically by African-American writers (405).

Because of his deep concern with Black heroes, Killens was predictably outraged along with many African Americans by William Styron's 1967 novel, *The Confessions of Nat Turner*, a number one best-seller that was awarded the Pulitzer Prize. John Henrik Clarke solicited responses from ten writers, of whom Killens was one, for an anthology titled *William Styron's Nat Turner: Ten Black Writers Respond*, which was published in 1968. In "The Confessions of Willie Styron," Killens suggests that the white public loved the book because it confirms myths and prejudices against the Black man and attempts to reduce Turner's stature as a historical figure. Killens complains that "Nat Turner, in the tradition of most black Americans, was a man of tragedy, a giant, but William Styron has depicted him as a child of pathos" (34). In Killens's eyes, Styron should never even have attempted the novel because his own paternalism and racism necessarily blocked him from apprehending Turner's true motivation. Styron's Turner dotes on kindly masters, an oxymoron to Killens, and is motivated more by lust for white women than the fact of slavery itself. To Killens, Styron's book is clearly inferior as a psychological profile of a Black rebel when juxtaposed against *Black Thunder*, Arna Bontemps's excellent historical novel about insurrectionist Gabriel Prosser.

In 1966 Killens wrote two pieces for *Negro Digest*. The first, "Brotherhood of Blackness," responds to both an essay by Thomas Echewa titled "Africans vs. Afro-Americans," which had appeared in an earlier issue, and a subsequent exchange in the journal between Echewa and African-American writer John A. Williams. Adopting a Pan-Africanist stance, like Du Bois and Malcolm X, Killens upbraids both men for engaging in superfluous and divisive discourse. Killens rejects the question, as it were, choosing instead to stress the interdependent nature of the struggles against racist oppression in Africa and the United States and urging, furthermore, as he recalls the warmth he felt during a 1962 trip to Africa, unity between continental Africans and their African-American brethren.

Killens received a subsequent invitation from the editors of *Negro Digest* to participate in a print forum: "The Meaning and Measure of Black Power." Along with eleven other writers and prominent figures—namely, Julian Bond, Eugene Walton, Anita Cornwell, Conrad Kent Rivers, Sterling Stuckey, Brooks Johnson, Francis Ward, Nathan Hare, Eloise Greenfield, Ronald Fair, and Dudley Randall—he would address two sets of questions: (1) Is the civil rights movement at the crossroads? And, if so, what are the practical alternatives to it? (2) What is your own reaction to the term "Black Power," and why do you feel the national press and the white public reacted as they did to the term? His response was that the civil rights movement had reached not a crossroads but a dead end and that an alternate strategy was required. Citing a growing schism between a Black middle class, wayward in its complacency, and the Black masses for whom economic conditions were worsening, he reiterates his belief that a Black nationalist unity is a necessary prelude to the integrationist aims of civil rights advocates. He embraces Black Power, which is essentially a restatement of OAAU doctrine, but couples the term, in another bit of *argumentum ad populum*, with the nation's supposedly cherished beliefs. Addressing the potential for African Americans to elect responsive Black leadership, as an alternative to unresponsive white leadership, he explains, "If Black Power means anything at all, it means 'one man, one vote.' It means an end to taxation without representation" (35). While Killens usually may have been a bit strident for mainstream civil rights supporters (this is indeed the same article to which King objected), they could hardly argue with a proposal to flex Black voting muscle.

Actually, the harshest criticism Killens received during the period was leveled against him by Harold Cruse, who disparages Killens and his entire career in his now classic *The Crisis of the Negro Intellectual*. Cruse depicts Killens as duplicitous, integrationist, and opportunist. He particularly disapproves of the latter *Negro Digest* article in which Killens wrote: "It seems to me there need be no strong schism at this moment between the advocates of black power and the 'black *bourgeoisie*.' If one of the principal tenets of Black Consciousness is economic power, the starting place is with the black middle class. May their tribes increase. Black Power advocates are no present danger to them" (34).

It was hard for Cruse to fathom that most Black Power theorists were much of a threat to anyone because he viewed their theorizing to be too amorphous and abstract to represent a coherent and powerful system of thought. Insofar as Cruse could decipher the rhetoric of Black Power, he viewed it as more reformist than revolutionary. His stated problem with the Killens article is that it represents, in his view, insufficient class analysis and a glib turnabout for one who previously championed the working class. Cruse flatly misrepresents Killens, giving the impression that the phrase "all power to the black bourgeoisie" is a quote from the article. Killens, who essentially called for a coalition across class lines, said no such thing. Cruse further accuses Killens of waffling on the question of nonviolence, which is certainly not evident from an examination of his essays and fiction. Nonetheless, Cruse vitriolically binds Killens, who never headed any formal political group, to the shortcomings of Black Power in general:

> Nothing better demonstrates the reformist ideology behind Black Power than the Killens stamp of approval. Never the originator of a single new concept, style, or exposition whether in literature or politics, Killens has been the neutralizing temporizer, the non-controversial, moderating lid-sitter par excellence. He is not averse to changing his position when necessary; but he possesses the reform politician's knack of catching on belatedly to all advanced demands and slogans, once it is certain that the establishment must bend to popular appeal. He then becomes the propagandizing expert just as if he were *always* of that opinion. (561–62)

To be dismissive is one thing, but to be accurately so is quite another. It is certainly not true that Killens made no innovative literary contribution. Addison Gayle and William Wiggins Jr., among others, describe his unique achievement. Nor is it the case that Killens was uncontroversial. As indicated previously, King was moved to rebuke Killens in print. And at the same time *The Crisis of the Negro Intellectual* was published, the so-called lid-sitting Killens was in the middle of an embattled stint as writer-in-residence at Fisk University because he chose to honor the memory of Malcolm X during a campus ceremony. That Killens changed his position when necessary was not the worst of traits. Many have applauded Malcolm X, whom Cruse deems an outstanding leader, for his facility at self-reinvention. Repositioning is not the important issue; our main interest should be in whether the ideological shifts are reasonable. Cruse charges that Killens was largely motivated by crass opportunism. But Killens's 1966 writing is a virtual restatement of what he was writing in 1964, some of it in conjunction with Malcolm, a fact Cruse fails to acknowledge. Indeed, *Black Man's Burden*, written before "Black Power" was a popular slogan and a book that is a must read for anyone who would evaluate Killens in 1967, is a work Cruse fails to mention. While it is true that Cruse's problem with Killens was not simply about ideas expressed in the mid-1960s but was based on experiences, like the Ellison review, extending back two decades, the point to be made here is that Cruse, who argues the need for a rigorous assessment of creative output, fails to make such assessment in the case of Killens. He virtually ignores Killens's writings, except for a phrase or two with which he wishes to take exception. However, he offers no real appraisal of the long-standing traits or evolving features of Killens's work.

Killens was not, as Cruse avers, bringing up the ideological rear. After slamming the 1966 article, Cruse writes, "One cannot analyze leadership trends unless it is done within the context of the role of the black bourgeoisie. The problem is—the Black Power theorists have not done so" (562). That is exactly what Killens was trying to do by considering Black Power and the Black bourgeoisie together.

Cruse's criticism of Killens smacks of a personal vendetta, one that perhaps had its basis in old disagreements that took place when they moved in overlapping cultural and political circles in Harlem. Cruse is critical of the entire *Freedom* newspaper crowd and sees Killens as a central figure of a group that Cruse claims never reached out sufficiently to the Black masses. Cruse also ridicules *The Urbanite*, a short-lived magazine Killens wrote for, as a middle-class, integrationist vehicle dominated by the old *Freedom* writers like Killens and Cruse's favorite foil, Lorraine Hansberry. He furthermore deems worthless a debate held at Town Hall in June 1964 during which Killens, along with Hansberry, Ossie Davis, Ruby Dee, Amiri Baraka (then known as LeRoi Jones), Paule Marshall, and Louis Lomax unwisely, according to Cruse, attacked the white liberal establishment as represented at the session by television personality David Susskind, *New York Post* editor James Wechsler, and *Fortune* editor Charles Silberman. He remarks of the affair that "they were accusing white liberals of not being radicals when they themselves did not compose a group with a radical Negro philosophy of any kind" (200–201). Also coming under fire is the Killens-led writers' conference that was held in April 1965 at the New School for Social Research as a tribute to the recently deceased Hansberry. Of the conference he writes, "The Killens literary and cultural entourage [was] approaching the end of its fifteen-year-old reign. This conference was painfully frenetic and pitifully rhetorical, attempting to analyze the Negro writer's cultural precariousness in American society, and the fate of the American Negro in American culture, as a people" (500).

It would be too much of a digression to explore Cruse's problem with Killens in greater detail. Nonetheless, it should be evident that much of Cruse's analysis is exaggerated and fragmentary. For example, Killens, unlike Hansberry, was not the major player relative to *Freedom* that Cruse would have us believe he was. Although *Freedom* was published monthly from 1951 to 1955, Killens did little, if any, writing for the newspaper other than the brief review of *Invisible Man*.[10] And in his diatribe against the so-called backward, upscale publication *The Urbanite*, Cruse, being characteristically short on specifics, never discusses the exact contribution Killens made to the magazine. If he had done so, he would have been forced to reveal that Killens wrote exclusively about blues and spirituals, hardly highbrow preoccupations.

In March 1961, Killens began to write a proposed series of monthly articles about music, but the publication lasted only long enough to feature two pieces. The first, "A Good Man Feeling Bad!" was a tribute to W. C. Handy, widely known as the Father of the Blues. Killens praises Handy as a vernacular artist who forged masterful music from the cultural testimony of common, everyday African Americans. Killens also posits that Handy's long productivity resulted perhaps from the fact that Handy was a "race" man who "never wandered away from the roots of his creative life" (24). Of extreme importance to Killens, consonant with his own artistic aims, was to demonstrate the generative potential of mass African-American sensibility. This aim, as well as the connection to his own fiction, is made even clearer in his second and last article for *The Urbanite*, "The Negro as Music Maker: Some Reflections on the Origins of Jazz." In a virtual reprise of the Jubilee section of *Youngblood*, Killens stresses that the roots of jazz lie in the Negro spirituals and then devotes most of the article to explaining, this time without the service of Robby Youngblood and Reverend Ledbetter, the double meanings, the fundamental resisting nature of such songs as "Go Down, Moses," "Swing Low Sweet Chariot," "Steal Away Jesus," and of course, Joe Youngblood's top pick, "Walk Together Children." Killens admits that he took some flak from his editor because it was thought he "had gone too far afield or too far back into the field (of cotton)" to suit the magazine's image (7). Indeed, his essay stood as an anomaly in the section of the magazine that was labeled "Classics and All That Jazz" and included reviews of the Modern Jazz Quartet, Antonio Vivaldi, and Brahms. But Killens never wavered either in his general enthusiasm for African-American folklore or in his campaign to alter any perception that Black slaves had been a contented, servile, totally unrebellious lot. He would use any forum, and he used *The Urbanite* quite ably, to propagate his message.

Concerning the charge that the Black writers lacked a radical philosophy at the Town Hall event, one need only recall that the affair at Town Hall took place a mere one week before the release of the OAAU charter, which suggests that even by Cruse's standards, Killens ought to be credited with possessing "some kind" of radical Negro philosophy.

Cruse would have Killens shoulder the entire blame for the ideological and artistic deficiencies of any group of which Killens was part, yet, as mentioned earlier, Cruse has not demonstrated that he has given the major portion of Killens's own writing a serious read. There is absolutely no discussion of the three books Killens had written by 1967. And what Cruse could not have known is that Killens would engineer, over the course of the next twenty years, even larger and more important conferences than the New School event. His entourage, if that is the proper term, had not even peaked, much less reached the end of its reign.

What Cruse saw in Killens over time—and what he *knows* he saw, though he is unsympathetic toward it—is the sort of double consciousness described by Du Bois (which Cruse experienced as well). This tension is a major feature of Killens's fiction, most expertly symbolized by the character Solly Saunders. It is also a quality he addresses in both interviews and autobiographical statements. But Killens was never an integrationist of the sort Cruse imagines. He was much more concerned with justice than mixing. Nor did nationalism ever grab full hold of his intellect, the reason he modifies, in his typical utopian way, certain OAAU statements.

Killens never addressed directly in print the comments made by Cruse, though he was certainly cognizant of them.[11] In fact, he appeared, along with John Henrik Clarke, another Cruse target, on panels with Cruse. Clarke, who eventually did respond to Cruse in print, wrote that "his book is full of anger without creative direction and facts without adequate explanation" (368). Clarke later confided in an interview that the panels they appeared on together were productive and that he and Killens preferred to support the best aspects of Cruse's thinking rather than to squabble with him about personal attacks.[12] Killens was less generous in private, referring to Cruse as "the establishment's informer and a literary hatchet man." He added that "his book might have been important. It could have been something of value, but he flubbed it, due to his own self-destructive vindictiveness and subjectivity."[13]

Killens's problem in the 1960s was not insincerity, conceptual sloppiness, or lack of community commitment. He could theorize well enough and his involvement and generosity are well established. The more problematic quest was for rhetorical effectiveness. Not wedded to narrow nationalism or mainstream integrationism, and operating in a popular sphere dominated by ideas associated with Malcolm X and Martin Luther King Jr., he tried to reach audiences whose interests were varied. Like any good rhetor, he chose the means of persuasion most suitable to a given situation. In this regard he resembled both Malcolm himself, who did not deliver quite the same message in the mosques that he did on college campuses, and the great Frederick Douglass, who habitually surveyed his audience, checking its ethnic composition, before deciding the specific content and tone of his speech. Killens led no movement, betrayed no organizational trust, promised no social deed he did not perform, impeded nobody else's progressive actions, or promoted any cause incompatible with Black liberation. It made little sense to criticize acrimoniously someone of this character who was grappling with important ideas and struggling to participate in the major discourse relative to those ideas.

The best essay by Killens during the 1960s and early 1970s, "Black Labor and the Liberation Movement," appeared in *Black Scholar* in 1970. He announces that

> between us club members in the Brotherhood of Blackness, it is no secret that the Black Liberation Movement is running out of steam. The Civil Rights Integrationist organizations are deathly stricken with senility and obsolescence. The Black Power detachments are at the moment powerless. "Race riots" as a form of struggle have become a terrible bore to the sophisticated White Establishment. Indeed in many cases the metropolitan police forces looked forward eagerly to those famous long hot summers as a means of killing off a few of the "natives" and as a proving grounds for testing new anti-riot weapons. (33)

The biggest weakness the author then saw in the movement was its failure to organize the Black labor force, the most numerous and potentially dynamic segment of the Black community. The working class outnumbered both the African-American middle class, which according to Killens had set too much of the Black political agenda, and the lumpen element romanticized by groups like the Black Panthers. "The vanguard is beautiful, dramatic, inspirational and necessary," he writes, "but the army is where it's at" (34). Black labor is seen as the army, the "Great Black Hope" (34). Killens, the former union official, no longer had faith (if he ever really had) that white labor could organize in the interests of African Americans. Commenting on Marxist thinking, for example, he argues that Marx himself undertheorized the influence of racism and the corruption of the white working class in industrialized nations. He calls for the creation of a National Black Labor Congress and closes the essay with "*All Power to Black Labor!*"

Cruse might call this an example of flip-flopping, and might even take some credit for influencing it. But there is nothing in the article not foretold in Killens's union activities or earlier writing. Notwithstanding, he may still have been thinking of Cruse when he offered in his 1971 self-interview, "Rappin' with Myself":

> I think I'm a man who has made a helluva lot of mistakes in my time, but I have always been in there pitching. I have always worked for Black liberation, but I've changed my mind a million times about how we are going to achieve it. For two years I was a CIO organizer. I had hopes that we could liberate the nation by joining hands with the white working class. Big mistake, but I learned from it. The thing is to learn

> from your mistakes. I was not disillusioned when the working class joined the KKK and voted for Wallace (I don't mean Henry). I wasn't disillusioned because I had no illusions in the first place. I just had high hopes. I was optimistic. When the labor movement didn't make it and was co-opted by the establishment, I said to myself, "Okay, that's that." I didn't really believe it anyhow. How could I? Growing up as I did in Macon, Georgia. I don't want to make a fetish or a religion out of mistake making. But I do insist upon my right to make them if they're not too costly to me and my people, and also my right to change my mind, to change me. (121–22)

It remains an open question whether Killens *really* had no illusions about cross-ethnic workers' solidarity. But whatever illusions may have existed could not have been simplistic. He was a brooding thinker and of Georgia, Harlem, Brooklyn, the 1930s, the 1960s, universities, World War II, and the labor movement. His essays reveal this range of experiential tension, the same territory explored in his novels, and make up an impressive complement.

4

Cultural Heroes

In 1968, in the aftermath of the assassination of Martin Luther King Jr., Killens wrote an essay, partly in tribute to the civil rights martyr, titled "The Black Writer and the Revolution." He urged African-American writers to remain up to the task of political and cultural transformation. "Make the revolution," he exhorted. "You can be rebels **with** a cause. A rebel-with-a-cause **plus** a program equals a revolutionary" (397). He issued his familiar call for a literature of Black legends, myths, and heroes, works that would incorporate historical reconstruction and visionary insight. The collective African-American literary project, in other words, should celebrate African-American people and promote resistance against oppression, and this artistic outpouring should be presented, according to the Killens prescription, in the African-American vernacular:

> Western man has used language, words, as a powerful weapon to enslave the rest of mankind, and now we black writers must use our language, Afro-Americanese, to redefine ourselves. We black folk are a colony on the mainland. I have heard colored musicians themselves say, "I don't play jazz, spirituals, rhythm and blues and that kind of stuff. I play serious music." I'm saying, these brothers have been had. The language has enslaved them just as it has enslaved, on one level or another, every black brother and sister in this nation. One of the black writer's tasks is to decolonize the language. "Good hair" and "high yaller" and "a nigger ain't shit" will have no place in Afro-Americanese one of these days, and soon, if the black writer does his job. (397)

Killens himself was just beginning to generate a new strand of prose to fit the bill. His first three novels were all developed from notes, scenes, and drafts traceable to the beginning of his career in the 1940s. They sprang largely from his early experiences in Southern and segregated environments. The publication of *'Sippi* in 1967, when Killens was fifty-one years old, marked the last major mining of that creative vein. In *The Cotillion*, published in 1971, Killens turns his attention to the Black, urban North of the late 1960s—sometime after the assassination of Malcolm X but before the murder of King—to continue his abiding interest in exploring and trumpeting African-American communal and political possibilities.

The genesis of *The Cotillion*, as with most Killens stories, was autobiographical. Club women were trying to get his daughter, Barbara, to become involved in a cotillion at the Waldorf-Astoria. Barbara, however, preferred to be immersed in political protest activities. According to her father, "she was into demonstrating, picket lines, sitting down in front of trucks, getting arrested, etc." ("The Half Ain't Never Been Told" 306). Nonetheless, Killens seized on the vehicle presented to turn out a hilarious satire of the Black middle class and disingenuous Black nationalism, a novel many regard as his best.

Harlem resident Yoruba Evelyn Lovejoy, the story's protagonist, has been invited by the Femmes Fatales, a group of bourgeois Black women who supposedly represent the "first Black families of Brooklyn," to participate in the Grand Cotillion to be held at the Waldorf. Yoruba and four other "disadvantaged" Harlem girls are slated to "benefit" from the missionary kindness of Mrs. Patterson and other members of the organization, who all reside in the relatively upscale district of Crowning Heights, a fictionalized version of the Crown Heights neighborhood in which Killens lived. Yoruba, however, is ambivalent about participating in the pageantry. Her budding Black nationalist identity and aesthetic do not easily accommodate the role of Black debutante, essentially seen as mimicry of white middle-class mating rituals and standards of beauty. The pressure to participate, to which she succumbs, is applied by her mother, Daphne Braithwaite Lovejoy, a light-skinned West Indian mulatto who identifies much more with European culture than that derived from Africa. By contrast, Matt Lovejoy, who bestowed the name Yoruba on his only child, is a Georgia-born, coal-black, frustrated nationalist who has no allegiance to white mythology and symbolism. He has no illusions about the value of a cotillion for Blacks. White folks, he understands, devised these events so their daughters would have a chance to meet, mingle with, and perhaps snare the most desirable, wealthy bachelors. But he sees no benefit in slavish imitation that amounts to no more than "just some more white folks' foolishness that don't git Blacks folks nowhere except in debt" (139).

The folly of valorizing alien mores and symbols, without even understanding them no less, is further dramatized at a tea hosted by the Jeffersons, one of the more earthy families associated with the Grand Cotillion. Mrs. Jefferson strikes up a conversation with Mrs. Robinson, the mother of Charlene, one of the other "disadvantaged" Harlem girls:

> "Do you dig Ray Charles?"
>
> Charlene's mother answered in a vague and horrifying mixture of assorted and affected accents: "Oi don't like jazz, blues, spearchals and that kind of common averday music. Oi prefer the classics. Oi like Chopping."
>
> Mrs. Jefferson said, "I'm hip. Everybody like chopping. You have to eat to live, but I thought we were discussing music."
>
> "Chopping!" Mrs. Robinson repeated softly, desperately, breaking into a sweat. "He's a great European musician. He lives in Paris." Could she be wrong about this too? Why was Mrs. Jefferson staring at her as if she were a total idiot? Mrs. Brap-bap saved the day, so to speak. "She means Chopin," she explained to Mrs. Jefferson. Then to Mrs. Robinson she said, "Honey, you can't even pronounce him, let alone appreciate him." (121)

Matt ultimately agrees to support Yoruba's involvement in the pageantry because he unequivocally loves and supports *her*, not because he believes in the activity sponsored by the Femmes Fatales, whom he sarcastically calls the "Fat Asses." His demeanor differs from his wife's, which, though also loving, rests on browbeating and emotional blackmail. She wants to make her daughter as "European" as she can.

Yoruba's very body signifies the ideological struggle between her parents. Her father never fails to appreciate her natural African-derived beauty, as does the author; she is repeatedly described as "Black and princessly." Yoruba's mother, on the other hand, has always sought to refigure her. She used to make her daughter hold her lips in, hoping that would make them grow thin. She also would keep Yoruba out of the sun as much as possible and, following an old superstition familiar to many

African Americans, would never allow her to drink coffee. Both actions were taken, of course, to prevent Yoruba from becoming any darker in complexion. Daphne does not hold Matt's color against him. She married him because she figured that he respected and adored her in a way that no white man she had ever met did. But because she felt she had disadvantaged her daughter color-wise, she desired to keep the damage to a minimum and not ruin her chances to mix among light-skinned "cultured" Blacks, marry one, and have light-skinned children with straight hair.

Ben Ali Lumumba, Yoruba's boyfriend and the story's narrator, plays a crucial role in assisting her to prepare for the Grand Cotillion while she, in turn, helps him clarify cultural and political conceptions and resolve some of his own self-doubts about Black identity and activism—his own shaky reliance on symbols, for example, including the phony British accent with which he sometimes speaks. Lumumba is also the key agent in the eventual psychological liberation of Daphne. Originally too dark and woolly headed for Yoruba's mother, who is appalled that Yoruba dates him and has chosen him as her escort, Lumumba gradually succeeds in altering her perspective. Her resistance is first diminished when she discovers that the *New York Times* had featured an article about him, portraying him as an up-and-coming writer. Although quick to discount the capabilities of a "darkie," Daphne decides he must have worth if important white folks deem it so. After meeting with Lumumba, who removes his beard, trims his hair, and dons a suit to impress her, Daphne admits to his charm, though she could envision no serious romantic relationship between Lumumba and Yoruba.

Daphne's outlook changes even more when she works as a servant at a white cotillion held in Southhampton. Yoruba and Lumumba also take jobs at the affair, Yoruba because of her mother's pressuring and Lumumba because he has decided to write a satirical novel titled *The Cotillion*. Lumumba wants to work the rich white folks' cotillion, the source of the imitative Black ones, both to gather material for his book and to show Daphne what impoverished and silly events all cotillions are. He explains to Daphne—and Killens explains to us—that he would only attack the African-American bourgeoisie in the context of scrutinizing the actions of the European-American bourgeoisie.

For Lumumba's purposes, the trip to Long Island could not have worked out better. In a scene reminiscent of the party at the Wakefield residence in *'Sippi*, the debutante ball degenerates, after parents and press depart, into a raucous orgy. Spurred on by alcohol and marijuana, the partygoers fornicate, or attempt to, all over the estate, engage in drunken brawls, and set the mansion on fire. The police and fire departments are summoned and the "riot" is later reported in the *New York Times*. Throughout the spectacle, Lumumba directs Daphne's gaze to various scenes, working to shatter her belief that the white bourgeoisie possess superior culture and refinement. "Look! Look, Miss Daphne! So this is the great white upper class, the cream of the crop! Wow!" (213). In the face of such stark evidence, Daphne capitulates. Although her psychic movement toward full acceptance of Black culture remains tentative, she nevertheless finds the display of white culture repulsive. She hurriedly leaves the Long Island cotillion, preferring to walk to the train station rather than wait around for the limousine and the return ride to New York City.

While the party only costs Daphne some of her illusions, it cost Killens a measure of commercial success. Motown optioned *The Cotillion* and planned to develop it into a Broadway musical. Smokey Robinson and Willie Hutch were slated to write the music. However, negotiations broke off over the Long Island scene. According to Killens, Bob Cohen, who was in charge of Artistic Productions, was troubled by the depiction of the white characters. The option was allowed to lapse as Killens stood his artistic ground.[1]

Daphne is nearly as stubborn. Not willing to abandon all her dreams for Yoruba, she rationalizes that the Femmes Fatales, unlike the folks in Southhampton, can imbue a cotillion with respect and dignity. She still views the imitation of whiteness to be a legitimate objective. To the contrary, Yoruba and Lumumba decide to subvert the Grand Cotillion, to make it truly Black and beautiful by using it as a platform to critique the festivities. They don African garb; Yoruba wears her hair natural for the first time. After they reach the stage, in a ballroom designed, in line with that year's theme, as a plantation, Lumumba seizes the microphone and, during an uproarious conclusion, exclaims, "Be done with false illusions! Come with us to the real world! . . . Up the Black Nation" (255). Ironically, the Grand Cotillion does serve as the "coming out" for Yoruba—and for Daphne, who joins them, and perhaps Lumumba as well. It was, as Fred Hord points out in *Reconstructing Memory*, "the culmination of their demystification of colonial cultural repression and their resistance to its dehumanization" (100). Priscilla Patterson, who boasts of having the whitest blood in the Femmes Fatales, tries to persuade Daphne to remain with them in their cause. She shouts at her, "You understand!" Daphne responds by standing tall, "taller than she'd ever stood," and declaring, "I understand. Finally I understand. And that's exactly why I going with my people" (255). It is an ending that prompted Charles Johnson to remark, in *Being & Race*, that *The Cotillion* is a "'positive' Cultural Nationalist comedy shaped entirely by radical black views on art" (91).[2]

Although *The Cotillion* is probably discussed most often because of the degree to which the Black bourgeoisie is ridiculed, Killens criticized members of the Black privileged class in fiction as far back as *Youngblood*. A more significant development is how those "radical black views on art" are structured. The main rhetorical strategies of the novel involve the "Du Boisian veil," the elaborate use of signifying, the recurring figure of Malcolm X, and the revision of community texts both sacred and secular.

As Daphne begins to recognize the silliness of the Long Island affair, her reactions are so described: "Now, at this, the 'really real thing,' the epitome of WASPY culture, a misty veil was slowly lifting from her eyes, even as she struggled valiantly to remain behind the veil of her darling innocence" (213). Du Bois often uses the metaphor of the veil in *The Souls of Black Folk* to represent the effects of racism.[3] The veil does not totally block African Americans' view of the larger society, but it affords a dim and distorted perspective that Blacks must continually labor to transcend. As Stephen Carey points out, an aspect of the "darkened view" is that it produces feelings of cultural inferiority in Blacks (66). Du Bois himself wrote with guarded optimism that "if somewhere in this whirl and chaos of things there dwells Eternal Good, pitiful yet masterful, the Anon in His good time in America shall rend the veil and the prisoned shall go free" (*The Souls of Black Folk* 215). Fortunately, this is the journey Daphne gets to take in the novel, the Anon in this case being the novelist.

Black satire, not merely an adornment, also holds the basic story together. As Lumumba, the narrator of *The Cotillion*, frames the matter in the foreword, "I meant to do myself some signifying. I meant to let it all hang out" (6). Just as examples of Daphne's alienation build toward the lifting of the veil, a series of clever barbs throughout the novel inexorably leads to the conclusion, which is, in essence, one big put-down of a cultural ritual deemed backward by the author. Also targeted for signifying, as a major strand of the book, are so-called Black Powerists who evidence more lip service than long-term productive engagement. They are unable to achieve positive communal construction of any sort, much less the "nation-building" about which they speak so freely. The Killens humor, always a central quality of his prose, is keenly sharpened to attack negative or compromising behavior manifested within or on the fringes of the Freedom Movement.

In the opening pages, Killens symbolizes the disarray of African-American political activity. The Black and Beautiful Burlesque, a strip joint featuring Afro-wearing Black beauties, has become the focus of "pickets picketing pickets picketing pickets, who were picketing" (15). Nationalists were demonstrating against the idea of Black nudity, while integrationists pushed for integrated burlesque queens. The burlesque club, we are told, "was where the action was, and there were fist fights every other night" (15).

Immediately afterward, we meet Billy "Bad Mouth" Williams, "mayor of Black nationalist Harlem," pontificating on the corner of 125th Street and Seventh Avenue. Billy is presented as totally self-absorbed: "God and/or Allah's most precious gift to the lucky Harlem masses. Don't take anybody else's word for it. Check it out with Bad Mouth himself. He'd tell you he was the last of the great Black Nationalists. Uncrowned prime minister of the Black government in exile. Hey! There was Garvey, Malcolm, Bad Mouth Williams. After that—well, Armageddon" (16). Bad Mouth has a variety of stock speeches to appeal to the Harlem masses. He knows the tropes, so to speak. Yoruba does also, for after only a few minutes of Bad Mouth's diatribe against hustling preachers, she muses, "It's preachers today. Yesterday it was 'Negro' leaders. The day before it was the 'white Communist liberals.' Tomorrow he would be doing a putdown on something else. The labor movement. The NAACP. The President." Bad Mouth's talk is not entirely unworthy. The author's own perspective is evident in the accusation that "You don't want no power. You just want to intergrate" (20). But Bad Mouth *only* talks; there is no sign that he is committed to organized and protracted struggle.

Lumumba is cast similarly early in the novel. As the "author," he can be said to be satirizing himself. Discussing with Yoruba his plans to become a writer, he dismisses the poetry he had just performed before a crowd at the Café Uptown Society: "Oh I don't mean that jive I just read. That's for the birds, the Black ones I mean. All you got to do for this crowd here is call whitey a bunch of mother-humpers and say that Black is beautiful, and like you got it made" (68). Later, in a restaurant, a series of Black men approach Lumumba, each offering a creative but overly complicated handshake. Lumumba says to one, "Brother, we got to get ourselves a quicker handshake. Whitey be kicking our heads in while we going through the ritual" (92). Definitely more style than substance are teenage members of the BBBMF, the Black and Beautiful Bad Mother Fuckahs. They cannot even recognize Lumumba without his beard, but once they hear him speak and are certain it is he, they assure him, "You're our main man" (172). They give Lumumba a business card, promise to T.C.B. if he ever needs them, and strut off in their dashikis and alligator boots.

The most memorable political caricature in the novel is that of Jomo Mamadou Zero the Third. Years before Paddy Chayefsky's *Network*, a film in which Black radicals are solicited for a television series in order to boost ratings, the self-styled revolutionary makes an appearance on *The Johnny Carson Show*.[4] Lumumba, a former seaman, shipped out with Jomo off and on for more than a year. That is why he knows that Jomo was not, as he claims, in prison during that time for dealing drugs and pimping. Lumumba anxiously awaits Jomo's appearance, though, because he feels his rap is "good therapy for the souls of Black folks" (173). But if Mr. Zero cannot fool Lumumba, he certainly isn't tricking or co-opting NBC either. To them, he's simply an exotic entertainment pawn. As Carson introduces him:

> And now ladies and gentlemen, it is my proud pleasure to introduce to you that greatest revolutionary of all times. He's greater and more dangerous than the late lamented Malcolm X, may he rest in peace and nonviolence, heh heh heh, and with all due respect. When he was two years old, our distinguished guest witnessed his father beat his mother to death with a large hambone. He swore off swine from that day forward. He was raised up by himself in the very jungle wilds of Harlem, hustled heroin and prostitutes since he was eight years old, raped his grandmother at the age of nine. Did five years in Sing Sing. And now he's making plans to overthrow our beloved country and systematically murder all us white folks. Isn't that wonderful? Isn't it

> truly tremendous? Give him a big hand, fellow Americans. He's gonna kill every white man in this nation. Bring him on with grand applause. Make this great one feel at home. (175)

When Jomo makes his entrance, to wild cheers and applause, Carson greets him, "Jomo Mamadou Zero the Third, ladies and gentlemen. Jomo Mamadou the Third! Sit down right here, Jomo, my main man, and tell us how you're going to overthrow the government and kill all the white folks in the world" (175). Jomo fulfills his part of the bargain as Lumumba watches in silence:

> His main man, Jomo Mamadou Zero the Third, in his boss dashiki, with large black glasses covering the upper regions of his face, glared out from behind his bad black beard at the ocean of pink-white faces in the TV audience. He spat across the footlights at them. And they applauded. He growled, "I wished all of you pale-faced pigs a bad damn evening, you swinish cannibalistic motherfuckas! And after them few kind words of salutation, I'm going to say some mean things to you." And the place exploded with applause. Pale-faced Johnny Carson shouted, "Isn't he wonderful, ladies and gentlemen!" (175–76)

While Killens criticizes some of the affectations and commercialism of 1960s-style Black nationalism and emphasizes that Blacks themselves are sometimes the enemies of Black progress, he yet is dedicated to the idea, as he is in his previous novels, that African-American self-love and unity are the first principles of a true Black liberation movement. Yoruba, for instance, would remind herself that the "hustlers, thugs, hoodlums, and pimps" who memorized catchphrases, bought dashikis, and changed their names were not the essence of the Freedom Movement (69–70).

The core of the movement, in Killens's view, are the vast number of everyday hardworking African Americans who would be receptive to responsive and responsible leadership. The role model in this regard, the standard by which all leaders are to be measured, is Malcolm X. At least a dozen times in the story his name is used, his nobility and dignity evoked, to point out the limitations of some would-be leader or to affirm a positive action or decision. Although Malcolm himself did not get to articulate fully his political program, his intellect intrigued Killens, and he celebrates this attribute along with Malcolm's love and commitment. *The Cotillion*, as Norman Harris observes, "asserts that symbolic political activity not directed by goals derived from an articulative philosophical framework is often futile and sometimes cruelly humorous" (154). Malcolm's promise, the potential of coherent and sustaining direction, the framework Harris speaks of, undergirds the novel. Killens thus aims to preserve the most generative aspect of Black nationalism—that is, the ethnic cohesion that can ultimately lead to fundamental social change. He realizes that the universal, whether in politics or art, is only approachable by way of a nationalist trail. Or as Hord phrases it, "Killens' correct politics calls for a hold on transcending nationalism until the prospects for universalism are black brighter" (87).

The intellectual heart of the novel is Matt Lovejoy. Georgia-born and in his fifties, like the author in both respects, he is the most grounded character in the text, and he is the one with a consistently secure and positive view of himself. Like his biblical namesake, who provided the first gospel of the New Testament, Matt preaches his own "first gospel," an amalgam of the Scriptures, still the most powerful text in the Black community, and Black nationalist myth. His "preaching" sustains his family and influences the broader community. For example, when conversation in the Jenkins Palace Barbershop gets around, as one can easily imagine it often does, to the ethnicity of Jesus Christ, Matt assumes the "pulpit":

> "Let me run it down for you. Fact of the business, Jesus' mother, Mary, was white. Right? But old Joseph was Black. Yes he was. That's how come they couldn't find no place to stop at in any of them Bethlehem hotels. That's how come there wasn't no place in the inn, cause them peckerwoods couldn't stand to see old Black Joe miscegenating all day and all night with little Miss Mary Anne."
>
> Suddenly, it got so quiet you could have heard a bedbug making water on a snowbank in Siberia. They never knew whether to take old Matt Lovejoy seriously or not. He was always coming out of a weird bag nobody else had ever heard of. Matt continued running down his thing.
>
> "All them Jews were colored in them days. And the white man, talking about the Romans, they had colonialized them, and Jesus was a Black Power man and he was trying to freedomize them. That's how come they crucifixed him. A lot of them Jews were toms, and they

> panicked after Jesus split, and they went off to Europe for two thousand years and miscegenated with them white Europeans and passed on into the white race. That's how come some of them suckers still got kinky hair, I mean till this very day. They ain't nothing but light-complected Negroes passing." (32–33)

Killens also links the Bible to popular community discussions of the question of nonviolence and to his own disagreement with King. After a character voices support for civil disobedience, one of the barbers respectfully, though disapprovingly, responds: "I'm with Rev. Luther all the way. He a good man. God-fearing and all that jive. But I just can't see myself letting a paddy beat on me, and I'm just standing around telling the sucker how much I love him. Telling him to be my guest. I believe in an eye for an eye and a tooth for a tooth. That's in the Good Book too. And a head for a head, and some ass for some ass. That's America to me. That's the true Christianity" (40). Even though Killens began work on this comedic novel to work out of a depression following King's bitterly ironic assassination, he would never embrace the nonviolent aspect of his friend's philosophy. He never believed King got it right and gives Matt Lovejoy the final, homespun word on King's approach: "I know one thing. It stands to reason, if the rabbits took rock-throwing lessons, there wouldn't be all them many hunters pitching boogie in the forest" (41).

As is evident, the political vision and primary topoi are cast in the Black vernacular. Although Killens had admirably employed such discourse as a significant feature in his prior novels, particularly with respect to dialogue and folklore, such discursive practice was framed by or entwined with naturalism or social realism and was never the dominant stylistic feature of those texts. He had written what Gayl Jones terms "composite novels" (13). With the 1970 publication of the short story "Rough Diamond," he freed his voice, as Jones might say (178), and devoted his complete literary canvas to showing off urban Black orality. Of course, this advent squares with the ideas espoused in "The Black Writer and the Revolution," but Killens was able to pull off the maneuver because by then, having lived in Harlem and Brooklyn for more than two decades, his ear had become finely attuned to the Black urban rhythms that surrounded him. "Rough Diamond," especially given its satirical bent, is a warm-up act for *The Cotillion*.

The story lampoons the Black writer-as-charlatan and centers on Bill Yardbird, who wins the National Book Award in 1964 for a book on Harlem in which he mostly traded in social pathology and "showed that jungle in all its true savagery and degradation" (171). Reminiscent of his 1952 review of *Invisible Man*, though ironically Yardbird is his Rinehart, Killens has the narrator exclaim, "I went Ellison one better, baby, ten times better. The father of the hero of my book had knocked up his wife, his mother, his three daughters, all in the same damn month" (171). The Black press denounces Yardbird for being an Uncle Tom or Gunga Din instead of an authentic "diamond in the rough," and he is chased from the community. He lives in Greenwich Village while also maintaining a Harlem address. Yardbird, the ever-backward pseudo-militant, eventually ends up behind the Iron Curtain and in bed with Elsatanya, his Russian guide and interpreter. The inspiration for Yardbird is a real writer, whom Killens declines to name, who was on television talking about how he had to get away from the "niggers" in Harlem. The use of the N-word alone, especially when not assigned to a fictional character, was enough to prompt Killens to respond. In current N-word debates, he would surely argue against its general use. He often summed up slavery and colonialism as the niggerizing of the earth and saw no positive place in the lexicon of Afro-Americanese for the word, which he termed the "alpha and omega word of our degradation" ("Rappin' with Myself" 118). To revel in "niggerness," he adds, "is to wallow complacently on the dunghill of our white-imposed degradation like a pig in a pool of mud" (118).

The Cotillion itself reads like a long Black Arts prose poem. The flowing, fast-paced, lean, sparse, "freed-up" writing is inspired by Amiri Baraka, for starters, as Johnson points out, and by Haki Madhubuti as well. As Yoruba is on the "A" train coming from work, "hot air, baby, by the ton, hot air was blown, stirred together by the whirligig electric fans overhead and shaken up by this St. Vitus-dancing, boogalooing, epileptic 'A' Train. Funky Broadway all the time. Funky! Oooh! Yeah! Dig it! Creating one overwhelming impact which rendered Yoruba's senses numb, and the dear child almost senseless" (10).

When Yoruba, now aboveground, strides toward her home, we get the type of impressionistic tribute to jazz that was commonplace among poets of the Black Arts era: "One Hundred and Twenty-fifth Street was also the street of sounds. Magnificent sounds. Jukeboxes all along the main stem blasting out the classics. Blowing love and hate and sorrow. Black classics. Serious music by serious musicians. Max Roach, Ray Charles, Lou Rawls, Etta Jones, Archie Shepp, John Coltrane, horn-blowing hornblowers" (14).

At the Uptown, Yoruba's initial perception of Lumumba is similar to the narrator's in Madhubuti's 1969 poem "But He Was Cool." Yoruba thinks "the cat on stage was clean. Not clean like Mister TV Clean, but handsome clean, hip clean, fine clean. Clean clean. Black clean" (64). In Madhubuti's poem, a character is depicted as "cool-cool ultracool was bop-cool/ice box cool" (39).

During a prep session for the Grand Cotillion, several members of the Femmes Fatales discover that Matt Lovejoy is a redcap at Penn Station, Pamela La-Smyhte's father is a janitor, and Charlene Robinson's writes the numbers. They exclaim, "Integration with white folks, yes, even with Jews and Jewesses, but to integrate with Black nobodies, this was carrying things too far" (84–85). Playing it straighter than Killens, Madhubuti delivers the same critique in his 1968 poem "The New Integrationist" by asserting, "I seek integration of negroes with black people" (21).

Other aspects of *The Cotillion* represent obvious verbal links to the author's own earlier efforts. For example, the frequent use of the phrase "Black and comely" to describe Yoruba is a twist, first used in *'Sippi*, on the biblical "black, but comely."[5] In this respect the novel can also be seen as companion and counterpart to one composed at almost exactly the same time, Toni Morrison's *The Bluest Eye*. Although the authors share a fundamental thesis—namely, that standards of beauty made pervasive by the dominant image machine often damage the self-esteem of African Americans—the resolution of the Morrison novel, given Pecola's insanity, is much more grim, an ending possible in the context of the novel because the Breedloves are incapable of providing the support and guidance (and thus the bitter irony of their names) to Pecola that the Lovejoys (whose name is apropos) can for Yoruba.

The Cotillion stands as one of Killens's most successful books. It proved commercially viable, received critical acclaim, and was nominated for the Pulitzer. The plot, as Addison Gayle notes, is a bit slight, but Killens gets all his licks in, explaining his poetic license in the foreword by means of Lumumba. Having experienced the "downtown white workshops" that stifled his creativity, the narrator makes a calculated decision to ignore their advice about craft: "I will intrude, protrude, obtrude or exclude my point of view any time it suits my disposition" (6). Of course, those familiar with Killens's prose, and with the rhetorical nature of prose in general, already knew this.

5

More Heroes

At the same time that he was composing *The Cotillion*, Killens was exploring other literary avenues for advancing his Black heroism project. The novels *Slaves*, *Great Gittin' Up Morning*, *A Man Ain't Nothin' but a Man*, and *Great Black Russian* all stem from this period. None has received much critical attention. *Slaves* is a novelization, *Great Gittin' Up Morning* and *A Man Ain't Nothin' but a Man* are usually classified as young adult stories, and *Great Black Russian* was passed over by commercial publishers. Nonetheless, they manifest many of the traits typical of Killens's more celebrated works and thus contribute to a coherent view of his rhetoric and poetics.

Slaves actually appeared before *The Cotillion*, being published in 1969. A film tie-in to the motion picture of the same title (in which Stephen Boyd, Ossie Davis, and Dionne Warwick starred), the novel details the events that lead to a slave insurrection. As a reviewer correctly noted in *Publishers Weekly*, *Slaves* "reads like the black answer to *Mandingo*" (99). But this comment was not an endorsement. The notion seemed to be that Killens counters a simplistic, psychologically underdeveloped tale of Black sexual animals lusting more after whites than after freedom by offering an equally simplistic, psychologically underdeveloped tale of slaves obsessed only with freedom. Perhaps so. However, such countering was considered a strong literary move among, say, some proponents of the Black Aesthetic. They would support an expanded fictional treatment, regardless of how stylized, of the point that Killens had been making all along—that is, the main preoccupation of slaves was emancipation, not lust for whites or servile adaptation to the fact of enslavement. *Slaves* furthers his project, begun in *Youngblood*, to render Southern experience with his sense of historical accuracy.

The plot is a slim one. Because of impending financial ruin, Mr. Stillwell separates Luke from his family and sells him, along with his sidekick Jericho. They end up on a cotton plantation in Mississippi owned by

Nathan Mackay, and labor under physically harsher conditions than had existed on the Stillwell horse farm in Kentucky. Nonetheless, Luke's pride and spirit are never broken, even by beating, in the way his master sees fit. Eventually, spurred on by the birth of a girl he helped to deliver, whom he named after his wife, Luke plots an escape and enlists the aid of Jericho. They plan to take along Cassy, who is Mackay's long-standing but now rebellious mistress, Evaline, his recent purchase, and the baby girl. The plan is discovered, and although the others actually do escape, Luke is killed by Mackay. But despite the simple plot and beyond the generally accepted evil of enslavement, there are ethical issues at the heart of the story worth pondering.

As the novel opens, Luke, the head slave on the Stillwell farm, is returning to Kentucky after being sent by his master to Ohio on a business mission. Luke voluntarily returns from the North to the South, a decision that puzzles his friend Jericho, who dubs him the "slavest slave of all" (11). Luke's decision to forgo his best chance at freedom is even questioned by his wife, Esther, who feels that Luke has acted irresponsibly, family ties notwithstanding. Luke's rationale for his return is that his "kindly" master has promised to manumit him and his family. His mistake lies in not reckoning that the master's economic self-interest would supersede so-called good intentions. So Luke is separated from his family anyway. Having blown his chance at freedom in the North, he is separated from them in slavery.

A second issue involves the slave's view of the sanctity of Black life under slavery. Cassy, as Sethe later would in *Beloved*, kills her own child rather than have it grow up a slave. Years later, after a decade as Stillwell's house mistress, her senses dulled by a steady supply of rum, she has not relented in her view, at least not during the early stages of the novel. She shows no sympathy toward baby Esther, who happens to be Mackay's daughter. She sees no point in the birth.

Slaves also represents Killens's fullest commentary on Christianity. He recognizes that Christianity is the most powerful system of values and beliefs among African Americans, so he chooses to encode his appeals for resistance inside a revolutionary interpretation of the Scriptures. Indeed, the rhetoric of and about Christianity serves as the binding structural element. Just as the gospel of Matthew (as in Lovejoy) appears in condensed form in *The Cotillion*, the evolving gospel of Luke (as in Stillwell) is central to *Slaves*. Although ironically, like Matt Lovejoy, Luke bears a New Testament name, his stance toward the Bible shifts from a more passive read to a rebellious one aligned more, at least in Killens's thinking, with the Old Testament.[1] At the outset of the novel, Luke takes solace in the fact that he lives on a so-called Christian plantation. All the Stillwell slaves have been baptized. Luke does not see as does Jericho (walls come tumbling down) that slavery is wrong in the absolute and is always to be opposed actively. Jericho believes that if the basic message is to be subservient, then the God in the Bible is the Massa's God. When Luke recalls that the Bible says "Servant, obey your master," Jericho rejoins that "If the Good Book say that, I don't need to learn to read" (22). As noted earlier, Luke's obedience is for naught, for Mr. Stillwell's so-called faith crumbles under economic pressure. As Mrs. Stillwell protests the sale of slaves, reminding her husband that as Christians they promised never to sell slaves to the South, Mr. Stillwell replies, "Christianity is one thing—slavery is something else altogether. . . . I have no intention of having my son come home from college to find I've let them take Stillwell Farms away from him" (20–21). Although Jericho would have Luke renounce the Bible at that point, arguing that it is the wrong JuJu for them, Luke takes his Bible with him when they are shipped off to New Orleans. Several weeks later, on a Sunday morning, with church bells ringing all over the city as backdrop, Luke and Jericho are auctioned, along with Evaline, to Mackay.

Mackay makes no pretense of being Christian. As he puts it, "I don't believe in villainy or virtue. Only in reality" (40). When he interrogates Luke back at his plantation, he asks Luke about his Bible and about Mrs. Stillwell's teaching him to read. Then Mackay remarks sarcastically, "Taught you to read, gave you the Bible, then took and sold you down the river. That's a Christian for you. . . . Here. I'm giving you the Bible too, but *I'm* going to keep you, Understand?" (47).

Even as the everyday backbreaking labor and repression of life on the Mackay plantation set in, Luke lies awake at night thinking wistfully about the past, not fruitfully confronting his present circumstances:

> It was a bad dream that he was dreaming and he would soon wake up in his neat little cabin with Esther in his arms and the children in their beds and old Massa and ol' Missus in the Big House, Kindly Christian people, and God was good and just and worked in mysterious ways but

> performed his wonders in due time, and Massa would keep his promise and set Luke free, the Lord looked out for his Chosen people. Wake up, Luke! He tried his damneddest to wake up from this nightmare. Wake up, Luke! Wake up, Luke and stop your dreaming and face this nightmare of reality. (56)

Only when Luke's faith evolves to the point where he can be as realistic as Mackay does he stand a chance of changing his condition. Jericho has insisted all along that if they are to embrace God, they must also embrace the idea, as generations of African Americans have been taught, that God helps those who help themselves.

While Luke is recovering from a brutal beating administered by overseers, he begins to gravitate more toward the Old Testament, in particular the story of Moses leading the Israelites from bondage. Luke doubts that he could be a Moses, but he views the birth of baby Esther as a providential sign and vows to make a good life for her somehow. Luke is further motivated after he works a party at the Big House. Like Daphne in *The Cotillion*, Luke is profoundly moved by a conversation he overhears that dispels any notions he still retained about a master's intentions. He hears Mackay lecture to his friends: "I took artists, sculptors, and turned them into niggers. And you got to keep them niggers twenty-four hours a day. You got to make them believe deep down in their hearts and souls they're niggers. The moment they stop thinking of themselves as niggers, you're in trouble. I wouldn't tolerate slaves on my farm that wouldn't call each other nigger" (95).[2] Later that night, down in the slave quarters, Luke acknowledges that Jericho has in fact been a true Christian all along because he never tried to be a "good nigger" and never believed in "good massas." "You a Christian," Luke tells him, "cause you always knew slavery was the Devil's workhouse, and you always worked to bring the building down" (101). In this spirit of understanding and brotherhood, the insurrection is planned. Unfortunately, Luke becomes a martyr, but baby Esther and Jericho, Cassy, and Evaline do leave the plantation with the help of several slaves and white sympathizer Mrs. Bennett. As in his other novels, Killens defines success for African Americans, even that laced with tragedy, as resulting from communal action and belief in common ideals. If Christianity is to be prominent among those ideals, then Killens clearly aims to promote a Christianity that is revolutionary.

Several other aspects link *Slaves* to Killens's other fiction. Jericho is the resident folk wit. Luke is cast physically in the Youngblood-Chaney-Lumumba mode, "tall and straight and handsome-black" (7). Cassy imagines him as a tall, Black, handsome Ashanti warrior, a man of supreme dignity. It is this image, this fearlessness, that awakens feelings of love and admiration in her. Cassy herself is described much like Yoruba Lovejoy: "Black and comely. . . . She was lovely, she was statuesque and queenly" (46). Cassy is sustained in part by the collection of African masks, a link to the African past, that is kept in the Big House.

The premises in *Slaves* are restated with even greater force in Killens's 1972 adolescent novel, *Great Gittin' Up Morning*. The plot also revolves, naturally, around a slave insurrection, in this case, Denmark Vesey's famous attempt at revolution in South Carolina. Vesey, in fact, managed to mobilize more than one thousand slaves to participate in a rebellion to take place in Charleston on June 16, 1822.[3] But perhaps the most intriguing aspect of the revolt to Killens was Vesey's status: a fairly prosperous free man even though his wife and children were slaves. Thus Killens is able to portray a hero whose love for family and brethren, and absolute hatred of American slavery, compels him to arms despite his own relatively secure status. Vesey is a more compelling figure than the equivocating though ultimately heroic Luke. Vesey already has what Luke and the others seek, namely freedom, and risks it in an attempt to liberate masses of Blacks.

Details of Vesey's early life are sketchy, and Killens takes the novelist's license to create events and character, such as predictably casting Vesey as uncommonly handsome and imposing, as are all his male protagonists up to that point. However, the latter parts of the novel are quite faithful to the historical record and to Vesey's character and temperament as a Talented Tenth role model. The fifty-five-year-old Vesey is described as critically literate and extremely well read. And as in many African-American stories, including several by Killens, we see the explicit connection between Black literacy and Black liberation:

> Denmark read everything he could get his hands on—newspapers, books, periodicals, magazines. He had a reading acquaintance with the abolitionist movement, the antislavery movement Quakers, the Underground Railroad. . . . He kept up with the debates in the United

> States Congress. He had read antislavery pamphlets smuggled into town by seamen. He knew the U.S. Constitution and the Declaration of Independence and the Bill of Rights. He could recite each one verbatim. The more he read, the more he heard from the mouths of seamen, the more he overheard from Haitian refugees, the more bitter was the pill of slavery for this proud Black man to swallow. (10–11)

This depiction of Vesey probably derives from one provided by historian John Lofton in *Insurrection in South Carolina*.[4]

Although Denmark Vesey was a great man, it is not a great man theory of history that produces him in Killens's novel. The author recognizes the relative prosperity of Blacks in Charleston and the unusual mobility that slaves in the area enjoyed. Because the city was an important commercial port, there was great demand for artisan labor such as carpenters (as Vesey was), blacksmiths, mechanics, and lumberyard workers. Blacks vastly outnumbered working-class whites (as well as whites overall); thus, they were the major part of the workforce. Slaveowners hired out their slaves, many of whom were skilled, with the bulk of the wages earned going to the masters. This arrangement was generally more profitable than using those slaves to pick cotton. So, ironically, it was the slaveowners' greed that helped establish the fluid community in which the idea of insurrection would take hold. The fact of this historical development supported Killens's belief that slaves, as well as truly conscious and committed free Blacks, were in general not appeased by halfway measures. Vesey, therefore, was supported by numerous co-conspirators who were also free men or relatively privileged slaves, such as Ned and Rolla Bennett, the governor's own servants.

Killens extends the commentary about liberatory religion embedded in *Slaves*. Vesey "preached freedom and liberation right out of the Holy Bible" (61). Like Luke Stillwell, Killens's Vesey gravitates toward the story of Moses, positing that God will turn on Blacks if they do not attempt to liberate themselves. Justifying his decision not to spare women or children during the planned rebellion, Vesey quotes Joshua 6:21, "and they utterly destroyed all that was in the city, both man and woman, young and old, and ox, and sheep, and ass, with the edge of the sword" (63–64). Down to the particular citing of the Scriptures, this passage is historically accurate. But for Killens, Christianity has no automatically privileged place among religious rituals, as indicated by his description of the conspirators on the verge of action. "Some had engaged in voodoo rites all night long the night before. Some prayed to the Christian god, Jehovah, others prayed to the god of Islam, Allah, before whom there was no other. Some prayed to three or four gods simultaneously" (101–2). Killens's concern is not with a particular deity; any god is fine who sanctions Black revolution.

The rebellion is ultimately thwarted. One hundred seventeen Blacks are charged as a result; of that number seventy-nine are put on trial. Thirty-four are hanged, including all the principal leaders except Monday Gell, who turns informant. Thirty-nine of the convicted and many of the innocent are exiled from the state. Laws subsequently passed by the state legislature include one that bars Blacks who leave the state from returning; another requires that after June 1, 1823, every free Black over fifteen years of age have a white guardian who would be legally responsible for him.

At Vesey's trial, witnesses who testified against him, like William Paul and George Wilson, argued that Vesey had misused the Bible to foment an uprising. The presiding judge, Lionel H. Kennedy, in pronouncing the sentence, declared (and Killens takes this from the actual trial report):

> In addition to treason, you have committed the grossest impiety, in attempting to pervert the sacred words of God and torture them into a sanction for the crimes of the blackest hue. It is evident, that you are totally insensible of the divine influence of that Gospel, "all of whose paths lead to peace." It was to reconcile us to our destinies on earth, and to enable us to discharge with fidelity, all the duties of life, that those holy precepts were imparted by heaven to fallen man.
>
> If you had searched them with sincerity, you would have discovered instructions, immediately applicable to the deluded victims of your artful wiles—"Servants (says Saint Paul) obey in all things your masters, according to the flesh, not with eye-service, as men-pleasers, but in the singleness of heart, fearing God." And then again, "Servants (says Saint Peter) be subject to your masters with all fear, not only to the good and gentle, but also to the forward." (*Great Gittin' Up Morning* 123–24; *The Trial Record of Denmark Vesey* 136)

For Killens's Vesey, however, his own take on the Bible is correct. As he thinks to himself in the courtroom, "The master and the slave would never have identical interpretations" (125).

Killens turns to another familiar icon in his 1975 adolescent novel *A Man Ain't Nothin' but a Man*, a book based on John Henry, the legendary steel driver who reportedly worked for the Chesapeake and Ohio Railroad in the 1870s on the dangerous Big Bend tunnel project in West Virginia. He has been the source of numerous songs and tales. The most common versions, as well as most tame, are that John Henry, a former slave, was a proud and stubborn man who pitted his enormous strength and ability against a steam drill in an attempt to delay mechanization. Although John Henry won the contest, he died when it was over from a stroke or heart attack. The fundamental structure of any John Henry tale derives from the basic ballad, more accurately termed a matrix of ballads. As identified by Norm Cohen, there are five elements:

> 1. an infantile premonition,
> 2. preparation for the contest (including the challenge, a financial incentive, John Henry's request for hammers of a specific weight, and the like),
> 3. the contest itself (usually limited to such information as who stood where, how rapidly each contestant drove, John Henry's comments as the contest proceeded, and praise for John Henry's powerful strokes),
> 4. the hero's last words, death, and burial, and
> 5. much editorializing on his woman (the clothes she wore, her behavior at his funeral, sometimes her own steel-driving prowess) (72)

All the details that would make up a lengthy narrative have been subjected to the interpretation of various storytellers, including the specific motivation for the contest, how John Henry obtained his freedom, the nature of his personality, his relationship to his family and home, whether he had a son or not, whether his main love interest was Lucy or Polly Ann, whether he was married, what feats of heroism were performed, the margin of his victory over the steam drill, the length of the contest, and even where he was born (he's been claimed by every state in the South).

As a boy growing up in Georgia, Killens undoubtedly heard a variety of John Henry songs and stories. He probably became aware at some point of the version published in the *Messenger* in 1925 by A. Philip Randolph and Chandler Owen. In their version, John Henry receives his freedom because he saves his master from drowning, not an action Killens would advocate. John Henry and his former master are described as best friends, yet John Henry's girlfriend, Lucy, remains enslaved on the plantation. Therefore, John Henry is largely motivated to work in order to purchase Lucy's freedom from someone who is supposed to be his best friend. Randolph and Owen do portray John Henry as "pure Negro" and deem him noble, but his facial features are described as ugly. The showdown with the steam drill is to help his master win a $500 bet, of which John Henry is promised $50. When Captain Walters informs a dying John Henry that they won the contest, John Henry affirms in third-person plural, "We've beat him" (75).

Perhaps the dominant John Henry story by the 1970s, as W. Nikola-Lisa suggests, was Ezra Jack Keats's *John Henry: An American Legend*. Keats's tale is not political with respect to the African-American community. As Nikola-Lisa notes: "John Henry's death symbolizes for Keats the waning of the prized American ideal of individualism. It is in this respect that Keats' John Henry gains widespread appeal, but at the price of ignoring the underlying racial tension inherent in the conflict between John Henry, an ex-slave, and white railroad bosses notorious for their exploitation of black laborers" (54). Killens was likely aware of the Keats version as well. The episode where John Henry saves the lives of a work crew by bravely preventing an explosion probably is drawn from that source. But as Brett Williams asserts, "Killens' John Henry is clearly a black hero and a laboring hero. He does not represent dumb brute strength, but rather links his contest with the machine drill to human dignity" (93).

Killens's John Henry thus evokes memories of Joe and Robby Youngblood although in real time, of course, John Henry was one of the models that shaped the Youngblood males. At any rate, like the Youngbloods and most of the writer's characters, his John Henry never learns to "grin and bow and scrape and take low in front of white folks" (18). Although the notion of being a steel driver, like his father, has been on John Henry's mind from the time he was a toddler, he actually chooses the vocation because it pays significantly higher wages than picking cotton on the plantation or rousting cotton on the waterfront. As such, the job increases the prospects that he and his wife, Polly Anne, can purchase a farm. As he explains to her: "We done worked on somebody else's land all our natcherl born days, and I'm working for the day to come when we can work our own soil and for our own selves and our chilluns. That's what I'm looking forward to. That's what freedom got to mean to all us Black folks. . . . Our own sweet black earth. Freedom don't mean nothin' if it don't mean that" (75–76). That all political power is based on the ownership of land, that it is the basis of nation building, has been, of course, a key principle of Black nationalist discourse.

On the other hand, what does not fit easily into Black nationalist discourse are the images of fellowship involving John Henry, Uncle Buddy, Ben Lawson, a white coworker, and the Chinese-American worker George Ling Lee. As a group they regularly dine at John Henry's home. Notwithstanding, ethnic differences do remain, and they are exploited by Captain Joe Brad, who spreads racist rumors to drive a wedge between the workers. Only Polly Anne's intervention keeps a confrontation between John Henry and Ben Lawson from becoming tragic. As they all afterward talk in Ben Lawson's home, John Henry discusses the limitation of ethnic alliances, telling Lawson that "when it come down to a test where a man really live at, you a white man first and a good man afterwards" (151). Lawson vehemently denies the charge, eventually arguing that he treats all men fairly regardless of color. He blames one of the captain's instigators, Will Hodge, for the trouble and plans to shoot him. John Henry counters by interceding, and he explains that Will Hodge is but a pawn being used by management. The more the men talk and understand management's tactics, the more the story turns back toward a transethnic leftist awareness reminiscent of portions of *Youngblood*, *And Then We Heard the Thunder*, and *Black Man's Burden*. John Henry, Uncle Buddy, Lawson, and Lee understand, a lesson Killens himself recalls from his union organizing days, how racism is employed to undermine working-class solidarity, with the result that management increases the profit margin at the expense of workers' well-being. As they wind up their session, John Henry reminds the others, "Just remember, a man ain't nothin' but a man, don't care what color he be. It seem such a hard thing to remember, especially hard for the poor white working folks" (154).

A popular song version recorded by Harry Belafonte, to whom Killens's novel is in fact dedicated, expresses the same sentiment about manhood:

> John Henry said to his Captain,
> "A man ain't nothin' but a man,
> And before I'll let your steam drill beat me down
> Gonna die with my hammer in my hand, Lord, Lord,
> Gonna die with my hammer in my hand."

The lyrics Killens uses in his novel are more explicit concerning ethnicity:

> A man ain't nothin' but a man—
> A man ain't nothin' but a man.
> He can be white or Black,
> He can be yellow or tan,
> It makes no difference when it's man to man.
> It's been like that since the world began.
> A man ain't nothin' but a man. (24)

By the time we get to the climactic challenge, the story is more complicated than the usual John Henry tale because of the merger of Black nationalist and broader leftist sentiments. In order to prevent cuts in wages or layoffs, John Henry tries to prove that a full complement of men is more economically expedient than machines. He feels a particular responsibility to save jobs for Black workers, knowing that other job prospects for them almost always mean a return to some plantation and a menial existence. After he wins the contest by drilling ten inches deeper than the drill, and presumably saves the jobs, he admits, facing his death, that mechanization is inevitable. In his view, the enemy is not machines, the unwise use of them is. The implied line of reasoning, of course, is that if economic inequality that damages Blacks were to persist, then that would constitute evidence that machines were indeed being misused.

Williams labels *A Man Ain't Nothin' but a Man* the best of the popular fiction about John Henry. While faithful to the Cohen outline, Killens writes an unusually political, family-oriented tale. In addition, he breaks the cycle of tragedy often indicated in the ballads. As Williams writes of

John Henry, "Often he addresses his last words to this child, and often he warns the boy that he too will die a steel-driving man" (124). In the Killens story the child has yet to be born and its sex is unknown. Beyond that, John Henry has agreed with Polly Anne that if they have a son he would not become a steel driver. "I wants him to be a doctor or a school-teacher, a leader of the people or something like that whatsonever he be" (127). Here is another Du Boisian, Talented Tenth twist to a Killens novel. Thus Polly Anne does not demonstrate any steel-driving prowess at the close of the novel, as is the case in many other versions of the tale. She makes no attempt to replicate John Henry's life, but by picking up his hammer she does intend to feel his strength and goodness as a source of inspiration: "And understood she must be strong. For their unborn child. And for the things for which he fought and died. And for all the future generations" (176).

Killens's last published novel, *Great Black Russian: A Novel on the Life and Times of Alexander Pushkin*, was also directly inspired by Harry Belafonte, who suggested in the 1960s that a biographical treatment of Pushkin could be a viable film project. Killens began the background research, became hooked on the subject, and for well over a decade studied materials about the man generally considered the greatest of all Russian poets. Unfortunately, the novel (the movie never happened) was not published until 1989, two years after the author's death.

There are several reasons Killens would be enamored of Pushkin. He was a poet in a culture where writers could achieve great fame and stature. He was a vernacular artist who spoke, unlike many of his French-worshipping predecessors, in the voice of the Russian masses. He wrote in support of revolutionary causes. Obviously, however, the irresistible attraction was Pushkin's African ancestry, thus the chance to portray in fiction another Black hero. Addison Gayle writes of Killens in the introduction to the novel:

> He is, like Pushkin, "the people's poet," one for whom concern with people is more important than wealth or fame. It is this concern which enables both him and the subject whose life he carefully researched and ably presented in fiction to remain vibrant forces in the daily lives of revolutionaries/romantics everywhere. When he visited Moscow and was taken on a tour which included the shrine to Pushkin, he stood

> looking down at the crypt of this black Russian poet. At that moment, two centuries of history merged and one poet reached across the vast expanse of time and distance to embrace another. (13)

Pushkin's great-grandfather on his mother's side was Ibrahim Hannibal, also known as the Negro of Peter the Great. This fact is highlighted throughout the first quarter of the novel—with both negative and positive connotations. As the elder Pushkin argues with his son and tries to persuade the budding poet to stop writing poems in Russian as opposed to French, he cruelly refers to young Pushkin as "you little African bastard!" (39). As his mother scolds young Pushkin to be more like his little brother and sister, who incidentally do not look Africoid, she remarks that "he just has the devil in him. It's his African blood rising up in him" (43). Positive comments about his African heritage come from his grandmother. Referring to Hannibal, using a favorite Killens description, she allows that "he was so tall and Black and comely" (47). On several occasions, suffering from stress and loneliness, Pushkin himself conjures up visions of Hannibal, who apparently enjoyed a distinguished career in Czar Peter's court. The first apparition occurs when Pushkin (also known as Sasha) is a student at the Lyceum, which he attended between the ages of twelve and eighteen. As Pushkin lies on his bed after a talk with his grandmother, "the tall Black man with dark eyes that seemed to pierce the darkness with their intensity came to his bedside and talked with him about times gone by, when he himself was a boy in far away Africa, a young Ethiopian prince" (77). Shortly thereafter, Pushkin declares to a schoolmate, a point he repeats on several occasions, "I'm an African-Russian. . . . A Russian with an African descendancy" (79).

Killens provides what is perhaps the most "African read" possible of Pushkin's life given the available data. He is joined in this effort by Gayle, who, depicting Pushkin, writes of the "overwhelming impact made upon him by his African ancestor" (Introduction 11). Gayle also credits Ibrahim Hannibal with much of Pushkin's moral development as the "poet who loved human freedom and who despised chains and shackles everywhere" (11). However, it can be argued, and many have, that Pushkin was far more Russian than anything else. Nor could Killens seriously dispute that claim, a point he conceded during a 1983 interview with Kenneth Peeples. It ought to be noted as well that the Pushkin name, traceable to the early fifteenth century, was one of the oldest among the nobility in Russia, and although Pushkin was indeed fascinated with his Ethiopian ties, he was also proud of his father's lineage. He named his younger son Grigorii after the first known male in the Pushkin line. But Killens, defending his strong Africanist rendering, emphasized that Pushkin acknowledged and took pride in his African heritage. This is certainly true as indicated by the fact that Pushkin left behind an unfinished novel titled *The Negro of Peter the Great*. Additionally, that sense of pride apparently influenced his views on the plight of fellow Blacks, including those enslaved in the West. Avrahm Yarmolinsky notes that Pushkin spoke on at least one occasion of "my brother Negroes" (14). It would be hard, though, to credit Hannibal, who owned a thousand slaves according to Killens himself, with his great-grandson's antislavery sentiment. The more immediate source was always before him—millions of peasants and serfs whose suffering was understood and detested by a sensitive and sympathetic artist.

So Pushkin is not solely a Black hero, but he is enough of one to fit easily among the Killens line of protagonists. He resembles Luke Stillwell, for example, when he argues that he is morally right to deceive oppressive rulers. To recall part of the climactic scene in *Slaves*:

> Mackay said, "You were lying through your teeth, weren't you, Boy?"
>
> Luke pondered the master's words, then said, in a trembly voice, "Man, I don't owe you the truth." (131)

During his meeting with Nicholas, Pushkin remembers how he had once replied to a fellow student who chided him for lying to the authorities: "There are Imperial truths and there are gospel truths, and they are just about the same, mostly lies. . . . Then there are truths that liberate the people, which are altogether different. I do not owe the Imperial Court the people's truth. All I owe it is damnation and exposure" (266).

Pushkin also favors a host of Killens characters, stretching all the way back to Big Mama in *Youngblood*, when he instructs a serf, Olga Kalasnikova, never to love her master, even if it is he. He is not to be admired for impregnating the woman, but he does sign manumission papers to set her free in the days following their most important conversation. As Olga expresses love and a desire to remain his serf girl, Pushkin instructs her that "you must learn to hate your master, sweet woman. You want to be free, don't you?" (230).

Pushkin was not a thoroughly committed and uncompromising rebel like Denmark Vesey, yet his influence was profound, an impact Killens understood well. To the extent that Russian workers read any poetry, it was Pushkin's that they read. Subversives were often caught with copies of his poems in their possession. Masses of people responded favorably to poems like his "Ode to Freedom."[5] Such writing and other agitation led to his being exiled by Czar Alexander.

In terms of concrete political acts, Pushkin is best known as the "Bard of the Decembrists." After the death of Czar Alexander in 1825, his brother Nicholas ascended to the throne. A rebellion was planned for December 14 but was crushed by the emperor's Horse Guards. Five members of the group, which became known as the Decembrists, were hanged and several others banished to Siberia. Many were Pushkin's friends and, in fact, had been inspired by him. The following year, Pushkin was summoned from his exile in Mikhailovskoye by Nicholas for a face-to-face meeting at the conclusion of which Nicholas announced a "new" Pushkin. The next eleven years, the last of his life, were spent in an uneasy relationship with the czar.

Ironically, though he is indeed born of nobility, Killens's Pushkin is less noble than his other tragic heroes. Despite his genius and impact, he is a brooding, often depressed talent, who spends far too much time dissipating, playing cards, and being complicit in the exploitation of serfs. He is the product of a decadent family that has no particular commitment to social justice. He dies at the age of thirty-seven, not mortally wounded in the fight against racism and economic exploitation, but as the result of a duel fought because of a love affair between his wife and the Frenchman George Charles d'Anthes. Nor is he anywhere near the Killens physical prototype at a diminutive five-feet-four inches, with "sallow jaundiced" skin (17).[6] Yet he was of African descent and, in general, valiantly for the people.

Yarmolinsky thinks that Alexander Pushkin is best understood as a poet who, "though not a man of the masses, felt with them by reason of his deep humanity, and had their emancipation at heart" (13). Those qualities—and Ibrahim—are his ticket into the Killens pantheon.

6

Ideology and Writers' Conferences

A serious survey of the impact of John Oliver Killens on public discourse must include attention to the literary conferences he organized. They function as "texts" that amplify his views on literary politics. This is not to suggest that Killens could script any of the conference participants. Sophisticated and articulate on their own, they capably spoke for themselves, sometimes, in turn, influencing Killens. The point, however, is that Killens generally knew who could be counted on to deliver messages he favored; therefore, the conferences largely functioned as elaborate sets of testimonials. It is in this sense that novelist Arthur Flowers, a Killens protégé, likes warmly to regard him as an "ideological orchestrator."[1] On the other hand, one can hardly help but recall the dim view of such orchestration expressed by Harold Cruse, who, referring specifically to a 1965 conference directed by Killens, wrote that "Negro Writers Conferences settle nothing, solve nothing, pose nothing, analyze nothing, plan nothing, create nothing—not even a decent new literary review—which is the least any bunch of serious, self-respecting writers with a gripe ought to do" (*Crisis of the Negro Intellectual* 498). Cruse does allow that at the 1965 conference, he heard papers that were "informative, eloquent, and pointed" (501). One should suppose that a paper that is informative demonstrates at the very least a posing of some sort, likely involves a modicum of analysis, and potentially resolves some issues or ambiguities as well. It is true that these affairs do not put to rest great cultural questions, no more than a church resolves everyone's moral dilemmas because services happen to be held. For example, utter repudiation of socialist realism in exchange for a strict Black nationalist aesthetic or detailed proposals for building a Black cultural infrastructure, items that supposedly were on Cruse's agenda, obviously cannot be treated with finality in such affairs.

While one can certainly sympathize with Cruse's frustration concerning the immediately generative limitations of conferences, the Killens record on developing cultural mechanisms is actually impressive. The

Harlem Writers Guild, which he cofounded in 1950, remains an important workshop more than fifty years later and currently operates out of the Schomburg Center for Research in Black Culture. Its members—ranging from the late John Henrik Clarke to Maya Angelou to Terry McMillan to Walter Mosley—have produced literally hundreds of books. In addition to workshop activities, the guild sponsors outreach activities in venues such as libraries and schools to promote African-American literature. Some of the growth and success of the guild has to be attributed to Killens's high profile as a literary organizer, an element that was part and parcel of the writers' conferences he directed. In addition, Killens was a member of the collective that founded *Freedomways: A Quarterly Review of the Negro Freedom Movement*, which was one of the more notable journals founded in the 1960s and which largely served as a publishing outlet for the Harlem Writers Guild.[2] Although not strictly a literary organ, *Freedomways* featured creative writing and literary reviews (all of Killens's major books were reviewed) because its founders were extremely interested in the relation of the arts to the Black freedom struggle.[3] Writers whose work appeared in the journal include Alex Haley, Alice Walker, Pablo Neruda, Derek Walcott, Mari Evans, Langston Hughes, Sterling Brown, James Baldwin, Gwendolyn Brooks, Nikki Giovanni, Arna Bontemps, and June Jordan.

Writers' conferences, while not perfect, can and in fact do serve as important vehicles of inspiration and cultural diffusion. Attendance now numbers in the thousands at the occasional Black Writers Conferences convened at Medgar Evers College, where Killens sparked the inaugural meeting in 1986.[4] An annual conference, a goal of Killens, has been conducted since 1991 by Haki Madhubuti, whose first national exposure came at an event led by Killens in 1968.[5]

Despite whatever shortcomings, then, the conferences Killens spearheaded between 1965 and 1986 remain a noteworthy contribution and are important milestones in Black literary history. The focus here is on the major lines of argument, developed by both Killens and several key panelists, which bind the occasions into a coherent whole.

Killens's affinity and agenda for writers' conferences can be traced back to one sponsored in 1959 by the American Society of African Culture (AMSAC). The theme was "The American Negro Writer and His Roots," and the author sat as chairman of the planning committee, which included William Branch, John Henrik Clarke, Julian Mayfield, Loften Mitchell, and Sarah Wright. In addition to the members of the planning group, panelists included Samuel Allen, Arna Bontemps, Arthur P. Davis, Langston Hughes, and J. Saunders Redding. In his own paper, Killens sounded a theme most urgent to him—that is, the production of positive, optimistic, affirming Black literature. He also outlined the following five-point proposal to be presented to the general body of AMSAC, a proposal to provide incentives for African-American authors:

> 1. The establishment of an annual award for creative writing in the area of Negro life.
> 2. The establishment of annual grants to send one or more Negro writers to Africa for a period of six months or longer, with the hope that they may be inspired to write a novel or a play on some aspect of this gigantic subject.
> 3. The establishment of a theatre for producing and encouraging plays on Negro life.
> 4. The publication of a periodical for Negro writers and for material about the Negro.
> 5. The establishment of an annual conference for Negro writers. ("Opportunities for Development of Negro Talent" 70)

The last point, of course, is the one in which Killens would invest the most energy. AMSAC did not establish an annual conference, nor could he. But he pursued the idea doggedly and staged major conferences whenever he could command the necessary resources.

The 1965 conference, titled "The Negro Writer's Vision of America," was held at the New School for Social Research, where Killens served as writer-in-residence. Held in April, three months after the death of Lorraine Hansberry, the gathering was convened in honor of the late playwright. Panelists included John Henrik Clarke, Ossie Davis, Sarah Wright, Loften Mitchell, LeRoi Jones, and James Baldwin, all of whom shared amicable experiences with Killens.[6] A conspicuous development was that Ralph Ellison, who had an adversarial relationship with Killens dating back to Killens's review of *Invisible Man* in 1952, declined to attend. To expect Ellison to participate—and Cruse is right on this score—was unreasonable given the aesthetic and political bent of Killens and his associates in the Harlem Writers Guild, who formed the main strand of the event. Furthermore, critical remarks subsequently made at the conference, primarily by John Henrik Clarke and white historian Herbert Aptheker, practically assured that Ellison would never attend a gathering where Killens was at the helm. Clarke, for instance, in a response to positive comments about Ellison made by NAACP Labor Secretary Herbert Hill, asserted:

> I hope Mr. Hill can be brief with this exaggeration of the role of Ralph Ellison who has spent so much time in the last ten years in flight from his own people and has not even answered most mail addressed to him by his fellow black writers and has said positively that art and literature are not racial. He won't come into any Afro-American writer's conference. I think Ellison wrote one very interesting thing. From the point of view of craftsmanship it was a very good and powerful work. Whether Ralph Ellison will follow up, whether Ralph Ellison has grown up is open to question in many quarters starting with me. (qtd. in *Crisis of the Negro Intellectual* 507)

Aptheker added the opinion regarding Ellison that "in terms of what he has published and also his published assertions, he has made himself rather not particularly visible in the struggles of the Negro people" (508).

Although Clarke was particularly harsh on Ellison (Killens had softened his stance by then), it must be noted that criticism of Ellison was not isolated.[7] He was often received with hostility by African-American college students. Even if Clarke, as well as Killens, had been absent from the New School event, it is unlikely that Ellison, had he participated, would have been embraced by many in the audience, which consisted largely of Black cultural nationalists and old-line leftists.

Of the writers present at the conference, James Baldwin was the one who received the most attention, both positive and negative. He held the audience in suspense with his keynote address but by the end of the conference had been labeled, according to Gay Talese, "an extremely talented literary prostitute" by conferee Myrna Baines, who was reportedly on the staff of *National Review*, the conservative publication edited by William Buckley (26). However, for present purposes, the crucial aspect of the appearance of Baldwin, the star invitee, is the degree to which his rhetoric compared and contrasted to that of Killens. To be sure, the two had different artistic visions. One can imagine Killens, who invariably stressed Black nobility and heroism, cringing as Baldwin announced that "I modeled myself on the junkies and whores because they form my background" and that "my history began on the auction block." As Killens, and Malcolm X, had asserted, "It is important for us to know that our history did not begin with slavery's scars."[8] On the other hand, Baldwin offered a revisionist take on American history and insisted that the moral obligation of artists was to fight for social justice. As described by M. S. Handler of the *New York Times*:

> One of the American tragedies, Mr. Baldwin said in his speech, is that the "white people cannot face the lies of their own history."
>
> He asserted that the "white Anglo-Saxons" had falsified the history of the United States and were today prisoners of their own myth-making. He scathingly spoke of the earliest settlers that had abandoned Europe out of sheer poverty or had come out of English jails only to manufacture "aristocratic" status for themselves in the colonies. "Who," he asked, "knows anything about the Virginia aristocrats outside of Virginia?"
>
> Mr. Baldwin continued, "The liberation of the people of this country, our lowly people, our junkies, and, yes, our middle class, depends on whether we are able to make a real confrontation with our history. For you face more terrible trials before you can emerge from the age of puberty."
>
> All the black artist is trying to do, he told his stunned audience, is "to make you remember who you really are." (31)

This second strand of Baldwin's presentation suited Killens just fine. One may even wonder, given the previous interactions between Killens and Baldwin, and recalling once again the collaboration between Killens and Malcolm X, how much of Baldwin's speech was directly influenced by the conference director. Or how responsible was Baldwin for the content of some of Killens's later speeches? Either way, the emphasis on American history as a literary and rhetorical battle was often part of Killens's opening remarks at subsequent conferences, including the last one he organized. As he spoke of history at the National Black Writers Conference in 1986:

> Americans have never been able to face their history, which is why the American people are inflicted with a Cowboy-Indian mentality, like the clannish cowboy in the White House with a mind set that imagines still charging up San Juan Hill with the white man's burden, with Teddy Roosevelt with his Big Stick Policy. Think of Manifest Destiny, Monroe Doctrine, Gun Boat Diplomacy. That's a hell of a lot of historical distortion to carry around from year to year. It is up especially to the writer to do the American people a favor and rub America's nostrils in the dung heap of its history, which is genocide and murder in the hundred millions of black and red men and women, and thievery of an entire North American land mass. That is the history of this country that it has never faced. Until America faces its history there will continue to be police actions, Vietnams, Bays of Pigs, Grenada invasions, overthrows of democratically elected governments such as in Chile, counterrevolutionary activities in central America, presidential schizophrenia and on and on.[9]

In "Reverberations from a Writers' Conference," Hoyt Fuller, one of the proponents of the emerging Black Arts Movement, noted that the 1965 conference reflected "the deepening estrangement of the Negro writer from the so-called 'mainstream' of American literature" (78). In particular, he cited the disparaging remarks made by white critic Richard Gilman, drama critic for *Newsweek* magazine, and the rebuttal by LeRoi Jones. On a panel titled "What Negro Playwrights Are Saying," Gilman argued Black playwrights were only in a preliminary stage, a notion dismissed by Jones and, subsequently, by Fuller as well.[10] For Fuller, Gilman's comments illustrated a problem faced by Black writers, artists whose commercial success was often jeopardized because of unfavorable reviews by white critics. The eventual solution, in Fuller's view, entailed cultivating a strong relationship between Black writers and Black audiences. If Black writers turned to their community, Fuller reasoned, the community would be supportive, forcing a change in the white critical reception, which, in turn, would lead to a larger readership overall for Black writers. As Fuller concludes, "Once Negro writers are honored in Harlem, then the critics will come to Harlem, bringing with them the general public. But this time around, the critics will have accepted Negro writers on the writers' own terms, and that will make all the difference" (84). Fuller deemed the conference a success in terms of popular support and apparently hoped it could spur the activity he advocated.

By the time the New School conference was held, Killens had accepted a position as writer-in-residence at Fisk University. There he organized conferences in 1966, 1967, and 1968. The 1966 conference was convened around the theme "The Image of the Negro in American Literature." Esteemed social critic J. Saunders Redding, who participated in the AMSAC conference, served as the opening keynote speaker and charged that some African-American writers were developing an inappropriate line of characters, arguing that they were "making heroes out of heels" (Llorens 55). He specifically mentioned John A. Williams, Chester Himes, Rosa Guy, and James Baldwin. The respective works in question were *Night Song*, *If He Hollers Let Him Go*, *Bird at My Window*, and *Another Country*. While the remarks proved provocative, and expressed sentiments not wholly shared by Killens, it was evident that the morally upright characters that Killens created met with the approval of Redding, as well as much of the audience, and were his preferred prototypes.

Redding's remarks would not have been surprising to those, like Killens, who were aware of his previous and consistent pronouncements about African-American literature. As far back as 1945, in an essay titled "The Negro Author: His Publisher, His Public and His Purse," Redding criticized the likes of Wallace Thurman (*Blacker the Berry*) and Claude McKay (*Banana Bottom*) for producing "empty, banal, pseudo-exotic tripe that is sometimes taken as the substance of Negro life in America" (146). Similarly, in his 1949 essay "American Negro Literature," he inveighed against negative stereotypes of Blacks reflected in the writing of both Black and white authors.[11] Those ideas were basically restated ten years later, often verbatim, in his address at the AMSAC conference, which was titled "The Negro Writer and His Relationship to His Roots," and in the 1965 *Negro Digest* print symposium, "The Task of the Negro Writer as Artist." Most recently, in the April 1966 issue of *The Crisis*, which was published just before his appearance at Fisk, he reviewed Guy's novel and made the "heroes out of heels" comment that he repeated at the conference. The criticism of Himes was ironic, though, because in the 1949 essay he praised Himes's *If He Hollers Let Him Go* and *Lonely Crusade* as notable literary achievements and examples of successful appeals to both Black and white audiences.

Killens himself sat on the panel titled "The Novel and Its Social Relevance to the Negro Revolution." After stating his familiar claim, inspired by Du Bois, that all art is propaganda, he went on to insist that "our literature should have social relevance to the world struggle and *especially* to the struggle of black Americans" (Llorens 57). In a similar vein, novelist William Melvin Kelley declared that "the task of the Negro writer should differ from that of the white writer in that, among other things, he should be addressing himself to the Negro" (Llorens 64). Overall, ideas about Black consciousness, Black affirmation, and politically useful art—core values to Killens—received considerable play and were compatible with the prevailing mood of the conference attendees.

Perhaps the most inspirational, strategic, and consequential articulation of the identity politics most promoted at the conference was voiced by Melvin B. Tolson. Tolson served partly as a counterpart to the thought and presence of Robert Hayden, the distinguished poet who was a professor at Fisk during Killens's tenure. The relationship between the two faculty members was contentious at best because of institutional decisions and openly expressed disagreements between the two about literary politics. Hayden had been at Fisk for twenty years, had been continually saddled with a heavy teaching load that hampered his poetic productivity, and had covered everything the English department had demanded of him. Yet he was deprived of opportunities to teach creative writing courses once Killens arrived. Furthermore, Hayden decried Killens's views about art and politics, and he disapproved of how popular those views were among the student body. Maybe mindful of an earlier time when writing by African Americans was sometimes described as "okay for a Negro," Hayden characteristically referred to himself as a poet who only happened to be Negro.[12] Although he wrote several of the most accomplished poems about the Black experience and social justice, pieces like "Middle Passage," "Runagate, Runagate," "Frederick Douglass," and "Homage to the Empress of the Blues," he would not embrace Black cultural nationalism. At any rate, Hayden, who served on the conference planning committee, knew he would be facing a largely hostile audience—not as a poet, he was warmly applauded at the literary reading—but as a panelist. *Negro Digest* editor David Llorens captures his performance:

> Reading lines from Yeats, Hayden solemnly commented, "I don't have to be Irish to love those lines.

> "Let's quit saying we're black writers writing to black folks—it has been given importance it should not have." Hayden's anticipation of opposition gave way to a slight stutter. "I don't think we're consciously trying to escape."
>
> His sensibility shaken to the point of anger, Hayden continued: "Please notice this—all you folks sitting out there waiting to jump down my neck." He proceeded to define poetry as "the beauty of perception given form . . . the art of saying the impossible." (Llorens 62)

Hayden's proposal for a more nuanced understanding of any writer's role and work failed to sway many in the crowd.

Tolson indeed proved dynamic. Although in his mid-sixties and battling stomach cancer to which he would succumb only four months later, he turned in a performance that Killens surely appreciated. As depicted by Llorens: "The audience, now spellbound, listened as the man who might affectionately be called the grandfather of the conference spoke of the tridimensionality of man, 'A man has his biology, his sociology, and his psychology—*and then he becomes a poet*'" (62). "Tolson then looked mischievously at Hayden and bellowed, 'I'm a black poet, an African-American poet, a Negro poet. I'm no accident—and I don't give a tinker's damn what you think'" (63).

Tolson, a former dramatist and longtime debate coach, probably would have been too much of a match for Hayden rhetorically even if the audience had been neutral. In front of the assemblage in Jubilee Hall, incited by Killens, both before and at the conference (to be partial to Tolson's analysis), Hayden had no shot. Ironically, Hayden and Tolson were not that far apart aesthetically, often grouped together as examples of technically excellent Black modernists (which also drew Tolson, the more obscure of the two, some criticism from Black Aestheticians).[13] And there was considerable mutual respect between the two poets, who had known each other for years. In 1952 they both participated in the landmark Festival of Negro Poets at Jackson State College, and Tolson recalled how impressed he was with Hayden's ability to transfix the audience by reading "Homage to the Empress of the Blues."[14] Hayden included Tolson in the 1967 anthology *Kaleidoscope*, writing in the head notes, seemingly in appreciation, that in Tolson's poetry exists "the consciousness, expressed very often with ironic humor, of what it means to be a Negro in the Western World" (57). Obviously the crowd at Fisk was not choosing between the two based on an assessment of their writing.

In any event, Tolson's conception both echoed and prefigured words uttered by Killens. In the 1965 *Negro Digest* symposium, Killens wrote, "I am not just *any* American. I am a special kind of an American, known as the Negro, invented by America for the special purpose of exploitation. Therefore, I *am* different. I look at life from the vantage point (for better or worse) of being an American Negro" ("Task of the Negro Writer as Artist" 74). In his 1971 self-interview, "Rappin' with Myself," he asked, "How in the hell could I be a writer who happens to be Black? I wasn't born pecking on a typewriter" (103). He argued that every African American is born Black in a racist nation and that the crucial facts for African-American writers are their roots and Black cultural frame of reference. In his view, "a cat would have to be really out to lunch to give up all that just for the questionable distinction of being 'a writer who happens to be a colored man'" (103).

The theme of the 1967 conference, held April 21–23, was "The Black Writer and Human Rights." Along with Killens, the speakers were John Henrik Clarke, LeRoi Jones, Ron Milner, Ronald Fair, Lerone Bennett, Margaret Danner, and Gwendolyn Brooks. The audience thus heard several speeches that continued the dominant, revolutionary tenor of the previous year's event, addresses that aligned with the general sensibility of the students, who made up most of the crowd, and the sentiments of the popular conference director. *Negro Digest* reported:

> The growth of Black consciousness on the Fisk campus was evident. It is not possible to gauge novelist John O. Killens' direct influence on this phenomenon, but the writer's relaxed, informal manner, and his total lack of pomp and preten[s]ion, cannot but have proved a remarkable change for a faculty member on the campus. The thrust of his relationship with the student has been to narrow the distance between teacher and student rather than to expand it. ("On the Conference Beat" 92)[15]

The most significant occurrence, a development that widely influenced discourses on African-American cultural politics, was the "rebirth" of Gwendolyn Brooks. Although the work of the celebrated poet had always reflected deep concern for and understanding of Black humanity, her artistic vision had been mostly connected, according to biographer George Kent, to the white liberal critical consensus. "Suddenly," as Brooks writes in her autobiography *Report from Part One*, "there was New Black to meet" (84).[16]

Although not youngsters, the historians Clarke and Bennett functioned as "New Blacks" who served to persuade Brooks about the virtues of Black Power and Black cultural nationalism. Clarke described enslavement as an assault on African identity and asserted that literature like the slave narratives was survival oriented. He then traced a movement from the slave narratives through a literature of restoration, as typified by the work of Du Bois, a literature of protest, as exemplified by the fiction of Richard Wright, to the advent of neo-slave narratives, as demonstrated by the writings of Killens, Baldwin, and Kelley. Clarke summed up by stating, "It is singularly the mission of the Black writer to tell his people what they have been in order for them to understand what they are. And from this the people will clearly understand what they must be" (qtd. in Kent 197). Bennett had argued in the 1965 *Negro Digest* symposium for a politically engaged art that would create new forms of expression and divorce itself from the "white culture structure" (78). He conveyed a similar message at Fisk, finding it astonishing that "a man or an oppressed person would choose to address his oppressors, primarily" (qtd. in Kent 198).

On her own subsequent panel, Brooks and fellow poet Margaret Danner were introduced somewhat rudely, a fact that perturbed Killens, by a student who suggested that no African-American poetry of relevance to the Black struggle had been published between the Harlem Renaissance and contemporary outpourings by Black cultural nationalists. Both Danner and Brooks, whose work had been done during the in-between period, took exception, but Danner, scheduled to speak first, was the one who reproached the student. Before her own presentation, which consisted mostly of reading poetry, Brooks issued a brief statement. Allowing that "race fed testimony" will find itself into Black art, she concluded, "I continue and violently to believe that, whatever the stimulating persuasion, poetry, not journalism, must be the result of involvement with emotions and ideas and ink and paper." Then she remarked, "And that's all the vital prose that I have for you, Mr. Killens" (qtd. in Kent 199).

Brooks's remarks were respectfully received as were her verses, which included selections like "Malcolm X," "Kitchenette Building,"

"The Mother," "We Real Cool," and "The Ballad of Rudolph Reed." She apologized for the fact that some of her poems treating the issue of social justice were too long to read. Concerning the response by the students, Kent notes that "although they would have to admit that Gwendolyn's poetry was a powerful element in the human rights struggle, their ultimate demand came closer to being satisfied by a literature that asserted a hearty rejection of middle-class values, a violent response to oppression, and an exclusive identification with the black community" (200). In other words, they were more interested in Ron Milner and the conference's biggest draw, LeRoi Jones. Near the end of Brooks's performance, Jones entered the hall and Brooks announced his arrival. Kent observes that "from that moment, the conference was in the hands of the more radical social critics and the visionary young" (200).

On the drama panel, Milner avowed, "If a new Black theater is to be born, sustain itself, and justify its own being, it must go home. Go home psychically, mentally, aesthetically, and I think physically" (qtd. in Kent 201). Jones's comments about theater complemented Milner's; then, at the audience's request, he turned into a performing poet, reading works like "A Poem for Halfwhite College Students." Given the rapturous response of the students, Kent concludes that "the Milner-Jones panel fully dramatized the marriage of the Black Power and Black Arts movements and the hard tones and desperation of life in the Northern ghettoes" (201–2). Brooks's immersion into the environment of the conference—proud and angry students denouncing integration—caused her to reconsider her specific notions of art and its relationship to the African-American social and political struggle. She later wrote, "I didn't know what to make of what surrounded me, of what with hot sureness began almost immediately to invade me. I had never been before, in the general presence of such insouciance, such live firmness, such confident vigor, such determination to mold or carve something DEFINITE" (85). Back home in Chicago, she became active in working with young African-American writers. Some, like Don L. Lee, would become important in their own right. She supported Black cultural initiatives and, ultimately, severed her long-standing ties with Harper and Row. In 1969 she began publishing with Broadside Press, a Black independent publishing company in Detroit founded by poet Dudley Randall. She became perhaps the major African-American author who most put her manuscripts where her mouth was, and she has been seen as a model of commitment for numerous African-American writers and publishers.

The 1968 conference took place two weeks after the assassination of Martin Luther King Jr. In his opening address, Killens urged the mostly student body to agitate for political and cultural change. A later version of his speech would be published as the essay "The Black Writer and the Revolution." The conference theme, "The Black Writer's Vision for America," harkened back to the New School affair (*Black* replacing *Negro* to reflect changing linguistic and cultural consciousness). Featured were Lee and such panelists as Charles V. Hamilton, Piri Thomas, and Sarah Webster Fabio. Julian Mayfield—novelist, essayist, playwright, and actor—delivered the keynote address.

In the context of Killens's "orchestration," the involvement of Mayfield is especially worth noting. Mayfield, an original member of the Harlem Writers Guild, had been abroad since 1961, residing in Ghana (a neighbor to Du Bois in the latter's final years) until 1966, and then in Europe and Asia until 1967. He was among the creative and literary artists criticized in the then newly published *Crisis of the Negro Intellectual*, and he was the first to issue a rebuttal. That statement was titled "Crisis or Crusade?" and appeared in the June 1968 issue of *Negro Digest*, which means that it is likely that the lengthy, fifteen-page review was both finished and the subject of some discussion between Mayfield and Killens prior to the Fisk gathering. However, Killens's letter of invitation to Mayfield dated January 10, 1968, is very brief and perfunctory, providing no sense that the two writers even knew each other on a personal level.[17] It is still possible, though, that the featuring of Mayfield, who defends Killens, can be viewed as an indirect response to Cruse.

Aside from dismissing Cruse's book as a dismal failure overall, despite its often brilliant economic analyses, Mayfield cites several of the expressions of petty jealousy, historical inaccuracies, and telling omissions that mark Cruse's work. For example, he attributes the harsh chapter on Lorraine Hansberry to the fact that Hansberry had refused to read the manuscript of a play Cruse had written. He accuses Cruse, justly so, of trying to pass himself off as a longtime Black nationalist while not revealing that he was a Marxist theoretician in the 1940s, a favored Black son of the organized left wing in Harlem, and had been ideologically in league with many people he later scorns. Mayfield clinches his argument by recounting an incident that occurred when he traveled to Cuba with a delegation that included Cruse in 1960, an episode during which Cruse reportedly, backed by two white women, berated a Cuban aide because food and drink were not readily available. Cruse is alleged to have exclaimed, "You damn well better get us something to eat and drink or I'll go back to the States and write the worst things I can think of about you and your damned Revolution!" (23–24). Mayfield claims that he wrote those words down that night, words that in his view spoke to an essential vindictiveness that lay at the heart of Cruse's character, and checked them against the recollections of others before publishing the 1968 review. He then remarks that "the man who screamed that blackmail threat, merely for food and water, is the author of *The Crisis of the Negro Intellectual*, the political pundit who presumes to sit in moral judgment on almost every black person who has written and published a book, a play or a poem" (24).[18]

Another interesting twist to the 1968 conference, a case of planting literary seed that would bear fruit, was the appearance of Lee, who had been recommended by Gwendolyn Brooks and was attending his first Black Writers Conference. Both Lee, later Haki Madhubuti, of course, and Killens served as writers-in-residence at Howard University in the 1970s and worked together on several conferences there. Ultimately, it has been Madhubuti who has since 1991 been able to maintain the annual writers' conference for which Killens called.

Of the Howard University conferences held between 1974 and 1978, the first, held in November 1974, was the most significant. By the beginning of the 1970s, the ranks of African Americans who were optimistic about social and political revolution had apparently thinned, which is not hard to fathom. Much crucial Black leadership had been eliminated—whether they were far left exemplars like the Black Panthers, nationalist visionaries like Malcolm X, or mainstream direct actionists like King. Such events bred nihilism or a belief that an oppressive establishment will always prevail. To demonstrate that Black was Beautiful could be done rather quickly, but to demonstrate that Black was powerful enough to sustain Black beauty over the long haul was another matter. It seemed that the symbolic Black transformation of the 1960s was waning—fewer Afros, dashikis, tiki sticks, rallies, slogans. Killens himself had treated these affectations satirically in parts of *The Cotillion*. The post-riots, "Great

Society" influx of money into the Black community was diminishing. Nixon was in the White House, Moynihan a chief advisor, and the age of "benign neglect" was underway. Thus the 1974 conference at Howard stands as the first major African-American writers' conference of a new political era.[19]

Killens directed this conference under the auspices of the Institute for the Arts and Humanities using the same theme as the 1966 conference at Fisk, only the title was changed, again to reflect new thinking, from "The Image of the Negro in American Literature" to "The Image of Black Folk in American Literature." The scale was larger than it had been at Fisk. Whereas there had been eight to ten panelists at the Fisk conferences, there were twenty-nine at Howard. Participants quite familiar to Killens like John Henrik Clarke, Ossie Davis, Maya Angelou, Alice Childress, Piri Thomas, Paule Marshall, Ron Milner, Mari Evans, and Haki Madhubuti were on hand as well as writers who had gained prominence since the Fisk conferences like Ishmael Reed, Quincy Troupe, Kalamu ya Salaam, and Richard Wesley.

In his expansive opening remarks that were titled the same as the conference theme, Killens urged fellow writers to unify in an effort to change the negative images that many Black people had of themselves, conceptions that were created and/or reinforced by media moguls on Madison Avenue and in Hollywood. He noted the recent proliferation of Blaxploitation movies like *Superfly* and the frequent use of the word "nigger" by Redd Foxx and Richard Pryor, informing the audience that in the words of Louis Reyes Rivera, "There ain't no chinks in the People's Republic. There ain't no spicks in Cuba" ("The Image of Black Folk in American Literature" 49). The creation of the "nigger," to his way of thinking, was the work of oppressors who attempted to justify the inferior status of slaves to themselves, to the outside world, and to the enslaved populace. He also spoke of the role that writers like Mark Twain, William Faulkner, Margaret Mitchell, and Robert Penn Warren played in promoting stereotypes of Blacks. Even while acknowledging that Harriet Beecher Stowe's *Uncle Tom's Cabin* was a "powerful weapon against American slavery," Killens suggested that the novel made widespread a host of stereotypes like the "loyal slave," the "kindly master," the "mulatto slave whose rebelliousness is solely the product of his or her white blood," and the contrasting "naturally submissive pure African" (49–50). Killens pointed out that these stereotypes cannot account for Nat Turner, Denmark Vesey, Harriet Tubman, Ann Nzinga, Toussaint L' Ouverture, Gabriel Prosser, and Cinque. He stressed that if African-American writing were to be geared toward liberation, a rhetorical purpose he felt was proper, then constructing images that contributed to "debrainwashing," to "deniggerizing," had to be a primary activity for African-American writers. Speaking more broadly, he proposed that African-American writers create a new vision, perhaps socialist or Pan-Africanist, that privileges people over things. And speaking organizationally, he suggested the formation of a national Black Writers Congress to "deal with the special and mutual problems faced by all Black writers, literarily, politically and economically" (51). Attempting to move beyond largely symbolic gestures or what he termed the "rap-style rhetoric" of the 1960s, he offered the offices of the institute as a means to found such an entity (45, 51).

Killens, again reflecting on what he regarded as weaknesses evident in the previous decade, wove a feminist strand into his speech. He argued for women's equality in the Black Liberation Movement, reminding the audience that "no revolution has made it in this Twentieth Century without the liberation of their woman being one of the top priorities" (47). He posited (and read from them) that the two most revolutionary poems of the previous forty years were written by Black women, Margaret Walker's "For My People" and Mari Evans's "Speak the Truth to the People" (51–52).

According to Carole A. Parks, there was a supportive consensus among the participants regarding Killens's perspective on the hazards of negative images and the exigence to create positive ones. As playwright-critic Eugene Perkins remarked, "Image-making should be a part of Black theater because from images we get models, from models, direction" (qtd. in Parks, "National Black Writers Convention" 88). But the group also expressed concerns, even disagreement, about how to disperse the magnificent images generated. Ossie Davis, delivering the keynote address, declared that technical expertise, access to mechanisms of production, and a broad yet sharply focused political outlook were necessary for all the proposed creation of positive images to have maximum impact. As he reasoned, "Seldom do we show our images connected with *power*. There is time for continuing to show how clever, how beautiful and talented we are. But we must have an international perspective on power" (qtd. in "National Black Writers Convention" 88). Despite exhortations like

Davis's and the fact that 250–600 people jammed the meeting sessions, less than 100 showed up to discuss the most concrete organizational proposal made at the conference, the formation of a Black Writers Congress. Undoubtedly, some were wary about which artistic tastes and policies would be dominant in such a group. Nonetheless, Ron Milner's comments rang ironically. Defending certain achievements of the 1960s, Milner argued that "rhetoric was tested right in the middle of rhetoric. The fire burned off the fat, left the lean, so we knew what and who was real" (qtd. in "National Black Writers Convention" 90). To Killens's dismay, apparently real was the lack of a strong enough collective will to establish a Black writers' association.

Even in the 1980s, Killens took every opportunity he could to push the idea that African-American writers should place their creative energies in the service of Black liberation efforts. However, his particular message may not have been reaching many ears by then. To be sure, there was still considerable talk about positive and negative images in the African-American community, but much of it had splintered along gender lines. The 1970s and 1980s had seen the spectacular rise and commercial success of Black female writers. Some of the more popular, Ntozake Shange and Alice Walker in particular, were often accused of "bashing" Black men. Many women, in turn, claimed that Black men, particularly writers, who as a whole had not painted flattering portrayals of Black women, were simply jealous. Shange's controversial choreopoem, *for colored girls who have considered suicide/when the rainbow is enuf*, was staged on Broadway in 1976, won an Obie Award, and was nominated for a Tony, an Emmy, and a Grammy. In 1983, Alice Walker received the Pulitzer Prize for *The Color Purple*. Killens, fully aware of those developments, made critical remarks about both *colored girls* and Walker's novel, although those comments were more tempered than those he made in 1952 about Ellison's *Invisible Man*. He spoke about the absence of "hero dynamics" in *colored girls*. And while acknowledging that he considered Walker a fine writer craftwise, he added that he sometimes had problems with her content. As was the case with the Ellison article, he proved to be a somewhat stern reviewer in his search for positive literary role models.[20]

By the mid-1980s, Killens, then writer-in-residence at Medgar Evers College in Brooklyn, was angling toward directing yet another conference. This one would be held March 21–23, 1986, and titled "The

Social Responsibility of the Writer to the Community." The topic was certainly timely once again given the intense discussions about stereotypes underway in African-American literary circles. However, after the film release of *The Color Purple* near the end of 1985, the issue of negative and positive images became the hottest cultural topic in virtually all quarters of the Black community. This partly explains why more than two thousand registrants turned out for what became the largest event that Killens directed. Another key factor was that many folks turned out in tribute to a man, now seventy years old, who still was working tirelessly to promote literature as a tool for radically democratic social change. On hand were thirty invited speakers, including many who by then had long-standing ties to Killens or had participated in one or more of the previous conferences, writers such as Margaret Walker, Maya Angelou, Toni Cade Bambara, Ishmael Reed, Calvin Hernton, Phil Petrie, Samuel Yette, Sonia Sanchez, Quincy Troupe, Amiri Baraka, Lonne Elder III, Richard Wesley, Addison Gayle, and Mari Evans. In fact, it was Evans, just as she had informed Killens's comments at the 1974 Howard conference, who provided the impetus for the conference director's greetings that were printed in the program: "During the glorious and turbulent Sixties, our poet Mari Evans called upon us to SPEAK THE TRUTH TO THE PEOPLE. Yet, to follow her counsel today may very well be to risk banishment from the publishing establishment. Faced with this harsh reality, the question of the writer's 'Social Responsibility' becomes crucial to our cultural survival" (3).

In his welcoming remarks at the conference on the morning of March 22, Killens began by telling the audience that writers, educators, and communicators have a responsibility to remain angry, though not despairing, about racism in the country. As mentioned earlier, he spoke, as Baldwin had at the 1965 New School conference, of the need to get America to face up to its history. Again he railed against negative depictions of African Americans in the mass media. Then, for maybe the final time in the public gaze, certainly the final time before an audience that large, he turned forcefully to his favorite topic, one that had consumed so much of his life's energy and creative effort. Using his own previous books as sources for anecdotes, he spoke, naturally, of the centrality of Black literary heroes to social struggle:

We are a great people. But where are the novels, the dramas, the epics about Saint Harriet of the Eastern Shore? Saint Medgar and Saint Fannie Lou of 'Sippi? Saint Rosa of Montgomery? Saint Malcolm of Nebraska? Saint Martin of Atlanta? The great Saint Paul of Rutgers? Where are the epics? Where are the monuments to their greatness? We need more literature and celebration of our nobility as a people. However, some of our writers are too busy getting over with the people that despise us, which means that fundamentally some of us despise ourselves. Too many of us are afraid to rock the boat. . . .

Our purpose must be to capsize that sucker, if necessary, and construct a boat which will, in the immortal words of Margaret Walker, "accommodate all the faces/all the Adams and Eves and their countless generations." Black writers must be boat rockers. Rock the boat. Capsize it. Drown the racist occupants.

Sisters and brothers, the Black writer, educator, and communicator are in an all out war for the minds of our own people, especially with the corporate media. It is total war sisters and brothers. And in this cultural revolution, we must wage guerilla warfare, even as this country did in the revolution against the British, even as the valiant guerilla fighters did in Vietnam against the greatest amassment of power the world has ever known, the armed might of the U.S.A. Even as our oppressors have used the English language as a weapon to degrade us, we must use the language to our own purposes. Metaphorically speaking, we must ambush the bastards, capture their weapons—the Anglo-Saxon language—and beat the hell out of them with their own weaponry. As my comrades used to say in the Army during World War II, "kicking asses and taking names." And in my humble opinion, that is precisely what the Black writer must be about. Excuse me. Take note. I said "kicking," not "kissing," "k-i-c-k," not "k-i-s-s." Life can be so confusing if you prefer to be confused.[21]

At that evening's dinner in his honor, Killens thanked all in attendance for their support and allowed that such support encouraged him in his efforts. Although he was visibly tired, even seriously ill, he read from Langston Hughes's poem "Mother to Son" and announced that he fully intended to "keep on keeping on." He asserted that the powers that be, chief among them the media and the board of education, were in a countercultural revolution. And as he had done at previous conferences dating back to 1959, he called for a permanent National Black Writers Conference, adding to that call a reiteration of the writers' union idea and the question of forming an "amalgamated Black press" to ensure that Black myths, legends, plays, and films are disseminated. He closed by reading from the greetings in the conference booklet: "We can take this beachhead and maintain it, if we work tirelessly, and fearlessly. We must push forward, for there is nought behind us save the open sea. The open sea and vicious sharks. And Moby Dick" (3).

As to be expected, much of the Killens viewpoint was amplified at the conference by Margaret Walker, Maya Angelou, Toni Cade Bambara, Mari Evans, Sonia Sanchez, Amiri Baraka, Addison Gayle, and Samuel Yette. They all urged in some way the Black writer or cultural worker to show a commitment to the Black community. For example, Margaret Walker, herself seventy years old and introduced by Killens as the "Empress of the Black Experience," noted that "Black writers are tied to the Black world and are responsible to it." However, Walker's nationalism, like Killens's, opened onto a broader outlook as she forecast a "new people's socialism of the twenty-first century" and a "pluralistic people's world." She urged African-American writers to "behold the vision and begin the task."

Maya Angelou spoke of a double responsibility: individual concern for one's artistic development and collective concern for the advancement of Black people. Making veiled references to the controversy surrounding *The Color Purple*, she stressed the need for African Americans to exhibit love toward one another if they aim to progress as a group. And she noted that the theme of love has always been a central although perhaps overlooked quality of African-American poetry.

Toni Cade Bambara and Mari Evans directly addressed the disputes over *The Color Purple*. Bambara, who saw the responsibility of the Black writer to be that of reminding people of what they are pretending not to know, denounced the round of "*Purple* debates" as largely a diversion promoted by elements of the media to diminish efforts to dismantle apartheid in South Africa or mobilize protest around the MOVE bombing in Philadelphia.

Evans argued that "our first responsibility to the community is to be at peace with our African selves, with that matrix, with who we really are before we're Republican, Democrat, hippie, flower child, feminist, gay, lesbian, universal, whatever. If we're clear about that, we can be clear about everything else." She offered that "the real issue is not Alice Walker." Evans suggested that those in attendance focus on what they could, in fact, control: things like the building of a Black cultural infrastructure and being proactive with respect to issues like the disproportionately high incarceration rate of Black people and the proper care of Black children. Evans added that the African-American artist draws from the group, thus owes the group, and she cited Du Bois's "Criteria of Negro Art" (Killens could think of no better reference) as a rationale for self-consciously political literary works.

Sonia Sanchez, in one of the most moving presentations at the conference, exhorted artists and others to form a broad progressive alliance to combat racism and economic exploitation. She mentioned the Middle Passage, the genocide of Native Americans, South African apartheid, the expanding prison-industrial complex in the United States, the invasion of Grenada, the danger posed by nuclear waste, the MOVE bombing, and the Atlanta child murders as political developments to which there had been inadequate responses. Asserting that "Americonomics" (her synonym for the economic policies of the Reagan administration) was a systematic attack on people to discourage activism, she called for the "building of institutions and consciousness not tied to the swing of capital." Also alluding, somewhat obliquely, to the *Purple* brouhaha, Sanchez admonished, "If you are doing, you don't have time to talk about other writers."

Amiri Baraka contended that the crucial issue with respect to literary assessment is the political allegiance of the artist and that all artists have an objective relationship to society despite whatever subjective pronouncements they may make. He rejected pure formalism as "complete freak out and denial of responsibility" and added that the African-American artistic movement always proceeded hand in hand with social struggle. The primary responsibility of the artist, Baraka espoused, is to "reflect the community at its most conscious," to compose work that is democratic and revolutionary.

Addison Gayle, always among the most sympathetic of literary critics when it came to Killens, sounded much like him as he declared, on the screenwriting panel, that "we need movies, good ones, about Malcolm X, Martin Luther King, Jr., and Sojourner Truth." Gayle added that as a writer, "you're always responsible to somebody."

Samuel Yette, from whom, in fact, Killens borrowed the term "hero dynamics," warned that the media were dangerously monopolized and too closely aligned with the government, with the result being that "a true adversarial relationship is lost, so is freedom of the press, and so is freedom."[22] As expected, he also pointed to the media's role in "devaluing Blacks and other people of color and fostering self-hate and other destructive behavior patterns." To Yette, Black journalists should "view their time in white media as tentative" and work toward owning their own outlets.

The 1986 conference proved to be the last formal set of affirmations and testimonials that Killens would hear in person, the final punctuation mark of his "public text." The voices he called on and merged with over the course of several decades helped him place before thousands the cultural initiatives he outlined in 1959. More efforts than we can yet tally with regard to literary output, publishing, and cultural organizing have been spawned by his continual need to discuss collective improvement and his willingness to assemble the folks.

Conclusion

In her 1971 essay "Tripping with Black Writing," Sarah Webster Fabio identifies a group of daring writers whom she labels "escapees from the prisons of Anglo rhetoric" and "frontiersmen in the lumbering netherlands of Black language" (228). She lists each member of the group and adds succinct phrases about his or her achievement and influence.[1] About John Oliver Killens, one of the escapees, she writes, "Killens. Killens' chilluns. On their jobs. Taking care of business. 'Deniggerizing the world'" (228). If this is now understood to be Killens's essential impact as a writer—that is, creating and inspiring Black vernacular art that promotes positive images of African Americans—he would find that a fairly acceptable outcome. He certainly sought, especially through his fiction, to ennoble people of African descent and to celebrate their culture.[2] As indicated, that mission led him to settle for characters that, with their Du Boisian uprightness, are somewhat thin psychologically. In fact, Robby Youngblood, Solly Saunders (an exception to the rule), Chuck Othello, and Killens's Pushkin, at a minimum, can be considered one serial character. However, the fictional whole in this case is greater than the sum of its parts. The uncompromising central intelligence at the heart of the Killens oeuvre, one that moves beyond glorifying to keep the volume pumped up about anti-Black racism and white supremacist brainwashing, is a precious entity in African-American literature. That such wisdom is encoded artistically in Black verbal forms, especially African-American humor, and has served as a model for younger writers stands as one of Killens's major rhetorical accomplishments. Fabio was also alluding, I imagine, to a political platform endorsed by the writer, one that stressed Black unity, Black commitment, Black self-determination, Black resistance, and Black self-defense.

Included in Killens's attempt to change or deniggerize the world was a continual verbal assault on literary, media, and educational establishments relative to their collectively abysmal record of promoting positive Black images. This question of portrayal was central to the many literary gatherings he spearheaded, although the issue hardly represented a new concern in the wider discourse on cultural politics. As far back as 1926, the same year Du Bois published "Criteria of Negro Art," *The Crisis* was already reporting on the "long controversy" about how Blacks should be depicted by writers and visual artists ("Questionnaire" 165). A questionnaire containing seven items concerning the obligation of writers and publishers appeared in the February 1926 issue.[3] Responses, including those by Carl Van Vechten, H. L. Mencken, Langston Hughes, Walter White, Alfred Knopf, Jessie Fauset, Georgia Douglas Johnson, and Charles Chesnutt, were featured in subsequent issues throughout the year. Although some conference participants undoubtedly found it irksome to have to revisit such a troublesome topic again and again, Killens remained passionate about the matter and steadfastly assembled voices around him to call for a mostly heroic treatment of African-American characters.

Beyond the dimension of Black nationalism, we can perceive other aspects of the Killens project, political and economic elements that were never totally submerged. Surely, Killens would speak passionately about the revolutionary possibilities of Black art in terms of the Black Liberation Movement, pressing the fact that "I write in a Black idiom to be dug by Black folks in the first instance" ("Rappin' with Myself" 103). But he would just as frequently add, sometimes immediately, that he also composes "for all people in the second" (103–4). Concern with the secondary audience, the "all people," marked his work with a broad, even socialist, humanism, which is especially evident in the jeremiad *Black Man's Burden*, a book that notably informed the political and economic positions taken by Stokely Carmichael and Charles V. Hamilton in *Black Power: The Politics of Liberation in America* (see 38–41). After Killens warns the nation against valuing free enterprise rather than free people, he advises, "We in America need to reconstruct our society so that people take precedence over property, and all men—white, black, brown, yellow—are masters, and only things are slaves" (166–67). He could otherwise envision no humane, truly prosperous, or stable nation, or entire world for that matter, as suggested by the utopian conclusion of *And Then We Heard the Thunder*. Ironically, in October 1987, as Killens lay upon his deathbed, the Dow Jones Industrial Average plunged 508 points in one day, sending financial markets into panic. Was it eerie affirmation of his views?

Killens was an artist very secure among Black people, Black fellow artists and activists in particular. In a 1984 interview he pointed out, "The writer has to reconcile the very serious contradictions: the absolute need for solitude to do his or her work and the absolute need for experiences with other people" (Peeples, "Artist as Liberator" 14). He offered further, "It would seem to me the writer should be a writer/activist. The writer should involve himself or herself wherever his or her people are struggling so that he or she can understand the meaning of struggle and interpret the struggle in his or her work" (14). It appears that the string of writers' conferences Killens organized also functioned as partial attempts to bridge realities that some, although not the majority of the panelists he would invite, would consider forever to be mutually exclusive. He put in his long and isolated hours at the typewriter, but as a naturally gregarious person he had an insatiable need, despite the great demand on his time, to convene events that drew others around him for discussions and presentations about literature and politics. The conferences he directed between 1965 and 1986 (he had begun planning another for 1988) stand alongside his writing as important milestones in African-American literary history.

A compulsive storyteller even away from the typewriter, Killens left behind a series of rich oral narratives. Some we're still trying to figure out. He related one about the discipline involved in cutting two hundred pages, at the publisher's request, from the manuscript that became *Youngblood*, which originally ran more than one thousand pages; another about that trimmed text turning up in *'Sippi* and other pieces. He told how a branch of the military purchased (or at least he heard so) thousands of copies of *And Then We Heard the Thunder* to dump into the ocean. One more about looking out from a hotel room in Tashkent in the Soviet Union, a place he had heard about from Langston Hughes, and watching native Blacks slap each other five in greeting. This was a favorite as it spoke to a worldwide brotherhood and sisterhood of Blackness that was in line with his vision.[4]

Intending to convey political messages with his stories, Killens was in league, in this regard, with Hughes, Richard Wright, Margaret Walker, and, of course, Du Bois. "All art is propaganda," he would agree with Du Bois, then counsel, but "all propaganda is not art" ("Rappin' with Myself" 135).

Last but not least, he was truly his great-grandmother's literary and rhetorical heir. As they sat around the fireplace or walked the streets of his childhood Macon together, she would spin tales of the nobility of her people and inform young John, "Aaah, Lord, Honey, THE HALF AIN'T

NEVER BEEN TOLD," thereby directing him toward his life's work ("The Half Ain't Never Been Told" 279). Killens later reflected, remembering images of his great-grandmother, "I could see her cocoa-colored face deepened with reddish-purple tones of African sunsets, hear her voice and it became a challenge to me to one day to try to tell that half that had not been told. It was the half that I would tell part of, at the very least. I felt I owed that much to Granny" (279). He kept alive the flame of her African-American pride all the way to the end.

John Oliver Killens was a great storyteller—and story.

Notes

Introduction

1 The Harlem Writers Guild was founded in 1950. Original members included Rosa Guy, John Henrik Clarke, and Walter Christmas. Members and alumni of the guild—such as Maya Angelou, Ossie Davis, Paule Marshall, Terry McMillan, and Walter Dean Myers—have produced hundreds of book-length or feature-length works of fiction, nonfiction, poetry, drama, and film. The Pulitzer Prize nominations were for the 1962 novel *And Then We Heard the Thunder* and the 1971 novel *The Cotillion*. Addison Gayle dubbed Killens the "spiritual father of the new novelists" in *The Way of the New World*, 261. Surprisingly, however, Gayle omits serious discussion of Killens's 1967 novel, *'Sippi*, from his analysis.

2 See Gayle, *The Way of the New World*, 261–77; and Bell, *The Afro-American Novel and Its Tradition*, 247–52.

3 See Neal, "And Shine Swam On"; and Neal, "The Black Arts Movement."

4 This definition of *rhetoric* is admittedly reductive. However, no consensus definition has emerged; the purpose of the one I offer is to focus attention on certain aspects of Killens's prose.

5 See Rampersad, *The Life of Langston Hughes*, 221–23.

Chapter 1

1 In "The Ethics of Living Jim Crow" Wright describes how he was beaten by his mother for participating in a fight with white boys. Although he had gotten the worst of the battle, he was punished because his mother wanted him to learn deference toward whites in order to improve his chances of survival in the South.

2 Killens, for example, titled an essay "Downsouth-Upsouth." See *Black Man's Burden*, 55–96. He subsequently references that essay in his introduction to *Black Southern Voices*, 2–3.

3 This excerpt is from a speech delivered by Douglass, "The Significance of Emancipation in the West Indies," 204.

4 Du Bois's 1903 essay "The Talented Tenth" and the 1948 essay "The Talented Tenth Memorial Address" are reprinted back-to-back in Henry Louis Gates Jr. and Cornel West's *Future of the Race*, 133–77. In the latter essay, Du Bois writes:

> Karl Marx stressed the fact that not merely the upper class but the mass of men were the real people of the world. He insisted that the masses were poor, ignorant, and sick, not by sin or by nature but by oppression. He preached that planned production of goods and just distribution of income would abolish poverty, ignorance and disease, and make the so-called upper-class, not the exception, but the rule among mankind. He declared that the world was not for the few, but for the many; that out of the masses of men could come overwhelming floods of ability and genius, if we freed men by plan and not by rare chance. Civilization not only could be shared by the vast majority of men, but such civilization founded on a wide human base would be better and more enduring than anything that the world has seen. The world would thus escape the enduring danger of being run by a selfish few for their own advantage.
>
> Very gradually as the philosophy of Karl Marx and many of his successors seeped into my understanding, I tried to apply this doctrine with regard to Negroes. My Talented Tenth must be more than talented, and work not simply as individuals. Its passport to leadership was not alone learning, but expert knowledge of modern economics as it affected American Negroes; and in addition to this and fundamental, would be its willingness to sacrifice and plan for such economic revolution in industry and just distribution of wealth, as would make the rise of our group possible. (162–63)

5 Killens wrote about his reverence for Du Bois, whom he termed Big Grand Daddy, on several occasions, including in "Rappin' with Myself," a self-interview. He speaks of Du Bois as Big Grand Daddy on pp. 114–15 and observes, "I was too much in respectful awe of this man Du Bois to call him my personal friend. You, a part of the great unwashed, do not call yourself a personal friend of the Patriarch, no matter how much you revere him. And that's the image he evoked for me. He was a beautifully arrogant aristocrat with a biting sense of irony and humor, and affected no false modesty. He had an objective evaluation of his importance and was not about to let you waste his time in discussion of the weather" (115). Also see Killens, introduction to *An ABC of Color*, 9.

6 In response to criticism from clergymen in Alabama, King's comments were made to justify his activism in sites beyond Atlanta and beyond the current legal system.

7 The "Sorrow Songs" is Du Bois's term for the spirituals in *The Souls of Black Folk*, 204–16.

8 For further views on the liberatory aspects of the spirituals, see Cone, *The Spirituals and the Blues*, 9–19; and Newman's introduction to *Go Down, Moses*, 23–24.

9 On page 93 of *The Cotillion*, Killens describes Lumumba's book collection as including works from "Du Bois, Baldwin, Spengler, Jones, Marx, Engels, Malcolm, Freud, Franklin, Bennett, Giovanni, Frazier, Hare, Douglass, Fair, Mitchell, Randall, Wright, Fanon, Hamilton, Ellison, Williams, Killens."

10 Killens made this comment to me during a series of conversations that took place between 1984 and 1986.

11 I was among a group of guests in 1986 to whom Killens proudly pointed out the Robeson poster.

12 Killens repeated these remarks on March 22, 1986, at the National Black Writers Conference at Medgar Evers College of the City University of New York.

13 This is one of several instances where Killens alludes to the comments made by Faulkner in the March 4, 1956, edition of the London *Sunday Times* that he would "fight for Mississippi against the United States, even if it meant going out into the street and shooting Negroes" (7) and to remarks made in a "A Letter to the North" that suggested that many Negroes in the South agreed with his views on gradualism and Northern agitators.

14 Black modes of discourse encompass, according to Smitherman, (1) call-and-response (Smitherman uses "call-response"), a series of spontaneous interactions between speaker and listener; (2) signification, the art of humorous putdowns, usually through verbal indirection; (3) tonal semantics, the conveying of meanings in Black discourse through specific kinds of voice rhythms and vocal inflections; and (4) narrative sequencing, the use of stories to explain and/or persuade. See *Talkin and Testifyin*, 101–66.

15 Ruth Finnegan observes that in *parallel phrasing*, "Each episode is related as a unit, and this full repetition of nearly similar events is one among the several means by which a skillful story-teller effectively heightens the tension and climax in his narration." See *Limba Stories and Story-Telling*, 79. She specifically defines *parataxis* as a construction where "sentences follow on one after the other as parallel formations complete in themselves rather than making up long periods of complex subordinate clauses" (75).

16 Concerning African-American ballads, N. I. White remarks, "There is hardly any such thing as a stanza belonging particularly to one song and to that alone. Generally speaking, practically any stanza is at home in practically any song." Qtd. in Gerould, *The Ballad of Tradition*, 268. LeRoi Jones comments in *Blues People* about how "certain technique and verses came to be standardized among blues singers" (67). With respect to hip-hop, a more recent genre, borrowed phrases include "you jes tall, that's all" and some version of "we ain't stoppin til 6 (sometimes 8) in the mornin." A more lengthy example of borrowing is Jay-Z's "I Just Wanna Love U (Give It to Me)." The following lines are taken almost verbatim from his close associate The Notorious B.I.G.'s "The World Is Filled": "When the Remi's in the system, ain't no tellin' / When I fuck 'em, will I diss 'em / That's what they be yellin': / I'm a pimp by blood, not relation / y'all be chasin', I replaced 'em, huh? / Drunk off Crys." Biggie's version goes: "When the Remi's in the system, ain't no tellin / Will I fuck em will I diss em, that's what these hoes yellin / I'm a pimp by blood, not relation / Y'all still chase on, I'll replace on, punks / Drunk off Dom, silk and gators." Further linking the borrowing in hip-hop to older musical forms and expanding the concept, scholar Marcyliena Morgan notes in "Nuthin' But a G Thang":

> The recognition of influences—*giving props, representin', recognizin'*—as well as exposing artists who do not acknowledge the source of their materials, is accomplished by directly stating the name of a person or group during a rap and/or using the words or phrases of another artist who belong to the same crew. This often includes the use of simile and metaphor, which requires "local" Hip Hop knowledge in order to be understood. Local knowledge includes lived experiences as well as familiarity with popular culture. For instance, the use of the word "CREAM" indicates both respect for the group who popularized the term (the Wu-Tang Clan) and its meaning (Cash Rules Everything Around Me). (194)

17 Song of Solomon 1:5.

18 There are numerous versions of this tale, one of which is included under the title "One Negro on Rye, Please!" in Spalding, *Encyclopedia of Black Folklore and Humor*, 488.

19 Gayle, *The Way of the New World*, 261.

20 Novels in question include Williams, *The Man Who Cried I Am* and *Captain Blackman*; Gaines, *Of Love and Dust* and *The Autobiography of*

Miss Jane Pittman; and Kelley, *A Different Drummer* and *Dunsfords Travels Everywhere*.

21 In "Rappin' with Myself," Killens speaks of Hughes's Pan-Africanism and love of Black people. He also addresses the impact on him of Margaret Walker's memorable poem "For My People" (101–3).

Chapter 2

1 Du Bois opens "The Talented Tenth" with the statement, "The Negro race, like all races, is going to be saved by its exceptional men." He closes with the almost identical statement, "The Negro race, like all other races, is going to be saved by its exceptional men" (133, 157).

2 About double consciousness, Du Bois wrote, "It is a peculiar sensation, this double-consciousness, this sense of always looking at one's self through the eyes of others, of measuring one's soul by the tape of a world that looks on in amused contempt and pity. One ever feels his twoness,—an American, a Negro; two souls, two thoughts, two unreconciled strivings; two warring ideals in one dark body, whose dogged strength alone keeps it from being torn asunder" (*The Souls of Black Folk*, 5).

3 In a conversation with me on December 31, 1999, Grace Killens took issue with Vincent and maintained that *Youngblood* was destined all along to be her husband's first novel. She recalls papers being shipped home during the war with the title "Stony the Road We Trod," which was indeed the working title of the manuscript that became *Youngblood*. Killens himself, however, stated in a 1978 *Black Forum* interview with Revish Windham (5–6) that the work he sent home to his wife was about his war experiences. He said he decided to explore his childhood experiences in his first novel because the material about the war was too close to him for him to interpret it then.

4 In contrast, the "inside" method begins with identification and analysis of broad social contradictions within the system and then moves outward to consider character in relation to such social forces (Bell, *The Afro-American Novel and Its Tradition*, 247). Bell draws from Lukács, *Realism in Our Time*.

5 Langston Hughes opens the chapter "Harriet Tubman: The Moses of Her People" with this quote (35) in his *Famous American Negroes*, which he presented to the Killens children. See Killens, *Black Man's Burden*, 36.

6 In personal correspondence to me dated February 19, 1998, Deborah Breen wrote: "The Bainbridge story is based on the Brisbane riots, but

there were also similar events in other cities, including Townsville and Cairns. . . . Killens may have chosen the name Bainbridge because similar riots occurred in England around the same time, near a town called Bainbridge. The basis of all these riots (as far as I know) was conflict between black American soldiers and white American soldiers, or conflict over enforced segregation." Breen also wrote: "It is very unlikely that John Oliver Killens was in Australia at the time of the riots, and his wife Grace Killens says it is more likely that he heard about the story from other soldiers he met after the incident. Coverage of the riots was censored in both the US and Australia at the time, but I have seen a couple of veiled references in letters from African American soldiers stationed in Australia who were writing back to newspapers in Baltimore and Chicago."

7 Often attributed to Solomon, in addition to Song of Solomon, are Proverbs, Ecclesiastes, and Psalms 72 and 127.

8 The idea of the crossroads or reckoning point is a recurrent theme in African-American culture exemplified by Robert Johnson's "Crossroads Blues": "I went to the crossroad, fell down on my knee, / Went to the crossroad, fell down on my knee, / Asked the Lord above to have mercy, save poor Bob if you please." See Hill, *Call & Response*, 802–3. Also note the ending, once again, of *12 Million Black Voices* and the town Crossroads, Georgia, in *Youngblood*.

9 The "call me Mister" phrase is taken from the title of a section in Spalding, *Encyclopedia of Black Folklore and Humor*, 446–60.

10 In Smitherman, *Black Talk*, 47, Amen Corner is defined as: "1) In the Traditional Black Church (TBC), originally the place where the older members sit, especially older women, the Church 'mothers,' who are perceived as the 'watchdogs of Christ' and who often lead the congregation in responsive *Amens*. 2) Any section of the Church where the congregation uses many verbal responses and *Amens*. 3) By extension, outside the Church world, a reference to any area where there are expressions of strong support and high feeling for a speaker or performer."

Chapter 3

1 A second founding charter, dated February 15, 1965, was not released before Malcolm's assassination. The reason for the second "founding" was doubtlessly connected to the OAAU's slow start. No more than a couple of hundred people joined, and financial support proved meager. Malcolm,

because he embarked on a second and longer trip to Africa in 1964, had little time for hands-on involvement in the organization's development.

2 For detailed discussion of Malcolm X's 1964 politics, see Breitman, *The Last Year of Malcolm X*, 26–69, 141–52. Dyson's full discussion is in *Making Malcolm*, "X Marks the Plots: A Critical Reading of Malcolm's Readers," 21–76.

3 In 1962 Ossie Davis invited Malcolm X to his home in Mount Vernon to meet John Oliver Killens and others; Peter Bailey recalls that Killens was in Harlem at the first planning meeting, in December 1963 or January 1964, of what would become the OAAU. See Hampton and Fayer, *Voices of Freedom*, 250–52, 256–57. Taylor Branch reports a 1964 meeting between Clarence Jones, the New York attorney for Martin Luther King Jr., and Malcolm X that took place at Sidney Poitier's home. Malcolm was escorted there by Killens. See *Pillar of Fire*, 345.

4 In "The Half Ain't Never Been Told," Killens reflects on Malcolm: "All of us loved Malcolm. He had been at our home where we now lived on Union Street. We were home owners by now. Malcolm was a shy man with a tough and tender strength. A very sensitive human being. We had been valued friends. I had helped him put together the Organization for Afro-American Unity. Philosophically speaking, Du Bois was my grandfather, Robeson was my father, Malcolm was my brother" (296). In "Rappin' with Myself," he writes:

> I loved Malcolm because he loved Black people and because he was the antithesis of Gunga Din. He had a Black sense of humor that would crack you up with laughter. He was an artist of the spoken word. And like all true artists he was self-critical. He was getting Black folk ready for the moment, for the national and international revolutionary moment, so the establishment figured he had to go. Brother Malcolm's mission was to deniggerize the earth. To rid the world of niggers. And so like David Woodson said in *'Sippi*, the establishment took notice of him like the Romans did Jesus, and they said to themselves, "There's a man teaching niggers to love themselves, teaching them that they ain't niggers. He's a dangerous man. He'll mess up our whole damn game if we ain't careful. We must get rid of him. We must get some niggers to do him in." (118–19)

5 In a phone interview with Yusuf Nuruddin in 1998, Clarke suggested that the help he and Killens gave Malcolm was more technical than substantive.

6 Killens visited Du Bois's home in Brooklyn Heights and had several occasions to visit and talk with King in Alabama. Killens alludes to these activities in "Rappin' with Myself," 115, 119–20. Ralph Abernathy recounts in his autobiography that Killens was on the bill for the performance to be given at the conclusion of the famous Selma-to-Montgomery March in 1965. See *And the Walls Came Tumbling Down*, 355. For evidence of correspondence and meetings between King and Killens, see Carson, *The Papers of Martin Luther King, Jr.*, 3:314–15, 4:46, 345, 605.

7 "Winter patriots" derives from Thomas Paine's *American Crisis*, originally published in 1776. Paine asserted, "The summer soldier and the sunshine patriot will, in this crisis, shrink from the service of their country; but he that stands it *now*, deserves the love and thanks of man and woman" (890). In 1965, Killens and Loften Mitchell coauthored a play titled *Ballad of the Winter Soldier*. Mitchell attributes the title to Paine. See Peterson, "John Oliver Killens," 293.

8 King wrote, in one of his characteristic statements about nonviolence,

> The ultimate weakness of violence is that it is a descending spiral, begetting the very thing it seeks to destroy. Instead of diminishing evil, it multiplies it. Through violence you may murder the liar, but you cannot murder the lie, nor establish the truth. Through violence you may murder the hater, but you do not murder hate. In fact, violence merely increases hate. So it goes. Returning violence for violence multiplies violence, adding deeper darkness to a night already devoid of stars. Darkness cannot drive out darkness: only light can do that. Hate cannot drive out hate: only love can do that.
>
> The beauty of nonviolence is that in its own way and its own time it seeks to break the chain reaction of evil. With a majestic sense of spiritual power, it seeks to elevate truth, beauty and goodness to the throne. Therefore I will continue to follow this method because I think it is the most practically sound and morally excellent way for the Negro to achieve freedom. (*Where Do We Go from Here*, 62–63)

9 The stanza from "Gunga Din" reads:

> With 'is mussick on 'is back,
> 'E would skip with our attack,
> An' watch us till the bugles made "Retire,"
> An' for all 'is dirty 'ide

'E was white, clear white, inside
When 'e went to tend the wounded under fire! (Kipling, *Rudyard Kipling*, 328)

Gunga Din, in movie form, was released in 1939. William Faulkner contributed to the story, a fact that would not have surprised Killens at all.

10 There were a few issues missing from the collection at the Schomburg Center for Research in Black Culture. No other articles by Killens appeared in the issues on hand.

11 In letters to literary agent Ronald Hobbs dated January 6, 1968, and January 20, 1968, Julian Mayfield responds to a proposed book project that would deal with issues raised by Cruse's book. Contributors would include himself as well as Julius Lester, John Henrik Clarke, and Killens. The project, however, never came to fruition.

12 Clarke interview by Nuruddin.

13 See Hart, "The Black Aesthetic and the Novels of John Oliver Killens," 74. In a letter to me in 2000, Hart recalled Killens's response when she broached the subject of Cruse during a meeting at Howard University: "It was as if his regard for Cruse was that of a person who is annoyed by a gnat on his arm and who has just to flick the bug away to be done with it!"

Chapter 4

1 Killens, "The Half Ain't Never Been Told," 304.

2 In addition to the readings by Hord and Johnson, see Dickson-Carr, *African American Satire*, 142–49.

3 For a fairly elaborate discussion of the veil metaphor, see Gibson, introduction to *The Souls of Black Folk*, xi–xv.

4 I have in mind scenes involving the characters Althea Hobbs, Sam Haywood, and the Great Ahmed Khan, which are described in the latter half of the script (90–160).

5 Song of Solomon 1:5.

Chapter 5

1 In "Rappin' with Myself" Killens writes, "I come right out of the Old Testament. I believe like Nat Turner, Fred Douglass, Denmark Vesey, Malcolm X, I believe in an eye for an eye, a tooth for a tooth" (106).

2 Killens also reflects Douglass's observation about the imperatives of masters to suppress the aspirations of the enslaved. Like Luke, Douglass heard his master express views about education for the people he owned. Similar to MacKay's admonition that "the moment they stop thinking of themselves as niggers, you're in trouble," Mr. Auld argued that learning and literacy would make slaves unmanageable. See Douglass, *Narrative*, 29.

3 The Vesey rebellion was originally scheduled to take place July 14, 1822. Because of concerns about security leaks, the date was moved up to June 16. However, the rebels did not strike then because the whites in Charleston seemed to have been tipped off. Subsequently, the movement was infiltrated before the rebellion could be enacted.

4 Killens mentions Lofton's book in his introduction to *The Trial Record of Denmark Vesey*, vii–xxi. The similar passage from Lofton, *Insurrection in South Carolina*, reads: "Schooled by long experience as a slave himself and acquainted through his reading with many expressed aspirations for freedom, Vesey had his own opinions as to what the liberties and the rights and privileges of Negroes should be. His notions did not conform to the white views that mere liberation from bondage was the ultimate reward for a black man and that freed slaves should be grateful for small blessings. He was annoyed by the obsequious forms which anyone with dark skin was expected to observe" (132).

5 The lines, as recorded in the novel:

> I will sing of freedom
> And scourge the evil that sits on the throne . . .
> Shudder, pupils of blind fortune
> Tyrants of the world;
> But lend an ear, ye fallen slaves,
> Gain courage and arise!
> It was law, not nature, tyrants,
> Put the crown upon your heads. (114)

6 Pushkin's height is not mentioned by Killens. However, it is noted by Robin Edmonds in *Pushkin*, 132.

Chapter 6

1 Arthur Flowers told me this several times between 1997 and 1999 during conversations at Syracuse University.

2 *Freedomways* was published from 1961 to 1985. The word "Negro" was dropped from the subtitle beginning with the summer 1968 issue. For a statement on Killens's role in the founding of the journal, see Jackson, *Freedomways Reader*, xxii, 335. Cruse acknowledges that members of the Harlem Writers Guild were the central figures of *Freedomways*. See *The Crisis of the Negro Intellectual*, 247. Not surprisingly, the longest book review *Freedomways* ever featured was Ernest Kaiser's of *Negro Intellectual*. Killens himself did not contribute much to *Freedomways*, only tributes to Lorraine Hansberry ("Lorraine Hansberry") and Charles White ("He Took His Art More Seriously Than He Did Himself") and a two-part story, "Run Like Hell and Holler Fire!"

3 Although reviewed in *Freedomways*, Killens received no free pass in terms of criticism. John Clarke's review of *And Then We Heard the Thunder* was enthusiastic, and John Henry Jones's review of *'Sippi* was even more favorable. But lukewarm at best were reviews by Earl Durham of *Black Man's Burden* and by Jean Carey Bond of *The Cotillion*.

4 Under the directorship of Elizabeth Nuñez, who was coordinator for the 1986 event, subsequent conferences were held in 1988, 1991, 1996, and 2000. Participants included Houston Baker Jr., Amiri Baraka, Gwendolyn Brooks, Henry Louis Gates Jr., Charles Johnson, Terry McMillan, Haki Madhubuti, Walter Mosley, Arnold Rampersad, Ishmael Reed, Sonia Sanchez, Ntozake Shange, Derek Walcott, Alice Walker, and John Edgar Wideman.

5 Madhubuti founded the Gwendolyn Brooks Writers Conference, which is annually sponsored by the Gwendolyn Brooks Center at Chicago State University.

6 All these authors were members of the Harlem Writers Guild and/or members of a second group cofounded by Killens, the Association of Artists for Freedom.

7 Killens would never supply a ringing endorsement of Ellison's work. But in *Black Man's Burden* he remarks that "a puny achievement is what Ellison's novel was not" (30). In "The Smoking Sixties," he noted, "We waited with great expectations for the second novel of Ralph Ellison, author of the powerful *Invisible Man*" (xvii).

8 Killens, *Black Man's Burden*, 45; Malcolm X, "Statement of Basic Aims and Objectives of the Organization of Afro-American Unity," 563.

9 Unless otherwise indicated, quotations from the 1986 conference were transcribed from tapes.

10 As reported by Fuller, Gilman's specific charge was "Negro playwrighting, as I see it thus far, is in a preliminary stage. It could not be otherwise. It is in the stage of being an arm of Negro awakening, of Negro political action, of Negro insistence, not on rights, but on being. Yet drama, as an art, cannot be concerned with an insistence on the right to be, but on the nature of being. In this, it is totally democratic and totally aristocratic. Any white dramatist is compelled to place his head under the guillotine when he writes, and it will fall off if what he writes is untrue—untrue, need I say, in aesthetic terms." Fuller's response:

> Negro writers *are*, just as Negroes *are*, and they accept their own being. It is not the Negro writer insisting on "the right to be" but the white critic who, because of his very special attitude and relationship *vis-à-vis* Negroes, visualizes the Negro as struggling to *become*—and *become*, in all probability, like white people. It is Mr. Gilman, the white critic, who imagines that Negroes are insisting on "the right to be." But the truth is that Negro writers have no doubts at all about their "right to be"; they are describing in their work "the nature of being," the nature of *their* being, the nature of being as reflected through their eyes and through their experience, which is all any writer ever does.
>
> And what Mr. Gilman has done—what many white critics invariably do—is to pass judgment on the quality of the *being* of Negro writers. He has said, in effect, that because Negro writers are involved in the struggle against those forces in the society which tend to dehumanize their *being* they, therefore, lack the maturity and the artistry to produce drama which is also art. The "nature of being" as Negro playwrights must see it, Mr. Gilman has implied, inhibits their creating a work of art. And then, to heap insult upon his wild, slashing wound, Mr. Gilman declared that the best play about Negroes ever written was the work not of a Negro but of the Frenchman Jean Genet, *The Blacks*, a fantastic pageant of masks and symbols which no Negro anywhere in the world could accept as having relevance to his life in strictly human terms. (82)

11 In the 1949 essay, Redding argued, for example, that Dunbar in his short stories succumbed to depicting simplistic characters. He saw Chesnutt as overriding stereotypes in *The Colonel's Dream* and the *Marrow of Tradition*, which, in Redding's view, is why Chesnutt was ignored by many readers in his day. For Redding, examples of works with artistic integrity

that were also successful appeals to Black and white audiences were Richard Wright's *Uncle Tom's Children* and *Native Son*, Chester Himes's *If He Hollers Let Him Go* and *Lonely Crusade*, Margaret Walker's *For My People*, Willard Motley's *Knock on Any Door*, and Frank Yerby's *The Foxes of Harrow*, *The Vixens*, and *The Golden Hawk*.

12 For further comments on Hayden's views and life at Fisk, see Hatcher, *From the Auroral Darkness*, 19–30, 36–40, 76–81. Also note Hayden's own accounts and actions: On April 27, 1965, he submitted a letter of resignation to Fisk president Stephen J. Wright. Explaining his reasons, he wrote, "I have endured the increasingly onerous teaching load you have required of me, hoping that eventually I might have earned the right to a lighter schedule which would have left more time and energy for writing. However, your recent appointment of a Writer in Residence has shown me how ill-founded my hopes were. And it seems to indicate a complete disregard for the work I have done over the years with the Creative Writing course here and for my own achievements as a writer. It augurs ill indeed for my future growth and productivity as a member of the Fisk faculty." Hayden retracted his resignation, perhaps because President Wright explained to him in a letter of June 17, 1965, that the funds designated for the residency carried the stipulation that an outside person be selected. In a letter dated February 15, 1968, Killens invited Hayden to be a part of a panel at the 1968 conference at Fisk, but Hayden did not appear on the program. He resigned permanently from Fisk in 1969. In 1974, he received a letter from Haki Madhubuti inviting him to participate in the 1974 conference at Howard University, but he declined.

13 Dudley Randall considers Tolson and Hayden together, along with Gwendolyn Brooks, in "The Black Aesthetic in the Thirties, Forties, and Fifties," 37–40. Sarah Webster Fabio makes critical remarks about Tolson in "Who Speaks Negro?"

14 Along with Tolson and Hayden, participants in the Festival of Negro Poets, which took place October 19–24, were Langston Hughes, Margaret Walker, Zora Neale Hurston, Sterling Brown, Arna Bontemps, Owen Dodson, and Jacob Reddix. For Tolson's comment on Hayden's reading, see Farnsworth, *Melvin B. Tolson*, 203.

15 Of course, all were not in harmony at Fisk. The report also noted that few faculty members were in attendance, and for the most part, faculty, particularly faculty from the English department, did not receive or greet the guest writers.

16 For a more detailed report, see Kent, *A Life of Gwendolyn Brooks*, 153–230; and Brooks, *Report from Part One*, 83–86.
17 Julian Mayfield Papers, Schomburg Center for Research in Black Culture.
18 To follow the Cruse-Mayfield debate to its conclusion in print, see "Reply on a Black Crisis."
19 A complementary description of the period is found in Kelley, *Yo' Mama's Disfunktional*, 4–7.
20 See Windham, "The Long Distance Runner," 41–42; Peeples, "The Artist as Liberator," 10. For a sharply different perspective, see Hernton, *The Sexual Mountain and Black Women Writers*, especially chapters 1 and 2. Also see Walker's own provocative essays "Coming in from the Cold" and "In the Closet of the Soul" included in her collection *Living by the Word*, 54–68, 78–92.
21 Textual treatment of the "Saint Harriet" line of reasoning is traceable to *Black Man's Burden*, 45–46.
22 See Yette, "Black Hero Dynamics and the White Media."

Conclusion

1 The other escapees are LeRoi Jones, Don L. Lee, and Ishmael Reed.
2 The subsequent remarks appeared in slightly different form in Gilyard, "John Oliver Killens."
3 The questions posed were as follows: 1. When the artist, black or white, portrays Negro characters is he under any obligations or limitations as to the sort of character he will portray? 2. Can any author be criticized for painting the worst or the best characters of a group? 3. Can any author be criticized for refusing to handle novels that portray Negroes of education and accomplishment, on the grounds that these characters are no different from white folk and therefore not interesting? 4. What are Negroes to do when they are continually painted at their worst and judged by the public as they are painted? 5. Does the situation of the educated Negro in America with its pathos, humiliation and tragedy call for artistic treatment at least as sincere and sympathetic as "Porgy" received? 6. Is not the continual portrayal of the sordid, foolish criminal among Negroes convincing the world that this and this alone is really and essentially Negroid, and preventing white artists from knowing any other types and preventing black artists from daring to paint them? 7. Is there not a real danger that young colored writers will be tempted to follow the

popular trend in portraying Negro character in the underworld rather than seeking to paint the truth about themselves and their own social class?

4 These stories were told to me between 1984 and 1986 at Medgar Evers College.

Bibliography

Abernathy, Ralph. *And the Walls Came Tumbling Down*. New York: Harper and Row, 1989.

The American Negro Writer and His Roots: Selected Papers from the First Conference of Negro Writers, March, 1959. New York: American Society of African Culture, 1960.

Angelou, Maya. *The Heart of a Woman*. 1981. Reprint, New York: Bantam Books, 1982.

Baldwin, James. *Another Country*. 1962. Reprint, New York: Dell Books, 1963.

Baraka, Amiri. *Blues People: Negro Music in White America*. New York: William Morrow, 1963.

———. "Poem for Halfwhite College Students." In *Transbluesency: The Selected Poems of Amiri Baraka/LeRoi Jones, Selected Poems 1961–1995*, ed. Paul Vangelisti, 144. New York: Marsilio, 1995.

Basaninyenzi, Gatsinzi. "Ideology and Four Post-1960 Afro-American Novelists." Ph.D. diss., University of Iowa, 1986.

Belafonte, Harry. *Belafonte at Carnegie Hall*. RCA Victor LPC/LSO 6006, 1959.

Bell, Bernard. *The Afro-American Novel and Its Tradition*. Amherst: University of Massachusetts Press, 1987.

Bond, Jean Carey. "Killens' New Novel a Satire on Black 'Society.'" Review of *The Cotillion; or, One Good Bull Is Half the Herd*, by John Oliver Killens. *Freedomways* (spring 1971): 203–5.

Bontemps, Arna. *Black Thunder*. 1936. Reprint, Boston: Beacon Press, 1992.

Booth, Wayne. *The Rhetoric of Fiction*. 2nd ed. Chicago: University of Chicago Press, 1983.

Branch, Taylor. *Pillar of Fire: America in the King Years, 1963–1965*. New York: Simon and Schuster, 1998.

Breen, Deborah. Letter to Keith Gilyard. February 19, 1998.

Breitman, George. *The Last Year of Malcolm X: The Evolution of a Revolutionary*. New York: Pathfinder Press, 1967.

Brooks, Gwendolyn. *Report from Part One*. Detroit: Broadside Press, 1972.

Carey, Stephen Anderson. "Black Men's Du Boisian Relationships to Southern Social Institutions in the Novels of John Oliver Killens." Ph.D. diss., University of Texas at Dallas, 1992.

Carmichael, Stokely, and Charles V. Hamilton. *Black Power: The Politics of Liberation in America*. New York: Random House, 1967.

Carson, Clayborne, ed. *The Papers of Martin Luther King, Jr.* Vol. 3. Berkeley: University of California Press, 1997.

———. *The Papers of Martin Luther King, Jr.* Vol. 4. Berkeley: University of California Press, 2000.

Chander, Harish. "John Oliver Killens." In *Contemporary African American Novelists: A Bio-Bibliographical Critical Sourcebook*, ed. Emmanuel S. Nelson, 250–59. Westport, CT: Greenwood Press, 1999.

Chayefsky, Paddy. *Network*. Hollywood: Script City, 1976.

Chesnutt, Charles W. *The Colonel's Dream*. 1905. Reprint, Miami: Mnemosyne Publishing, 1969.

———. *The Marrow of Tradition*. 1901. Reprint, Ann Arbor: Ann Arbor Paperbacks, 1969.

———. "Response to Questionnaire about the Negro in Art." *The Crisis* (November 1926): 28–29.

Clark, Steve. Introduction to *By Any Means Necessary*, by Malcolm X. New York: Pathfinder Press, 1970.

Clarke, John Henrik. "*The Crisis of the Negro Intellectual* by Harold Cruse: A Reappraisal of Some Neglected Aspects of the Crisis." In *Africans at the Crossroads: Notes for an African World Revolution*, 365–81. Trenton: Africa World Press, 1991.

———. "Negro Men at War." Review of *And Then We Heard the Thunder*, by John Oliver Killens. *Freedomways* (spring 1963): 227–29.

———. Review of *Youngblood*, by John Oliver Killens. *Freedom* (August 1954): 7.

Clarke, John Henrik, ed. *William Styron's Nat Turner: Ten Black Writers Respond*. Boston: Beacon Press, 1968.

Cohen, Norm. *Long Steel Rail*. Urbana: University of Illinois Press, 1981.

Cone, James. *The Spirituals and the Blues: An Interpretation*. Maryknoll, NY: Orbis Books, 1992.

"On the Conference Beat." *Negro Digest* (March 1967): 90–93.

Corbett, Edward, and Robert Conners, eds. *Classical Rhetoric for the Modern Student*. 4th ed. New York: Oxford University Press, 1999.

Cruse, Harold. *The Crisis of the Negro Intellectual: A Historical Analysis of the Failure of Black Leadership*. 1967. Reprint, New York: Quill, 1984.

———. "Reply on a Black Crisis." *Negro Digest* (November 1968): 19–25, 65–69.

Dickson-Carr, Daryl. *African American Satire: The Sacredly Profane Novel*. Columbia: University of Missouri Press, 2001.

Douglass, Frederick. *Narrative of the Life of Frederick Douglass, An American Slave, Written by Himself*. 1845. Reprint, New York: W. W. Norton, 1997.

———. "The Significance of Emancipation in the West Indies: An Address Delivered in Canandaigua, New York, on 3 August 1857." In *The Frederick Douglass Papers, Series One: Speeches, Debates, and Interviews, Volume 3: 1855–63*, ed. John Blassingame, 183–208. New Haven: Yale University Press, 1985.

Dubey, Madhu. *Black Women Novelists and the Nationalist Aesthetic*. Bloomington: Indiana University Press, 1994.

Du Bois, W. E. B. "Criteria of Negro Art." *The Crisis* (October 1926): 290–97.

———. *The Souls of Black Folk*. 1903. Reprint, New York: Penguin, 1989.

———. "The Talented Tenth." 1903. In *The Future of the Race*, ed. Henry Louis Gates Jr., and Cornel West, 133–57. New York: Knopf, 1996.

———. "The Talented Tenth Memorial Address." 1948. In *The Future of the Race*, ed. Henry Louis Gates Jr. and Cornel West, 159–77. New York: Knopf, 1996.

Durham, Earl. "Capturing the Negro Mood." Review of *Black Man's Burden*, by John Oliver Killens. *Freedomways* (spring 1966): 182–84.

Dyson, Michael Eric. *Making Malcolm: The Myth and Meaning of Malcolm X*. New York: Oxford University Press, 1995.

Echewa, Thomas. "Africans vs. Afro-Americans." *Negro Digest* (January 1965): 33–38.

———. "Reply to an American Negro." *Negro Digest* (September 1965): 23–27.

Edmonds, Robin. *Pushkin: The Man and His Age*. New York: St Martin's Press, 1994.

Ellison, Ralph. *Invisible Man*. New York: Random House, 1952.

Evans, Mari. "Speak the Truth to the People." In *Call & Response: The Riverside Anthology of the African American Literary Tradition*, ed. Patricia Liggins Hill, Bernard Bell, Trudier Harris, William J. Harris, R. Baxter Miller, and Sandra O'Neale, 1575–76. Boston: Houghton Mifflin, 1998.

Fabio, Sarah Webster. "Tripping with Black Writing." 1971. In *Within the Circle: An Anthology of African American Literary Criticism from the Harlem Renaissance to the Present*, ed. Angelyn Mitchell, 224–31. Durham: Duke University Press, 1994.

———. "Who Speaks Negro?" *Negro Digest* (1966): 54–58.

Farnsworth, Robert. *Melvin B. Tolson, 1898–1966: Plain Talk and Poetic Prophecy*. Columbia: University of Missouri Press, 1984.

Faucet, Jessie. "Response to Questionnaire about the Negro in Art." *Crisis* (June 1926): 71–72.

Faulkner, William. "A Letter to the North." *Life*, March 5 1956, pp. 51–52.

Finnegan, Ruth. *Limba Stories and Story-Telling*. Oxford: Oxford University Press, 1967.

Fuller, Hoyt. "Reverberations from a Writers' Conference." *African Forum* 1, no. 2 (1965): 78–84.

———. "Towards a Black Aesthetic." 1968. In *Within the Circle: An Anthology of African American Literary Criticism from the Harlem Renaissance to the Present*, ed. Angelyn Mitchell, 199–206. Durham: Duke University Press, 1994.

Gaines, Ernest. *The Autobiography of Miss Jane Pittman*. 1971. Reprint, New York: Bantam Books, 1972.

———. *Of Love and Dust*. 1967. Reprint, New York: Bantam Books, 1969.

Gates, Henry Louis, Jr., and Nellie McKay, eds. *The Norton Anthology of African American Literature*. New York: W. W. Norton, 1997.

Gayle, Addison. Introduction to *Great Black Russian*, by John Oliver Killens. Detroit: Wayne State University Press, 1989.

———. *The Way of the New World: The Black Novel in America*. Garden City, NY: Doubleday, 1975.

Gerould, Gordon Hall. *The Ballad of Tradition*. Oxford: Oxford University Press, 1932.

Gibson, Donald. Introduction to *The Souls of Black Folk*, by W. E. B. Du Bois. New York: Penguin, 1989.

Gilyard, Keith. "Genopsycholinguisticide and the Language Theme in African American Fiction." *College English* 52 (1990): 776–86.

———. "John Oliver Killens." In *The Before Columbus Foundation Fiction Anthology: Selections from the American Book Awards 1980–1990*, ed. Ishmael Reed, Kathryn Trueblood, and Shawn Wong, 389–91. New York: W. W. Norton, 1992.

Guy, Rosa. *Bird at My Window*. Philadelphia: J. B. Lippincott, 1966.

Hampton, Henry, and Steve Fayer, eds. *Voices of Freedom: An Oral History of the Civil Rights Movement from the 1950s through the 1980s*. New York: Bantam Books, 1990.

Handler, M. S. "2 Negro Writers Open Talk Series." *New York Times*, April 25, 1965, p. 31.

Harris, Norman. "Understanding the Sixties: A Study of Character Development and Theme in Seven Recent Afro-American Novels." Ph.D. diss., Indiana University, 1980.

Hart, Betty. "The Black Aesthetic and the Novels of John Oliver Killens." Master's thesis, West Virginia University, 1974.

Hatch, Gary Lane. *Arguing in Communities*. Mountain View, CA: Mayfield, 1996.

Hatcher, John. *From the Auroral Darkness: The Life and Poetry of Robert Hayden.* Oxford: George Ronald, 1984.

Hayden, Robert. "Frederick Douglass." In *Collected Poems*. New York: Liveright, 1985.

———. Letter to Stephen J. Wright. April 25, 1965. Robert Hayden papers, National Baha'i Archives.

———. "Homage to the Empress of the Blues." In *Collected Poems*. New York: Liveright, 1985.

———. "Middle Passage." In *Collected Poems*. New York: Liveright, 1985.

———. "Runagate Runagate." In *Collected Poems*. New York: Liveright, 1985.

Hayden, Robert, ed. *Kaleidoscope: Poems by American Negro Poets*. New York: Harcourt, Brace and World, 1967.

Henderson, Stephen. *Understanding the New Black Poetry: Black Music and Black Speech as Poetic References*. New York: William Morrow, 1973.

Hernton, Calvin. *The Sexual Mountain and Black Women Writers*. New York: Doubleday, 1987.

Hill, Patricia Liggins, Bernard Bell, Trudier Harris, William J. Harris, R. Baxter Miller, and Sandra O'Neale, eds. *Call & Response: The Riverside Anthology of the African American Literary Tradition*. Boston: Houghton Mifflin, 1998.

Himes, Chester. *If He Hollers Let Him Go*. 1945. Reprint, New York: Signet, 1971.

———. *Lonely Crusade*. 1949. Reprint, Chatham, NJ: Chatham Bookseller, 1973.

Hord, Fred Lee. *Reconstructing Memory: Black Literary Criticism*. Chicago: Third World Press, 1991.

Howard-Pitney, David. *The Afro-American Jeremiad: Appeals for Justice in America*. Philadelphia: Temple University Press, 1990.

Howe, Russell. "New Civil War If Negro Claims Are Pressed: An Exclusive Interview with William Faulkner." London *Sunday Times*, March 4, 1956, p. 7.

Hughes, Langston. *Famous American Negroes*. New York: Dodd, Mead, 1954.

———. "Mother to Son." In *The Collected Poems of Langston Hughes*, ed. Arnold Rampersad and David Roessel, 30. New York: Vintage, 1995.

———. "The Negro Mother." In *The Collected Poems of Langston Hughes*, ed. Arnold Rampersad and David Roessel, 155–56. New York: Vintage, 1995.

Jackson, Esther Cooper, ed. *Freedomways Reader: Prophets in Their Own Country*. Boulder, CO: Westview Press, 2000.

Jay-Z. "I Just Wanna Love U (Give It to Me)." *The Dynasty: Roc La Familia*. Polygram Records, 2000. ASIN: B000050HS9.

Johnson, Charles. *Being & Race: Black Writing since 1970*. Bloomington: Indiana University Press, 1988.

Johnson, Georgia Douglas. "Response to Questionnaire about the Negro in Art." *The Crisis* (August 1926): 193.

Jones, Gayl. *Liberating Voices: Oral Tradition in African American Literature*. 1991. Reprint, New York: Penguin, 1992.

Jones, John Henry. "Killens' Fine, Sensitive New Novel." Review of *'Sippi*, by John Oliver Killens. *Freedomways* (fall 1967): 373–75.

Jones, LeRoi. See Amiri Baraka.

Kaiser, Ernest. Review of *The Crisis of the Negro Intellectual*, by Harold Cruse. *Freedomways* (winter 1969): 24–41.

Keats, Ezra Jack. *John Henry: An American Legend*. New York: Pantheon, 1965.

Kelley, Robin D. G. *Yo' Mama's Disfunktional: Fighting the Culture Wars in Urban America*. Boston: Beacon Press, 1997.

Kelley, William Melvin. *A Different Drummer*. 1962. Reprint, New York: Anchor Books, 1989.

———. *Dunsfords Travels Everywhere*. Garden City, NY: Doubleday, 1970.

Kent, George. *A Life of Gwendolyn Brooks*. Lexington: University Press of Kentucky, 1990.

Killens, John Oliver. *And Then We Heard the Thunder*. 1962. Reprint, Washington, DC: Howard University Press, 1983.

———. "An Appreciation." In *This Child's Gonna Live*, by Sarah Wright. New York: Feminist Press at City University of New York, 1986.

———. "The Artist and the Black University." *The Black Scholar* (November 1969): 61–65.

———. "The Black Culture Generation Gap." *Black World* (August 1973): 22–33.

———. "Black Labor and the Liberation Movement." *The Black Scholar* (October 1970): 33–39.

———. *Black Man's Burden*. New York: Trident Press, 1965.

———. "The Black Writer and the Revolution." *Arts and Society* 5 (1968): 395–99.

———. "Broadway in Black and White." *African Forum* 1, no. 3 (1966): 66–76.

———. "Brotherhood of Blackness." *Negro Digest* (May 1966): 4–10.

———. "The Confessions of Willie Styron." In *William Styron's Nat Turner: Ten Black Writers Respond*, ed. John Henrik Clarke, 34–44. Boston: Beacon Press, 1968.

———. *The Cotillion; or, One Good Bull Is Half the Herd*. New York: Trident Press, 1971.

———. "God Bless America." 1952. In *Black American Stories: A Century of the Best*, ed. Langston Hughes, 204–9. New York: Hill and Wang, 1966.

———. "A Good Man Feeling Bad!" *The Urbanite* (March 1961): 22–24.

———. *Great Black Russian: A Novel on the Life and Times of Alexander Pushkin*. Detroit: Wayne State University Press, 1989.

———. *Great Gittin' Up Morning: The Story of Denmark Vesey*. Garden City, NY: Doubleday, 1972.

———. "The Half Ain't Never Been Told." In *Contemporary Authors Autobiography Series*, Vol. 2. Ed. Adele Sarkissian, 279–306. Detroit: Gale, 1985.

———. "He Took His Art More Seriously Than He Did Himself." *Freedomways* (summer 1980): 192–94.

———. "Hollywood in Black and White." In *White Racism: Its History, Pathology and Practice*, ed. Barry Schwartz and Robert Disch, 398–407. New York: Dell, 1970.

———. "The Image of Black Folk in American Literature." *The Black Scholar* (June 1975): 44–52.

———. Introduction to *An ABC of Color*, by W. E. B. Du Bois. New York: International Publishers, 1969.

———. Introduction to *Black Southern Voices: An Anthology of Fiction, Poetry, Drama, Nonfiction, and Critical Essays*, ed. John Oliver Killens and Jerry Ward Jr. New York: Meridian, 1992.

———. Letter to Julian Mayfield. Jan. 16, 1968. Julian Mayfield Papers, Schomburg Center for Research in Black Culture.

———. Letter to Robert Hayden. February 15, 1968. Robert Hayden Papers, National Baha'i Archives.

———. "Lorraine Hansberry: On Time!" *Freedomways* (fall 1979): 273–76.

———. *A Man Ain't Nothin' but a Man: The Adventures of John Henry*. Boston: Little, Brown, 1975.

———. "The Negro as Music Maker: Some Reflections on the Origins of Jazz." *The Urbanite* (April 1961): 7, 29, 33.

———. "Opportunities for Development of Negro Talent." *The American Negro Writer and His Roots: Selected Papers from the First Conference of Negro Writers, March, 1959*. New York: American Society of African Culture, 1960.

———. "Rappin' with Myself." In *Amistad 2: Writings on Black History and Culture*, ed. John A. Williams and Charles Harris, 97–136. New York: Vintage Books, 1971.

———. "Reflections from a Black Notebook." *Black Creation* (April 1971): 12–14.

———. Review of *Invisible Man*, by Ralph Ellison. *Freedom* (June 1952): 7.

———. "Rough Diamond." In *Harlem: Voices from the Soul of Black America*, ed. John Henrik Clarke, 169–84. New York: Signet, 1970.

———. "Run Like Hell and Holler Fire!" *Freedomways* (fall 1983): 244–56; (fall 1984): 260–66.

———. *'Sippi*. 1967. Reprint, New York: Thunder's Mouth Press, 1988.

———. *Slaves*. New York: Pyramid, 1969.

———. "The Smoking Sixties." In *Black Short Story Anthology*, ed. Woodie King Jr., xi–xviii. New York: Columbia University Press, 1972.

———. "Wanted: Some Black Long Distance Runners." *The Black Scholar* (November 1973): 2–7.

———. *Youngblood*. 1954. Reprint, Athens: University of Georgia Press, 1982.

———, ed. *The Trial Record of Denmark Vesey*. Boston: Beacon Press, 1970.

King, Coretta Scott. *My Life with Martin Luther King, Jr.* 1969. Reprint, New York: Penguin, 1993.

King, Martin Luther, Jr. "Letter from Birmingham Jail." 1963. In *The Norton Anthology of African American Literature*, ed. Henry Louis Gates Jr. and Nellie McKay, 1854–66. New York: W. W. Norton, 1997.

———. *Where Do We Go from Here: Chaos or Community?* 1967. Reprint, Boston: Beacon Press, 1968.

Kipling, Rudyard. "Gunga Din." In *Rudyard Kipling: The Complete Verse*. London: Kyle Cathie Limited, 1990.

Knopf, Alfred. "Response to Questionnaire about the Negro in Art." *The Crisis* (April 1926): 280.

Lee, Don L. See Haki Madhubuti.

Lehman, Paul Robert. "The Development of a Black Psyche in the Works of John Oliver Killens." Ph.D. diss., Lehigh University, 1976.

Llorens, David. "Writers Converge at Fisk University." *Negro Digest* (June 1966): 54–68.

Lofton, John. *Insurrection in South Carolina: The Turbulent World of Denmark Vesey*. Yellow Springs, OH: Antioch Press, 1964.

Lukács, Georg. *Realism in Our Time: Literature and the Class Struggle*. 1963. Reprint, New York: Harper Torchbooks, 1971.

McDowell, Deborah. "Boundaries: Or Distant Relations and Close Kin." In *Afro-American Literary Study in the 1990's*, ed. Houston A. Baker Jr. and Patricia Redmond, 51–77. Chicago: University of Chicago Press, 1989.

McKay, Claude. *Banana Bottom*. 1933. Reprint, New York: Harvest Books, 1970.

Macon, Wanda. "John O. Killens." *The Oxford Companion to African American Literature*, ed. William Andrews, Frances Smith Foster, and Trudier Harris, 419–20. New York: Oxford University Press, 1997.

Madhubuti, Haki. "But He Was Cool, or: He Even Stopped for Green Lights." In *GroundWork: New and Selected Poems of Don L. Lee/Haki R. Madhubuti from 1966–1996*. Chicago: Third World Press, 1996.

———. "The New Integrationist." In *GroundWork: New and Selected Poems of Don L. Lee/Haki R. Madhubuti from 1966–1996*. Chicago: Third World Press, 1996.

Magill, Frank, ed. *Masterpieces of African-American Literature*. New York: HarperCollins, 1992.

Malcolm X. "Basic Unity Program, Organization of Afro-American Unity." In *New Black Voices: An Anthology of Contemporary Afro-American Literature*, ed. Abraham Chapman, 564–74. New York: Mentor, 1972.

———. *By Any Means Necessary*. New York: Pathfinder Press, 1970.

———. "Statement of Basic Aims and Objectives of the Organization of Afro-American Unity." 1964. In *New Black Voices: An Anthology of Contemporary Afro-American Literature*, ed. Abraham Chapman, 558–64. New York: Mentor, 1972.

Mayfield, Julian. "Crisis or Crusade?" *Negro Digest* (June 1968): 10–24.

———. "Julian Mayfield's Response to Harold Cruse." *Negro Digest* (November 1968): 26–27.

———. Letter to Ronald Hobbs. Jan 6 1968. Julian Mayfield Papers, Schomburg Center for Research in Black Culture.

———. Letter to Ronald Hobbs. Jan 20, 1968. Julian Mayfield Papers, Schomburg Center for Research in Black Culture.

"The Meaning and Measure of Black Power." *Negro Digest* (November 1966): 20–37, 81–96.

Mencken, H. L. "Response to Questionnaire about the Negro in Art." *The Crisis* (March 1926): 219–20.

Miller, Keith. "Martin Luther King, Jr. Borrows a Revolution." *College English* 48 (1986): 249–65.

Morgan, Marcyliena. "'Nuthin' but a G Thang': Grammar and Language Ideology in Hip Hop Identity." In *Sociocultural and Historical Contexts of African American English*, ed. Sonja L. Lanehart, 187–209. Amsterdam: John Benjamins, 2001.

Morrison, Toni. *Beloved*. New York: Knopf, 1987.

———. *The Bluest Eye*. New York: Knopf, 1970.

Motley, Willard. *Knock on Any Door*. 1947. Reprint, New York: Signet, 1950.

Neal, Larry. "And Shine Swam On." In *Black Fire: An Anthology of Afro-American Writing*, ed. LeRoi Jones and Larry Neal, 638–56. New York: William Morrow, 1968.

———. "The Black Arts Movement." 1968. In *Within the Circle: An Anthology of African American Literary Criticism from the Harlem Renaissance to the Present*, ed. Angelyn Mitchell, 184–98. Durham: Duke University Press, 1994.

Newman, Richard. *Go Down, Moses: Celebrating the African-American Spiritual*. New York: Clarkson Potter, 1998.

Nikola-Lisa, W. "John Henry: Then and Now." *African American Review* (spring 1998): 51–56.

The Notorious B.I.G. "The World Is Filled." *Life after Death*. Bad Boy Records. 78612-73011-2, 1997.

Onstott, Kyle. *Mandingo*. Richmond, VA: Delinger, 1957.

Paine, Thomas. *American Crisis*. 1776. In *The Heath Anthology of American Literature Third Edition*. Vol. 1. Ed. Paul Lauter. Boston: Houghton Mifflin, 1998.

Parks, Carole A. "The National Black Writers Convention." *Black World* (January 1975): 86–92.

Peeples, Kenneth, Jr. "The Artist as Liberator: An Interview with John Oliver Killens." *Community Review* (fall 1984): 6–14.

Peterson, Bernard, Jr. "John Oliver Killens." In *Contemporary Black American Playwrights and Their Plays: A Biographical Directory and Dramatic Index*. New York: Greenwood Press, 1988.

"Questionnaire about the Negro in Art." *The Crisis* (February 1926): 165.

Rampersad, Arnold. *The Life of Langston Hughes*. Vol. 1: 1902–1941. Oxford: Oxford University Press, 1986.

Randall, Dudley. "The Black Aesthetic in the Thirties, Forties, and Fifties." In *Modern Black Poets: A Collection of Critical Essays*, ed. Donald Gibson, 34–42. Englewood Cliffs, NJ: Prentice Hall, 1973.

Randolph, A. Philip, and Chandler Owen. "The Steel Drivin' Man." 1925. In *African American Literature*, ed. Demetrice Worley and Jesse Perry Jr., 73–75. Lincolnwood, IL: National Textbook Company, 1993.

Redding, J. Saunders. "American Negro Literature." *The American Scholar* (spring 1949): 137–48.

———. "The Negro Author: His Publisher, His Public and His Purse." 1945. In *A Scholar's Conscience: Selected Writings of J. Saunders Redding 1942–1977*, ed. Faith Berry, 140–46. Lexington: University Press of Kentucky, 1992.

———. "The Negro Writer and His Relationship to His Roots." In *The American Negro Writer and His Roots: Selected Papers from the First Conference of Negro Writers, March, 1959*. New York: American Society of African Culture, 1960.

———. Review of *Bird at My Window*, by Rosa Guy. *The Crisis* (April 1966): 225, 227.

Review of *Slaves*, by John Oliver Killens. *Publishers Weekly*, April 14, 1969, p. 99.

Shange, Ntozake. *for colored girls who have considered suicide/when the rainbow is enuf*. 1975. Reprint, New York: Scribner, 1997.

Smith, Rochelle, and Sharon Jones, eds. *The Prentice Hall Anthology of African American Literature*. Upper Saddle River, NJ: Prentice Hall, 2000.

Smitherman, Geneva. *Black Talk: Words and Phrases from the Hood to the Amen Corner*. Boston: Houghton Mifflin, 1994.

———. *Talkin and Testifyin: The Language of Black America*. Boston: Houghton Mifflin, 1977.

Spalding, Henry, ed. *Encyclopedia of Black Folklore and Humor*. New York: Jonathan David Publishers, 1972.

Stowe, Harriet Beecher. *Uncle Tom's Cabin*. 1852. Reprint, Columbus, OH: Charles E. Merrill, 1969.

Styron, William. *The Confessions of Nat Turner*. New York: Random House, 1967.

Talese, Gay. "Many Words, Mostly Hot, Mark Writers' Parley." *New York Times*, April 26, 1965, p. 26.

"The Task of the Negro Writer as Artist: A Symposium." *Negro Digest* (April 1965): 54–70, 72–83.

Thurman, Wallace. *Blacker the Berry: A Novel of Negro Life*. 1929. Reprint, New York: Collier Books, 1970.

Van Vechten, Carl. "Response to Questionnaire about the Negro in Art." *The Crisis* (March 1926): 219.

Vincent, Theodore. *Black Power and the Garvey Movement*. San Francisco: Ramparts Press, 1972.

Walker, Alice. *The Color Purple*. San Diego: Harcourt Brace Jovanovich, 1982.

———. *Living by the Word: Selected Writings 1973–1987*. San Diego: Harcourt Brace Jovanovich, 1989.

Walker, Margaret. "For My People." 1937. In *The Norton Anthology of African American Literature*, ed. Henry Louis Gates Jr. and Nellie McKay, 1572–73. New York: W. W. Norton, 1997.

Welty, Eudora. *One Writer's Beginnings*. 1983. Reprint, New York: Warner, 1985.

White, Walter. "Response to Questionnaire about the Negro in Art." *The Crisis* (April 1926): 279–80.

Wiggins, William, Jr. "The Structure and Dynamics of Folklore in the Novel Form: The Case of John O. Killens." *Keystone Folklore Quarterly* (fall 1972): 92–117.

Williams, Brett. *John Henry: A Bio-Bibliography*. Westport, CT: Greenwood Press, 1983.

Williams, John A. *Captain Blackman*. 1972. Reprint, New York: Bantam Books, 1974.

———. *The Man Who Cried I Am*. 1967. Reprint, New York: Signet, 1968.

———. *Night Song*. 1961. Reprint, New York: Pocket Books, 1970.

———. "Open Letter to an African." *Negro Digest* (September 1965): 22, 28–35.

Windham, Revish. "The Long Distance Runner: An Interview with John Oliver Killens." *Black Forum* (fall/winter 1978): 4–7, 28–31, 40–43.

Wright, Richard. *12 Million Black Voices: A Folk History of the Negro in the United States*. 1941. Richard Wright Reader. New York: Da Capo Press, 1997.

———. *Black Boy: A Record of Childhood and Youth*. New York: Harper, 1945.

———. "The Ethics of Living Jim Crow: An Autobiographical Sketch." 1937. In *Richard Wright: Early Works*, 225–37. New York: Library of America, 1991.

———. *Native Son*. New York: Harper and Brothers, 1940.

———. *Uncle Tom's Children*. New York: Harper and Brothers, 1938.

Wright, Stephen J. Letter to Robert Hayden. June 17, 1965. Robert Hayden Papers, National Baha'i Archives.

Yarmolinsky, Avrahm, ed. *The Poems, Prose and Plays of Alexander Pushkin*. New York: Random House, 1936/1964.

Yerby, Frank. *The Foxes of Harrow*. New York: Dial, 1946.

———. *The Vixens*. 1947. Reprint, New York: Pocket Books, 1965.

———. *The Golden Hawk*. 1948. Reprint, New York: Dell Books, 1982.

Yette, Samuel. "Black Hero Dynamics and the White Media." *Black World* (January 1975): 22–28.

Index

About the Author

Keith Gilyard is the Edwin Erle Sparks Professor of English and African American Studies at the Pennsylvania State University and a former president of the National Council of Teachers of English. He has published widely on the topics of language and rhetoric. He is the recipient of two American Book Awards and the Penn State Faculty Scholar Medal for Outstanding Achievement in the Arts and Humanities.